The Research Process

What's your next step? Use this guide to help you along the way.

P9-DHT-621

The Bedford
RESEARCHER

Mike Palmquist

Colorado State University

Bedford/St. Martin's   Boston ◆ New York

For Bedford/St. Martin's

Developmental Editor: Sara Eaton Gaunt
Production Editor: Deborah Baker
Senior Production Supervisor: Joe Ford
Editorial Assistant: Joanna Lee
Copyeditor: Paula Woolley
Text Design: Claire Seng-Niemoeller
Cover Design and Art: Billy Boardman
Composition: Stratford Publishing Services, Inc.
Printing and Binding: R. R. Donnelley & Sons Company

President: Joan E. Feinberg
Editorial Director: Denise B. Wydra
Editor in Chief: Karen S. Henry
Director of Marketing: Karen Melton Soeltz
Director of Editing, Design, and Production: Marcia Cohen
Managing Editor: Elizabeth M. Schaaf

Library of Congress Control Number: 2005927769

For information, write: Bedford/St. Martin's, 75 Arlington Street, Boston, MA 02116 (617-399-4000)

ISBN: 0–312–43392–1
EAN: 978–0–312–43392–5

Acknowledgments

Figure 2.1: Reprinted with the permission of Colorado State University Libraries.
Figure 2.3: Reprinted with the permission of EBSCO Information Services.
Figure 2.6: Copyright © 1998–2005 by Netscape Communications Corporation.
Figure 2.7: Mariët Westermann, from *A Worldly Art: The Dutch Republic 1585–1718.* Copyright © 1996. Reprinted with the permission of Harry N. Abrams, Inc.
Figure 2.7: Gerard Dou, *Old Woman Reading,* early 1630s. Oil on panel, 28 x 21 in. (71 x 55.5 cm). Rijksmuseum, Amsterdam. Reprinted with permission.
Figure 2.8: Reprinted with the permission of CNN.com.
Figure 2.9: Roddy Scheer, excerpt from "A Mighty Wind" from *E: The Environmental Magazine* (September/October 2003). Copyright © 2003. Reprinted with the permission of E/The Environmental Magazine.

Preface for Instructors

Since the first edition of *The Bedford Researcher* was published, the amount of information available online has grown rapidly. *Google* has become a verb. Blogs have emerged as important players in shaping public opinion and disseminating information. Databases have become more comprehensive and, increasingly, are offering access to the complete text of the articles they reference. Libraries have responded to these changes by making significant investments in online information resources, including online access to scholarly journals and books.

Research writers, understandably, have struggled to keep up with the rapid pace of change. They might think blogs are important, but they're uncertain which blogs best meet their needs. They've heard about news search sites, such as Google News or Yahoo! News, but wonder about the credibility of the content they deliver. They've read about advances in new instant messaging programs but struggle to understand the role these tools might play in their research.

With this situation in mind, I began the second edition of *The Bedford Researcher* by revisiting the question that guided my work on the first edition: *What significant new challenges face today's research writers?* As before, I found the answers by turning to the work I've done with students in my own research writing classes:

- Choosing the most relevant sources for a research writing project continues to challenge less experienced writers. They are often overwhelmed by the large number of sources produced by their initial searches of library catalogs, databases, and Web sites. Helping students develop strategies for refining research questions and identifying relevant search terms is critical to their success.

- The explosive growth of the Web and the increasing number of full-text documents available through databases make understanding how to read critically, evaluate, and work with sources both more difficult and more essential than ever before.

- Managing the sources collected during a research project and ensuring that each source is cited appropriately remains of central importance.

- The ease with which students can misuse electronic sources continues to grow. Understanding plagiarism and fair use — not just of text but also of images, audio, and video — continues to rank among the most significant challenges facing research writers.

- Finally, the range of documents created by research writers continues to expand. When research writers understand the concept of genre and how genres respond to specific writing situations, they can present their work in the most effective manner and in the most appropriate medium.

These challenges strongly shaped my work on this new edition of *The Bedford Researcher*. But, as in the first edition, I also focused on the enduring challenges that have faced writers since they began working with sources: considering purpose and audience; taking notes carefully and accurately; developing clear and appropriate thesis statements; integrating information from sources into a draft; and revising and editing efficiently and effectively. The result is a textbook that addresses the rapidly changing conditions under which research writers work without sacrificing its strong foundation of proven strategies for conducting research, working with sources, and drafting, revising, and editing.

Like the first, this edition of *The Bedford Researcher* offers writers and teachers a strong set of instructional technology resources. We've taken great pains to ensure that these tools are relevant, easy to use, and focused on the needs of research writers. The companion Web site (bedfordresearcher.com) is genuinely interactive, presenting both tutorials and the new Bedford Bibliographer. The tutorials provide clear illustrations of research processes, guide students as they progress on their own work, and allow them to share their work with teachers and classmates. The Bedford Bibliographer, a comprehensive bibliography builder, significantly improves the first edition's bibliography tool.

FEATURES

The Bedford Researcher is based on the premise that the decisions good research writers make are shaped primarily by rhetorical concerns—by the writer's purposes and interests, by the readers' needs and interests, by setting, and by course requirements, time limitations, and opportunities. To illustrate this premise, the book presents research writing as a process of choosing, learning about, and contributing to a conversation among readers and writers.

A Familiar Organization   The text is divided into five parts. The first four parts correspond to the stages of an idealized research writing process, although the book stresses the recursive nature of research writing. The fifth part focuses on documentation systems. Part One, Joining the Conversation, introduces the concept of research writing as a social act. It helps students understand that research writing involves exploring conversations among writers and readers, narrowing their focus to a single conversation, and developing a research question to guide their inquiry into that conversation. Part Two, Collecting Information, helps students create a search plan based on their research question and then search for information using print resources, electronic resources, and field research methods. Part Three, Working with Sources, discusses critical reading strategies, evaluation criteria, and note taking. Part Four, Writing Your Document, helps students develop their thesis, organize their information and ideas, develop an outline, plan and draft their document, integrate source material, avoid plagiarism, revise and edit their drafts, and design their document. Finally, Part Five, Documenting Sources, provides comprehensive chapters on MLA, APA, *Chicago*, and CSE styles. An appendix presents a comprehensive, annotated list of print, database, and Web resources for more than forty disciplines.

Complete Coverage of the Research Writing Process Combined in an Easy-to-Use Handbook The book is designed so that students can find information quickly and work competently through each stage of their projects. Each chapter is structured around a set of Key Questions that enables students to find information quickly. The strategic design employs clear and accessible illustrations, checklists, activities, and documentation guidelines—the parts of the text students will return to as they write. A thorough cross-referencing system directs students to the help they need—within the text or on the companion Web site—when they need it.

A Conversational, Student-Friendly Tone *The Bedford Researcher* is written in an accessible, easy-to-follow style that treats students with respect. A new section, Getting Started with Confidence, gives students an early overview of the entire research process and how to approach it. And easy-to-understand examples are used throughout the book.

Detailed Case Studies of Student Researchers Discussions throughout the text are illustrated by the writing processes of six Featured Writers—students with whom I worked as they undertook a variety of research writing projects, including traditional research essays, Web sites, and feature articles. Your student writers will be able to understand and learn from these real-life examples as they plan and conduct their own research, and draft and revise their own project documents.

Emphasis on Project Management When we surveyed teachers on which part of the research process students find most difficult, managing a research project ranked first. To that end, numerous prompts throughout the text help keep researchers on track. In Chapter 1, for example, students learn how to create and use a research log and a project timeline to plan and manage their work. *My Research Project* activities also provide comprehensive support for project management.

A Cross-curricular Companion Because students need a research text suitable for various academic purposes, *The Bedford Researcher* and its companion Web site feature examples and models that span the disciplines, providing research writing help for composition courses and beyond. Part Five provides guidelines for writing papers in MLA style, APA style, *Chicago* style, and CSE style. Each style is illustrated through example documents created by the featured writers and each is supported by the Bedford Bibliographer on the companion Web site.

NEW TO THIS EDITION

This edition of *The Bedford Researcher* has undergone a thorough revision, guided by a comprehensive set of reviews and the survey responses of students, instructors, and academic librarians. Key updates include:

A Streamlined Text with a More Navigable Design The new full-color design makes key information even easier to find. I've included more tips and checklists—including new *Quick Reference* boxes at the end of every chapter—so students can interact with the text at a glance.

Answers to Students' Real Questions about Research   The text addresses students' real questions about research writing, taken from surveys. A list of these most frequently asked questions on the inside front cover gives students a new way to access the text.

New Tutorials Focusing on the Most Challenging Topics in Each Part of the Book   I've introduced visually engaging tutorials in the text—and expanded them on the companion Web site—to provide interactive guidance for the real problems students have, such as developing a research question, evaluating Web sites, and integrating quotations.

Straightforward Discussions of Plagiarism, Research Ethics, Common Knowledge, and Fair Use   In the new chapter on avoiding plagiarism, Chapter 14, I provide clear models to help students avoid potential trouble spots when quoting, paraphrasing, summarizing, integrating, and documenting sources. I've also expanded the section on ensuring accuracy and avoiding plagiarism during note taking.

Updated Coverage of Working with Electronic Sources and Tools   The text offers up-to-date advice for searching for and evaluating electronic sources; saving and organizing such sources; integrating images, audio, and video; and revising and editing with electronic tools.

An Extended Treatment of Recognizing Sources   Throughout the text, I advise students on how to distinguish among materials such as scholarly and popular sources, primary and secondary sources, Web sites and databases.

A Stronger Emphasis on Audience and Purpose   In addition to an already strong focus on rhetorical concerns throughout the text, new *What's My Purpose?* boxes remind students to constantly reflect upon—and reconsider—their purpose at every stage of the research writing process.

COMPANION WEB SITE

The Bedford Researcher Web site (bedfordresearcher.com) provides an extensive collection of online materials, including tools and content designed specifically for an interactive environment.

The Bedford Bibliographer   New for this edition, I developed this straightforward, easy-to-use research tool to help students evaluate sources and create an annotated bibliography in MLA, APA, *Chicago,* or CSE style.

Interactive Tutorials   Also new to this edition, the tutorials let students practice the key research writing strategies they learn about in the book, such as developing a thesis, evaluating Web sites, and integrating quotations.

Research Project Activities   Each *My Research Project* activity in the text can be downloaded or printed from the companion Web site.

Annotated Links for Research Writing   The companion Web site gives students access to an extensive annotated list of Web-based resources for research writing. They can also access Web search sites and directories for more than forty disciplines.

Featured Student Writers   The Web site includes detailed profiles of the six student writers whose work is featured in the text. Students can view selected notes, completed activities, and rough and final drafts of their research writing projects. They can also view edited transcripts of interviews in which the featured writers discuss their research writing processes.

Research Writing Guides   Updated for this edition, these guides provide details about using online library catalogs, databases, Web search sites and directories, and other online resources. They also offer updated support for using word processors and creating Web sites.

Teaching with *The Bedford Researcher*   The instructor's manual can be downloaded from bedfordresearcher.com. In addition to chapter overviews and specific teaching goals and tips, the manual directs you to specific resources for each skill that you'll teach (for example, refining a thesis statement or integrating sources) and illustrates how the book's content aligns with content on the companion Web site.

ACKNOWLEDGMENTS

I am most grateful to my family—my wife Jessica, my daughter Ellen, and my son Reid—for their support as I've worked on this edition of *The Bedford Researcher*. I am grateful as well for the guidance and support I've received from David Kaufer, Chris Neuwirth, and Richard Young, who have helped me, in graduate school and in the many years since, to think critically and carefully about the relationships among rhetoric, pedagogy, and technology. I am indebted to my colleagues Kate Kiefer, Stephen Reid, Sarah Sloane, Lisa Langstraat, Tobi Jacobi, Sue Doe, Liz Jackson, Kerri Mitchell, Will Hochman, and Nick Carbone for their willingness to share ideas and offer support as I worked on this book. I also thank Chris Arigo, who updated the lists of disciplinary and writing resources, and Liz Jackson, who updated and expanded the instructor's manual.

I am also grateful for the opportunity to work with reviewers who provided thoughtful advice and honest reactions to drafts of this new edition: Cora

Agatucci, Central Oregon Community College; Wendy Warren Austin, Edinboro University of Pennsylvania; Lisa Babinec, Cascadia Community College; Roger Bacon, Northern Arizona University; Sonia Apgar Begert, Olympic College; Lisa Bernhagen, Highline Community College; Deborah D. Borchers, Pueblo Community College; Arnold Bradford, Northern Virginia Community College; Rachael L. Brooks, Texas A&M–Corpus Christi; Lynda Bryson, Front Range Community College; Beth Camp, Linn-Benton Community College; Gail Corso, Neumann College; Katherine Frank Dvorsky, Colorado State University–Pueblo; Teri Ferguson, Oklahoma State University–Oklahoma City; Jane Fife, Western Kentucky University; Michael Galaviz, Texas A&M–Corpus Christi; Kevin J. Gardner, Baylor University; Stuart Greene, University of Notre Dame; Betty L. Hart, The University of Southern Indiana; Fran B. Holt-Underwood, Georgia Perimeter College–Lawrenceville; Jennifer Jett, Bakersfield College; Allen Learst, Mesa State College; Lindsay Lewan, Arapahoe Community College; Kari Miller, Georgia Perimeter College–Lawrenceville; Rebecca Mitchell, University of California, Santa Barbara; Marcella Munson, Florida Atlantic University; Matthew Parfitt, Boston University; Marnie Jo Petray, Slippery Rock University; William Mark Poteet, Indiana University of Pennsylvania; Colleen Rudman, Suffolk County Community College; Randy Russell, Red Rocks Community College; Carol Smith, Chandler-Gilbert Community College; Kathleen E. Studebaker, Missouri Southern State University; Kristie Sweet, Northeastern Junior College; Madelyn Troxclair, Seattle Central Community College; Jay VerLinden, Humboldt State University; Laura Ponder Wavell, Texas A&M–Corpus Christi; and Pavel Zemliansky, James Madison University. Their reactions, observations, and suggestions led to many of the improvements in this edition.

I am continuously impressed by the extraordinary support offered by the editors at Bedford/St. Martin's. Development editor Sara Eaton Gaunt's careful and thoughtful edits made it possible to streamline the textbook even as we increased our coverage of key research writing issues. Nick Carbone's able leadership of the new media group—along with his good humor, patience, and generosity of spirit—made the revisions of the Web site and the development of the Bedford Bibliographer pleasant and rewarding. Tari Fanderclai's insights into the needs of students and teachers who use the Web site led to significant improvements in its usability and usefulness and helped make the Bedford Bibliographer a success. I am indebted, as well, to Deborah Baker, who has once again done a superb job directing the production of the book, and to Barbara Flanagan and Paula Woolley, who have done such a careful job of copyediting. I am pleased, once again, by the extraordinary design work of Claire Seng-Niemoeller, who redesigned the book, and Jennifer Smith, who designed the new companion Web site. My thanks are offered as well to editor in chief Karen Henry, who so ably coordinated the preparation of this project, offering good advice at critical points in the process and bringing together a superb editorial team. And I am grateful for the tireless work of editorial assistant Joanna Lee.

The Bedford Researcher would not exist without Rory Baruth, regional sales manager for Bedford, Freeman, and Worth Publishers, who introduced me to the editors at Bedford/St. Martin's many years ago. I am indebted to Rory for his interest in the work I've done in technology-supported writing instruction and for his encouragement as I've worked on this and other projects for Bedford/St. Martin's. I am grateful as well to Joan Feinberg and Denise Wydra for their support of *The Bedford Researcher* and for their thoughtful suggestions about the directions this second edition might take. Their experience and understanding of the needs of writers and teachers have resulted in a stronger book and a more useful Web site.

Finally, I offer my thanks to the six student writers who shared their work, their time, and their insights into their research writing processes with the readers of this book: Jenna Alberter, Alexis Alvarez, Patrick Crossland, Kevin Fahey, Pete Jacquez, and Maria Sanchez-Traynor. The many hours we spent discussing their research writing processes helped focus my exploration of the roles textbooks can play in teaching and learning. As I wrote and revised this book, their work served as a constant reminder that research writing is a process of continuous discovery and reflection.

Mike Palmquist
Colorado State University

Introduction for Writers

You live in the information age. You surf the Web, use email, send instant messages, carry a mobile phone, watch television, read magazines and newspapers, view advertisements, attend public events, and meet and talk with others. Understanding how to work with information is among the most important writing skills you can have. In fact, most of the writing that you'll do in your lifetime—in college courses or for a career or community project—requires this skill. Take as examples the following types of documents—all of which require a writer to use information from sources:

- college research essays
- informative Web sites
- letters of complaint about a product or service
- product brochures or promotional literature
- market research analysis to help start a new business or launch a new product
- feature articles in a newspaper or magazine
- proposals to a school board or community group
- PowerPoint presentations at fund-raising events
- restaurant reviews or travel guides

Because such a wide range of documents relies heavily on a writer's ability to work with information, *The Bedford Researcher* is not so much about research papers as about research writing. What I hope you'll take from this text is a way of thinking about how to conduct research and write a document based on the sources of information you find.

The primary goals of *The Bedford Researcher* are to help you learn how to:

- choose the topic on which you'll develop a research question and thesis statement
- collect information about your topic from electronic, print, and field sources
- read critically, evaluate, and take notes on the information you've collected
- plan, write, and design an effective document
- document your sources of information

Meeting these goals requires thinking about research writing in a new way. Research writing is more than simply collecting and reporting information; it is a process of inquiry—of asking and responding to key questions. Instead of thinking of research writing as an isolated activity, think of it as a social act—a conversation in which writers and readers exchange information and ideas about a topic.

The research writing process you'll follow in this book consists of five main activities, which correspond to the five parts of this book:

Part I: Joining the Conversation	⊘	Chapters 1, 2, and 3 focus on getting started; exploring and narrowing your topic; and developing your research question and proposal.
Part II: Collecting Information	⊘	Chapters 4 through 7 discuss getting ready to collect and keep track of information; and searching for information with electronic resources, print resources, and field research methods.
Part III: Working with Sources	⊘	Chapters 8, 9, and 10 address reading critically, evaluating sources, and taking notes.
Part IV: Writing Your Document	⊘	Chapters 11 through 16 focus on organizing your ideas, developing a thesis statement, drafting, integrating sources, and revising, editing, and designing your document.
Part V: Documenting Sources	⊘	Chapters 17 through 21 discuss the reasons for documenting sources and provide detailed descriptions of four of the most commonly used documentation systems—MLA, APA, *Chicago*, and CSE.

As you read about these activities and carry them out in your own research project, keep in mind that they reflect a typical writing process—not a step-by-step recipe. Whatever your process turns out to be, remember that the order you follow is far less important than adapting these processes to the needs of your particular project.

SUPPORT THROUGHOUT YOUR RESEARCH WRITING PROCESS

The Bedford Researcher offers a wealth of support—in the book and on the companion Web site—to help you complete a research project.

In the Text

The textbook you are holding provides step-by-step guidance for writing research documents. It includes clear descriptions of research writing strategies, examples, activities, documentation guidelines, and help with finding resources in over forty disciplines, such as biology, history, marketing, and women's studies.

Color-coded tabs help you find information quickly.

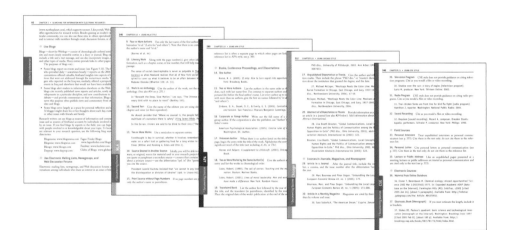

Key Questions begin each chapter and enable you to match your research writing needs to the material in the chapter.

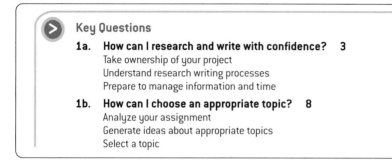

> **Key Questions**
>
> **1a.**   **How can I research and write with confidence?**   3
>   Take ownership of your project
>   Understand research writing processes
>   Prepare to manage information and time
>
> **1b.**   **How can I choose an appropriate topic?**   8
>   Analyze your assignment
>   Generate ideas about appropriate topics
>   Select a topic

Process Boxes and Checklists offer at-a-glance views of a specific research or writing process.

EXPLORING YOUR TOPIC

Step 1	Create a plan to explore your topic
Step 2	Discuss your topic with others
Step 3	Conduct preliminary observations
Step 4	Find and review sources

CHECKLIST FOR PARAPHRASING

To paraphrase, follow these guidelines:

- ✔ Be sure that you understand the passage by reading it and the surrounding text carefully.
- ✔ Restate the passage in your own words. Make sure that you do more than simply change a few key words.
- ✔ Avoid unintentional plagiarism by comparing the original passage with your paraphrase. Make sure that you've conveyed the meaning of the passage but that the wording and sentence structure differ from those in the original passage.
- ✔ Note the author, title, and the page or paragraph where the passage can be found.

What's My Purpose? **Boxes** help you consider—and reconsider—your purpose at every stage of the research writing process.

? WHAT'S MY PURPOSE?

Your research question focuses your attention on a specific aspect of the issue you've decided to address. Your decisions about how to collect and manage information should reflect that focus.

Consider featured writer Maria Sanchez-Traynor's research question and the different plans she might have used to collect and manage information. Maria's research question asks how English is taught to foreign-language speakers at the Intensive English Program (IEP) at Colorado State University. Her plan led her to collect information though interviews with students and teachers at the IEP, observation of IEP classes, and analysis of promotional materials from the program. Had she written an article that analyzed or critiqued the instructional practices of IEP instructors, she would have followed a different plan, one that expanded the range of sources she collected to include interviews with ESL (English as a Second Language) specialists from other institutions, database and library catalog searches for scholarly work on ESL, and ESL textbooks.

As you decide how to collect and manage information, keep your research question in mind. Doing so will help you determine the types of sources, resources, and search strategies you'll need to investigate the issue you've decided to address.

Read more about Maria Sanchez-Traynor at **bedfordresearcher.com**. Click on Featured Writers.

Annotated Examples make it easier for you to learn from the many illustrations and screen shots throughout the text.

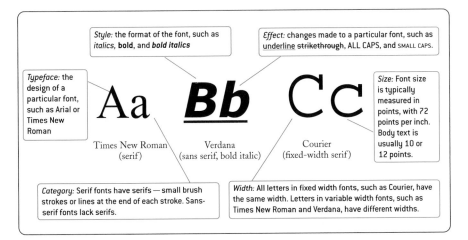

Style: the format of the font, such as *italics*, **bold**, and ***bold italics***

Effect: changes made to a particular font, such as underline strikethrough, ALL CAPS, and SMALL CAPS.

Typeface: the design of a particular font, such as Arial or Times New Roman

Size: Font size is typically measured in points, with 72 points per inch. Body text is usually 10 or 12 points.

Times New Roman (serif)

Verdana (sans serif, bold italic)

Courier (fixed-width serif)

Category: Serif fonts have serifs — small brush strokes or lines at the end of each stroke. Sans-serif fonts lack serifs.

Width: All letters in fixed width fonts, such as Courier, have the same width. Letters in variable width fonts, such as Times New Roman and Verdana, have different widths.

Tutorials in the book—and expanded on the companion Web site—provide you with extra help for important research writing issues, such as developing a research question, evaluating Web sites, and integrating quotations.

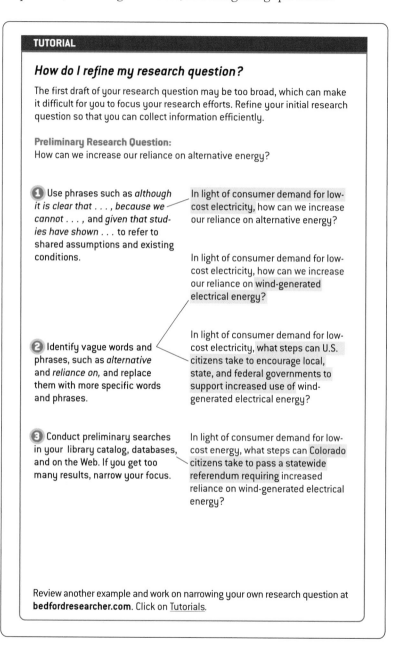

TUTORIAL

How do I refine my research question?

The first draft of your research question may be too broad, which can make it difficult for you to focus your research efforts. Refine your initial research question so that you can collect information efficiently.

Preliminary Research Question:
How can we increase our reliance on alternative energy?

1 Use phrases such as *although it is clear that . . . , because we cannot . . . ,* and *given that studies have shown . . .* to refer to shared assumptions and existing conditions.

In light of consumer demand for low-cost electricity, how can we increase our reliance on alternative energy?

In light of consumer demand for low-cost electricity, how can we increase our reliance on wind-generated electrical energy?

2 Identify vague words and phrases, such as *alternative* and *reliance on,* and replace them with more specific words and phrases.

In light of consumer demand for low-cost electricity, what steps can U.S. citizens take to encourage local, state, and federal governments to support increased use of wind-generated electrical energy?

3 Conduct preliminary searches in your library catalog, databases, and on the Web. If you get too many results, narrow your focus.

In light of consumer demand for low-cost energy, what steps can Colorado citizens take to pass a statewide referendum requiring increased reliance on wind-generated electrical energy?

Review another example and work on narrowing your own research question at **bedfordresearcher.com**. Click on <u>Tutorials</u>.

My Research Project Activities connect what's in the text with your own research writing.

My Research Project

USE YOUR RESEARCH QUESTION TO GENERATE SEARCH TERMS

To generate keywords for your searches, write your research question on a piece of paper or in a word processor and then underline or boldface the most important words and phrases in the sentence. Brainstorm a list of related words and phrases:

Example:

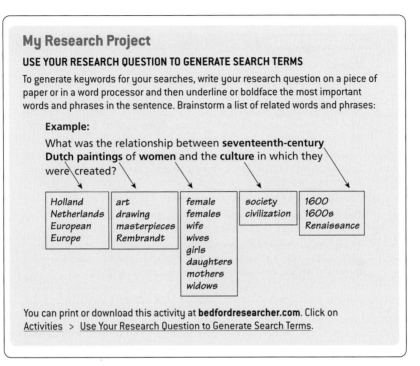

What was the relationship between **seventeenth-century Dutch paintings** of **women** and the **culture** in which they were created?

| Holland Netherlands European Europe | art drawing masterpieces Rembrandt | female females wife wives girls daughters mothers widows | society civilization | 1600 1600s Renaissance |

You can print or download this activity at **bedfordresearcher.com**. Click on Activities > Use Your Research Question to Generate Search Terms.

Quick Reference Boxes at the end of every chapter give you a brief overview of steps to take before you move on.

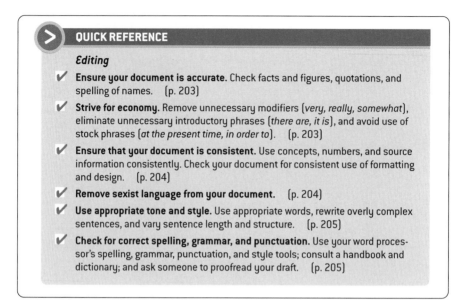

> **QUICK REFERENCE**
>
> *Editing*
>
> ✔ **Ensure your document is accurate.** Check facts and figures, quotations, and spelling of names.   (p. 203)
>
> ✔ **Strive for economy.** Remove unnecessary modifiers (*very, really, somewhat*), eliminate unnecessary introductory phrases (*there are, it is*), and avoid use of stock phrases (*at the present time, in order to*).   (p. 203)
>
> ✔ **Ensure that your document is consistent.** Use concepts, numbers, and source information consistently. Check your document for consistent use of formatting and design.   (p. 204)
>
> ✔ **Remove sexist language from your document.**   (p. 204)
>
> ✔ **Use appropriate tone and style.** Use appropriate words, rewrite overly complex sentences, and vary sentence length and structure.   (p. 205)
>
> ✔ **Check for correct spelling, grammar, and punctuation.** Use your word processor's spelling, grammar, punctuation, and style tools; consult a handbook and dictionary; and ask someone to proofread your draft.   (p. 205)

Cross-references to the companion Web site direct you to related material online at bedfordresearcher.com.

Find a list of Web sites about conducting interviews at **bedfordresearcher .com**. Click on <u>Links</u> > <u>Resources for Conducting Field Research</u>.	Learn how to use bullets, numbering, and indentation to create outlines at **bedfordresearcher.com**. Click on <u>Guides</u> > <u>How to Use Your Word Processor</u>.	For additional help, consult the St. Martin's Tutorial on Avoiding Plagiarism at **bedfordstmartins.com/ plagiarismtutorial**.

On the Web Site

The Bedford Researcher Web site at bedfordresearcher.com offers tools and resources to aid you with the most challenging parts of the research writing process.

The Bedford Bibliographer.   Use this online tool to evaluate your sources and generate an annotated bibliography in MLA, APA, *Chicago*, or CSE style.

Tutorials.   The tutorials in this book are expanded online, giving you more help with your most pressing research-related problems and helping you make progress with your research project.

Activities.   *My Research Project* activities throughout the text allow you to apply what you learn to your own projects. The activities can be downloaded or printed from the Web site.

Links.   Carefully chosen and collected in one convenient place, hundreds of links point you to research-related resources on the Web on a wide variety of topics. You'll also find comprehensive lists of databases and print resources for research in more than forty disciplines.

Featured Writers.   Read notes and drafts written by the six students featured in the text; interviews with the students explain how they tackled their research writing projects.

Guides.   Online advice for using search engines, word processors, and other digital research and writing tools offer you extra assistance when you need it.

Brief Contents

Contents

I Joining the Conversation   1

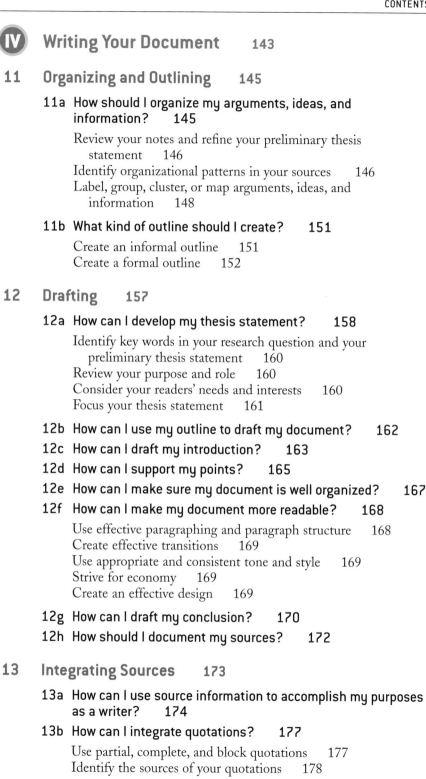

The Bedford Researcher

I	**Joining the Conversation**
II	Collecting Information
III	Working with Sources
IV	Writing Your Document
V	Documenting Sources

PART I

Joining the Conversation

 Getting Started 3

2 Exploring and Narrowing Your Topic 15

3 Developing Your Research Question and Proposal 32

Working on a research writing project is similar to joining a conversation. Before you contribute to the conversation, listen carefully to what others are saying. By reading widely, talking with knowledgeable people, and making firsthand observations, you can gain the knowledge you need to add your voice to the discussion.

In Part One of *The Bedford Researcher,* you'll read about how to get started, how to choose an appropriate topic, how to explore and narrow that topic, and how to develop a clearly stated research question and a proposal.

Part I
Joining the Conversation

> 1   Getting Started
2   Exploring and Narrowing Your Topic
3   Developing Your Research Question
and Proposal

1

Getting Started

> **Key Questions**

Getting started can be the hardest part of a research writing project. You'll likely find yourself staring at a blank computer screen or twirling a pen in your fingers as you ask, "Is this project really necessary?" or "What in the world should I write about?"

This chapter helps you get started. It provides an overview of research writing processes and project management strategies and discusses how to select an appropriate topic.

1a

How can I research and write with confidence?

Even writers who are new to research writing can approach it confidently. All that's needed is personal investment in your writing project, a clear understanding of the processes involved in research writing, and an awareness of strategies for managing them.

Take Ownership of Your Project

Confident research writers have a strong personal investment in their research writing project. Sometimes this investment comes naturally. You might be interested in your topic, committed to achieving your purposes as a writer, intrigued by the demands of writing for a particular audience, or looking forward to the challenges of

3

writing a new type of document, such as a Web site or a magazine article. At times, however, you need to create a sense of personal investment by looking for connections between your interests and your writing project. This can be a challenge, particularly when you've been assigned a project that wouldn't normally interest you.

The key to investing yourself in a project you wouldn't normally care about is taking ownership of the project. To take ownership, ask yourself how your project might help you pursue your personal, professional, or academic interests. Think about how the project might help you meet new people or learn new writing or research strategies. Or look for unique challenges associated with a project, such as learning how to develop arguments or use document design techniques more effectively. Your goal is to feel that you have a stake in your research writing project by finding something that appeals to your interests and helps you grow as a researcher and writer.

● Understand Research Writing Processes

Research writing involves learning about a topic, drawing conclusions about that topic, and sharing your conclusions with your readers. Many factors affect how you will accomplish your goals. If you are writing an argument, your overall process will be somewhat different than it would be if you are writing to inform your readers. Similarly, the type and length of document you are planning to write will shape your approach. Despite the unique characteristics of each research writing project, most research writers use the processes shown in Figure 1.1.

● Prepare to Manage Information and Time

There are two primary strategies for managing your writing project: managing the information you collect as you work, and managing your time.

Managing Information   If you've ever forgotten a phone number or misplaced tickets to a concert, you know how frustrating it can be to lose something. It can be just as frustrating to lose your interview notes or forget where you found a quotation or fact. As you begin your research writing project, decide how you'll keep track of what you'll learn. You might want to start a research log—a place where you can keep the sources you collect and record your thoughts and progress. A research log can take many forms:

- a notebook
- a word processing file or a folder on your computer
- a folder or binder
- a set of note cards
- notes taken on a personal digital assistant (such as a Palm handheld or a Pocket PC)
- a tape recorder or voice recorder

Choosing, exploring, and narrowing a topic (Chapters 1 and 2)	• • • Pick a topic; talk about it with others and browse sources; focus on an issue within the topic.
Developing and refining a research question (Chapter 3)	• • • Ask a question that will guide your collection and use of information.
Collecting information (Chapters 4–7)	• • • Use print and electronic resources and field research to locate appropriate, relevant sources.
Reading critically, evaluating, and taking notes (Chapters 8–10)	• • • Read and evaluate with a critical, questioning attitude; mark and take notes on key ideas and information.
Organizing and planning (Chapter 11)	• • • Map the shape of your document, refine your thesis statement, and prepare to draft.
Drafting (Chapters 12–14)	• • • Create a document that helps you achieve your purposes and address your readers.
Revising and editing (Chapter 15)	• • • Review and refine your document.
Designing (Chapter 16)	• • • Use document design to enhance the effectiveness of your document.
Documenting sources (Chapters 17–21)	• • • Cite your sources accurately and appropriately.

FIGURE 1.1   Research Writing Processes As you learn about your topic and reflect on your progress, you'll move back and forth among these processes.

Although it might seem like extra work now, creating a research log as you begin your project will save time in the long run.

My Research Project

CREATE A RESEARCH LOG

Create your research log now so you'll be prepared to face the challenges of planning and carrying out your project.

The Bedford Researcher Web site at **bedfordresearcher.com** can help you create your research log. You'll find electronic versions of the "My Research Project" activities as well as interactive versions of the tutorials found throughout this book. You'll also find the **Bedford Bibliographer**, a tool that allows you to save bibliographic information and brief annotations for your sources as you work on your project.

Managing Time   Time management should be a high priority as you begin your research writing project. If you don't schedule your time well, for example, you might spend far too much time collecting information and far too little working with it.

As you begin thinking about your research writing project, consider creating a project timeline. A timeline can help you identify important milestones in your project and determine when you need to meet them.

My Research Project

CREATE A PROJECT TIMELINE

In your research log, start a project timeline like the one shown here. The steps in your process might be slightly different, but most research writing projects follow this general process. As you create your timeline, keep in mind any specific requirements of your assignment, such as handing in a first draft, revised drafts, and so on.

PROJECT TIMELINE		
ACTIVITY	START DATE	COMPLETION DATE
Select your topic		
Explore your topic		
Narrow your topic		
Develop your research question		
Get ready to collect and manage information		
Collect information		
Read and evaluate information		
Take notes		
Organize your information		
Develop your thesis statement		
Plan your document		
Write the first draft of your document		
Review and revise your first draft		
Write and revise additional drafts		
Edit your draft		
Design your document		
Finalize in-text and end-of-text citations		
Submit your document		

You can download or print this activity at **bedfordresearcher.com**. Click on Activities > Create a Project Timeline.

FEATURED WRITERS

Discussions throughout this book are illustrated by six Featured Writers — real students who crafted a variety of research projects, including traditional essays, Web sites, and feature articles. You can learn from these real-life examples as you plan and conduct your own research, and draft and revise your own document.

Jenna Alberter • Writing about Images of Women in Seventeenth-Century Dutch Art
Jenna wrote a research essay for an art history course. She explored the general topic of seventeenth-century Dutch art and then narrowed her topic to images of women in this art and the way these images "influenced and were influenced by the culture in which they were created." You can read her research essay on p. 266.

Alexis Alvarez • Writing about the Impact of Competitive Sports on Adolescent Girls
Alexis wrote an argumentative essay about the effects competitive sports can have on adolescent girls. She explored the general topic of competitive sports and women before narrowing her topic to the use of steroids by female teenaged athletes. You can read her essay on p. 292.

Patrick Crossland • Writing an Informative Research Paper about College Admissions Standards
Patrick wrote a research essay about college admissions standards. Throughout the semester, Patrick worked in a group with four classmates. Although each student wrote his or her own essay, the students shared ideas and sources. You can read his essay on p. 320.

Kevin Fahey • Writing an Analytic Research Essay about Ernest Hemingway's Characterization of Nick Adams
Kevin wrote a research essay about Ernest Hemingway's description and development of Nick Adams, the character Hemingway scholars agree most closely resembles Hemingway himself.

Pete Jacquez • Writing about the Benefits of Wind Power
Pete created a Web site about the benefits of wind-generated electrical power. His site provides both information about wind power and an argument in favor of increasing reliance on wind power.

Maria Sanchez-Traynor • Writing an Article about the Intensive English Program at Colorado State University
Maria wrote a feature article about the Intensive English Program (IEP) at Colorado State University. The IEP provides instruction in written and spoken English for students whose first language is not English. Maria explored her topic by observing classes, visiting the IEP Web site, reading promotional literature, and conducting interviews with the program's assistant director, two of its students, and a teacher.

You can follow the featured writers' research writing process by visiting the Bedford Researcher Web site at **bedfordresearcher.com** and clicking on <u>Featured Writers.</u> Here you'll find interviews in which the writers discuss their work, and you can read their assignments, the notes they took as they worked on their projects, and drafts of their documents.

1b

How can I choose an appropriate topic?

In the most general sense, your topic is what you will research and write about—it is the foundation on which your research writing project is built. An appropriate topic, however, is much more than a simple subject heading in an almanac or encyclopedia. It is a subject of debate, discussion, and discovery.

Thinking of your topic as a topic of conversation is critical to your success as a research writer. Research writing goes beyond merely locating and reporting information. Instead, it is an ongoing process of inquiry in which you must consider your purposes, your readers, and the conventions associated with the type of document you plan to write.

Although locating a topic is as easy as visiting your library, reading the newspaper, or browsing the Web, choosing a topic that is well suited to your research writing project requires additional work. It involves reflecting on your assignment, your interests, and your readers. To choose a suitable topic, work through these steps.

CHOOSING AN APPROPRIATE TOPIC

Step 1　　Analyze your assignment

Step 2　　Generate ideas about appropriate topics

Step 3　　Select a topic

● Step 1: Analyze Your Assignment

Research writers in academic and professional settings usually work in response to an assignment. You might be given general guidelines, such as "choose a topic in your major"; you might be asked to choose a topic within a general subject area, such as race relations; or you might be given complete freedom in your choice of topic.

> Download or print a list of useful prompts from **bedfordresearcher.com**. Click on Activities > Analyze Your Research Writing Assignment.

Be aware, however, that no matter how much freedom you have, your assignment will provide important clues about what your instructor and your other readers will expect. To analyze your assignment, ask yourself the following questions about your research writing situation.

? WHAT'S MY PURPOSE?

Every writer has a purpose, or reason, for writing. In fact, most writers have multiple purposes. If you are writing a research project for a class, your purposes might include completing the assignment as required, learning something new, improving your writing skills, convincing others to adopt your point of view about an issue, and getting a good grade. If you are an employee working on a project status report, your

↓

WHAT'S MY PURPOSE? (continued)

purposes might include conveying key information to your superiors, performing well enough to earn a promotion, and gaining valuable experience in project management. Whatever your purposes for conducting a research project, your topic should help you accomplish them.

"What's My Purpose" boxes like this one, located throughout this book, will help you consider and reconsider your purpose throughout your research writing process.

Who Are My Readers and Why Would They Read My Document?   Your assignment might identify your readers, or audience, for you. If you are writing a research project for a class, one of your most important readers will be your instructor. You are also likely to have additional readers, such as your classmates, people who have a professional or personal interest in your topic, or, if your project will be published in print or online, the readers of a particular newspaper, magazine, or Web site. If you are writing in a business or professional setting, your readers might include supervisors, customers, or other people associated with the organization. In some cases, you might be asked to define your own audience. As you consider possible topics, ask yourself which subjects these readers would be most interested in learning about. Featured writer Kevin Fahey, for example, would probably not have written about the literature of Ernest Hemingway if his target audience had been the readers of a magazine such as *PC World* or *Street Rod.*

Regardless of who your readers are, remember that they aren't empty vessels waiting to be filled with information. They will have their own purposes for reading your document. If the topic you select doesn't fit those purposes, they're likely to stop reading.

What Will Influence Me and What Will Influence My Readers?   Research writers aren't mindless robots who churn through sources and create documents without emotion or conviction—or at least they shouldn't be. Your topic should interest you. An appropriate topic will keep you motivated as you carry out the work needed to complete your research project successfully. Your project should also be your own, even if it's been assigned to you. One of the most important things you can do as a research writer is to make a personal connection with the topic. To make that connection, look for topics that can help you pursue your personal, professional, and academic interests.

Readers are influenced by their interest in a particular topic, their knowledge of the topic, and their values and beliefs. If your readers have no interest in your topic, know little about it, or are offended by it, you aren't likely to meet with much success.

What Type of Document Am I Writing?   Assignments often specify the type of document you will be writing. You might be asked to write essays, reports, or Web sites. You might also write articles, opinion columns, letters to the editor, multimedia presentations, brochures, or flyers. Decide whether your topic suits the type of document you are writing.

What Will Affect My Ability to Work on This Project?   The requirements of your assignment, the limitations you will face as you work, and the opportunities you can capitalize upon will affect your ability to work on your research project.

Requirements and Limitations   If you are writing your research project for a class, examine the requirements of your assignment:

- the required length or page count
- the project due date
- the number and type of sources you can use (electronic, print, and field)
- any suggested or required resources
- specific requirements about the organization and structure of your document (a title page, introduction, body, conclusion, works cited list, and so on)
- expected documentation format (such as MLA, APA, *Chicago*, or CSE)
- any intermediate reports or activities due before you turn in the final project document (such as thesis statements, notes, outlines, and rough drafts)

You might also face limitations, such as lack of access to information or lack of time to work.

Determining your requirements and limitations will help you weigh the potential drawbacks of a topic. You might find that you need to narrow the scope of your topic significantly given your time and page limit.

Opportunities   Sometimes writers get so wrapped up in the requirements and limitations of the assignment that they overlook their opportunities. As you think about your topic, ask yourself whether you can take advantage of opportunities such as

- access to a specialized or particularly good library
- personal experience with and knowledge about a topic
- access to people who are experts on a topic

For example, featured writer Alexis Alvarez thought about her personal experiences and those of her friends before deciding to focus on the impact of competitive sports programs on adolescent girls.

Step 2: Generate Ideas about Appropriate Topics

By now you might have some ideas of topics that interest you and that fit your research writing situation. Your next step is to think more carefully about potential topics by using prewriting activities such as brainstorming, freewriting, looping, and clustering. You can use these activities to generate possible topics and narrow your focus from broad, general topics to those that would be more appropriate for a research project.

Brainstorming   Brainstorming involves listing ideas as they occur to you. This list should not consist of complete sentences—in fact, brainstorming lists are meant to record the many ideas that come into your head as you think of them. Brainstorming is most successful when you avoid censoring yourself. Although you'll end up using only a few of the ideas you generate during brainstorming, don't worry until later about weeding out the useful ideas from the less promising ones.

Brainstorming sessions are usually conducted in response to a specific question. Featured writer Patrick Crossland generated the following list in response to the question, "What interests me personally about this project?"

how people decide they like colleges

who goes to which colleges? Breakdown by academic ability, income, social class, race?

how colleges select students

what colleges look for in students

secret standards used by colleges?

Freewriting   When freewriting, you write full sentences quickly, without stopping and—most important—without editing what you write. You might want to start with one of the ideas you generated in your brainstorming activity, or you can begin your freewriting session with a phrase such as "I am interested in my topic because. . . ." After brainstorming about the general topic of college admissions, Patrick Crossland focused his freewriting on his readers' purposes and interest. The following is an excerpt from Patrick's freewriting:

> People love stats. My readers may want to know about the statistics of who's getting into what colleges and why. My readers may want to use my info as a source for their own writing or thinking about the subject—they may want to contest/agree with my stand and viewpoints about how students are admitted to college—may even think they know how schools go about the process, like using SAT scores and activities and sometimes race.

> *Patrick did not edit his freewriting or worry about spelling, grammar, or style.*

Some writers set a timer and freewrite for five, ten, or fifteen minutes; others set a goal of a certain number of pages and keep writing until they have met that goal. (Hint: If you find it difficult to write without editing, try blindwriting—freewriting on a computer with the monitor turned off.)

Looping   Looping is an alternative form of freewriting. During a looping session, you write for a set amount of time (say five minutes) and then read what you've written. As you read, identify one key idea in what you've written and then write for five minutes with the new key idea as your starting point. Patrick Crossland, for example, wrote in response to a sentence he had generated during freewriting, "My readers may want to know about the statistics of who's getting into what colleges and why."

My readers will be both my professor, who has already gone through college, and my fellow students, who may be looking to transfer to other colleges or apply to graduate schools someday—what aspect of college admissions will all of these readers be interested in?

Clustering   Clustering involves presenting your ideas about a potential topic in graphical form. Clustering can help you gain a different perspective on a topic by helping you map out the relationships among your ideas. It can also help you generate new ideas. Patrick Crossland used clustering to map out his ideas and further narrow his topic (see Figure 1.2).

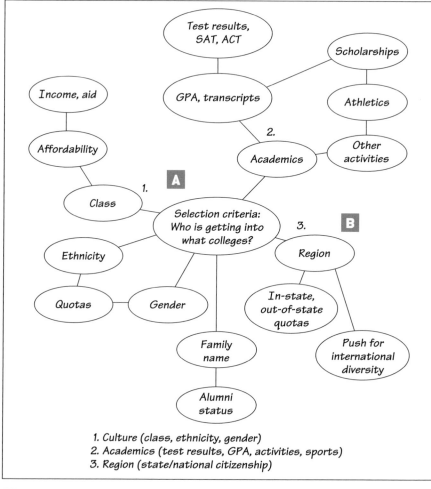

1. Culture (class, ethnicity, gender)
2. Academics (test results, GPA, activities, sports)
3. Region (state/national citizenship)

FIGURE 1.2   A Cluster of Ideas Created by Patrick Crossland

A Patrick listed a central idea and three key areas to explore.

B Key areas are also linked to related ideas.

When you have completed your brainstorming, freewriting, looping, and clustering activities, review what you've written. You'll most likely find that these prewriting techniques have generated a useful list of ideas for a topic.

My Research Project

GENERATE IDEAS FOR A TOPIC

In your research log, use brainstorming, freewriting, looping, and clustering to generate ideas for a topic.

Brainstorm responses to the following questions:

- What do I want to accomplish with this project?
- What interests me personally about this project?
- What interests me academically about this project?
- Who are my readers?
- What topics do my readers need to read about?
- What topics would my readers like to read about?

Freewrite in response to one of the following prompts, replacing the *X*'s with the ideas for topics that you generated during your brainstorming session. Before you begin, set a goal of a certain number of minutes or a set amount of pages you will write.

- Writing about *X* will help me accomplish the following purposes:
- I am personally interested in *X* because . . .
- I am academically interested in *X* because . . .
- My readers need or would like to know about *X* because . . .

Select a response from your freewriting activity and carry out the following **looping** exercise.

1. Paste the response at the top of your word processing file or write it at the top of a page in your notebook. Then freewrite for five minutes about the response.
2. Identify the best idea in this freewriting.
3. Freewrite for five more minutes about the idea you've identified.
4. Repeat the process until you've refined your idea into a potential topic.

Generate additional ideas about your potential topic by using a **clustering** exercise.

1. In the middle of a sheet of paper, or in the center of an electronic document (word processing file or graphics file), write your potential topic.
2. Identify ideas that are related to your central topic and list them near it. Think about the importance and relevance of each related idea, and draw lines and circles to show the relationships among your ideas.
3. Write additional ideas related to the ideas in Step 2. In turn, draw lines and circles to show their relationships to the other ideas in your cluster.
4. Repeat the process until you've created a cluster of ideas that represents your current understanding of the topic you are considering.

You can download or print this activity at **bedfordresearcher.com**. Click on Activities > Generate Ideas about a Topic.

Step 3: Select a Topic

After you've spent time thinking and prewriting about potential topics for your research project, you should select the strongest candidate.

As you make your choice, think carefully again about the level of interest both you and your readers might have in the topic. Some topics, such as Patrick Crossland's, will appeal to a large number of people, including high school students applying to colleges, college students who might not have been accepted by their top choices, and the parents of these students. Other topics, such as Jenna Alberter's focus on seventeenth-century Dutch art, might appeal to a somewhat smaller group of readers—in her case, art historians or readers of the book *Girl with a Pearl Earring*. The key is to identify which topics—whether they will attract many readers or only a handful of researchers—are compatible with your purpose and interests and those of your readers.

In addition, remember that your topic is subject to change. It's a starting point, not a final destination. As you explore your topic, you'll begin to narrow it to a specific issue—a point of disagreement, uncertainty, concern, or curiosity—that is being discussed by a community of readers and writers.

> **QUICK REFERENCE**

Getting Started

✔ Gain confidence about research writing by becoming acquainted with the research writing process.   (p. 3)

✔ Create a research log to manage information and ideas as you work.   (p. 5)

✔ Develop a project timeline to help manage your time.   (p. 6)

✔ Analyze your assignment by reflecting on your research writing situation — purposes, influences, type of document, requirements, limitations, and opportunities.   (p. 8)

✔ Generate ideas about appropriate topics by brainstorming, freewriting, looping, and clustering.   (p. 10)

✔ Choose the most promising and appropriate topic.   (p. 14)

2

Exploring and Narrowing Your Topic

Exploring involves gaining a general understanding of the issues—points of disagreement, uncertainty, concern, or curiosity—within a topic. Narrowing your focus to a single issue lays the groundwork for developing the research question that will frame your thinking about that issue and guides your efforts to gain a comprehensive understanding of it.

2a

How can I explore my topic?

Beginning to explore your topic is similar to attending a public meeting on a controversial issue. Imagine yourself at a meeting about a proposed development in your neighborhood. You're uncertain about whether to support or oppose its construction, but it seems as though all the others at the meeting have made up their minds. After an hour of people shouting back and forth, the moderator suggests a break to allow tempers to cool.

During the break, you wander from one group of people to another. Everyone is talking about the same topic, but the conversations are radically different. In one group, four people who bitterly oppose the development are talking about how to stop it. In another group, a developer is explaining the steps that will be taken to minimize the project's impact on the neighborhood. Yet another group is discussing alternative uses of the building site. As you walk around the room, you listen for information to help you decide which conversation you want to join. Eventually, you join the group discussing alternatives to development because this issue interests you most.

This process is similar to the strategies you'll use to explore and narrow your topic. At this early stage in your research project, you are listening in on conversations about specific issues in order to choose one that most intrigues you. To explore your topic, follow these steps:

EXPLORING YOUR TOPIC

Step 1   Create a plan to explore your topic
Step 2   Discuss your topic with others
Step 3   Conduct preliminary observations
Step 4   Find and review sources

Step 1: Create a Plan to Explore Your Topic

Before you start exploring your topic, create an informal research plan.

❓ WHAT'S MY PURPOSE?

Review your purpose in your research log. As you develop your research plan, remember that it should reflect your purpose for working on the project and provide directions for locating, collecting, and managing information.

The most common elements of a research plan include:

- a list of people with whom you can discuss your topic, including people who know a great deal about or have been involved with the topic, and people, such as librarians, who can help you locate information about your topic
- a list of questions to ask people who can help you explore your topic
- a list of settings you might observe to learn more about your topic
- a list of resources to search and browse, such as library catalogs, databases, Web search engines, and Web directories
- a system for keeping track of the information you collect

After you create your plan, use it to guide your work and to remind yourself of steps you might overlook. A note such as "talk to Professor Garvey about recent clinical studies" can come in handy if you've become so busy searching the Web or your library's catalog that you forget about your other plans for exploring your topic.

After you've drafted your plan, share it with your instructor, your supervisor, or a librarian, who might suggest additional resources, shortcuts, and alternative strategies. Take notes on the feedback you receive and, if necessary, revise your plan.

My Research Project

CREATE A RESEARCH PLAN

In your research log, answer the following questions.

- Who can help me learn more about my topic?
- What questions should I ask people on my list?
- What settings can I observe to learn more about my topic?
- What resources can I search or browse to learn more about my topic?
- How can I keep track of information I collect as I explore my topic?

Using your responses, write your plan as a series of steps and ask your instructor, your supervisor, or a librarian to review it.

You can download or print this activity at **bedfordresearcher.com**. Click on Activities > Create a Research Plan.

Step 2: Discuss Your Topic with Others

Talking about your topic with people who know about it or have been affected by it can provide you with insights that are not available through other sources. An instructor, a supervisor, or a librarian can also help you identify additional resources.

Featured writer Alexis Alvarez explored her topic—women and competitive sports—in part by talking with family members and friends who had competed in organized sports. These discussions helped Alexis better see the many different issues she could pursue within her topic.

You can also explore a topic by conducting formal interviews (see p. 95) or by writing letters and email messages (see p. 104). If you are uncertain about how to find people you can interview about your topic, you

Learn more about chat at **bedfordresearcher.com**. Click on Guides > How to Use Chat, Instant Messaging, and MOOs.

might start by visiting an Internet chat room devoted to discussion of serious issues. (For example, visit the chat rooms in the community section of CNN.com.)

Step 3: Conduct Preliminary Observations

Observation is a powerful tool, especially when you are just getting started on a research project. Like discussing your topic with others, observing can provide you with valuable information that isn't available from other sources.

Featured writer Maria Sanchez-Traynor used observation to help explore her topic—the Intensive English Program at Colorado State University. Maria observed two classes in the program, which provided her with a different perspective than she could have gained through other information-gathering techniques.

Step 4: Find and Review Sources

After you've talked with others about your topic and observed relevant settings, take advantage of the work other writers have done on the topic by finding and reviewing sources.

Search Your Library's Online Catalog. Online library catalogs allow you to search for sources by title, author, and subject words. Before you begin your search, generate a list of words and phrases associated with your topic. If you already know the names of authors or the titles of books or periodicals related to your topic, search for them. At this point, however, you'll usually conduct a subject search on your topic.

Featured writer Jenna Alberter wrote a research essay about images of women in seventeenth-century Dutch paintings. She began exploring her topic by conducting a word search in her library's online catalog on the broad topic of seventeenth-century Dutch art (see Figure 2.1).

For more about searching online library catalogs, see p. 63.

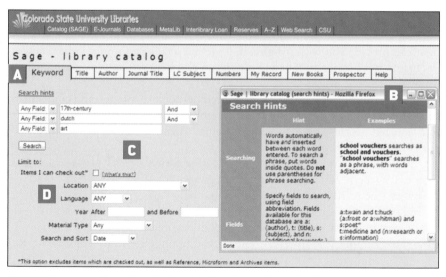

FIGURE 2.1   Jenna Alberter's Initial Search in Her Library's Online Catalog

A Available search types

B Search tips open in a new window

C Jenna's word search

D Searches can be limited (see p. 63)

FIGURE 2.2   Browsing the Shelves in a Library

A If you located the book *The Golden Age of Dutch Art* . . .

B . . . browse the shelves to find related works, such as *Flemish and Dutch Painting.*

Browse Your Library's Shelves.   Once you've located a relevant book or periodical through your library's online catalog, you can usually find other sources about your topic on the same or nearby shelves (see Figure 2.2). Scan the titles of those works to locate additional sources you might not have found in your online catalog search.

As you browse your library, be aware of differences in the types of sources you find. Depending on your topic, some types of sources will be more appropriate than others. For example, if you are interested in a topic such as featured writer Pete Jacquez's (wind-generated electrical power), and want to learn about the latest developments in wind turbine design, you might focus on trade and professional journals, newspapers, and magazines. If you are interested in a topic such as Ernest Hemingway, as Kevin Fahey was, you would focus on books and articles in scholarly journals. Note the following characteristics of sources you might find as you browse the shelves at your library:

- **Books** undergo a lengthy editorial process before they are published, and librarians evaluate them before adding them to the library collection.

- **Articles in scholarly journals** also undergo a lengthy editorial process before they are published. Most are reviewed—evaluated for accuracy, completeness, and methodological soundness—by experts in the field before they are accepted for publication.

- **Articles in trade and other professional journals** do not always go through a strict review process. You can find out whether articles are reviewed by looking at the submission policies printed in the journal.

- **Articles in magazines and newspapers** are usually reviewed only by the editors of the publication. Editorials typically represent an editor's or editorial board's opinion on an issue and are not subject to review. Similarly, opinion columns and letters to the editor seldom go through a review process.

- **Theses and dissertations** are final projects for students in graduate programs. Theses and dissertations vary in quality and reliability, although they have been reviewed and approved by committees of professors.

- **Microfilm and microfiche** are methods of storing documents such as older issues of newspapers and magazines or government documents and reports.

- **Other sources** include maps, videotapes, audiotapes, and multimedia items such as CD-ROMs and DVDs.

When you locate a source that seems particularly useful, read its works cited list, footnotes, endnotes, or in-text citations for related sources and then find and evaluate them.

Browse Newsstands and Bookstores.   If your topic is a current one, browse at a newsstand for specialty newspapers and magazines to which your library doesn't subscribe. If your topic has a broad, popular appeal, you might look at the books in a large bookstore or on a bookseller's Web site.

Search Available Databases.   Databases organize information as records (or entries) on a particular topic. You can search these records just as you would search an online library catalog (see Figure 2.3). If you have difficulty locating databases or aren't sure which databases are appropriate for your topic, ask a reference librarian for assistance.

For more on searching databases, see p. 68.

Conduct Web Searches.   Web searches allow you to locate quickly a great deal of information about your topic—although not all of it will be as reliable as the sources you locate through a library catalog or database. To start searching the Web, visit one of the leading search engines, such as Google (www.google .com), AllTheWeb.com (www.alltheweb.com), or MSN Search (search.msn.com).

> Learn more about locating information on the Web at **bedfordresearcher.com.** Click on Guides > How to Use a Web Search Site and Guides > How to Search a Web Directory.

Once you visit a site, you can begin to browse the Web. Browsing the Web is similar to browsing the shelves in the library. That is, once you've located a Web site that is relevant to your research question, you can usually follow links from that site to related sites. For instance, one of the Web sites Pete Jacquez visited as a result of his initial search on MSN Search (see Figure 2.4) was the National Renewable Energy

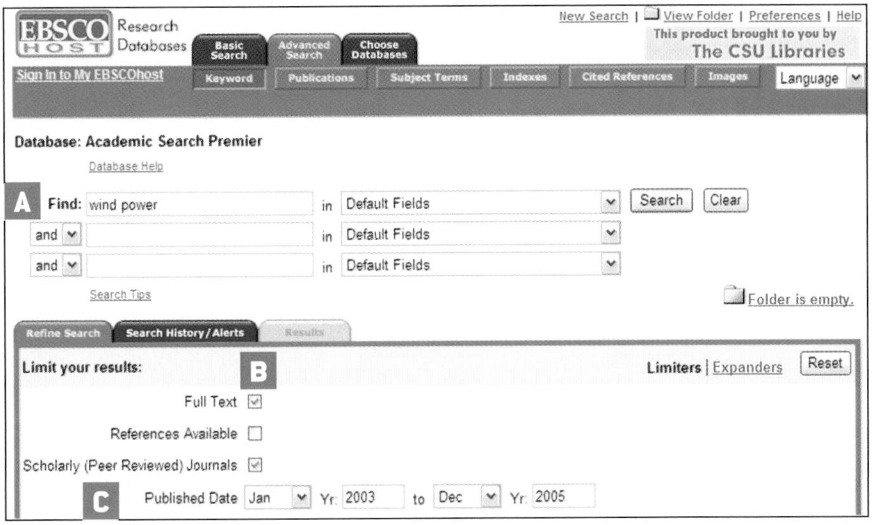

FIGURE 2.3   Pete Jacquez's Initial Search in the *Academic Search Premier* Database

A Pete searched for *wind power.*

B Pete limited his search.

C Pete set a date range to locate only recent articles.

D Other options (not shown): Pete limited his search to articles. He expanded his search to "Also search within the full text of the articles" and "Also search for related words."

Laboratory's National Wind Technology Center Web site, which contains a list of Web sites related to wind power (see Figure 2.5).

For more on Web searches, see p. 68.

Browse Web Directories.   Unlike Web search engines, which automatically search the Web and enter each new site they find into large databases, Web directories, such as Open Directory (www.dmoz.org) and Google Directory

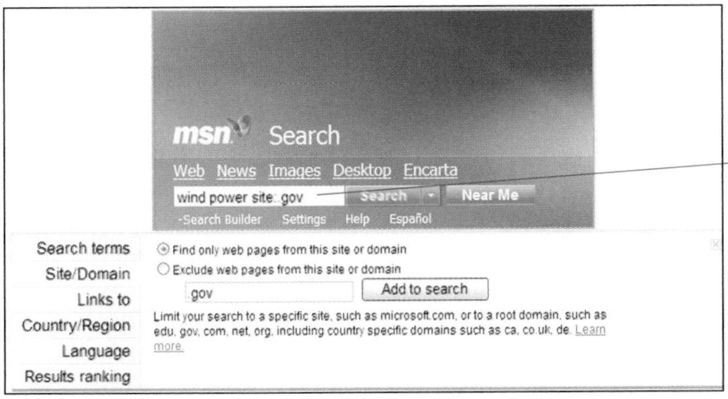

FIGURE 2.4
Pete Jacquez's
Initial Search on
MSN Search

Pete restricted his search for *wind power* to government sites.

FIGURE 2.5 A Site Listed in Pete Jacquez's Initial Search Results

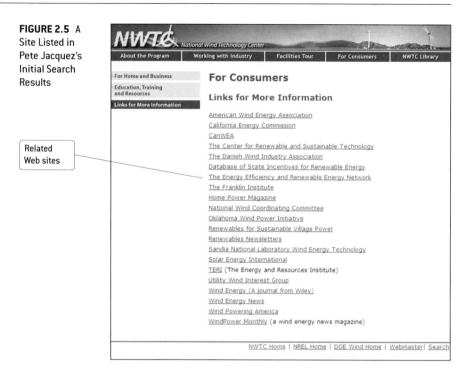

Related Web sites

(directory.google.com) use editors—real people—to organize their links to Web sites by categories and subcategories (see p. 70 to learn more about Web directories). When Pete Jacquez visited Open Directory, he found information on his topic by clicking on the general category Science and then by clicking in succession on the subcategories Energy and Wind Power (see Figure 2.6).

Browse Electronic Mailing Lists, Newsgroups, Blogs, and Web Discussion Forums. Electronic mailing lists, newsgroups, blogs, and Web discussion forums can be excellent sources of information, but they can also contain some outrageous misinformation. Because most of these resources are unmoderated—that is, anything sent to them is published—you'll find everything from expert opinions to the musings of folks who know little or nothing about your topic. When read with a bit of skepticism, however, the messages can help you identify issues within your topic. For more on these online resources, see p. 81.

Learn more at **bedfordresearcher.com**. Click on Guides > How to Research Newsgroups, Mailing Lists, and Web Discussion Forums.

Record Your Search Results. As you explore your topic, record your searches: Identify the library catalogs, databases, and Web sites you search; list the words and phrases you use in your searches; and note the quality and quantity of results produced by each search. This information will be useful if, later on, you want to conduct these searches again or conduct the same searches on different search sites or databases.

Joining the Conversation

FIGURE 2.6
Searching the
Open Directory

Skim Your Sources. Skimming—reading just enough to get a general idea of what a document is about—enables you to gather information quickly from the sources you've located as you've explored your topic. You can skim books, articles, Web pages, newsgroups, chat transcripts, interview notes, observation notes, or anything else in written form.

Figures 2.7 and 2.8 illustrate strategies for skimming brief print documents and Web pages. Key strategies include identifying the type of document you are skimming; scanning titles, headings and subheadings, and figure captions; reading the first and last sentences of paragraphs; scanning menus and other navigation aids; and looking for information about authors and publishers. If you are reading a longer document, such as a book or report, consider these additional strategies:

- **Check the table of contents,** if one is provided. This provides a useful overview of the document's content and organization.

- **Check the index,** if one is provided, to learn more about the content of the document.

- **Check the glossary,** if one is provided. The terms that are defined can provide clues about the focus of the document.

- **Check the works cited list,** if one is provided, to learn about the types of evidence used in the document.

- **Check for pull quotes** (quotations or brief passages pulled out of the text and set in larger type elsewhere on the page), which often call attention to important arguments, ideas, and information in a document.

- **Check for information about the author** to learn about the writer's background, interests, and purposes for writing the document.

FIGURE 2.7   Skimming a Print Document

Source: Mariët Westermann, *A Worldly Art: The Dutch Republic, 1585–1718* (New York: Harry N. Abrams, 1996).

A **Check the title** for cues about content.

B **Skim opening paragraphs** for the purpose and scope of the document.

C **Check headings and subheadings** to learn about content and organization.

D **Read the first and last sentences of paragraphs** to find key information.

E **Skim captions of photos and figures**, which often highlight important arguments, ideas, and information.

Mark, Annotate, and Take Brief Notes on Your Sources.   As you skim your sources, do the following:

- Mark them by highlighting or underlining important passages so that you'll be able to easily locate key passages later in your research writing process (see Figure 2.9).

- Annotate them by briefly recording in the margins your initial reactions to a source.

- Take brief notes in your research log. For example, you might note similarities or differences among your sources, such as different proposals for solving a problem or different interpretations of an issue. These notes allow you to start to pull together the arguments, ideas, and information that several of your sources touch on.

FIGURE 2.8 Skimming a Web Page

Source: CNN, www.cnn.com/2004/BUSINESS/03/09/australia.windfarm/index.html

A **Check the page title** in the title bar of the browser for the purpose and content of the page.

B **Check the URL** to learn about the purpose of a Web page. Look for cues such as .edu for education, .gov for government, and .com for commercial and business sites.

C **Read the navigation headers and menus** to learn about the content and organization of the site.

D **Read the title.**

E **Scan for boldface, colored, or italic text.** Important information is often highlighted in some way on the page.

F **Skim captions of photos and figures**, which often highlight important arguments, ideas, and information.

G **Check for links to other sites** to learn more about the issue.

H **Read the first and last sentences of paragraphs** to find key information.

Check for information about the author to learn about the author's background, interests, and purposes for writing the document.

I Joining the Conversation

FIGURE 2.9
Pete Jacquez's
Annotations and
Highlighting on a
Printout of a Page
from an Online
Magazine

My Research Project

EXPLORE YOUR TOPIC

As you work through the strategies discussed in this chapter, use the following activity to keep track of your topic exploration in your research log.

1. What is my topic?

2. Have I discussed my topic with others? If so, what have I learned? If not, who are likely candidates for interviews — such as librarians, instructors, and people involved with or affected by my topic — and what questions should I ask them?

3. Are there any preliminary observations I should conduct? Have I done so? If so, what have I learned?

4. Have I found and reviewed sources? Have I searched the library catalog and browsed the shelves? Have I searched databases and the Web? Have I skimmed, marked, annotated, and taken brief notes on the sources I've found? If so, what have I learned about my topic?

You can download or print this activity at **bedfordresearcher.com**. Click on
Activities > Explore Your Topic.

2b

How can I narrow my topic?

Once you've explored your topic, your most important goal is to narrow it to a specific issue. Issues are points of disagreement, uncertainty, concern, or curiosity that are being discussed by communities of readers and writers.

As she explored the general topic of seventeenth-century Dutch art, featured writer Jenna Alberter read sources, viewed reproductions of Dutch paintings, talked with her professor about her topic, and kept a running list of ideas and information that interested her. Jenna started to make connections among the wide range of arguments, ideas, and information she encountered, and she was ultimately able to focus on the single issue that interested her most: the mutual influences of art and women's social roles in seventeenth-century Holland.

Moving from your topic to a single issue about that topic involves three main steps.

NARROWING YOUR TOPIC

Step 1   Identify conversations about issues in your sources
Step 2   Assess the importance and relevance of issues
Step 3   Select an issue

Step 1: Identify Conversations about Issues in Your Sources

Identifying conversations about issues in your topic is the first step in determining which issue is most appropriate for your research project. As you work through this process, look for patterns in the arguments, ideas, and information you encounter.

Find Central Concepts Repeated in Your Sources.   When several sources refer to the same idea, you can assume that this information is central to the topic. For instance, as Alexis Alvarez looked at articles and Web sites about the impact of competitive athletics on adolescent girls, she found repeated references to self-esteem, confidence, and performance-enhancing drugs. Noticing this repetition enabled Alexis to identify some of the important conversations about her topic.

Find Broad Themes Discussed in Your Sources.   Sources that discuss the same general theme are most likely involved in the same conversation. Among the sources that Jenna Alberter explored, she found that some focused on what images of women in seventeenth-century Dutch painting reveal about the status of women at the time, others focused on the style and technique used to create portraits of women, and still others focused on the role these images played in helping women understand their place in society. By noting these broad themes, Jenna was able to identify some of the key conversations taking place about her topic.

Find Disagreements among Your Sources.   Some sources will explicitly indicate that they disagree with arguments, ideas, or information in other sources. For example, Pete Jacquez found that some sources reported on the cost effectiveness of wind-generated electrical power, while others argued that electricity generated from burning gas, coal, or oil is more cost-effective. Looking for such explicit statements of disagreement helped Pete identify a group of sources that were engaged in conversation with one another.

Find Recurring Voices in Your Sources. As you read sources, you might find that some authors write frequently about your topic or that some authors are referred to frequently by other writers. These authors might have significant experience or expertise related to the topic, or they might represent particular perspectives on the topic. Stay alert for these recurring voices.

Step 2: Assess the Importance and Relevance of Issues

After you have identified issues that are being discussed in your sources, you are ready to assess the importance and relevance of those issues. Determine your personal interest in each issue and the relevance of the issue for your writing situation.

Determine Your Personal Interest in an Issue. As you review the issues you've identified, ask what interests you most about each one. By identifying personal connections between your sources and your own interests, you are more likely to focus on an issue that will sustain your interest throughout the course of your research project.

Consider Your Writing Situation. Evaluate each issue by asking yourself the following questions:

- **Will selecting this issue help me achieve my purposes as a writer?** Review your purpose and examine how each of the issues you have identified will help you best accomplish it.
- **Will my readers want or need to read about this issue?** Ask yourself which issue your readers would be most interested in or would most need to know about.
- **Is this issue appropriate for the type of document I plan to write?** Some issues that are well suited for editorials and opinion columns in your school newspaper, for example, might not be suitable for an academic or professional paper.
- **Is this issue compatible with my requirements and limitations?** Determine whether you can address an issue reasonably, given your assignment due date.
- **What opportunities do I have if I choose this issue?** For example, featured writer Pete Jacquez found that he could interview the directors of a program encouraging the use of wind power in his local community.

Step 3: Select an Issue

After you've assessed the issues you've found during your exploration of your topic, select the strongest candidate and the one that interests you most. Think, too, about the level of interest you and your readers might have in the issue and whether writing about this issue will allow you to achieve your purposes as a writer.

Table 2.1 shows the topics explored by the featured writers and the issues they decided to address.

TUTORIAL

How can I identify conversations in my sources?

You can identify conversations taking place in your sources by looking for patterns. Creating a five-column table like the one below can help you sort things out.

1 Record the source. Here, the writer uses the author's last names.

2 Record concepts that are repeated in your sources.

3 Record other broad themes that you've noticed in your sources.

4 Note points on which the sources disagree.

5 Note the sources that these sources are citing. You could make use of them later.

Source	Repeated Concepts	Broad Themes	Disagreements	Key Voices
Alpers	Women's social roles	Domestic life		Cats, Vermeer, de Hooch, Maes
Franits	Women's social roles	Domestic life Stages of life	Should be focusing on family life, not just vice	Cats
Westermann	Women's social roles	Domestic life Stages of life		Cats, Vermeer, de Hooch

In this example, featured writer Jenna Alberter has noted that three of her sources talk about women's roles in society. She used this conversation as the basis for her research on seventeenth-century Dutch art.

Review another example and work on narrowing your own research question at **bedfordresearcher.com**. Click on <u>Tutorials</u>.

TABLE 2.1   THE PROGRESSION FROM TOPIC TO CONVERSATION

FEATURED WRITER	TOPIC	CONVERSATION ABOUT AN ISSUE
Jenna Alberter	Seventeenth-century Dutch art	Mutual influences of art and women's social roles in seventeenth-century Holland
Alexis Alvarez	Women and competitive sports	Steroid use among adolescent girls involved in competitive sports
Patrick Crossland	College admissions	Impact of college admissions standards on the makeup of U.S. colleges and universities
Kevin Fahey	Ernest Hemingway	Varying interpretations of Hemingway's characterization of Nick Adams
Pete Jacquez	Wind-generated electrical power	Best strategies for increasing U.S. use of wind-generated electrical power
Maria Sanchez-Traynor	English as a second language (ESL)	Effectiveness of the Intensive instruction English Program (IEP) at Colorado State University

My Research Project

NARROW YOUR TOPIC TO AN ISSUE

In your research log, complete the following activity to narrow your topic to a single issue.

1. What are the three most important issues I have identified so far?
2. Of these issues, which one will best help me sustain my interest in this project?
3. Which one will best help me achieve my purposes as a writer?
4. Which one will best address my readers' needs and interests?
5. Which one best fits the requirements of my assignment?
6. Which one is most appropriate for the type of document I plan to write?
7. Which one has the fewest limitations?
8. Which one allows me to best take advantage of opportunities?
9. Based on these answers, the issue I want to choose is:

You can download or print this activity at **bedfordresearcher.com**. Click on <u>Activities</u> > <u>Narrow Your Topic to an Issue</u>.

> **QUICK REFERENCE**

Exploring and Narrowing Your Topic

✔ Get organized by creating a plan to explore your topic.   (p. 16)

✔ Discuss your topic with people who know about or have been affected by it. (p. 17)

✔ Conduct preliminary observations.   (p. 17)

✔ Find and review written sources by searching your library catalog, browsing its shelves, searching databases, searching the Web, and skimming your sources. (p. 18)

✔ Identify issues related to your topic.   (p. 27)

✔ Evaluate the issues in light of your research writing situation.   (p. 28)

✔ Select an issue.   (p. 28)

Part I
Joining the Conversation

1	Getting Started
2	Exploring and Narrowing Your Topic
3	Developing Your Research Question and Proposal

3

Developing Your Research Question and Proposal

Key Questions

3a. **How can I develop and refine my research question?** 32
Consider your roles
Generate potential research questions
Select and refine your preliminary research question

3b. **What is a research proposal and how can I create one?** 42

Your research question directs your efforts to develop a research proposal, create a search plan, and collect information. It also provides the foundation for your thesis statement—a statement designed to help your readers understand your view of the issue—which you'll develop and refine as you work with sources and draft your document.

3a

How can I develop and refine my research question?

A research question is a brief question that directs your efforts to collect, critically read, evaluate, and take notes on your sources. An effective research question focuses on a specific issue, reflects your writing situation, and is narrow enough to allow you to collect information in time to meet your deadlines. Most research questions begin with the word *what, why, when, where, who,* or *how.* Some research questions use the word *would* or *could* to ask whether something is possible. Still others use the word *should* to analyze the appropriateness of a particular action, policy, procedure, or decision. Since your research question may change as you learn more about your issue, it's best to think of it as a flexible guide. By revising your research question to reflect your growing understanding of the issue you've decided to address, you will build a solid foundation for the thesis statement you'll create when you begin planning and drafting your document (see p. 143).

DEVELOP AND REFINE YOUR RESEARCH QUESTION

Step 1   Consider your roles

Step 2   Generate potential research questions

Step 3   Select and refine your preliminary research question

---

● Step 1: Consider Your Roles

A role is a way of relating to your readers. The roles you take on will reflect your purpose and your understanding of your readers.

? WHAT'S MY PURPOSE?

To help them achieve their purpose, research writers typically adopt one or more of the following roles:

- *Advocates* present evidence in favor of their side of an argument and, in many cases, offer evidence that undermines opposing views. If you plan to write an argument, you'll most likely adopt the role of advocate.

- *Reporters* often present themselves as experts and present detailed but neutral information on a topic. Their writing is authoritative and suggests that they are knowledgeable. A reporter might also write a document that provides an overview of competing ideas about a topic, such as a guide to the positions of candidates for public office.

- *Interpreters* analyze and explain the significance of ideas or events. In some ways an interpreter acts like a reporter. However, while reporters tend to present the information they've found in their sources as factual, interpreters are more likely to consider the accuracy and meaning of the sources they cite.

- *Inquirers* typically present new information about a topic. For instance, a scientist might conduct a study that tests the effects of a new diet; the report that emerged from the study would present the results. If you plan to conduct your own laboratory or field studies, you will most likely take on the role of inquirer.

- *Entertainers* attempt to amuse or divert their readers. Although entertainment is not a primary goal in academic or professional writing, it is often an important part of articles written for magazines, newspapers, and Web sites. Research writers often write informative articles in an entertaining way in an attempt to keep their readers interested.

Note that these roles are not mutually exclusive. For example, featured writer Pete Jacquez's initial purpose was to inform his readers about the potential benefits of wind power. Eventually he decided that he also wanted to advocate its use, suggesting strategies for increasing our reliance on wind power.

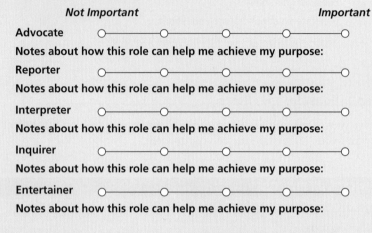

My Research Project

SELECT ROLES CONSISTENT WITH YOUR PURPOSE

The following activity can help you rank the relative importance of the potential roles you might adopt as you work on your project.

	Not Important				*Important*

Advocate ○———○———○———○———○
Notes about how this role can help me achieve my purpose:

Reporter ○———○———○———○———○
Notes about how this role can help me achieve my purpose:

Interpreter ○———○———○———○———○
Notes about how this role can help me achieve my purpose:

Inquirer ○———○———○———○———○
Notes about how this role can help me achieve my purpose:

Entertainer ○———○———○———○———○
Notes about how this role can help me achieve my purpose:

You can download or print this activity at **bedfordresearcher.com**. Click on Activities > Select Roles Consistent with Your Purpose.

● Step 2: Generate Potential Research Questions

Your next step is to generate a list of questions about the issue you've decided to address. Questions can focus on the following:

- **Information.** What is known — and not known — about an issue?
- **History.** What has occurred in the past that is relevant to an issue?
- **Assumptions.** What conclusions — merited or not — have writers and readers already made about an issue?
- **Goals.** What do the writers and readers involved in conversation about this issue want to see happen (or not happen)?
- **Outcomes.** What has happened so far? What is likely to happen?
- **Policies.** What are the best procedures for carrying out actions? For making decisions?

Questions can lead you to engage in the following kinds of thinking processes:

- **Definition.** Describing specific aspects of an issue.
- **Evaluation.** Asking about strengths and weaknesses or appropriateness.

- **Comparison/Contrast.** Asking about distinctions between aspects of an issue.
- **Cause/Effect Analysis.** Asking what leads to a specific result.
- **Problem/Solution Analysis.** Defining problems, considering outcomes of a problem, assessing potential solutions, and/or offering solutions.
- **Sequential Analysis.** Asking about step-by-step series of events.
- **Inquiry.** Seeking new information; conducting original research.
- **Reporting.** Conveying what is known about an event, idea, or phenomenon.

By combining a specific focus, such as assumptions, with a specific type of thinking process, such as definition, you can create carefully tailored research questions:

What assumptions have shaped debate about this issue?
What assumptions have worked against a resolution of this issue?

In Table 3.1, different focuses and types of thinking processes are used to generate questions about Pete Jacquez's issue, *best strategies for increasing U.S. use of wind-generated electrical power.*

As you begin generating potential research questions, ask yourself whether you are interested in focusing on such concerns as the current state of knowledge about your issue, its history, the assumptions informing the conversation about the issue, the goals of writers involved in the conversation, the likely outcomes of the issue, or policies associated with the issue. Then reflect on the range of options you have for thinking about these concerns. Are you interested, for example, in defining or evaluating? Are you interested in conducting such analyses as comparing alternatives, looking for cause/effect relationships, defining or solving problems, or tracing a sequence of events? Are you interested in conducting your own study? Are you interested in reporting what others have done or are doing?

Specific question words might also help you get started. If you are interested in conducting an analysis, for example, you might use the words *what, why, when, where, who,* and *how.* If you are interested in exploring goals and outcomes, you might use the words *would* or *could.* If the conversation focuses on determining an appropriate course of action, generate questions using the word *should.* Consider the differences between these questions:

- **What** are the benefits of wind power?
- **Would** it be feasible to require electrical companies to generate 20 percent of their power through wind turbines?
- **Should** the federal government pursue legislation to support wind power?

Each question would lead to differences in how to search for sources of information, which sources to use in a project document, what role to adopt as a writer, and how to organize and draft the document.

TABLE 3.1 GENERATING RESEARCH QUESTIONS

	DEFINITION	EVALUATION	COMPARISON/ CONTRAST	CAUSE/ EFFECT	PROBLEM/ SOLUTION	SEQUENCE	INQUIRY	REPORTING
Information	Where are the best locations for generating wind power?	How effective are current strategies for increasing use of wind power?	What are the similarities and differences among strategies to increase use of wind power?	What will lead to increased use of wind power?	What are the primary obstacles to increasing use of wind power?	What process is likely to be most effective at increasing use of wind power?	How could we increase U.S. use of wind power?	What strategies are now being tried to increase use of wind power?
History	Which strategies have been used to increase use of wind power?	Which strategies have been most effective at increasing use of wind power?	When will the costs of wind-generated electrical power rival that of power generated by natural gas, coal, and oil?	What has led to efforts to increase use of wind power?	How have obstacles to increased use of wind power been overcome?	What process has been followed to successfully implement wind power in other countries?	What can we learn from the past to increase use of wind power?	How are people using lessons from the past to increase current use of wind power?
Assumptions	Which values drive efforts to increase use of wind power?	Which assumptions have proven most damaging in efforts to increase use of wind power?	Which assumptions are driving efforts to increase use of wind power?	What faulty assumptions have led to failures in the wind-power industry?	What can be done to rescue efforts to increase reliance on wind power?	What has led to current assumptions about wind power?	How can we change assumptions about use of wind power?	What are the focuses of the debate about use of wind power?

	DEFINITION	EVALUATION	COMPARISON/CONTRAST	CAUSE/EFFECT	PROBLEM/SOLUTION	SEQUENCE	INQUIRY	REPORTING
Goals	What are the goals of wind-power advocates?	Which goals are most likely to be realized by advocates of wind power?	What are the differences among the goals pursued by different groups of wind-power advocates?	What is likely to occur if current goals of wind-power advocates are realized?	What are the primary obstacles to wind power and how can they be overcome?	How have the goals pursued by wind-power advocates developed over time?	Would advocates of wind power respond positively to a shift in short-term goals?	How is the goal of greater use of wind power being pursued by its advocates?
Outcomes	What is likely to result from efforts to increase use of wind power?	What are the best outcomes that can be expected from efforts to increase use of wind power?	Compared to the use of coal-based power plants, what are the advantages of outcomes from efforts to increase use of wind power?	Could advertising campaigns increase the likelihood of widespread adoption of wind power?	What undesirable consequences are likely to result from efforts to increase use of wind power?	When will wind power be an economically viable alternative to power from coal?	Why are legislators hesitant about supporting increased use of wind power?	Who are the most likely users of wind power?
Policies	What policies should the government implement to support wind power?	What are the advantages of pursuing a policy of increased use of wind power?	How do policy initiatives led by wind-power advocates differ from those of the coal industry?	What are the likely results of government support for wind power?	To what extent can a policy of greater reliance on wind power reduce reliance on petroleum imports?	How will the energy industry respond to passage of a national energy policy favoring wind power?	How do consumers respond to "extra-cost" wind-power initiatives?	Would it be feasible to require electrical companies to generate 20% of their power through wind turbines?

Step 3: Select and Refine Your Preliminary Research Question

Review your potential research questions and select a question that interests you, is consistent with the roles you have adopted, and is appropriate for your research writing situation. To refine your question, consider referring to shared assumptions and existing conditions, narrowing its scope, and conducting preliminary searches.

Refer to Shared Assumptions and Existing Conditions. You can refine your research question by using qualifying words and phrases to narrow its scope, by calling attention to assumptions that have been made by the community of writers and readers who are addressing your issue, or by referring to existing conditions relevant to your issue. Note the difference between these three versions of featured writer Alexis Alvarez's research question:

Original Question:

What should be done about steroid use by adolescent girls involved in competitive sports?

Alternative 1:

Even though we know that widespread drug testing of all athletes, younger and older, is impossible, what should be done about steroid use by adolescent girls involved in competitive sports?

Alternative 2:

Given the lack of knowledge about the health consequence of steroid use among athletes and their parents, what should be done about steroid use by adolescent girls involved in competitive sports?

As you refine your research question, you might use conditional words and phrases such as the following:

Mix . . .	and Match
Although	we know that . . .
Because	it is uncertain . . .
Even though	it is clear that . . .
Given that	studies indicate . . .
In light of	recent events . . .
Now that	it has been shown . . .
Since	the lack of . . .
While	we cannot . . .

Narrow the Scope of Your Research Question. Early research questions typically suffer from lack of focus. You can narrow the scope of your question by looking for vague words and phrases and replacing them with more specific words or phrases.

The process of moving from a broad research question to one that might be addressed effectively in a research essay might produce the following sequence:

Original Research Question:

What is behind the increased popularity in women's sports?

Refined:

What has led to the increased popularity of women's sports in colleges and universities?

Further Refined:

How has Title IX increased opportunities for women athletes in American colleges and universities?

Conduct Preliminary Searches. One of the best ways to test your research question is to conduct some preliminary searches in an online library catalog or database or on the Web. If you locate a vast amount of information in your searches, you might need to revise your question so that it focuses on a more manageable aspect of the issue. In contrast, if you find almost nothing in your search, you might need to expand the scope of your research question.

My Research Project

DEVELOP AND REFINE YOUR RESEARCH QUESTION

Complete the following activity in your research log to help you develop and refine your preliminary research question.

1. To develop potential research questions, identify the issue you are focusing on and write ten questions related to the conversation you have decided to join. Begin each question with one of the following words:

Could	What	Who
How	When	Why
Should	Where	Would

2. Choose the research question that best meets the needs of your writing situation, especially your purpose and roles and your readers' purposes, interests, values, and beliefs.

3. Refine your working research question by replacing vague words and phrases with more specific words and phrases.

4. Ask whether you should refine your research question by referring to shared assumptions and existing conditions.

5. Test your refined research question by conducting preliminary searches of library catalogs, databases, and the Web.

You can download or print this activity at **bedfordresearcher.com**. Click on Activities > Develop and Refine Your Research Question.

TABLE 3.2 THE FEATURED WRITERS' RESEARCH QUESTIONS

FEATURED WRITER	TOPIC	ISSUE	RESEARCH QUESTION
Jenna Alberter	Seventeenth-century Dutch art	Mutual influences of art and women's social roles in seventeenth-century Holland	What was the relationship between seventeenth-century Dutch paintings of women and the culture in which they were created?
Alexis Alvarez	Women and Competitive Sports	Steroid use among adolescent girls involved in competitive sports	What should be done about steroid use by adolescent girls involved in competitive sports?
Patrick Crossland	College admissions	Impact of college admissions standards on the makeup of U.S. colleges and universities	What cultural, academic, and regional factors affect college admissions decisions?
Kevin Fahey	Ernest Hemingway	Varying interpretations of Hemingway's characterization of Nick Adams	How is Nick Adams characterized by Ernest Hemingway?
Pete Jacquez	Wind-generated electrical power	Best strategies for increasing U.S. use of wind-generated electrical power	What strategies, if any, should Coloradoans use to encourage local, state, and federal governments to increase U.S. use of wind-generated electrical power?
Maria Sanchez-Traynor	English as a Second Language (ESL)	Effectiveness of the Intensive English Program (IEP) at Colorado State University	How is English taught to foreign-language speakers at the Intensive English Program?

TUTORIAL

How do I refine my research question?

The first draft of your research question may be too broad, which can make it difficult for you to focus your research efforts. Refine your initial research question so that you can collect information efficiently.

Preliminary Research Question:
How can we increase our reliance on alternative energy?

1 Use phrases such as *although it is clear that . . . , because we cannot . . . ,* and *given that studies have shown . . .* to refer to shared assumptions and existing conditions.

In light of consumer demand for low-cost electricity, how can we increase our reliance on alternative energy?

In light of consumer demand for low-cost electricity, how can we increase our reliance on wind-generated electrical energy?

2 Identify vague words and phrases, such as *alternative* and *reliance on,* and replace them with more specific words and phrases.

In light of consumer demand for low-cost electricity, what steps can U.S. citizens take to encourage local, state, and federal governments to support increased use of wind-generated electrical energy?

3 Conduct preliminary searches in your library catalog, databases, and on the Web. If you get too many results, narrow your focus.

In light of consumer demand for low-cost energy, what steps can Colorado citizens take to pass a statewide referendum requiring increased reliance on wind-generated electrical energy?

Review another example and work on narrowing your own research question at **bedfordresearcher.com**. Click on Tutorials.

I Joining the Conversation

3b

What is a research proposal and how can I create one?

A research proposal—sometimes called a prospectus—is a formal presentation of your plan for your research writing project. A proposal helps you pull together the planning you've done on your project and identify areas where you need additional planning.

Unlike a search plan (see p. 48), which is designed primarily to help *you* decide how to collect information, a research proposal is addressed to someone else, usually an instructor, supervisor, or funding agency. A research proposal typically includes the following:

- **A title page** serves as a cover for your research proposal. It should include the working title of your research writing project, your name and contact information, and the date.

- **An introduction** should identify the issue you've decided to address; state your research question and, if you have created one, your working thesis statement; describe your purpose; and identify your readers and describe their needs and interests.

- **A review of literature** provides a brief overview of the key arguments, ideas, and information in the sources you've collected so far. You should identify useful sources found during your exploration of your topic and explain why you've found them useful.

- **A plan to collect information** offers a brief description of the types of resources you'll use to locate information relevant to your issue and outlines the steps you'll take to collect it. You should indicate whether you'll consult reference librarians; whether you'll use library catalogs, databases, and Web sites; and whether you'll conduct field research.

- **A project timeline** will give your reader an indication of the range of days, weeks, or months over which you will be completing your research and writing your document.

- **A working bibliography** lists the sources you've collected so far. Sometimes you will be asked to create an annotated working bibliography, which contains a brief description of each source. Your working bibliography should conform to the documentation system (MLA, APA, *Chicago*, CSE) specified by your instructor, supervisor, or funding agency.

Optional elements include the following:

- **An abstract or executive summary** provides a brief summary—usually fifty to two hundred words—of your project. You should identify the issue you've decided to address and your research question. You should also indicate what type of document—such as a research essay, informative Web site, or magazine article—you'll write.

- **An overview of key challenges** encourages you to think about potential problems you will need to address as you work on your project. This section of your research proposal might discuss such difficulties as locating or collecting specific types of sources. It also provides an opportunity for your instructor, supervisor, or potential funder to respond by suggesting strategies for meeting specific challenges.
- **A funding request and rationale** provides a budget that identifies costs for key project activities, such as conducting your search, reviewing the sources you collect, writing and designing the document, and publishing the document.

A formal research proposal allows you to consolidate the work you've done so far and get feedback on your plans to carry out your project.

My Research Project

CREATE A RESEARCH PROPOSAL

Use the following activity to create a formal research proposal.

1. Provide the working title for your project.
2. Describe your issue.
3. Describe your purpose for working on this project.
4. Describe your readers' needs and interests.
5. State your research question.
6. Briefly review key findings about your issue from the sources you found as you explored your topic.
7. Indicate how you'll locate additional arguments, ideas, and information about your issue.
8. Include your project timeline.
9. Include your working bibliography.
10. Discuss the key challenges you face (optional).
11. Identify specific funding requests (optional).

You can download or print this activity at **bedfordresearcher.com**. Click on Activities > Create a Research Proposal.

> **QUICK REFERENCE**

Developing Your Research Question and Proposal

✔ Define your role as a research writer. (p. 33)

✔ Generate potential research questions. (p. 34)

✔ Select and refine your research question. (p. 38)

✔ If necessary, develop a research proposal. (p. 42)

The Bedford Researcher

I	Joining the Conversation
II	**Collecting Information**
III	Working with Sources
IV	Writing Your Document
V	Documenting Sources

PART II
Collecting Information

Learning how to collect information provides the foundation for a successful research project. As you begin to answer your research question, you'll want to know more about how and where to look for useful sources of information. In this section of *The Bedford Researcher,* you'll learn how to prepare to collect and manage information, and how to search for information using electronic resources, print resources, and field research methods.

4

Getting Ready to Collect and Keep Track of Information

> **Key Questions**
>
> **4a.** **How should I get ready to collect information?**   47
> Create a search plan
> Create a schedule for carrying out your plan
> Find out if your plan is a good one
>
> **4b.** **How can I save and organize the information I find?**   51
> Decide how to save and organize electronic sources
> Decide how to save and organize print sources
> Create a working bibliography

Your research question focuses your attention on the issue you've decided to address. Even with a narrowly defined research question, however, it's likely that your search for information will produce a large number of relevant sources. To use those sources most effectively, you should decide how you will collect and manage your information.

4a

How should I get ready to collect information?

Getting ready to collect information involves making decisions about

- the types of sources you want to collect (such as books, articles, and opinion columns)
- the types of resources you will use to locate sources of information (such as library catalogs, the World Wide Web, and surveys)

- the strategies you will use as you work with specific resources (such as key-word searches)
- the schedule you will follow as you conduct your research

To make these decisions, reflect on the plan you created in Chapter 2 to explore your topic. The goal of that plan was to gain a broad understanding of the conversations taking place about issues in your topic. Now you need to search for and collect sources that will help you answer your research question. Essentially, you need to shift from a broad overview of the conversations about a topic to an in-depth focus on a single conversation about an issue.

Making these decisions will take time. But this decision-making process will save far more time and effort than it takes to carry out. It will reduce time lost in poorly conceived searches for information, in locating misplaced sources, in last minute searches for incomplete citation information and in making up for a lack of relevant print, electronic, and field sources.

? WHAT'S MY PURPOSE?

Your research question focuses your attention on a specific aspect of the issue you've decided to address. Your decisions about how to collect and manage information should reflect that focus.

Consider featured writer Maria Sanchez-Traynor's research question and the different plans she might have used to collect and manage information. Maria's research question asks how English is taught to foreign-language speakers at the Intensive English Program (IEP) at Colorado State University. Her plan led her to collect information though interviews with students and teachers at the IEP, observation of IEP classes, and analysis of promotional materials from the program. Had she written an article that analyzed or critiqued the instructional practices of IEP instructors, she would have followed a different plan, one that expanded the range of sources she collected to include interviews with ESL (English as a Second Language) specialists from other institutions, database and library catalog searches for scholarly work on ESL, and ESL textbooks.

> Read more about Maria Sanchez-Traynor at **bedfordresearcher.com**. Click on Featured Writers.

As you decide how to collect and manage information, keep your research question in mind. Doing so will help you determine the types of sources, resources, and search strategies you'll need to investigate the issue you've decided to address.

Create a Search Plan

A search plan is an informal record of your decisions about how to search for and collect information. Unlike a research proposal (see p. 42), which is addressed to an instructor, supervisor, or potential funding agency, a search plan is written for *you*. As a result, your plan can be brief and informal. Creating a search plan involves three steps.

CREATING A SEARCH PLAN

Step 1   Identify the types of sources that seem most relevant.

Step 2   Identify the types of resources you might use to locate information.

Step 3   Identify the search strategies you might use as you work with resources.

Identify the Types of Sources That Seem Most Relevant.   Research writers use information found in a variety of sources—electronic, print, and field—to support the points they make in their documents. As you begin to create your search plan, think carefully about which types of sources are most consistent with the issue you plan to address. Will it be more useful to rely heavily on articles found in magazines, newspapers, and on Web sites? Should you rely primarily on scholarly books and articles in academic and professional journals? Could you make good use of field sources, such as interviews, observations, and surveys?

Maria Sanchez-Traynor, who wrote an informative article about teaching and learning at the Intensive English Program at Colorado State University, knew she wanted to focus on what was actually happening in the classes associated with the program. "I knew I wouldn't find anything in books or articles because it was such a specialized, local issue," she said, "so I decided to focus on interviews, observations, and the program's Web site." Featured writer Jenna Alberter, in contrast, knew that searching books and journal articles would be most productive. The issue she had decided to address, mutual influences of art and women's social roles in seventeenth-century Holland, was not likely to be addressed in recent newspaper or magazine articles. Nor was it well suited to observation or other types of field research, although she might have interviewed professors who were familiar with seventeenth-century Dutch art.

Identify the Types of Resources You Might Use to Locate Information.   Once you've identified the types of sources that seem most relevant, determine which resources you might use to locate those sources. In general, you can use three sets of resources to locate sources:

- **Electronic resources,** such as online library catalogs, databases, and Web search sites, allow you to search and browse for sources using a computer. Electronic resources provide access to publication information about—and in some cases to the complete text of—print, electronic, and multimedia sources.

- **Print resources,** such as bibliographies, indexes, encyclopedias, dictionaries, handbooks, almanacs, and atlases, can be found in library reference and periodical rooms. Unlike electronic resources, which typically cover recent publications, many print resources provide information about publications over several decades—and in some cases over more than a century.

- **Field research methods** allow you to collect information firsthand. These methods include conducting observations, interviews, and surveys; corresponding with experts; attending public events and performances; and viewing or listening to television and radio programs.

Identify the Search Strategies You Might Use to Work with Specific Resources. Your search plan should identify the strategies you will use for each type of resource. Search strategies include keyword searches, interview questions, and observation forms. If your topic lends itself to Web searches, for instance, your search plan should define the keyword searches you will use. If you need to interview people, your search plan should identify the questions you want to ask each person.

Because Maria Sanchez-Traynor was searching for information about a topic that was unlikely to be the subject of newspaper, magazine, or journal articles, her search plan focused on field research methods and searching the Web. In particular, she needed to develop interview questions, create a means of collecting information during her observations, and compile a list of potential search terms for Web search sites and directories. In contrast, because Jenna Alberter was searching primarily for books and journal articles, she based her search plan almost exclusively on searches in library catalogs and databases.

My Research Project

CREATE A SEARCH PLAN

In your research log, create a search plan using the following questions:

1. What types of sources are most relevant to my issue?
2. What types of resources should I use to locate information?
3. What search strategies should I use with each resource?

You can download or print this activity at **bedfordresearcher.com**. Click on <u>Activities</u> > <u>Create a Search Plan</u>.

Create a Schedule for Carrying Out Your Plan

After developing your search plan, schedule time to carry out specific searches for information. Next to each activity—such as searching databases, searching the Web, searching a library catalog, and conducting an interview—identify start dates and projected completion dates. Creating a schedule will help you budget and manage your time.

Find Out If Your Plan Is a Good One

Share your search plan with your instructor, your supervisor, or a librarian. Each might suggest additional resources, shortcuts, and alternative search strategies for your project. Take notes on the feedback you receive and, if necessary, revise your plan.

4b

How can I save and organize the information I find?

Before you begin to collect information, decide how you will save and keep track of it.

● Decide How to Save and Organize Electronic Sources

You will need to save the electronic sources you find before you can begin working with them. Decide which of the following techniques would be best:

Printing Printing out articles or Web pages allows you to highlight key passages, write comments in the margins, and circle text and graphics on a page. When you print out a Web page, make sure the URL and date are included on the printout and are readable. If they're not included or if they're incomplete (which can happen when URLs are very long), write them down on the first page of the printout.

Copying and Pasting You can use the COPY and PASTE commands in your browser and word processor to save electronic documents and graphics. Note that you also need to copy and paste the URL and record the date on which you accessed the page so that you can return to it if necessary and cite it appropriately.

> Learn more about copying and pasting at **bedfordresearcher.com**. Click on Guides > How to Use Your Word Processor.

Saving to Disk Toward the end of your research writing project, particularly when you are drafting your document, you might find yourself wishing that you'd saved all of your electronic sources to disk—a hard drive, a diskette, a Zip disk, a USB flash drive, or a writable CD or DVD. Saving sources to disk allows you to open them in a Web browser or word processor at a later time.

How you save your sources will vary according to the type of electronic source you're viewing. Web pages can be saved using the FILE > SAVE AS . . . or FILE > SAVE PAGE AS . . . menu command in your browser. Images and other media materials from the Web can be saved by right-clicking (in Windows) or control-clicking (on the Macintosh) on the item you want to save and selecting SAVE IMAGE AS . . . or SAVE PICTURE AS . . . or some variation of that command from the pop-up menu. Depending on the database, you might be able to mark a record returned by your search. Saving a source to disk does not automatically record the URL or the date on which you viewed the source for the first time. Be sure to record that information.

As you save information to disk, keep it organized. The simplest organizational strategy is to save your work in a single folder (see Figure 4.1). As you save your work, use descriptive file names. Rather than naming a file "Notes 1.doc," for instance, name it "Interview Notes from John Garcia, April 22.doc." Keep in mind that the single-folder approach might not work well for larger projects. At

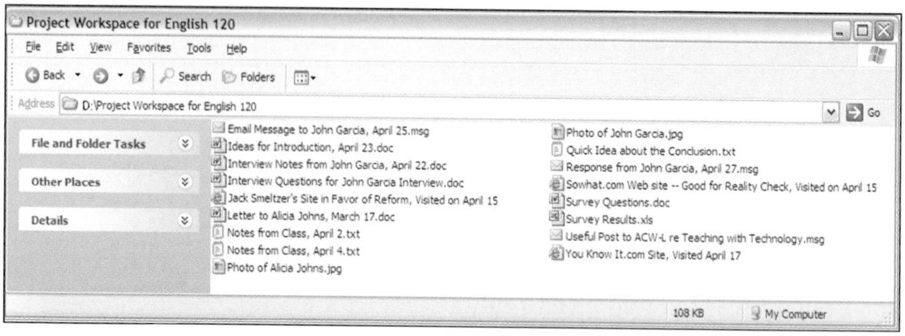

FIGURE 4.1   A Project Workspace Using a Single Folder

some point, the sheer number of files in the folder makes it difficult to find a single file easily. Rather than scrolling through several screens of files, you might find it more efficient to create multiple folders to hold related files (see Figure 4.2).

Using Email   You can email yourself messages containing electronic documents you've found in your research. Some databases, such as those from EBSCO and OCLC/FirstSearch, allow you to email the text of selected records directly from the database (see Figure 4.3).

Using Bookmarks and Favorites   You can use a Bookmarks or Favorites list in your Web browser to keep track of your sources (see Figure 4.4).

Be aware that Bookmarks and Favorites lists can become disorganized. To avoid this problem, change the order of the items in your list, put related items into folders, and give the items on your list descriptive names.

Note as well that there are drawbacks to relying on a Bookmarks or Favorites list as a place to "store" your sources. First, pages on the Web can and do change. If you suspect that the page you want to mark might change before you complete your research project, save it to disk or print it so that you won't lose its content. Second, some Web pages are generated by database programs. In such cases, you might not be able to return to the page using a Bookmarks or Favorites list. A URL like the following usually indicates that a Web page is generated by a database program:

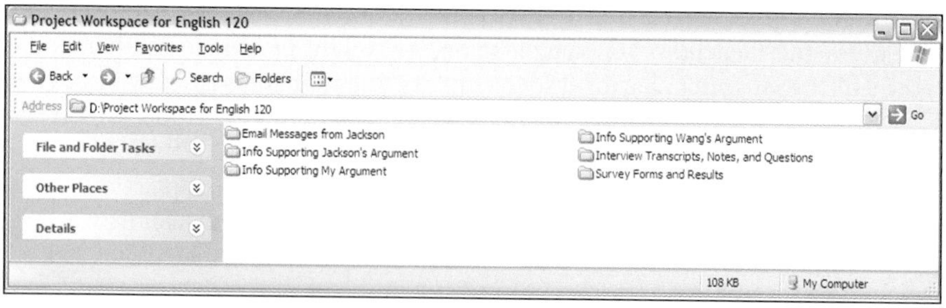

FIGURE 4.2   A Project Workspace Using Multiple Folders

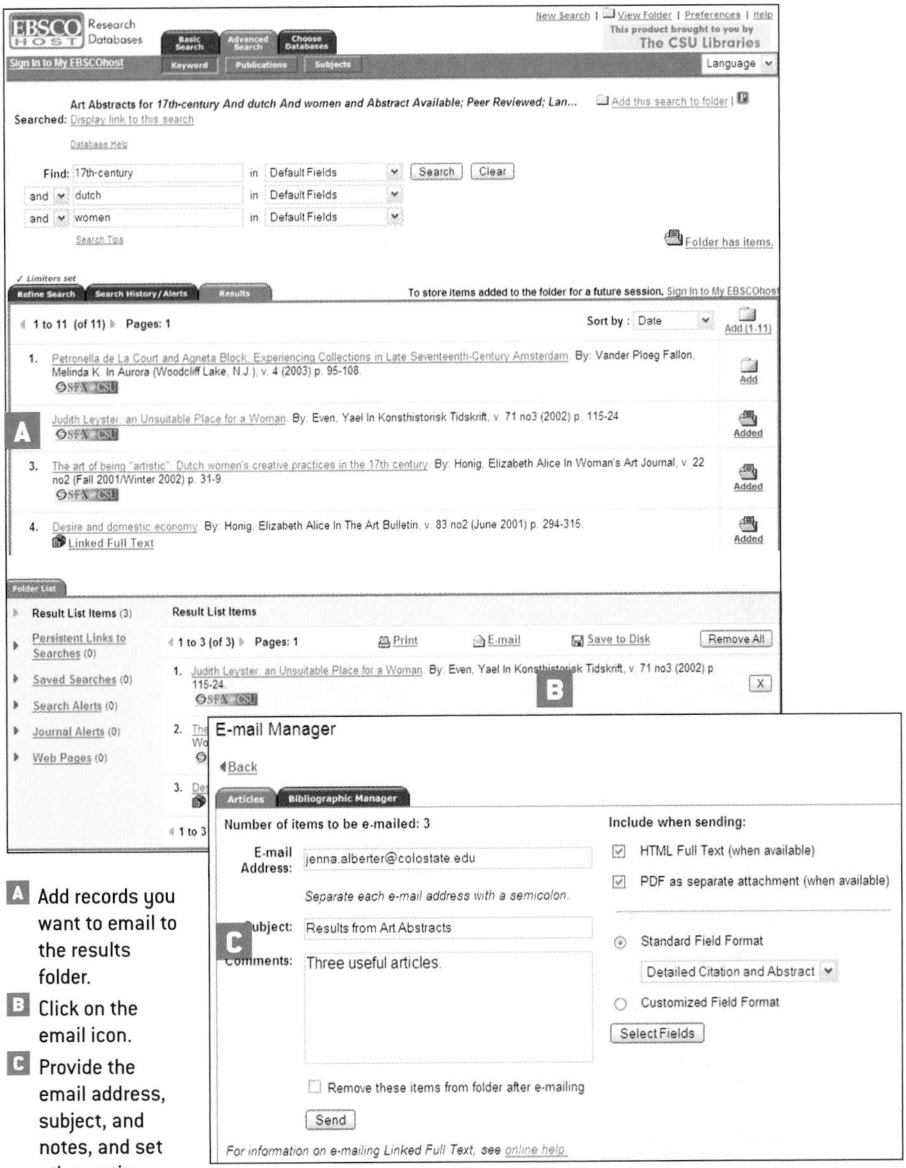

A Add records you want to email to the results folder.

B Click on the email icon.

C Provide the email address, subject, and notes, and set other options.

FIGURE 4.3 Sending Database Records via Electronic Mail

> http://firstsearch.oclc.org/FUNC/QUERY:%7Fnext=NEXTCMD%7F%22/
> FUNC/SRCH_RESULTS%22%7FentityListType=0%7Fentitycntr=
> 1%7FentityItemCount=0%7F%3Asessionid=1265726%7F4%7F/fsres4.txt

Although this long string of characters starts out looking like a normal URL, the majority of the characters are used by the database program to determine which

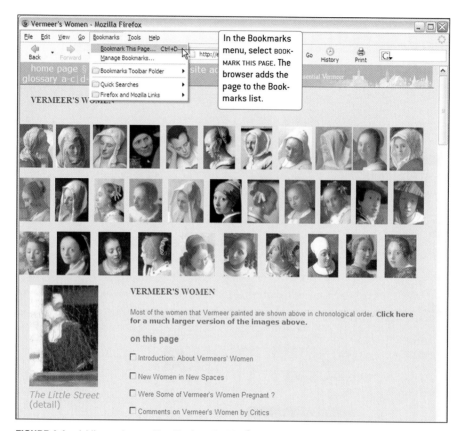

FIGURE 4.4   Adding an Item to Your Bookmarks List (Mozilla, Netscape Navigator, and Firefox)

records to display on a page. In many cases, the URL works only while you are conducting your search. If you add such a URL to your Bookmarks or Favorites list, there's a good chance it won't work later.

Using the Bedford Bibliographer   The Bedford Bibliographer tool at bedford researcher.com allows you to save bibliographic information about each of your sources, to write a brief note or annotation about each source, and to save text from electronic sources. The Bedford Bibliographer can also create a working bibliography formatted in MLA, APA, *Chicago,* or CSE style.

Whatever strategies you use to save and organize electronic sources, be sure to back up your work. Replacing lost information takes time and effort. Avoid the risk of lost information by taking the time to make copies of your electronic files, saved Web pages, email messages, and Bookmarks or Favorites list.

Decide How to Save and Organize Print Sources

During your research project, you'll accumulate a great deal of print information, such as

- your written notes (in a notebook, on loose pieces of paper, on Post-it Notes, and so on)
- printouts from Web pages and databases
- articles sent through a library's fax-on-demand service
- printed word processing documents, such as various drafts of your research question
- books, magazines, newspapers, brochures, pamphlets, government documents
- photocopies of articles, book chapters, and other documents
- letters, printed email messages, survey results, and so on

Rather than letting all this information build up in messy piles on your desk or stuffing it into folders in your backpack, create a filing system to keep track of your print documents. Filing systems can range from well-organized piles of paper labeled with Post-it Notes to three-ring binders to file cabinets filled with neatly labeled files and folders.

Regardless of the approach you take, keep the following principles in mind:

- **Create an organizational scheme that allows you to locate your print materials.** Decide whether you want to group material by topic, by date, by pro versus con, by type of material (Web pages, photocopies, original documents, field sources, and so on), or by author.
- **Stick with your organizational scheme.** You'll find it difficult to locate materials if you use different approaches at different points in your research project.
- **Make sure printed documents provide complete publication information.** If a source doesn't contain publication information, write it on the document yourself.
- **Date your notes.** Indicating dates when you recorded information can help you reconstruct what you might have been doing while you took the note. Dates are also essential for documenting Web sources and other sources obtained online.
- **Write a brief note on each of your print materials.** Indicate how it might contribute to your project.

Create a Working Bibliography

A working bibliography is a running list of the sources you've explored and plan to use in your research project—with publication information for each source.

The organization of your working bibliography can vary according to your needs and preferences. You can organize your sources in any of the following ways:

- in the order in which you collected your sources
- in categories
- by author
- by publication title
- according to an outline of your project document

The entries in a working bibliography should include as much publication information about a source as you can gather (see Table 4.1).

TABLE 4.1 INFORMATION YOU SHOULD LIST IN A WORKING BIBLIOGRAPHY	
TYPE OF SOURCE	**INFORMATION YOU SHOULD LIST**
All Sources	• Author(s) • Title • Publication year
Book	• Editor(s) of book (if applicable) • Publication city • Publisher • Series and series editor (if applicable) • Translator (if applicable) • Volume (if applicable) • Edition (if applicable)
Chapter in an Edited Book	• Publication city • Publisher • Editor(s) of book • Book title • Page numbers of chapter
Journal, Magazine, and Newspaper Article	• Title of journal, magazine, or newspaper • Volume number or date • Issue number or date • Page numbers of article
Web Page, Newsgroup Post, Email Message, and Chat and MOO Transcript	• URL • Access date (the date you read the source) • Sponsoring organization, if listed
Field Research	• Title (usually a description of the source, such as "Personal Interview with Jessica Lynn Richards" or "Observation of June Washington's Class at Tavelli Elementary School") • Date (usually the date on which the field research was conducted)

You may be asked to create an *annotated bibliography,* a formal document that provides a brief note about each of the sources you've listed, in addition to its complete citation information. These notes, or annotations, are typically brief—usually no more than two or three sentences. The content, focus, and length of your annotations will reflect your purposes for creating an annotated bibliography:

- In some research writing projects, you will submit an annotated bibliography to an instructor for review and comment. In this situation, your instructor will most likely expect a clear description of the content of each source and some indication of how you might use the source.

- In other research writing projects, the annotated bibliography might serve simply as a planning tool—a more detailed version of a working bibliography. As a result, your annotations might call your attention to key passages or information in a source, suggest where you might use information or ideas from the source in your project document, or emphasize relationships between this source and others you've collected.

- In still other research writing projects, the annotated bibliography might be the end product of your research efforts. In this case, you will write your annotations for your readers, keeping their needs and interests in mind.

Featured writer Pete Jacquez created an annotated bibliography that he included on his Web site about wind-generated electrical power. Because his bibliography was intended for readers who were interested in learning more about wind power, his annotations focused primarily on describing the arguments, ideas, and information in each source. The first four entries in his annotated bibliography are found in Figure 4.5.

> Find these and other annotated bibliographies at **bedfordresearcher.com**. Click on Featured Writers.

In contrast, featured writer Jenna Alberter created an annotated bibliography that her instructor used to assess her progress on her research writing project (see Figure 4.6).

Your working bibliography will change significantly as you work on your research writing project. As you explore and narrow your topic and, later, as you collect and work with your sources, you will add potentially useful sources and delete sources that are no longer relevant. Eventually, your working bibliography will become one of the following:

- A *works cited* or *references list*—a formal list of the sources you have referred to in a document.

- A *bibliography* or *works consulted list*—a formal list of the sources that contributed to your thinking about an issue, even if those sources were not referred to explicitly in the text of the document.

Keeping your working bibliography up-to-date is a critical part of your research writing process. The bibliography helps you keep track of your sources and increases the likelihood that you will cite all the sources you use in your document—an important contribution to your efforts to avoid plagiarism.

II Collecting Information

A Bisbee, D. W. (2004). NEPA review of offshore wind farms. *Boston College Environmental Affairs Law Review 31*(2), 349–385.

This review focuses on offshore wind farms and their efficiency at producing electricity. The article notes that offshore wind farms can sometimes be inconsistent in their output of electrical power due to variable winds. The article speculates about the extent to which this inefficiency resulting from inconsistent winds reduces the viability of offshore wind farms as an alternative to fossil fuel plants.

Bohlander, B. (2004). Colorado State first university in the United States to offer choice of wind power to campus residents. Colorado State University. Retrieved September 27, 2004, from http://newsinfo.colostate.edu/content/news_print.asp?news_item_id=627126272

B This news release announces that Colorado State University is the first university to offer students the option of purchasing wind-generated electrical power for their use in dormitories and other campus housing. The news release discusses the future of wind power and provides information about the specific costs for students who choose to utilize wind power while living on-campus.

Brown, L. R. (2003). Wind power is set to become world's leading energy source. *Humanist 63*(5), 5.

C This article addresses advancements in wind power technology and how further advancements will help in the push for wind-generated electricity. This article supports the ideas that wind power can and should be utilized as an alternative to fossil fuels.

Chasteen, S. (2004). Who owns wind? *Science and Spirit 15*(1), 12–15.

This article focuses on the economics aspect of implementing wind power. The author identifies the issue of economic motives behind wind power, which has become more relevant as large firms look to move into the wind power market.

FIGURE 4.5   Part of Pete Jacquez's Annotated Working Bibliography

A Entries follow APA style (see p. 274).
B Annotations provide brief summaries of the purpose and content of the sources.
C Annotations are intended for visitors to Pete's Web site, rather than for his instructor or himself.

You can read more about works cited and works consulted lists in Part Five, Documenting Sources.

> **A** Alpers, Svetlana. "De Hooch: A View with a Room." Art in America 86.6
> (1999): 92-99.
>
> In her review of an exhibition of 40 De Hooch paintings at the Wadsworth
> Atheneum, Alpers compares De Hooch with Vermeer, suggesting that the two were
> aware of each other's work and noting that Vermeer borrowed from De Hooch.
> Alpers argues that De Hooch presents a less complicated, more tolerant image of
> women than artists such as Gerard Ter Borch and Nicolaes Maes. This article is
> likely to be useful for my discussions of housewives. And Alpers also cites Cats's
> Houwelyck, so I can use Alpers to set up my discussion of--or vice versa.
>
> **Cats, Jacob. Houwelyck [Marriage]. 1625.**
>
> This book is quoted and excerpted in Franits, Paragons and in Westermann. It was
> one of many books published in the Netherlands and England during the seven-
> **B** teenth century and served as a comprehensive reference book for women of all
> ages, but especially young women, regarding matters of marriage and family. It
> contained instructions for women on proper behavior during the six stages of life:
> Maiden, Sweetheart, Bride, Housewife, Mother, and Widow--all defined in comparison
> to the roles of men. I am probably going to refer to this book early in the essay
> when I discuss how women were instructed about their roles in Dutch society.
>
> **Franits, Wayne E. Paragons of Virtue: Women and Domesticity in
> Seventeenth-Century Dutch Art. Cambridge: Cambridge UP, 1993.**
>
> Franits focuses on paintings of domestic life--particularly of women--by
> seventeenth-century Dutch artists. Franits uses books and other sources, such as
> Cats's Houwelyck, to give a context for and explore the significance of the paint-
> ings. A main argument is that these paintings reinforced the social status quo.
> **C** I'll use Franits's book for its discussion of Houwelyck and for its insights into the
> social values of the time.

FIGURE 4.6 Part of Jenna Alberter's Working Annotated Bibliography

A Entries follow MLA style (see p. 241).

B Annotations provide brief summaries of the purpose and content of the sources.

C Annotations are intended for Jenna and her teacher. They indicate how and where she will use these sources in her document.

TUTORIAL

How do I create an annotated bibliography?

Descriptive annotations are brief summaries of the source, no more than two or three sentences. For graded annotated bibliographies, ask your instructor what he or she expects.

1 Provide a complete source citation, following the guidelines of your documentation system (e.g., MLA, APA, *Chicago,* or CSE). This example uses APA style.

2 Format each citation so that it stands out from its annotation. You can use bold or a contrasting color.

3 In the annotation, identify the information and ideas most relevant to your project, such as significant arguments and findings.

4 Include relevant information about the background and qualifications of the author or key authorities mentioned in the source.

Costello, B. (2004, July 4). Too late? Survey suggests millions of kids could be juicing. *New York Post,* 059. Retrieved October 2, 2004, from http://www.nypost.com/sports/24424.htm.

This article discusses steroid and other performance-enhancing drug use among eighth- through twelfth-grade boys and girls and provides a number of relevant statistics. I'll use this source to support statements about steroid use among young female athletes.

DeNoon, D. (2004, August 4). Steroid use: Hitting closer to home. WebMD. Retrieved October 1, 2004, from http://my.webmd.com/content/Article/92/101457.htm.

This Web page provides information about increasing steroid use in America, quotations from scientists and physicians, as well as the latest statistical figures regarding this use. I'll use it for statistical evidence and to drive home the point that this is a problem that needs to be addressed.

Your instructor might also want you to note the type of the source (e.g., book, journal article, or Web site) and its length.

Review another example and work on your annotated bibliography at **bedfordresearcher.com**. Click on <u>Tutorials</u>.

My Research Project

CREATE A WORKING BIBLIOGRAPHY

You can create your working bibliography in print form — in a notebook — or in electronic form — in a word processing file. You can also use the the **Bedford Bibliographer** at **bedfordresearcher.com**, which allows you to

- create entries for new sources
- annotate sources
- evaluate sources
- copy and save some or all of the text from a source
- display your working bibliography in MLA, APA, *Chicago,* or CSE style
- print your working bibliography, save it as a file, or send it via email

> **QUICK REFERENCE**

Getting Ready to Collect and Keep Track of Information

✔ Prepare to collect information by reflecting on your purpose.   (p. 47)

✔ Create a search plan.   (p. 48)

✔ Create a schedule for carrying out your search plan.   (p. 50)

✔ Ask your instructor, your supervisor, or a librarian to review your plan.   (p. 50)

✔ Decide how you will save and organize electronic sources.   (p. 51)

✔ Decide how you will save and organize print sources.   (p. 55)

✔ Create a working bibliography.   (p. 55)

II Collecting Information

5

Searching for Information with Electronic Resources

> **Key Questions**

Since the computer became a research tool, the primary challenge associated with collecting information has changed. Research writers no longer worry about locating *enough* sources; instead, they worry about finding the *right* sources. This chapter addresses the important differences among online library catalogs, databases, Web search sites, and other electronic resources you can use to locate information, and explains how to use these resources to locate the best sources for your research writing project.

5a

How can I search for sources with online library catalogs?

Library catalogs provide information about the materials in a library's collection. Most libraries provide access to their catalogs through the Web, although some smaller libraries rely on traditional print catalogs. At a minimum, an online catalog will provide information about the author(s), title, publication date, subject, and call number for each source in the library's collection. Often it will also indicate the location of the source in the library and whether the source is available for checkout.

Online library catalogs give information on the print publications in a library collection. They can also provide information about publications in other media. Online catalogs typically help you locate

- books
- journals owned by the library (although not individual articles)
- newspapers and magazines owned by the library (although not individual articles)
- documents stored on microfilm or microfiche
- videotapes, audiotapes, and other multimedia items owned by the library
- maps
- theses and dissertations completed by college or university graduate students

Note that library catalogs are not well suited for locating journal, magazine, or newspaper articles or online sources such as Web pages.

Although you can limit your search to the online library catalog at your college or university, you can benefit from searching other catalogs available on the Web. The Library of Congress online catalog, for example, presents a comprehensive list of publications on a particular subject or by a particular author (visit catalog.loc.gov). Some sites, such as the Karlsruhe Virtual Catalog (www.ubka.uni-karlsruhe.de/hylib/en/kvk.html), allow you to locate or search multiple online library catalogs. If your library doesn't have a listed publication in its collection, you can request it through interlibrary loan. Most online library catalogs at colleges and universities allow you to search for sources by author(s), title, keyword, subject, publication date, and call number.

> Find other sites that list online library catalogs at **bedfordresearcher.com**. Click on Links > Resources for Conducting Electronic Searches.

Search by Author

Searching by author means looking for sources written by a specific author or authors. Most library catalogs assume that you will enter the last name of the author first, followed by a first name or initial. Some library catalogs and data-bases allow you to browse sources by entering all or part of the last name or by using wildcard symbols (symbols such as * or ? that stand in for one or more letters in a word; see p. 78). Figure 5.1 shows a search Jenna Alberter conducted for sources written by Patricia Phagan, one of the writers she'd learned about as she explored her topic.

> Read more about Jenna Alberter at **bedfordresearcher.com**. Click on Featured Writers.

Search by Title

If you know the exact title of a source, such as *Six Subjects of Reformation Art: A Preface to Rembrandt,* you can enter the entire title. If you know only part of the title, such as *Rembrandt* or *Reformation Art,* you might have to sift through a list of books whose titles contain the phrase or word you enter.

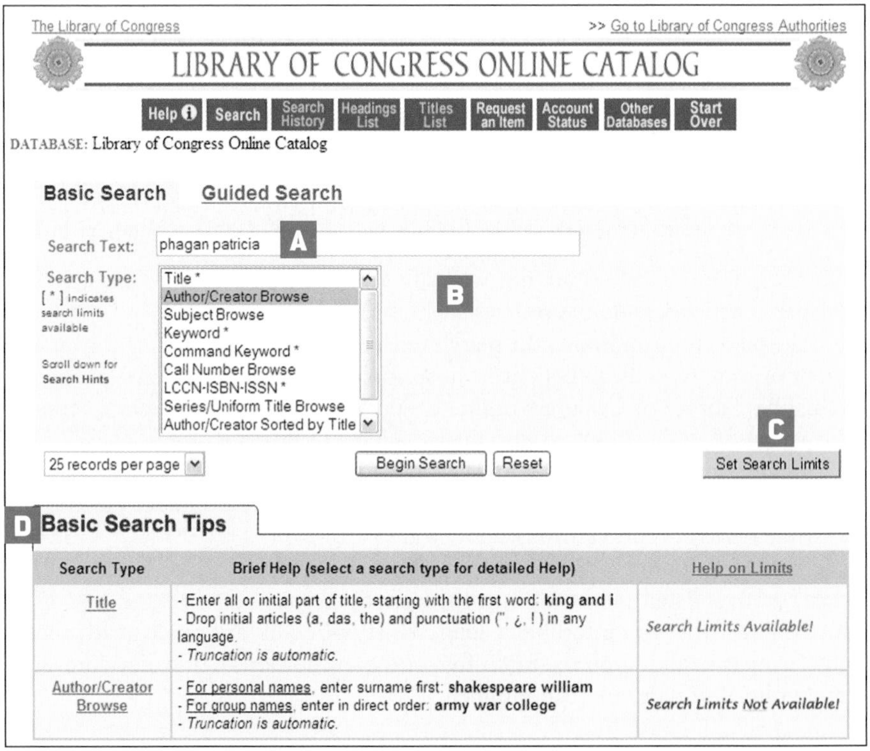

FIGURE 5.1 Searching by Author at the Library of Congress Online Catalog (catalog.loc.gov)

A The author's last name followed by first name.

B Other types of searches are available.

C Limits can be placed on searches.

D Tips are provided.

|| Collecting Information

Search by Word

Searching by keyword allows you to search for a specific word or phrase. In many online library catalogs, you can decide whether to search in all or only some parts (or fields) of a catalog record, such as title or subject (see Figure 5.2).

Search by Subject

When you search by subject, you look for sources cataloged under specific subject headings (see Figure 5.3). Many college and university libraries use the Library of Congress classification system to organize their collections, while others use the Dewey decimal classification system.

Search by Publication Date

If you're working on a subject that is time-sensitive — such as recent developments in gene therapy — limit your search by publication date. You can reduce the number of sources to those published during a certain time period.

Search by Call Number

Searching by call number allows you to take a virtual stroll through your library. To conduct this type of search, enter a call number from the Library of Congress

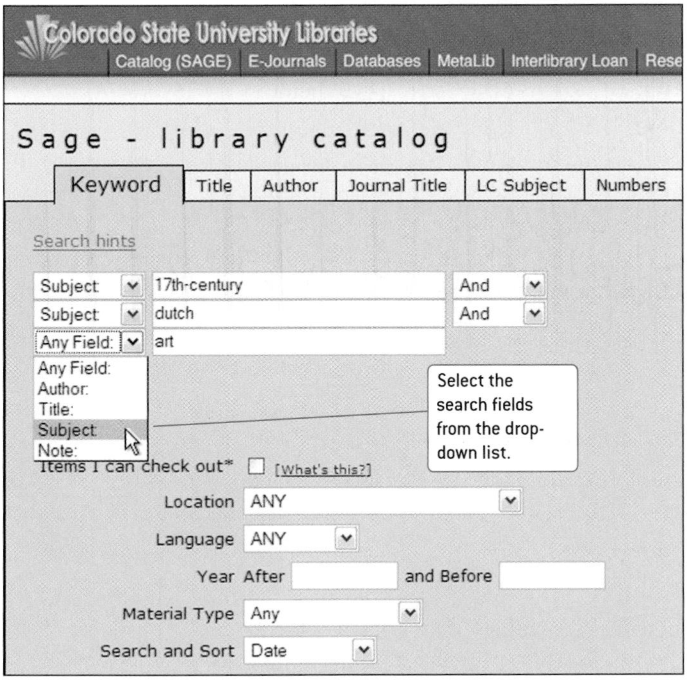

FIGURE 5.2
Searching by Word in an Online Library Catalog

FIGURE 5.3
Searching by Library of Congress Subject Heading

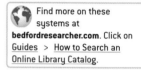

Colorado State University Libraries

Catalog (SAGE) | E-Journals | Databases | MetaLib | Interlibrary Loan | Reser

Sage — library catalog

| Keyword | Title | Author | Journal Title | **LC Subject** | Numbers |

art - dutch - 17th century   [Submit]

Type as much or as little of the subject as you want. For example:

- Trails -- Colorado -- Cache la Poudre -- Maps
- Indians of North America
- United States -- History -- Civil War, 1861-1865

classification system or the Dewey decimal system. If you are viewing the record for a book that you find interesting, you can often click on the call number to browse a list of sources with nearby call numbers.

> Find more on these systems at **bedfordresearcher.com**. Click on Guides > How to Search an Online Library Catalog.

Library of Congress Classification System

A   General Works
B   Philosophy, Psychology, Religion
C   Auxiliary Sciences of History
D   History: General and Old World
E   History: United States
F   History: United States Local and America
G   Geography, Anthropology, Recreation
H   Social Sciences
J   Political Science
K   Law

L   Education
M   Music and Books on Music
N   Fine Arts
P   Language and Literature
Q   Science
R   Medicine
S   Agriculture
T   Technology
U   Military Science
V   Naval Science
Z   Library Science and Information Resources

Dewey Decimal Classification System

000   Computers, Internet, and Systems
100   Philosophy
200   Religion
300   Social Sciences, Sociology and Anthropology
400   Language

500   Science
600   Technology
700   Arts
800   Literature, Rhetoric and Criticism
900   History

Search by a Combination of Terms

Online library catalogs can help you locate sources quickly, especially when you conduct simple searches, such as an author search by last name. If the last name is a common one such as Smith or Garcia or Chen, however, your search might produce far more results than you would like. In this case, it might help to search for more than one type of information—such as author and keyword—at the same time. The Library of Congress online catalog, for example, allows you to conduct this type of search through its Guided Search page.

My Research Project

PREPARE TO SEARCH ONLINE LIBRARY CATALOGS

As you get ready to search online library catalogs, return to your search plan and make a list of names, keywords, and phrases. Examine your working bibliography to identify the authors, titles, and subjects of your best sources. Then answer the following questions:

1. What are the names of authors I can use to search by author?
2. What are the titles of works that have been referred to me or that I have found in works cited pages that I can use to search by title?
3. What words and phrases can I use to search by word?
4. What words and phrases can I use to search by subject?
5. Does it make sense to search by date? If so, what are the dates I should search within?
6. Would call numbers in the Library of Congress or Dewey decimal classification systems be useful for me to browse? If so, what are these call numbers?

You can download or print this activity at **bedfordresearcher.com**. Click on Activities > Prepare to Search Online Library Catalogs.

5b

How can I search for sources with databases and Web search sites?

Databases operate much like online library catalogs, although they focus on a different collection of sources. Whereas an online catalog allows you to search for publications owned by the library, a database allows you to search for periodical articles, theses and dissertations, multimedia materials, papers presented at professional conferences, and government documents.

> Find an annotated list of print and electronic resources at **bedfordresearcher.com**. Click on Links > Resources for Specific Disciplines.

Web search sites allow you to search for Web sites that might be relevant to your issue. The most widely known Web search sites cover the entire Web, while specialized sites enable you to search for more specific content. Some Web search sites, such as Google's Image Search (www.google.com/imghp), also let you locate images or other multimedia materials.

Identify Relevant Databases

Databases vary in the topics they cover and the information they provide. Some databases provide information about newspaper, magazine, and journal articles addressing a general subject area, such as business or education (see Figure 5.4). Others focus on articles published in academic and professional journals on a specific field, such as microbiology or art history. Still others offer access to government documents, dissertations, and multimedia materials. Although most databases supply only publication information and brief descriptions of the information in a source, a growing number of databases allow you to view the complete text of a source. If the database you are using does not provide access to the source, check your library's online catalog for the title of the publication in which it appears. If your library does not own the publication, you can request it through interlibrary loan (see p. 86).

Although some databases can be accessed publicly through the Web, such as ERIC (eric.ed.gov/), most are available only through library computers or a library Web site. Four major types of databases are described in Table 5.1.

In addition to linking to online versions of articles, a number of databases allow you to save your searches and search results for later viewing. EBSCOhost Research Databases, for example, allows you to create an account on its "My EBSCOhost" site. Once you've created an account, you can save your searches, search history, and search results, among other options. Your work is saved in a folder that you can access as you use the database (see Figure 5.5).

Identify Relevant Web Search Sites

The Web has become the largest and most accessible "library" in the world. In addition to content developed for online use, the Web is home to a great deal of material that was once available only in print. For example, many magazines and journals are placing their back issues on the Web, and others are moving completely to online publication. In addition, groups such as Project Gutenberg (www.gutenberg.org) are providing access to literature published long before the information age.

> Find a list of additional Web search engines at **bedfordresearcher.com**. Click on Links > Resources for Conducting Electronic Searches.

Unfortunately, the Web is also the most disorganized library in the world, since it's being built by millions of people without a common plan or much communication among them. Thus, to locate sources, researchers have turned to Web search sites. Like online library catalogs and databases, Web search sites help you to locate information quickly and easily. However, while library catalogs and databases provide results that have been carefully selected by librarians and database editors, the Web pages produced by

TABLE 5.1 MAJOR TYPES OF DATABASES			
TYPE OF DATABASE	FUNCTION	EXAMPLE	GIVE FULL-TEXT OF ARTICLES?
Subject Databases	Provide publication information and abstracts (brief summaries) on sources about a broad subject area, such as education, business, or psychology	The Art Abstracts database (see Figure 5.4)	Generally no
Bibliographies	Provide publication information about publications in a specific discipline or profession, such as literary studies, computational linguistics, or the social sciences	*The MLA Bibliography* *The International Bibliography of the Social Sciences*	Generally no
Full-Text Databases	Provide publication information, abstracts, and the complete text of documents in a specific subject area, discipline, or profession	Lexis-Nexis Academic ACM Digital Library Academic Search Premier	Yes
Citation Indexes	Provide publication information and abstracts on sources that have referenced a specific publication	*Science Citation Index* *Social Sciences Citation Index* *Arts & Humanities Citation Index*	No

Web search sites can be uneven in quality, ranging from refereed articles in scholarly journals to home pages written by fifth graders.

Web Search Engines   When you use a Web search engine, you obtain information about Web pages and other forms of information on the Internet, including PDF files, PowerPoint files, Word files, newsgroup posts, blogs, and chat rooms (see p. 82). Web search engines keep track of these sources by locating documents on Web sites and entering them in a searchable database.

Keep two cautions in mind as you use Web search engines. First, because most search engines index only a portion of the Web — sometimes as much as 50 percent and sometimes as little as 5 percent — you should use more than one

EBSCO HOST | Research Databases | Basic Search | Advanced Search | Choose Databases | New Search | View Folder | Preferences | Help

Sign In to My EBSCOhost | Keyword | Publications | Subjects | Language ∨

◄ 3 of 3 ► | Result List | Refine Search | 🖶 Print | 📧 E-mail | 💾 Save | Add to folder | Folder is empty.

Formats: 📄 Citation

A

Title: *Dutch* culture and the politics of difference: Paragons of virtue; *Women* of the golden age; review article

Author: Vanhaelen, Angela

Source: RACAR, Revue d'Art Canadienne, Canadian Art Review, v. 21 no1-2 (1994) p. 137-43. Includes bibliography

B

Abstract: A review of Paragons of Virtue: *Women* and Domesticity in Seventeenth-*Century Dutch Art*, by Wayne Franits, and *Women* of the Golden Age: An International Debate on *Women* in Seventeenth-*Century* Holland, England and Italy, edited by Els Kloek, Nicole Teeuwen, and Marijke Huisman. These two recent publications show that gender issues are becoming increasingly central to the (re)writing of the history of *17th-century Dutch* culture, and they contribute significantly to considerations of the subject. An analysis of these two volumes accesses recent methodological debates that converge and often conflict at the intersection of the disciplines of *women's* history, literary studies, *art* history, and socioeconomic history. These works reveal that the study of *17th-century Dutch* culture can gain much from the theoretical rigor and contestatory politics of feminist interventions in history.

Descriptors: Women in art; Art, Dutch--17th century; Women--Social and economic status--History

Language: English

Document Type: Feature article

ISSN: 03159906

Entry Date: 19970213

Accession Number: BART96032917

Persistent link to this record: http://0-search.epnet.com.catalog.library.colostate.edu:80/login.aspx?direct=true&AuthType=cookie,ip,url,uid&db=ach&an=BART96032917

C

Database: Art Abstracts

View Links: 🔗 SFX CSU

FIGURE 5.4   A Record Retrieved from the *Art Abstracts* Subject Database

A Author, title, and other publication information.

B An abstract, or brief description of the article.

C Check for an online version of the article.

search engine to search the Web. If you don't find what you're looking for on one, it doesn't mean you won't find it on another. Second, because Web pages can be moved, deleted, or revised, you might find that a search engine's results are inaccurate. Some search sites, such as Google, provide access to cached versions of older Web pages. Leading Web search engines include

Google: www.google.com
AllTheWeb: www.alltheweb.com
AltaVista: www.altavista.com
Ask Jeeves: www.ask.com
Excite: www.excite.com

Gigablast: www.gigablast.com
MSN Search: search.msn.com
Teoma: www.teoma.com
WiseNut: www.wisenut.com
Yahoo! www.yahoo.com

Web Directories   Unlike Web search sites, Web directories employ human editors to organize information about Web pages into categories and subcategories. Directories allow you to browse lists of Web sites by clicking on general topics, such as Health or Education, and then successively narrow your search by clicking on subtopics. Many directories also permit you to conduct keyword searches

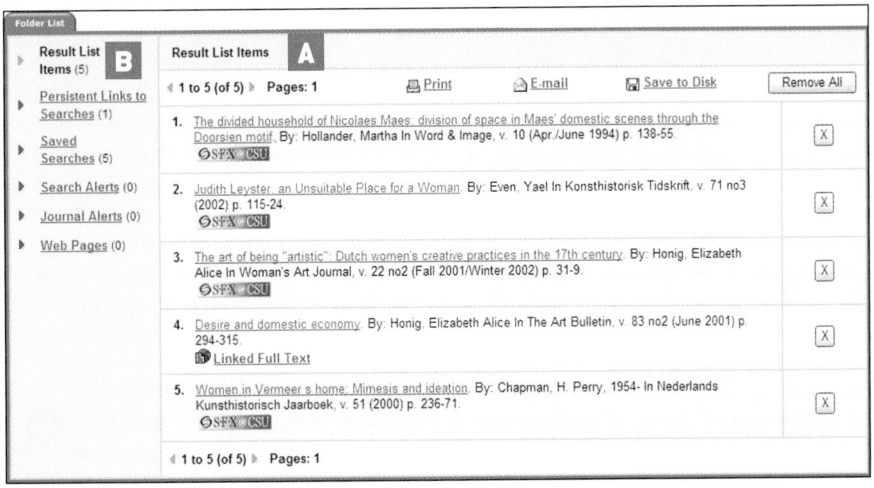

FIGURE 5.5 The EBSCOhost Folder

A Results saved from searches are displayed.

B Menu provides access to results and saved searches.

|| Collecting Information

within specific categories (see Figure 5.6). This enables you to search within a collection of Web sites that have already been judged by real people to be relevant to your topic. Leading Web directories include

About.com: about.com

AltaVista Directory: www.altavista.com/dir/

Google Directory: www.google.com/dirhp

Hoppa: hoppa.com

InfoMine: infomine.ucr.edu

Internet Public Library: www.ipl.org

Librarians' Index to the Internet: lii.org

LookSmart: search.looksmart.com

Open Directory Project: dmoz.org

Web World: www.webworldindex.com

Yahoo! Directory: dir.yahoo.com

Meta Search Sites   On a meta search site you can conduct a search on several Web search engines or Web directories at the same time. These sites typically search the major search engines and directories and then present a limited number of results on a single page. Some meta search sites such as ProFusion allow you to customize the list of sites that are searched (see Figure 5.7). ProFusion also lets you restrict your search to specific categories of information, such as movie reviews, astronomy, or bilingual education.

> Find a list of additional meta search sites at **bedfordresearcher.com**. Click on Links > Resources for Conducting Electronic Searches.

Use a meta search site early in your search for information on the Web. You might use a meta search site to do a side-by-side comparison of various search

FIGURE 5.6A   Searching a Web Directory

A Keyword searches produce a list of categories and Web pages.

B Categories, such as *Science* and *Health,* include subcategories, such as *Technology* and *Fitness.*

C Statistics about sites indexed, editors, and categories

sites and directories. When featured writer Pete Jacquez searched for the phrase *wind power* on ProFusion, for example, he found that the search sites Teoma and MSN Search produced more useful sets of results than the AltaVista and Netscape search sites. Leading meta search sites include

Dogpile: www.dogpile.com

ixquick: ixquick.com

Kartoo: www.kartoo.com

Mamma: www.mamma.com

Metacrawler: www.metacrawler.com

ProFusion: www.profusion.com

Search.com: www.search.com

SurfWax: www.surfwax.com

Vivisimo: vivisimo.com

News Search Sites   You can search for news on most major Web search sites and directories, such as Google, MSN Search, and Yahoo! (see Figure 5.8). In addition, specialized news search sites allow you to conduct focused searches for current and archived news reports. Leading news search sites include

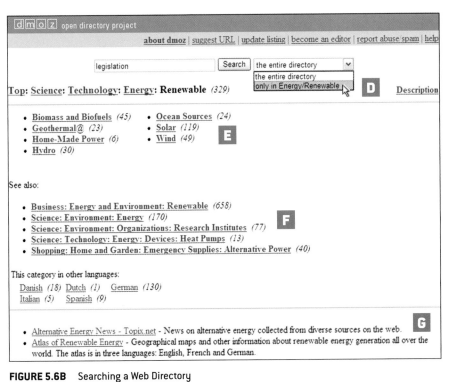

FIGURE 5.6B Searching a Web Directory

D Keyword searches can be restricted to one category.

E Subcategories

F Related categories

G Related Web pages

AllTheWeb News: www.alltheweb.com/?cat=news

AltaVista News: www.altavista.com/news/

Ask Jeeves News: news.ask.com

Daypop: www.daypop.com

Google News: news.google.com

MSN Search: search.msn.com

NewsTrove.com: www.newstrove.com

RocketInfo.com: www.rocketnews.com

Search.com: www.search.com

World News Network: www.wn.com

Yahoo! News: news.yahoo.com

Reference Search Sites On a reference search site you can search for information that has been collected in encyclopedias, almanacs, atlases, dictionaries,

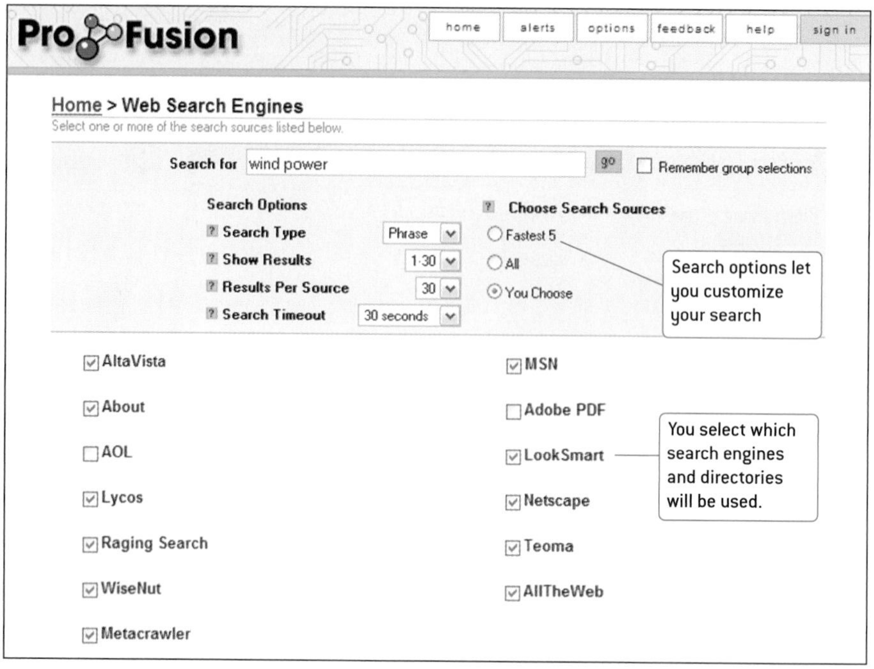

FIGURE 5.7   Customizing a Search on the ProFusion Meta Search Site (www.profusion.com)

and other reference resources. Some reference sites, such as MSN Encarta and Encyclopedia Britannica Online, offer limited access to information from their encyclopedias for no charge and complete access for a fee. Other sites, such as Information Please and Bartleby.com allow unrestricted access to recently published reference works, including the *Columbia Encyclopedia, The Encyclopedia of World History,* and *The World Factbook.* One widely used reference site is Wikipedia (en.wikipedia.org), a site that is collaboratively written by its readers. Because of its comprehensiveness, Wikipedia can serve as a useful starting point for research on a topic. However, because any reader can make changes to the site, it's best to double check the information you find there. Leading reference search sites include

Bartleby.com Reference: www.bartleby.com/reference

Encyclopedia.com: www.encyclopedia.com

Encyclopedia Britannica Online: www.britannica.com

Fablis: www.fablis.com

Information Please: www.infoplease.com

MSN Encarta: encarta.msn.com

Wikipedia: en.wikipedia.org

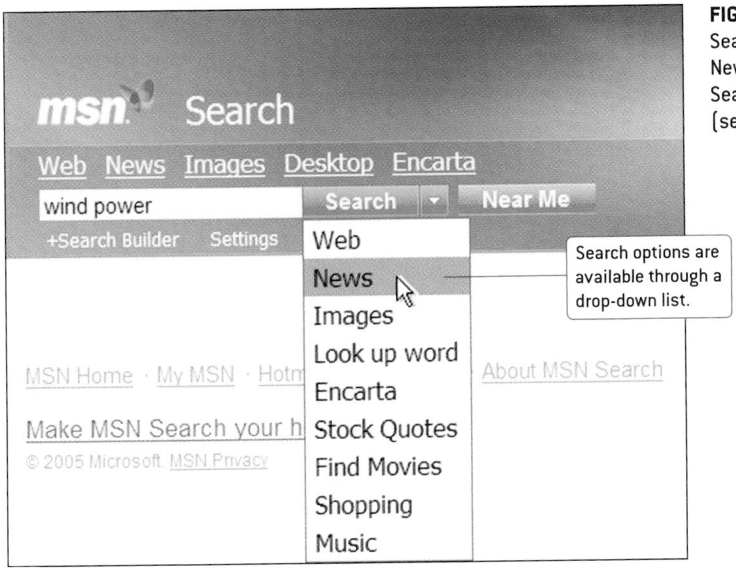

FIGURE 5.8
Searching for
News on MSN
Search
(search.msn.com)

Government Documents Search Sites and Directories   Many government agencies and institutions have turned to the Web as their primary means of distributing their publications. FirstGov, sponsored by the U.S. government, allows you to search the federal government's network of online resources. Government Printing Office Access provides publication information about print documents and links to those publications when they are available online. Sites such as Fed-Stats and FedWorld give access to a wide range of government-related materials. In addition to these specialized government Web sites, you can locate government publications through many Web directories, such as Yahoo! Leading government documents sites include

About.com's U.S. Government Information Directory: usgovinfo.about.com

Canadian Government Search Engines: canada.gc.ca/search/srcind_e.html

FedStats: www.fedstats.gov

FedWorld: www.fedworld.gov

FirstGov: www.firstgov.gov

Google UncleSam: www.google.com/unclesam

Government Printing Office Access: www.gpoaccess.gov

GovSpot.com: www.govspot.com

SearchGov.com: www.searchgov.com

State and Local Government Directory: www.statelocalgov.net

Deep Web Search Sites and Directories   Many specialized topics are addressed through databases or database-supported Web sites that, although accessible through the Web, are not indexed by conventional Web search sites such as Google or AllTheWeb. These sites are referred to collectively as the Deep Web or the Invisible Web because they are not easily found by the search technologies used by leading search sites. To search the Deep Web, try such search sites as Complete Planet, a directory of more than seventy thousand searchable databases and specialty search engines, and Turbo10.com, a meta search site focusing on specialized sites, directories, and Web-accessible databases. (For more on the Deep Web, read "The Deep Web" at library.albany.edu/internet/deepweb.html.) Leading Deep Web search sites and directories include

Academic Info:
www.academicinfo.net

Complete Planet:
aip.completeplanet.com

Direct Search:
www.freepint.com/gary/direct.htm

Invisible-web.net:
www.invisible-net.net

Profusion: www.profusion.com

Turbo10.com: turbo10.com

Answer Sites   Answer sites let you ask questions about a topic. At some sites, such as AllExperts.com, you can send questions to people who have listed themselves as "experts" on a topic and view responses to previously asked questions. Other sites, such as AskJeeves (www.askjeeves.com), display a list of Web sites and related searches in response to your question about a topic.

Several answer sites provide information for a fee. Google Answers (answers.google.com), for example, allows you to ask a question and indicate the fee you are willing to pay. You can also view answers to previously asked questions at Google Answers. Whether you are paying for answers or getting them for free, be wary of the quality of the answers you receive. Although you might sometimes receive useful advice, the "expert" replying to your question might actually know surprisingly little about the topic.

> **? WHAT'S MY PURPOSE?**
>
> As you decide which of the electronic resources discussed in this chapter you will use, keep in mind the differences among them. Understanding the different types of materials these resources offer will help you judge how much time to spend using them. If you are addressing an issue that is currently being debated in the popular press, news search sites might offer a good starting point. If you have chosen a historical topic, consider starting with your library's online catalog. If you are researching a topic that is addressed in scholarly articles, turn to databases. Your purpose as a writer will affect your decisions about which resources to use and how to use them.

Search with Keywords and Phrases

To search for sources, research writers type words and phrases in the search field of a database or Web search site. Featured writer Patrick Crossland used the keywords *college, university,* and *admissions* in some of his searches for information about his research writing project, while Alexis Alvarez used the phrases *competitive sports* and *adolescent girls.*

Keyword searches include

- **simple searches** that use one or more keywords, such as *college, university,* or *admissions*
- **wildcard searches** that use special characters, such as * or ?, to increase the scope of a search
- **searches for exact phrases** that locate sources containing words in a specific order, such as *competitive sports*
- **Boolean searches** that allow you to specify which keywords or phrases to include or exclude from a search
- **advanced operator searches** that use unique features of specific Web search sites

My Research Project

USE YOUR RESEARCH QUESTION TO GENERATE SEARCH TERMS

To generate keywords for your searches, write your research question on a piece of paper or in a word processor and then underline or boldface the most important words and phrases in the sentence. Brainstorm a list of related words and phrases:

Example:

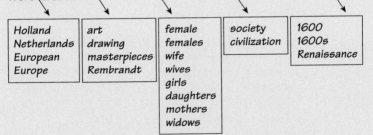

What was the relationship between **seventeenth-century Dutch paintings** of **women** and the **culture** in which they were created?

| Holland Netherlands European Europe | art drawing masterpieces Rembrandt | female females wife wives girls daughters mothers widows | society civilization | 1600 1600s Renaissance |

You can print or download this activity at **bedfordresearcher.com**. Click on Activities > Use Your Research Question to Generate Search Terms.

Simple Searches   Simple searches consist of one or more keywords. In some databases, library catalogs, and Web search sites, adding keywords to a search increases the number of sources you find (as in "find all sources containing the keywords *research* or *writing*"). In other cases, adding keywords decreases the number of sources you find (as in "find only sources containing both the keywords *research* and *writing*"). You can find out how your database, library catalog, or Web search site treats multiple keywords by consulting online help—or by conducting some test searches and reviewing your results.

Wildcard Searches   Sometimes you're not sure what form of a word is most likely to occur. Rather than conducting several searches for *compete, competes, competitive, competitiveness, competition,* and *competitions,* for example, you can combine your search into a single wildcard search. Wildcards are symbols that take the place of letters or strings of letters. By standing in for multiple letters, they allow you to expand the scope of your search.

The most commonly used wildcard symbols are

* usually takes the place of one or more characters, such as *compet**

? usually takes the place of a single character, such as *wom?n*

TABLE 5.2 COMMONLY USED BOOLEAN OPERATORS

BOOLEAN OPERATOR	FUNCTION	EXAMPLE
AND/+ (plus)	Finds sources that include both terms	adolescent AND girls
OR	Finds sources that include either term	sports OR athletics
NOT/− (minus)	Finds sources that include one term but not the other	girls NOT boys
ADJ (adjacent)	Finds sources in which the keywords appear next to each other	competitive ADJ athletics
NEAR	Finds sources in which the keywords appear within a certain number of words of each other (usually twenty-five; depending on the search engine, you may be able to change the default setting)	adolescent NEAR athlete
BEFORE	Finds sources in which keywords appear in a particular order	competitive BEFORE athletics
Parentheses ( )	Although not strictly a Boolean search term, parentheses are used to group keywords and Boolean operators	competitive AND (athletics OR sports) AND (girls NOT boys)

Other wildcard symbols include !, +, and $. Consult the help section in a database, library catalog, or Web search site to learn whether wildcard symbols are supported.

Searches for Exact Phrases Sometimes the best way to locate information in a keyword search is to search for an exact phrase. If you're interested in the economic impact of a damaging hurricane, such as Hurricane Ivan, for instance, you might search for sources containing the exact phrase *Hurricane Ivan.* This would eliminate sources in which the word *Hurricane* or *Ivan* appears by itself. Many databases and Web search sites permit you to specify phrases using quotation marks, and some provide a drop-down list where you can indicate whether a string of words consists of separate keywords or is a phrase.

Boolean Searches Boolean searches let you focus your search by specifying whether keywords or phrases *can* appear in the results of a search, *must* appear in the results, or *must not* appear in the results. Some forms of Boolean search also allow you to search for keywords or phrases that appear next to, before or after, or within a certain distance from one another within a document. Table 5.2 lists commonly used Boolean operators and their functions.

Many online catalogs, databases, and Web search sites include the use of Boolean search terms—typically AND, OR, and NOT or plus (+) and minus (−) signs—in their basic search forms (see Figure 5.9). Others allow Boolean searches in advanced search forms (see Figure 5.10).

Advanced Operator Searches A number of leading Web sites, such as Google, Yahoo!, and MSN Search, offer special operators that allow you to fine-tune a Web search. These special operators can be used in combination with keyword, phrase, wildcard, and Boolean searches. Table 5.3 illustrates the use of several special operators in Web searches.

FIGURE 5.9 Boolean Search in a Basic Search Form

‖ Collecting Information

FIGURE 5.10   Boolean Search in an Advanced Search Form

A Boolean AND
B Phrase required with Boolean AND
C Boolean OR
D Boolean NOT

TABLE 5.3 SPECIAL OPERATORS

FUNCTION	GOOGLE	YAHOO!	MSN SEARCH
Find synonyms	~writing	synonym writing	
Words in body text	intext:writing		
Words in title of page	intitle:writing	intitle:writing	
All words in title of page	allintitle: writing reading		
Locate similar Web pages	related: writing.colostate .edu		
Find a definition	define:writing	define writing	define writing
Search a single domain	site:writing .colostate.edu	site:writing .colostate.edu	site:writing .colostate.edu
Search for words in URL	inurl:writing	inurl:writing	
Locate sites linking to a page	link: writing.colostate .edu	link: writing .colostate.edu	link: writing .colostate.edu

My Research Project

RECORD SEARCHES

One of the most important research strategies you can use as you collect information is keeping track of your searches. Note not only the keywords or phrases and
the search strategies you used with them (wildcards, Boolean search, author search,
and so on) but also how many sources the search turned up and whether those
sources were relevant to your research project.

In your research log, record the following information for each source you search:

↓

1. Resource that was searched
2. Search terms used (keywords, phrases, publication information)
3. Search strategies used (simple search, wildcard search, exact phrase search, Boolean search)
4. Date search was conducted
5. Number of results produced by the search
6. Relevance of the results
7. Notes about the search

You can download or print this activity at **bedfordresearcher.com**. Click <u>Activities</u> > <u>Record Your Searches</u>.

5c

How can I search for sources with other online resources?

You can locate useful information about your conversation by using Web portals, blogs, and records of electronic discussions.

Use Web Portals and Communities

Many of the more successful Web search sites and directories, such as Yahoo!, MSN, and Lycos, have shifted their focus from merely helping readers locate Web sites to providing a comprehensive set of Web-based services, such as email, stock quotes, weather reports, news, entertainment, sports information, telephone directories, and online shopping. These sites attempt to offer a one-stop gateway—or portal—to the Web.

Portals offer several advantages to research writers. Most portals allow you to customize the content and layout of the page you see when you visit their site. My Yahoo! (my.yahoo.com), for example, gives you the ability to display the Yahoo! search field, a list of saved searches, bookmarks, and information from a variety of news, sports, and entertainment sources, among many other options. It also allows you to save notes and map your progress on a research project with a personal calendar. Perhaps most important, portals can be accessed from any computer with Internet access. Web portals that can be customized include

My Excite: my.excite.com   My Netscape: my.netscape.com
My Lycos: my.lycos.com   My Yahoo!: my.yahoo.com
My MSN: my.msn.com

Web communities are portals for specific groups. Some of the most popular community sites include iVillage.com, which is directed toward women; ZDNet .com and CNET.com, which are targeted at computer users; and Run the Planet (www.runtheplanet.com), which supports runners. Like portals, Web communities offer opportunities for research writers. Besides gaining an insider's view on a particular community, you can also use these sites to obtain specialized information and to interact with members through email, discussion forums, or chat.

Use Blogs

Blogs — short for Weblogs — consist of chronologically ordered entries on a Web site and most closely resemble entries in a diary or journal. Blog entries usually include a title and a text message, and can also incorporate images, audio, video, and other types of media. Many entries provide links to other pages on the Web.

The purposes of blogs vary:

- Some blogs report on events and issues (see Figure 5.11). The bloggers who provided daily — sometimes hourly — reports on the 2004 political conventions offered valuable, firsthand insights into aspects of the conventions that were not addressed through the mainstream media. The bloggers who reported on the Iraq war, similarly, offered a perspective on events in Iraq and elsewhere that would not have been available otherwise.

- Some blogs alert readers to information elsewhere on the Web. These blogs cite recently published news reports and articles, newly revealed developments in a particular discipline, and new contributions to an ongoing debate — and provide commentary on that information. Blogs created to serve this purpose often publish news and commentary from other Web sites and blogs.

- Some blogs serve largely as a space for personal reflection and expression. A blogger might share his or her thoughts about each day, current events, or other issues with friends and family.

Research writers can use blogs as sources of information and commentary on an issue and as sources of firsthand accounts by individuals involved in or affected by an issue. If you find blogs by experts in the field, you can begin a dialogue with people involved in or knowledgeable about your topic. To locate blogs that are relevant to your research question, use the following blog search sites and directories:

Blogarama: www.blogarama.com Fagan Finder Blogs:
Blogwise: www.blogwise.com   www.faganfinder.com/blogs
Bloogz: www.bloogz.com   Feedster: www.feedster.com
Daypop: www.daypop.com   Globe of Blogs: www.globeofblogs.com

Use Electronic Mailing Lists, Newsgroups, and Web Discussion Forums

Electronic mailing lists, newsgroups, and Web discussion forums support conversations among individuals who share an interest in an issue or belong to a par-

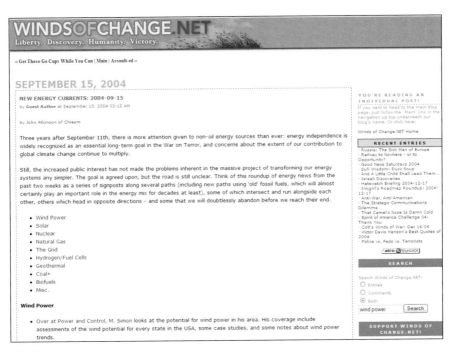

FIGURE 5.11   Blog Entry on Alternative Energy

ticular community. You can read a message sent to a mailing list, sometimes referred to as a listserv, in the same way that you read other email messages. Messages posted to newsgroups and Web discussion forums can be read using most Web browsers.

In addition to reading messages, you can post your own. Although there is no guarantee that you'll receive helpful responses, experts in a particular area often read and contribute to these forums. If you are fortunate enough to get into a discussion with one or more knowledgeable people, you might obtain useful information.

> Find a list of additional search sites for newsgroups and mailing lists at **bedfordresearcher.com.** Click on Links > Resources for Conducting Electronic Searches.

Mailing lists, newsgroups, and discussion forums can be located through the following search engines and directories:

Catalist: www.lsoft.com/lists/listref.html

CyberFiber: www.cyberfiber.com

Forum Zilla: www.forumzilla.com

Google Groups: groups.google.com

Newzbot: www.newzbot.com

Tile.net: tile.net/lists

My Research Project

DISCUSS YOUR RESEARCH PROJECT WITH OTHERS

Return to your research log and review your search plan. As you collect information about your issue, reconsider how your plan capitalizes on available electronic resources. If you are uncertain about how you might use these resources, discuss your project with a reference librarian or your instructor. Given the wide range of electronic resources that are available, a few minutes of discussion could save you a great deal of time searching for useful sources.

> ### QUICK REFERENCE

Searching for Information with Electronic Resources

✔ Search your library's online catalog.   (p. 63)

✔ Identify and search relevant databases.   (p. 68)

✔ Identify and use appropriate Web search sites.   (p. 68)

✔ Conduct keyword and phrase searches.   (p. 77)

✔ Search other online resources.   (p. 81)

6

Searching for Information with Print Resources

> **Key Questions**
>
> **6a.** **How can I use the library stacks to locate sources? 86**
> Browse the stacks
> Check out books and periodicals
> Use interlibrary loan
>
> **6b.** **How can I use a library periodicals room to locate sources? 87**
>
> **6c.** **How can I use a library reference room to locate sources? 88**
> Consult bibliographies
> Consult indexes
> Consult biographies
> Consult general and specialized encyclopedias
> Consult handbooks
> Consult almanacs
> Consult atlases

Contrary to recent claims, there is life (and information) beyond the World Wide Web. Print resources can help you locate a wealth of information relevant to your research project.

? WHAT'S MY PURPOSE?

To make the most effective use of the print resources available in a library, ask how the information they can point you toward will help you achieve your purposes as a writer. If you are working on a research project that has a historical component, as was the case with featured writers Jenna Alberter and Kevin Fahey, you'll find that

↓

WHAT'S MY PURPOSE? (continued)

print bibliographies and indexes can point you toward sources that cannot be located using a database. Moreover, because libraries organize their collections by subject, you can use the sources you locate through print resources as starting points for browsing the library stacks. By relying on the careful selections librarians make when adding to a library collection, you will be able to find useful, credible sources that reflect your purpose and address your issue.

6a

How can I use the library stacks to locate sources?

The library stacks—or shelves—house the library's collection of bound publications. You can locate publications by browsing the stacks and checking works cited pages for related publications. Once you've decided a source is relevant to your issue, you can check it out or request it through interlibrary loan.

Browse the Stacks

One of the advantages of the classification systems used by most libraries—typically the Library of Congress or Dewey decimal classification system—is that they are subject based. As a result, you can browse the stacks to look for sources on a topic because books on similar subjects are shelved together. For example, if your research takes you to the stacks for books about alcohol abuse, you're likely to find books about drug abuse, treatment programs, and codependency nearby.

When you find a publication that seems useful, check the works cited page for related works. The combination of browsing the stacks for sources and checking the works cited pages of those sources can lead you to publications relevant to your issue.

Check Out Books and Periodicals

In some cases, you'll discover that a publication you want is not available because it has been checked out, reserved for a course, or placed in off-site storage. If a publication is checked out, you may be able to recall it—that is, ask that it be returned to the library and held for you. If it has been placed on reserve, you may be able to photocopy or take notes on it. If it has been placed in off-site storage, you can usually request it at the circulation desk.

Use Interlibrary Loan

If you can't obtain the book or periodical you need from your library, use interlibrary loan to borrow materials from another library. Most libraries allow you to request materials in person or on the Web. Some libraries let you check the status of your interlibrary loan request or renew interlibrary loan materials through the Web. You can learn how to use interlibrary loan at your library by consulting its Web site or a librarian.

6b

How can I use a library periodicals room to locate sources?

Periodicals include newspapers, magazines, and academic and professional journals. A periodicals room—or journals room—contains recent issues for library visitors to browse. Many libraries also have a separate room for newspapers published in the last few weeks or months.

To ensure everyone's access to recently published issues, most libraries don't allow you to check out periodicals published within the last year, and they usually don't allow newspapers to be checked out at all. Older periodicals are sometimes placed in bound volumes in the stacks. Few libraries, however, keep back issues of newspapers in paper form. Instead, you can often find back issues of leading newspapers in full-text databases or in microforms. Microform is a generic name for both microfilm, a strip of film containing greatly reduced images of printed pages, and microfiche, film roughly the shape and size of an index card containing the same kinds of miniaturized images. You view these images using a microform reader, a projection unit that looks something like a large computer monitor. Many microform readers allow you to print full-size copies of the pages.

To help you locate articles in periodicals, most periodicals rooms provide access to electronic databases, which are more likely than print indexes and bibliographies to contain listings of recent publications. Once you've identified articles you want to review, you'll need to find the periodicals containing those articles. Most online library catalogs allow you to conduct a title search for a periodical, in the same way you conduct a title search for a book. The online catalog will tell you the call number of the periodical, and most online catalogs will give information about its location in the library. In addition, some libraries provide a printed list that identifies where periodicals are located. If you have difficulty finding a periodical or judging which publications are likely to contain articles relevant to your research project, ask a librarian for assistance.

> Learn more about using databases to locate sources at **bedfordresearcher .com** Click on Guides > How to Search a Database.

6c

How can I use a library reference room to locate sources?

Although many of the reference books in library reference rooms serve the same purposes as the electronic databases discussed in Chapter 5, others offer information not available in databases. Using reference books to locate print resources has several benefits:

- **Most databases have short memories.**   Databases seldom index sources published before 1970, and typically index sources only as far back as the mid-1980s. Depending on the conversation you've decided to join, a database might not allow you to locate important sources.

- **Most databases focus on short works.**   In contrast, many of the print resources in library reference rooms will refer you to books and longer publications as well as to articles in periodicals.

- **Many library reference resources are unavailable in electronic form.**   For instance, the *Encyclopedia of Creativity*, which offers more than two hundred articles, is available only in print form.

- **Entries in print indexes are easier to browse.**   Despite efforts to aid browsing, databases support searching far better than they do browsing.

Reference rooms contain print resources on a range of topics, from government to finance to philosophy to science. Some of the most important print resources you can consult in a reference room include bibliographies, indexes, biographies, general and specialized encyclopedias, handbooks, almanacs, and atlases.

● Consult Bibliographies

Bibliographies list books, articles and other publications that have been judged relevant to a topic. Some bibliographies provide only citations, while others include abstracts—brief descriptions—of listed sources.

Complete bibliographies attempt to list all of the sources published about a topic, while selective bibliographies attempt to list only the best sources published about a topic. Some bibliographies limit their inclusion of sources by time period, often focusing on sources published during a given year.

Types of Bibliographies   You're likely to find several types of bibliographies in your library's reference room or stacks, including trade bibliographies, general bibliographies, and specialized bibliographies.

- **Trade Bibliographies.**   Trade bibliographies allow you to locate books published about a particular topic. Leading trade bibliographies include *The Subject Guide to Books in Print, Books in Print,* and *Cumulative Book Index.* Kevin Fahey found a large number of books about Ernest Hemingway in *Books in Print* (see Figure 6.1).

> Read more about Kevin Fahey at **bedfordresearcher.com**. Click on Featured Writers.

A HEMINGWAY, ERNEST, 1899–1961

B Astro, Richard & Beason, Jackson, J., eds.
Hemingway in Our Time: Published Record of a
Literary Conference Devoted to a Study of the
Work of Ernest Hemingway Held at Oregon
C State University on April 26–27, 1973. LC 73-
18428. 222p. reprinted. Pap. 63.30 (0-317-28801-6.
2020634) Bks Demand.

Baker, Carlos. Ernest Hemingway Life Story. 1976. 47.50
(0-685-45827-X, Scribners Ref) Mac Lib Ref.
—Hemingway, the Writer as Artist, 45h rev. ed. 440p. 1972,
pap. Text 21.95 (0-691-01305-5, 86) Princeton U Pr.
Baldwin, Marc D. Reading "The Sun Also Rises"
Hemingway's Political Unconscious. (Modern American
Literature Ser.: Vol. 4). 168p. ©. 1997. 39.95
(0-8204-3033-1) P Lang Pubng.

FIGURE 6.1 An Entry from *Books in Print* on Ernest Hemingway

A Subject heading

B Recently published books listed in bold print; older books listed in
normal print

C Publication information

- **General Bibliographies.** General bibliographies cover a wide range of
  topics, usually in selective lists. For sources on humanities topics,
  consult *The Humanities: A Selective Guide to Information Sources.* For
  sources on social science topics, see *Social Science Reference Sources: A
  Practical Guide.* For sources on science topics, go to bibliographies such
  as *Information Sources in Science and Technology, Guide to Information
  Sources in the Botanical Sciences,* and *Guide to Information Sources in the
  Physical Sciences.*
- **Specialized Bibliographies.** Specialized bibliographies typically provide
  lists of sources—often annotated—about a topic. For example, *Art
  Books: A Basic Bibliography of Monographs on Artists,* edited by Wolfgang
  M. Freitag, focuses on sources about important artists.

Locating Bibliographies Although most general and trade bibliographies can
be found in your library reference room, specialized bibliographies are likely to
be located in your library's stacks. To locate bibliographies, follow these steps:

1. *Consult a cumulative bibliography.* Cumulative bibliographies provide an
   index of published bibliographies. *The Bibliographic Index: A Cumulative
   Bibliography of Bibliographies,* for instance, identifies bibliographies on a
   wide range of topics and is updated annually.

2. *Consult your library's online catalog.* When you search your library's online catalog, use keywords related to your issue plus the keyword *bibliography*. Featured writer Kevin Fahey searched his college's online catalog using the keywords *Hemingway* and *bibliography* (see Figure 6.2).

3. *If necessary, seek advice from a reference librarian.* Reference librarians will help you find bibliographies that are relevant to your issue.

● **Consult Indexes**

Indexes provide citation information for sources found in a particular set of publications. Many indexes also include abstracts—brief descriptions—that can help you determine whether a source is worth locating and reviewing. The following types of indexes can be found in libraries.

Periodical Indexes   Periodical indexes list sources published in magazines, trade journals, scholarly journals, and newspapers. Some periodical indexes cover a wide range of periodicals, others focus on periodicals that address a single subject, and still others focus on a small set or even an individual periodical:

- *The Readers' Guide to Periodical Literature* indexes roughly two hundred general-interest magazines. Updated monthly, the *Readers' Guide* organizes entries by author and subject.

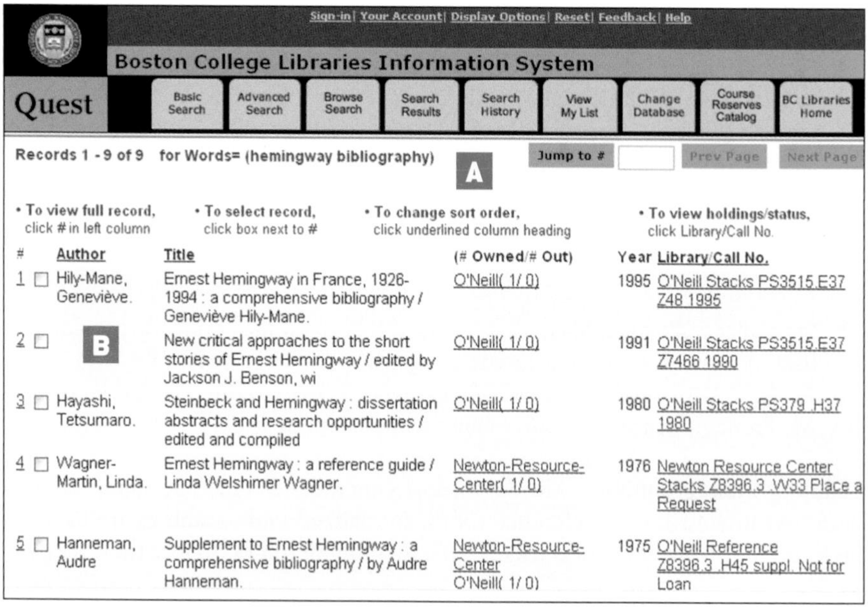

FIGURE 6.2   Searching an Online Library Catalog for Bibliographies
A Search for bibliographies by adding the keyword *bibliography*
B The list of results includes several bibliographies

- *Art Index* provides information about sources published only in art magazines and journals. Updated quarterly, *Art Index* orders entries by author and subject.
- *The New York Times Index* lists articles published only in that newspaper. Updated twice a month, the *Index* organizes entries by subject, geography, organization, and references to individuals.

Featured writer Patrick Crossland used the *Readers' Guide to Periodical Literature* to locate sources about college admissions (see Figure 6.3).

> Find an annotated list of periodical indexes at **bedfordresearcher.com.** Click on Links > Resources for Specific Disciplines.

Significant differences can exist between the print and electronic database versions of periodical indexes. For example, while the printed *Readers' Guide to Periodical Literature* covers publications since 1900, the *Readers' Guide* database only contains information on articles published since 1983.

Indexes of Materials in Books   To locate articles in edited books, turn to resources such as the *Essay and General Literature Index,* which indexes nearly five thousand book-length collections of articles and essays in the arts, humanities, and social sciences. You might also find subject-specific indexes of materials in books. *The Cumulative Bibliography of Asian Studies,* for example, covers articles in edited books.

Pamphlet Indexes   Libraries frequently collect pamphlets of various kinds. To help patrons find these materials, many libraries create a pamphlet index. Ask a reference librarian whether your library has a pamphlet index and where it is. You can also consult the *Vertical File Index.* Updated monthly, this index lists roughly three thousand brief sources on ten to fifteen newsworthy topics each month.

Government Documents Indexes   Government documents indexes list documents published by federal, state, and local governments.

A **Admissions**
B *See also*
College applications
Be sure the advice is worth the price [consultants] B. Wildavsky.
C il *U.S. News & World Report* v129 no10 p94-6 S 11 2000
Ben's life: getting in vs. going out. il *Seventeen* v59 no4 p82 Ap
D 2000
Berkeley's new colors [large Asian American population at university] K. Peraino. il *Newsweek* v136 no12 p61 S 18 2000

FIGURE 6.3   A Listing in the *Readers' Guide to Periodical Literature*
A Subject heading
B Other potentially relevant headings
C Publication information for one article (the letters *il* stand for "illustrated")
D Other articles related to the subject heading

- To find documents published by the federal government, consult the *Monthly Catalog of United States Government Publications.*
- To locate documents published by the U.S. Congress, look in the *CIS Index to Publications of the United States Congress.*
- To obtain information about the daily proceedings of the House of Representatives and the Senate, consult the *Congressional Record.*
- For documents published by the Supreme Court, consult *United States Reports,* the cumulative index of the *Official Reports of the Supreme Court.*
- To locate government documents containing statistical information, including census reports, look in the *Statistical Abstract of the United States.*

Many larger college and university libraries serve as depositories of government documents. As a result, indexes to government documents might be found in either the reference room or a separate government documents collection in your library. Ask a reference librarian for help.

Citation Indexes   Citation indexes allow you to determine which publications make reference to other publications, a useful strategy for finding sources that are engaged in the same conversation. To learn which sources refer to an article published in a scientific journal, for example, you could consult the *Science Citation Index.*

Consult Biographies

Biographies cover key figures in a field, time period, or geographic region. *Who's Who in America,* for instance, provides brief biographies of important figures in the United States during a given year, while *Great Lives from History* takes a broader view, offering biographies of key figures in world history.

Consult General and Specialized Encyclopedias

General encyclopedias attempt to provide a little knowledge about a lot of things. The idea behind a general encyclopedia, such as the *New Encyclopaedia Britannica,* is to present enough information about a topic to get you started on a more detailed search.

Specialized encyclopedias such as *The MIT Encyclopedia of the Cognitive Sciences,* for example, take a narrower focus than general encyclopedias, usually of a field of study or a narrow historical period. In addition, articles in specialized encyclopedias are typically longer than articles in general encyclopedias and offer more detailed coverage of topics.

Consult Handbooks

Like encyclopedias, handbooks provide useful background information about a topic in a compact form. Unlike encyclopedias, most handbooks, such as

The Engineering Handbook and the *International Handbook of Psychology,* cover a narrow topic area. Entries in handbooks are also much shorter than the articles found in encyclopedias.

Consult Almanacs

Almanacs contain lists, charts, and tables of information of various types. You're probably familiar with *The Old Farmer's Almanac,* which is known for its accuracy in predicting weather over the course of a year. Information in almanacs can range from the average rainfall in Australia to the batting averages of the 1927 Yankees to the average income of Germans and Poles prior to World War II.

Consult Atlases

Atlases provide maps and related information about a region or country. Some atlases take a historical perspective, while others take a topical perspective.

My Research Project
DISCUSS YOUR RESEARCH PROJECT WITH OTHERS

Return to your research log and review your search plan. As you collect information about your issue, reconsider how your plan capitalizes on the print resources available in your library reference room. If you are uncertain about how you might use these resources, discuss your project with a reference librarian. Given the wide range of specialized print resources that are available, a few minutes of discussion with a knowledgeable librarian could save you a great deal of time.

> **QUICK REFERENCE**

Searching for Information with Print Resources
- ✔ Use the library stacks to locate sources. (p. 86)
- ✔ Use the periodicals room to locate sources. (p. 87)
- ✔ Use the reference room to locate sources. (p. 88)

Collecting Information

7

Searching for Information with Field Research Methods

> **Key Questions**

Published documents aren't the only source of information for a research project. Nor are they always the best. Publications — such as books, articles, Web sites, or television reports — offer someone else's interpretation of an event or an issue. By relying on another person's interpretation, you're looking through that person's eyes rather than through your own.

Experienced research writers know that you don't have to use published reports to find out how an event or issue has affected people — you can ask the people yourself. You don't have to view television or radio coverage of an event — you can go to the event yourself. And you don't have to rely on someone else's survey of public opinion — you can conduct your own.

> ### ? WHAT'S MY PURPOSE?
>
> Your preparations for using field research methods will be most effective if you clearly understand your purpose for carrying out your research project and your purpose for using field research. Before committing yourself to designing and administering a survey, for example, ask yourself what kind of results you can expect to gain and what role those results will play in your project. Ask as well whether a certain field research method is the best technique for gaining that information, or whether you might gain it more effectively and efficiently in another way.

7a

How can I use interviews to collect information?

Interviews—in which one person seeks information from another—can provide firsthand accounts of an event, authoritative interpretations of events and issues, and reactions to an event or issue from the people who have been affected by it. Most interviews follow a question-and-answer format, but some more closely resemble a free-flowing discussion. You can conduct interviews face to face, over the telephone, via email, and even through an instant messaging program.

● Decide Whether to Conduct an Interview

Thinking carefully about the role an interview might play in your research project can help you decide whether and how to conduct it.

Sometimes the decision to interview is a natural extension of the kind of work you're doing. For example, although featured writer Alexis Alvarez was able to find plenty of information from other sources about the pressures that would lead adolescent female athletes to use performance-enhancing drugs, she decided to interview friends and family members who had played competitive sports because she knew that firsthand reports would strengthen her argument.

Sometimes the decision to conduct an interview isn't so much the result of careful planning as it is the recognition of an available opportunity. Featured writer Pete Jacquez, who created a Web site about wind-generated electrical power, learned that one of his friends had recently signed up for a wind power program offered by his university. His interviews produced a personal perspective about wind power that he wouldn't have been able to find through print or electronic sources.

> Read more about Alexis Alvarez and Pete Jacquez at **bedfordresearcher.com**. Click on Featured Writers.

● Plan Your Interview

The most important things to consider as you plan your interview are whom to interview and what to ask.

Deciding Whom to Interview   Your decisions about whom to interview should be based on the kind of information you want for your research project.

- If you're trying to better understand a specific aspect of a conversation, interview an expert in the field.
- If you want to learn what people in general think about an issue, interview a number of people who are affected by the issue.
- If you're hoping to collect quotations from people who are authorities on a subject, interview someone who will be recognized as an authority.

Once you've decided what sorts of people you want to interview, you'll need to identify and contact interview candidates. If you're working on a research project for a class, ask your instructor and classmates for suggestions. Then ask whether they can introduce you to the people they suggest. Before you call to set up an interview, make some preparations:

1. Write a script to help you remember what to say.
2. Prepare a list of dates and times that work for you.
3. Estimate how much time you'll need to complete the interview.
4. Be ready to suggest a location for the interview.
5. Leave your phone number or email address so that your interview candidate can get in touch with you if a conflict arises.

Deciding What You Should Ask   Your interview questions should focus on the issues you want to address in your project. As you prepare your questions, keep the following principles in mind:

1. *Consider your research question, the role you are adopting, and the kind of information you want to collect.* Are you seeking background information, or do you want someone's opinion? An answer to the question, "How did this situation come about?" will be quite different from an answer to the question, "What do you think about this situation?"
2. *Ask questions that require more than a yes or no answer.* You'll learn much more from an answer to a question such as, "What factors will affect your vote on referendum X?" than from an answer to "Will you vote for referendum X?"
3. *Prepare a limited number of main questions and many follow-up questions.* Good interviews seldom involve more than eight to ten main questions, but experienced interviewers know that each question can lead to several follow-up questions.
4. *Be flexible.* Be ready to ask follow-up questions.

> Find a list of Web sites about conducting interviews at **bedfordresearcher.com**. Click on Links > Resources for Conducting Field Research.

● **Conduct Your Interview**

Consult the following checklist before you conduct your interview.

CHECKLIST FOR CONDUCTING INTERVIEWS

✔ **Arrive early and review your questions.** If you are conducting your interview over the phone, set time aside before the call to review your questions and then call the person you are interviewing at the agreed-upon time.

✔ **Introduce yourself and ask for permission to record the interview.** Explain why you are conducting the interview. Ask for permission to record and use quotes from the interview.

✔ **Set up and test your recording equipment.** Ideally, use an audio or video recorder to make a complete record of your interview. At a later time, you can re-view what was said and carefully transcribe exact quotations from the tape.

✔ **Ask your questions clearly and be ready to respond with follow-up questions.** Allow the person you are interviewing a chance to answer your questions fully. Don't insist on strictly following your list of interview questions; if discussion naturally flows in another, useful direction, be prepared to shift your line of questioning.

✔ **Take notes, even if you are using a video or audio recorder.** A set of handwrit-ten notes will serve as a backup if there are technical glitches and will help you remember ideas you had during the interview.

✔ **Be alert for related sources mentioned in the interview.** If specific sources that might be relevant to your research writing project are mentioned during the in-terview, ask for copies of those sources, or for the exact title and where you might find it.

✔ **Leave your contact information when the interview is over.** Provide a way for the person you interviewed to reach you to change or add anything to his or her comments.

✔ **Send a thank-you note.** Let the person you interviewed know how much you appreciated the opportunity to learn from him or her.

7b

How can I use observation to collect information?

Like interviewing, observing a setting can provide you with valuable information you would not be able to find in other sources. Although some observations can involve a significant amount of time and effort, an observation need not be com-plicated to be useful.

Decide Whether to Conduct an Observation

The most important decision you'll make regarding an observation is whether to conduct it in the first place. Some topics are more suited for observation than others. For example, before writing her article on the Intensive English Program at Colorado State University, featured writer Maria Sanchez-Traynor observed students and teachers in the program. She went to two classes, watched, listened, and took notes. Seeing the classes gave Maria insights that she couldn't have gained simply by reading about the program or interviewing its students and teachers.

Plan Your Observation

As you plan your observation, determine the following:

What You Should Observe and How Often You Should Observe It   If, for example, you've decided to observe children in a day-care center, you'll quickly learn that there are not only many day-care providers in your community but also several different kinds of providers. Clearly, observing a large day-care center won't tell you much about what happens in a small center operated out of a home. In addition, there's no guarantee that what you'll see in one day-care center on any given day will be typical. Should you conduct multiple observations? Should you observe multiple types of day-care providers?

The answers to these questions will depend largely on what role the information you collect during your observations will play in your research writing project. If you want to learn more about the topic but don't plan to use anything you observe as a source of evidence in your project, then you might want to conduct a fairly limited observation. If you decide to use evidence from your observations throughout your project, then you will need to conduct multiple observations, possibly in more than one setting.

What to Look For   The biggest limitation of observation is that you can see only one thing at a time. Experienced observers focus their observations on activities that are most relevant to their research projects. As a result, their observations are somewhat selective. Spreading yourself too thin will result in fairly "thin" results. Then again, narrowing in too quickly can mean that you miss important aspects of the setting. Your reasons for conducting an observation and what you hope to gain from it are probably your best guide to what to focus on.

Whether You Need Permission to Observe   Seeking permission to observe someone can be complicated. People have expectations about privacy, but people can (and often do) change their behavior when they know they are being observed. As you consider whether to ask for permission, imagine yourself in the position of someone who is being observed. If you are still uncertain, ask your instructor for advice.

Find a list of Web sites about conducting observations at **bedfordresearcher.com**. Click on Links > Resources for Conducting Field Research.

Conduct Your Observation

You'll find a number of similarities between collecting information in an interview and collecting information during an observation. The checklist that follows will help you conduct your observation.

CHECKLIST FOR CONDUCTING OBSERVATIONS

✔ **Arrive early.** Give yourself time to get prepared.

✔ **Review your planning notes.** Remind yourself what you're looking for and how you will record your observations.

✔ **Introduce yourself.** If you have asked for permission to observe a setting (such as a class or a day-care center), introduce yourself before you begin your observation. Use your introduction as an opportunity to obtain signatures on consent forms if you need them.

✔ **Set up your recording equipment.** You'll certainly want to make sure you've got a notepad and pens or pencils. You might also have an audio or video recorder, a laptop computer, or a handheld, such as a Palm or Pocket PC. Test whatever you've brought with you to make sure it's working properly.

✔ **Take notes.** As with interviews, take notes during your observation even if you're using an audio or video recorder. Noting your impressions and ideas while conducting an observation can help you keep track of critical events. In addition, if your recorder doesn't work as expected, a set of notes can mean the difference between salvaging something from the observation and having to do it all over again. If you find yourself in a situation where you can't take notes — such as at a swimming lesson, when you're taking part in the lesson — try to write down your thoughts about what you've observed immediately after the session.

✔ **Leave contact information and send thank-you notes.** If you have asked someone for permission to observe the setting, give the person a way to contact you, and send a thank-you note after you have completed the observation.

7c

How can I use surveys to collect information?

Surveys allow you to collect information about beliefs, attitudes, and behaviors from a group of people. Typically, surveys help you answer *what* or *who* questions — such as "Who will you vote for in the next election?" Surveys are less useful in obtaining the answers to *why* questions. In an interview, for instance, you can ask, "Why did you vote the way you did in the last election?" and expect to get a reasonably well-thought-out answer. In a survey, however, people often neglect to write lengthy, careful responses. If you conduct a survey, remember to include a copy of your survey questions in an appendix to your project document.

Decide Whether to Conduct a Survey

Your decision about whether to conduct a survey should be based on the role it will play in your research project, the amount of work required to do a good job, and the kind of information you are seeking. In many cases, you'll find that other field research methods are more appropriate than surveys. Surveys are useful if you want to collect information about the attitudes and behaviors of a large group of people (more than five or ten). If you simply want opinions from a handful of people, you can gain that information more efficiently by interviewing or corresponding with them.

Plan Your Survey

As you plan your survey, determine the following:

Whom to Survey   You must decide whom and how many people to survey. For instance, if you're interested in what students in a specific class think about an issue, survey all of them. Even if the class is fairly large (say, one hundred students), you probably won't have too much trouble tabulating the results of a brief survey. Keep in mind, however, that most surveys aren't given to everyone in a group. National polls, for instance, seldom survey more than one thousand

> Find a list of Web sites about conducting surveys at **bedfordresearcher.com**. Click on Links > Resources for Conducting Field Research.

sand people, yet they are used to assess the opinions of everyone in the country. So how will you select your representative sample? One way is to choose people from the group at random. You could open your school's telephone book and then pick, say, every twentieth name. Another option is to stratify your sample. For example, you could randomly select a specific number of first-year, second-year, third-year, and fourth-year students—and you could make sure that the number of men and women in each group is proportional to their enrollment at the school.

What to Ask and How to Ask It   Designing effective surveys can be challenging. Understanding the strengths and weaknesses of the kinds of questions that are frequently asked on surveys is a good way to get started. Figure 7.1 illustrates the main types of questions found on surveys.

Whether You Are Asking Your Questions Clearly   Test your survey items before administering your survey by asking your classmates or family members to read your questions. A question that seems perfectly clear to you might cause confusion to someone else. Try to rewrite the questions that confuse your "testers" and then test them again. Doing so will help you improve the clarity of your survey. Consider the evolution of the following question:

Original Question:

What can be done about voter turnout among younger voters?

> Does "about voter turnout" mean increasing voter turnout, decreasing voter turnout, or encouraging younger voters to be better informed about candidates? Does the phrase "younger voters" mean 18-year-olds or 30-year-olds?

Revised Question:

In your opinion, what can be done to increase turnout among 18-to-24-year-old voters?

Election Survey

Thank you for completing this survey.

A 1. Did you vote in the last presidential election? ☐ yes ☐ no

2. I vote:

In every election	In most elections	In about half of the elections	Rarely	Never
☐	☐	☐	☐	☐

B 3. I have voted in the following types of elections (check all that apply):
   - ☐ Regular local elections
   - ☐ Special local elections
   - ☐ Regular statewide elections
   - ☐ National elections

C 4. Voting is a civic duty: ☐ true ☐ false

D 5. All eligible voters should participate in local, state, and national elections:

Strongly Agree	Agree	Not Sure	Disagree	Strongly Disagree
☐	☐	☐	☐	☐

6. Please rate the following reasons for voting on a 1-to-5 scale, in which 5 indicates very important and 1 indicates not at all important:

	1	2	3	4	5
To be a good citizen	☐	☐	☐	☐	☐
To have a say in how government affects my life	☐	☐	☐	☐	☐
To support a particular cause	☐	☐	☐	☐	☐
To vote against particular candidates	☐	☐	☐	☐	☐

E 7. Please rank the following types of elections from most important (4) to least important (1):
   - _____ Presidential elections
   - _____ Statewide elections
   - _____ Locale (city and county) elections
   - _____ Student government elections

F 8. Please tell us what influenced your decision to vote or not vote in the last election.

FIGURE 7.1 Sample Survey

A Yes/no items divide respondents into two groups.

B Multiple-choice items indicate whether a respondent knows something or engages in specific behaviors. Because they seldom include every possible answer, be careful when including them.

C True/false items more often deal with attitudes or beliefs than with behaviors or events.

D Likert scales measure respondents' level of agreement with a statement, their assessment of something's importance, or how frequently they engage in a behavior.

E Ranking forces respondents to place items along a continuum.

F Short-answer items allow greater freedom of response, but can be difficult to tabulate.

Collecting Information

TUTORIAL

How do I write a good survey question?

Developing a good survey question is challenging. The process is similar to writing an essay. Make the first draft of a survey question express your thoughts. Revise the question to clarify it for survey respondents.

1 Write a first draft of the question.

Did you vote or not vote in the last election and why or why not?

2 Simplify the question.

Why did you vote or not vote in the last election?

3 Identify and then clarify keywords and phrases.

What were your reasons for voting or not voting in the last election?

4 Consider alternative ways of asking a question — including whether it should be a question.

Explain your reasons for voting or not voting in the last election.

5 Ask for feedback from potential respondents. Review and clarify keywords and phrases. Consider potential reactions to phrasing.

Please tell us what influenced your decision to vote or not vote in the last election.

Review another example and work on refining survey questions at **bedfordresearcher.com**. Click on Tutorials.

Conduct Your Survey

The sheer number of surveys people are asked to complete these days has reduced the public's willingness to respond to them. In fact, a "good" response rate for a survey is 60 percent. The checklist that follows can help you achieve a high response rate:

CHECKLIST FOR CONDUCTING SURVEYS

☑ **Keep it short.** Surveys are most effective when they are brief. Don't exceed one page.

☑ **Format and distribute your survey appropriately.** If your survey is on paper, make sure the text is readable, there is plenty of room to write, and the page isn't crowded with questions. If you are distributing your survey through email, you can either insert the survey questions into the body of your email message or attach the survey as a word processing file. If you are distributing your survey on the Web, you can

- code your survey so that survey responses are added to a database (if you can create Web pages of this kind or know someone who can).
- ask respondents to copy the text on the page and paste it into an email message that they then send to you.
- link a word processing file containing your survey to a Web page and ask respondents to fill it out and return it to you as an email attachment.
- ask respondents to print the survey and fax or mail it back to you.

☑ **Explain the purpose of your survey.** Explaining who you are and how you will use the results of the survey in your research writing project can help increase a respondent's willingness to complete and return your survey.

☑ **Treat survey respondents with respect.** People respond more favorably when they think you are treating them as individuals rather than simply as part of a mailing list. When possible, use first-class stamps on surveys sent through the mail and, when appropriate, address potential respondents by name in cover letters or email messages.

☑ **Make it easy to return the survey.** If you are conducting a survey through the mail, be sure to include a stamped, self-addressed envelope. If you are conducting your survey on the Web or via email, be sure to provide directions for returning completed surveys.

II Collecting Information

Analyze Your Results

Once you've collected your surveys, you must tabulate your responses. It's usually best to tabulate survey responses using a spreadsheet program, which provides flexibility when you want to analyze your results. You can also organize the results in a table in a word processing program.

7d

How can I use correspondence to collect information?

Correspondence includes any textual communication—such as letters, faxes, and email. Correspondence can also take place through real-time communication using chat or instant messaging. If you use chat or instant messaging, be sure to save a record—or transcript—of the exchange.

Although many research writers benefit from corresponding with experts, correspondence need not be sent only to experts. If you are writing an article about the effects of recent flooding in the Midwest, you could correspond with relatives, friends, or even strangers to ask them about their experiences with the floods. You can use their responses to illustrate the impact of the flood on average folks. You can also correspond with staff at government agencies, corporations, and organizations. Many of these institutions hire public relations personnel to respond to inquiries from the public.

Courtesy is essential when corresponding. Introduce yourself and explain the goals of your research project. Make sure that you are clear and ask specific questions. Thank your reader and indicate that you look forward to hearing from him or her. If you decide to send a letter via regular mail, include a self-addressed, stamped envelope to increase your chances of getting a response.

7e

How can I use public events to collect information?

Public events, such as lectures, conferences, and public meetings and hearings, often provide research writers with useful information. As with observations, you can record public events by taking notes or bringing an audio or video recorder. In addition, a number of communities broadcast public events on local access cable channels. If you attend a public event in person or on the Web, find out whether a transcript of the event will be available.

Alternatively, you can create a transcript yourself. ABCNews.com, for instance, hosts chat sessions with leading authors, artists, politicians, news reporters, and entertainers and provides transcripts on its Web site. If your browser or your chat program doesn't allow you to save a transcript, you can copy relevant passages during the session and paste them into a word processing file.

7f

How can I use broadcast media to collect information?

Radio and television are sources of information that research writers frequently overlook. News and information programs on television, such as *The NewsHour with Jim Lehrer* and *60 Minutes,* might provide useful information about the conversation you plan to join. You may want to record the programs in order to examine them in detail. In addition, check the Web for radio programs and transcripts. National Public Radio's news information program *All Things Considered,* for instance, has audio archives going back to January 1996 that you can listen to on the Web (visit www.npr.org and search the program's archives).

My Research Project

ASSESS THE RELEVANCE OF FIELD RESEARCH METHODS

Think about whether the field research methods discussed in this chapter might contribute to your research project. If you decide to use observations, interviews, surveys, correspondence, or other forms of field research, seek advice from researchers who have used these methods, or from your instructor or a librarian.

QUICK REFERENCE

Searching for Information with Field Research Methods
- Plan and conduct interviews.   [p. 95]
- Plan and conduct observations.   [p. 97]
- Design, conduct, and analyze a survey.   [p. 99]
- Use correspondence to collect information.   [p. 104]
- Attend public events to gather information about your issue.   [p. 104]
- Use broadcast media to collect information.   [p. 105]

II Collecting Information

The Bedford Researcher

I	Joining the Conversation
II	Collecting Information
III	**Working with Sources**
IV	Writing Your Document
V	Documenting Sources

PART III

Working with Sources

After you've collected your information, you'll be ready to devote your complete attention to reading critically, evaluating, and taking notes on your sources. The next three chapters of *The Bedford Researcher* lead you through the process of deciding which information is most useful for your research writing project.

8

Reading Critically

Key Questions

Critical readers read actively and with an attitude. Reading actively means working with a text as you read: skimming, reading for meaning, and rereading passages that leave you with questions. It means underlining and highlighting text, noting your reactions in the margins, and responding to arguments, ideas, and information. Reading with an attitude means never taking what you read at face value. It means asking questions, looking for implications, making inferences, and making connections to other sources.

8a

How does reading critically differ from evaluating?

At first glance, reading critically might seem to be the same as evaluating, which is discussed in detail in the next chapter. Although the two processes are related, they're not identical. Critically reading a source—questioning what it says and thinking about what it means—focuses your attention on making sense of the source. In contrast, evaluation focuses your attention on determining how reliably a source presents its information and how well it meets your needs as a research writer.

8b

How can I use my research question to read critically?

Your research question focuses your attention on your issue, provides the foundation for your search plan, and directs you to specific sources as you collect information. Your research question also provides the basis for creating a preliminary thesis statement, which you will use to guide your critical reading.

A preliminary thesis statement is an answer to your research question. At this point in your research writing process, your answer to your research question is preliminary because it is neither as formal nor as complete as the thesis statement you'll use when you draft your document. However, a preliminary thesis statement is an important first step toward developing your thesis statement—your statement of your main point. Figure 8.1 shows the progression from research question to preliminary thesis statement to thesis statement in the context of the research writing process.

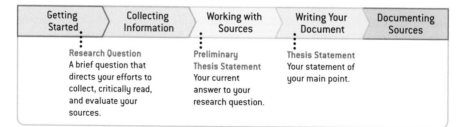

Getting Started	Collecting Information	Working with Sources	Writing Your Document	Documenting Sources
	Research Question A brief question that directs your efforts to collect, critically read, and evaluate your sources.	Preliminary Thesis Statement Your current answer to your research question.	Thesis Statement Your statement of your main point.	

FIGURE 8.1   Moving from a Research Question to a Preliminary Thesis Statement to a Thesis Statement

As an early response to your research question, your preliminary thesis statement can help you decide whether you agree or disagree with an author—and thus whether you want to align yourself with his or her position on the issue. It will also help you judge whether the evidence provided in a source is effective and how you might be able to use the new ideas and information you're reading about.

Use your preliminary thesis statement to test your ideas against the arguments, ideas, and information you encounter in your reading. As your ideas change, revise your preliminary thesis statement.

● Develop a Preliminary Thesis Statement

To draft your preliminary thesis statement, brainstorm or freewrite in response to your research question. After reviewing your response, settle on a preliminary thesis statement and use it to guide your critical reading.

Featured Writer Alexis Alvarez's Research Question:

What should be done about steroid use by adolescent girls involved in competitive sports?

Responses:

The typical response to steroid use in sports, such as the Olympics or professional football, seems to be some sort of punishment—losing a medal or being banned from competition for a period of time. But will this work with kids—especially kids who don't seem to have the same level of maturity as older athletes? And what about parents who encourage kids—and most likely provide the funds—to use steroids to get ahead (parents with college scholarship dollars in their eyes, no doubt)? So . . . maybe punishment isn't the answer—or at least it's only part of the answer. It seems from my reading so far that most kids don't understand the negative consequences of using steroids. They only see the potential benefits (making a team, performing at a higher level, getting famous, getting a scholarship, etc.). And parents might not understand those consequences as well. And then some coaches might even get into the act, "helping" kids compete at a higher level, and getting the wins they "need." If kids don't understand the consequences, then education might be useful. And most kids don't like to cheat, so maybe part of the answer is putting more of an emphasis on fair play. And you need to get parents and coaches into some sort of solution too.

Preliminary thesis statement:

Steroid use by adolescent girls involved in competitive sports might be addressed by educating athletes, parents, and coaches about health consequences and emphasizing fair play.

This statement is too vague to use as a thesis statement, but it would serve as an effective guide for critically reading sources. For example, if you read a source that argues for a solution to the problem of steroid use by young athletes, you could ask whether that solution makes sense in light of what you had read in other sources or whether it is based on a different set of assumptions.

Table 8.1 presents the movement from research question to preliminary thesis statement in the featured writers' projects. Note how the preliminary thesis statement attempts to answer the research question and thus lets readers know what the writer thinks an answer to the research question might be. The devel-

TABLE 8.1 THE FEATURED WRITERS' PRELIMINARY THESIS STATEMENTS

FEATURED WRITER	RESEARCH QUESTION	PRELIMINARY THESIS STATEMENT
Jenna Alberter	What was the relationship between seventeenth-century Dutch paintings of women and the culture in which they were created?	Seventeenth-century Dutch paintings reflected society's expectations of women and helped women understand their roles in society.
Alexis Alvarez	What should be done about steroid use by adolescent girls involved in competitive sports?	Steroid use by adolescent girls involved in competitive sports should be addressed by educating athletes, parents, and coaches about health consequences and emphasizing fair play.
Patrick Crossland	What cultural, academic, and regional factors affect college admissions decisions?	Factors affecting college admissions decisions include race, gender, and intellectual ability.
Kevin Fahey	How is Nick Adams characterized by Ernest Hemingway?	Nick Adams is a flawed character with whom readers can identify.
Pete Jacquez	What strategies, if any, should Coloradoans use to encourage local, state, and federal governments to increase U.S. use of wind-generated electrical power?	Coloradoans should encourage local, state, and federal governments to increase reliance on wind-generated electrical power through a mix of tax incentives and reduced regulation.
Maria Sanchez-Traynor	How is English taught to foreign-language speakers at the Intensive English Program?	Teachers use immersion techniques and explain the theory of the English language to help students at the IEP learn to speak and write in English.

opment of their preliminary thesis statements marked a significant step for the featured writers in their progress toward writing their final documents. By offering

Read more about the Featured Writers at **bedfordresearcher.com**.

a preliminary answer to their research questions, they began to take ownership of their work: They shifted their focus from learning about the conversations they had decided to join to deciding what contribution they might make to the conversation.

My Research Project

DRAFT A PRELIMINARY THESIS STATEMENT

In your research log, complete the following activity to draft your preliminary thesis statement.

1. Write your current research question.
2. Brainstorm or freewrite in response to your research question.
3. Select the response that best reflects your current understanding of the conversation you have decided to join. If appropriate, combine responses into one preliminary thesis statement.
4. Write your preliminary thesis statement.

You can print or download this activity at **bedfordresearcher.com**. Click on Activities > Develop and Refine Your Thesis Statement.

Working with Sources

8c

How can I read with an attitude?

Reading critically means reading with an attitude. Your attitude will change during your research writing process. As you begin to read your sources critically, your attitude might be one of curiosity. You'll note new information and mark key passages that provide you with insights into the conversation you're joining. You will adopt a more questioning attitude as you try to determine whether sources fit in your project or are reliable. Later, after you begin to draw conclusions about the conversation, you might take on a more skeptical attitude, becoming more aggressive in challenging arguments made in sources than you were at first.

Regardless of where you are in your research writing process, you should always adopt a critical attitude. Accept nothing at face value; ask questions about your topic; look for similarities and differences in the sources you read; examine the implications of what you read for your research project; be on the alert for unusual information; and note relevant sources and information. Most important, be open to ideas and arguments, even if you don't agree with them. Give them a chance to affect how you think about the conversation you've decided to join.

Approach a Source with Your Writing Situation in Mind

One way to get into the habit of reading critically is to approach a source with your writing situation in mind. To do so, think about your research question and preliminary thesis statement, your purpose, your readers' needs and interests, the context in which your project document will be read, your requirements and limitations, and your opportunities.

Your Research Question and Preliminary Thesis Statement   As you critically read your sources, answer the following questions:

- Are the arguments, ideas, and information in this source relevant to my research question and preliminary thesis statement?
- Does this source present arguments, ideas, and information that make me reconsider my research question or preliminary thesis statement?
- Does this source provide any new arguments, ideas, or information?
- Does this source offer a new perspective on the conversation?

? WHAT'S MY PURPOSE?

Return to your research log and review your purpose. Keeping your purpose in mind as you read will make it easier to recognize useful information when you come across it. As you read, keep in mind the following questions:

- Will the information in this source help me accomplish my purpose? Can I use the information in this source as support for points I want to make? Can I use it to illustrate ideas that differ from mine?
- Is the information in this source more useful for my purpose than what I've found in other sources?
- Does the source provide a good model of a convincing argument or an effective presentation of information? Can I learn anything from the presentation of the points and evidence in this source?

Your Readers' Needs and Interests   Consider your readers' needs and interests by asking the following questions as you read:

- Would my readers want to know about the arguments, ideas, and information found in this source?
- Would my readers find the source's information convincing or compelling?
- Would my readers benefit from a review of the argument and evidence presented in this source?
- What are my readers likely to think about the argument and evidence presented in this source? How will they respond to them?

Your Document and the Context in Which It Will Be Read   Research documents are presented in a variety of formats—for example, as printed texts, Web pages, or multimedia presentations. They're also read in a wide range of settings: in an office by someone sitting at a desk, on a bus or train by someone commuting to or from work, on a computer with a large, high-resolution monitor or a cramped screen. As you read your sources, be alert to what you can learn about organizing and formatting your document effectively. Answer the following questions about your document and the context in which it will be read:

- Does this source provide a useful model for organizing my document?
- Does this source provide a useful model for formatting my document?
- Can I learn anything from how figures, tables, or photos are used in the source?

Your Requirements and Limitations   As you read, keep your requirements and limitations in mind:

- If I find useful information in a source, will I be able to follow up on it with additional research? Will I have enough time to follow up on that information?
- How much information can I include in my document? Will my readers be looking for a general overview or a detailed report?

Your Opportunities   Instead of limiting your options, take advantage of them. As you read, ask yourself whether a source presents any possibilities or opportunities you have not discovered yet.

III Working with Sources

8d

What strategies can I use to read actively?

Once you have drafted your preliminary thesis statement and thought about your writing situation, you are ready to start reading actively. Reading actively means interacting with sources and evaluating them in light of the conversation you've decided to join. When you read actively, you might do one or more of the following:

- identify important passages for later rereading
- identify key ideas and information
- write questions in the margins
- jot down reactions to ideas and arguments
- link one part of the source to another visually

As you read sources, use two active-reading strategies: marking a source and annotating a source.

Mark Sources

Marking a source to identify key arguments, ideas, and information is a simple yet powerful active-reading strategy. Common marking techniques include

- using a highlighter, a pen, or a pencil to identify key passages in a print source
- attaching notes or flags to printed pages
- highlighting passages in electronic texts with your word processor

Annotate Sources

You can further engage with your sources by writing brief annotations, or notes, in the margins of print sources and by using commenting tools for electronic sources.

Many research writers use annotations in combination with marking (see Figure 8.2). If you have highlighted a passage (marking) with which you disagree, for instance, you can write a brief note about why you disagree with the passage (annotating). You might make note of another source you've read that could support your argument, or you might make a note about the need to look for information that will help you argue against the passage.

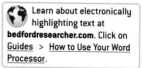 Learn about electronically highlighting text at **bedfordresearcher.com**. Click on Guides > How to Use Your Word Processor.

Learn about electronically highlighting text at **bedfordresearcher.com**. Click on Guides > How to Use Your Word Processor.

8e

What should I pay attention to as I read?

Different projects will require you to pay attention to different things as you read. In general, however, you should pay attention to the following:

- the type of source you are reading
- whether the source is a primary or secondary source
- the author's main point and other key points
- evidence offered to support points
- new information (information you haven't read before)
- ideas and information that you find difficult to understand
- ideas and information that are similar to or different from those you have found in other sources

Getting to the ivy league: How family composition affects college choice

go to Web site

Author: Lillard, Dean; Gerner, Jennifer **Source:** Journal of Higher Education 706–730 70, no. 6 (Nov/Dec 1999): p. 706–730 **ISSN:** 0022-1546 **Number:** 46386576 **Copyright:** Copyright Ohio State University Press Nov/Dec 1999

Introduction

A primary tenet of American society revolves around access to positions of influence and equality of opportunity. Educational attainment provides the central vehicle through which upward mobility can occur. Consequently, educational researchers have long been concerned about the extent to which higher education has been accessible to all students regardless of socioeconomic and racial characteristics. This study examines patterns of attendance at four-year and selective four-year colleges across students from single- and two-parent families. In particular, we examine whether these students differ in their choice of colleges to which they apply, are admitted, and which they attend.

A student's home life has an impact on college apps.

The college-aged population is increasingly characterized by the experience of family disruption. Rising rates of divorce and illegitimate births imply that an increasing number of children either directly experience the breakup of their parents' marriage or never live in traditional two-parent families. Among those children born in 1950, 28% of whites and 60% of blacks had at some time lived with only one (or no) parent by age 17. Of children born twenty years later, 41% of whites and 75% of blacks can expect to live with fewer than two parents by age 17. These figures imply that, in contrast to earlier cohorts, the experience of living in a single-parent home is increasingly common among children growing up in the late 1970s and 1980s.

Children from dysfunctional families less likely to apply

As family disruption becomes more prevalent, questions of equity and access arise if children from disrupted families are less likely to apply to and attend four-year colleges and selective four-year colleges. Differences in access might arise from two possible sources. First, disrupted and intact families may differ in the resources they can bring to bear to prepare their children for college. Second, the impact of these resources on college choices of children from disrupted and intact families may differ. Our results suggest that although both influences are present, differences in the levels of resources account for the largest proportion of the difference in the college choices between children from disrupted and intact families.

Two reasons why access to college varies with family makeup

Review of the Literature

In a general review of the college choice literature, Hossler, Braxton, and Coopersmith (1989) identify several important correlates of college choice. These include family socioeconomic status, student academic ability and achievement, parental levels of education, parental encouragement and support, student educational aspirations about career plans, and quality of the high school. Although many of these factors vary with family composition, little attention is paid in this literature to the role family composition plays in college choices.

FIGURE 8.2 A Source Highlighted and Annotated by Featured Writer Patrick Crossland

III Working with Sources

Noting these aspects of a source during your active reading will help you better understand the source, its role in the conversation you've decided to join, and how you might use it in your document.

Identify the Type of Source You Are Reading

One of the most important things to pay attention to as you read is the type of source you are reading. If a source is an opinion column rather than an objective summary of an argument, for example, you'll be less likely to be taken in by a questionable use of logic or analysis. If you are reading an annual corporate report for stockholders in a company, you'll recognize that the primary concern of the writers is to present the company in as positive a light as possible. If an article comes from a peer-reviewed academic journal, you'll be sure that it's been judged by experts in the field as well founded and worthy of publishing.

Recognizing the type of source you are reading will help you create a context for understanding and questioning the arguments, ideas, and information presented in the source.

Identify Primary and Secondary Sources

Primary sources are either original works or evidence provided directly by an observer of an event. Primary sources include

- poems, short stories, novels, essays, paintings, musical scores and recordings, sculpture, and other works of art or literature
- diaries, journals, memoirs, and autobiographies
- interviews, speeches, government and business records, letters, and memos
- reports, drawings, photographs, films, or video and audio recordings of an event
- physical artifacts associated with an event, such as a weapon used in a crime or a piece of pottery found in an archaeological dig

Secondary sources comment on or interpret an event, often using primary sources as evidence (see Table 8.2).

As a research writer, you should attempt to obtain as many primary sources as possible so that you can come to your own conclusions about your issue. If you rely entirely or mostly on secondary sources, you'll be viewing the issue through

TABLE 8.2 EXAMPLES OF PRIMARY AND SECONDARY SOURCES	
PRIMARY SOURCES	**SECONDARY SOURCES**
A short story by Ernest Hemingway	An article that presents a critic's analysis of the short story
A transcript of the statement made by President George W. Bush on September 11, 2001	A recording of an interview in which a historian discusses the significance of the statement
A laboratory study concerning the benefits of strength training for women with osteoporosis	A Web site that presents a review of recent research about prevention and treatment of osteoporosis

the eyes of other researchers. When you read a secondary source, ask yourself what factors might have affected the author's argument, presentation, or analysis.

Identify Main Points

Most sources, whether they are informative or argumentative, make a main point that you should pay attention to as you read critically:

- An editorial in a local newspaper urges voters to approve financing of a new school.
- An article reports a new advance in automobile emissions testing.
- A Web page provides information about the benefits of a new technique for treating a sports injury.

Identify Supporting Points

Once you've identified a main point, look for key points that support it. If an author is arguing, for instance, that English should be the only language used for official government business in the United States, that author might support his or her argument with the following additional points:

- Use of multiple languages erodes patriotism.
- Use of multiple languages keeps people apart—if they can't talk to each other they won't learn to respect each other.
- Use of multiple languages in government business costs taxpayers money because so many alternative forms need to be printed.

Identify Evidence

A point is only as good as the evidence—information or reasoning—used to support it. Evidence can take many forms, including the following:

- **Appeals to authority.**   Appeals to authority are often presented in the form of quotations by experts on the topic.
- **Appeals to logic.**   Appeals to logic often occur in the form of if-then reasoning, as in "if this is true, then we can expect such and such to happen."
- **Empirical evidence.**   Empirical evidence is often given in numerical or statistical form.

Identify New Information

As you read, mark and annotate passages that contain information that is new to you. Keep track of new information in your research log in the form of a list or as a series of brief descriptions of what you've learned and where you learned it.

III Working with Sources

Identify Hard-to-Understand Information

As you read, you might be tempted to ignore information that's hard to understand. If you skip over this information, you might miss something that is critical to the success of your research project. When you encounter information that's difficult to understand, mark it and make a brief annotation reminding yourself to check it out later.

Sometimes you'll learn enough from your reading of other sources that the passage won't seem as difficult when you come back to it later. And sometimes you'll still be faced with a passage that's impossible to figure out on your own. In this case, turn to someone else for advice.

- Ask a question about the passage on a newsgroup or electronic mailing list.
- Interview an expert in the area.
- Ask your instructor or a librarian for help.
- Search a database, library catalog, or the Web using words you didn't understand in the source.

Identify Similarities and Differences

You can learn a lot by looking for similarities and differences among the sources you read. For example, you might identify a group of authors who share a position on an issue, such as favoring increased government support for wind energy. You could then contrast this group with other groups of authors, such as those who believe that market forces should be the primary factor encouraging wind power and those who believe we should focus on other forms of energy. Similarly, you can make note of information in one source that agrees or disagrees with information in another. These notes can help you build your own argument or identify information that will allow you (and potentially your readers) to better understand the issue.

My Research Project

NOTE CONNECTIONS AMONG SOURCES

In your research log, identify connections among your sources. Ask whether information in one source agrees or disagrees with information in another. How might you handle these connections in your research project?

You can print or download this activity at **bedfordresearcher.com**. Click on Activities > Note Connections among Sources.

8f

How many times should I read a source?

As you work through your sources, you'll find that many are less relevant to your research project than you'd hoped when you collected them. When you come across one of these sources, move on to the next source.

Other sources are worth reading more carefully. When a source offers what seems like good arguments, ideas, or information, use a three-pass approach:

1. Skim the source to get a general idea of its organization and content.
2. Read actively, marking and annotating relevant passages in the text.
3. Reread passages that are either particularly promising or difficult to understand.

First Pass: Skim for Organization and Content

Before investing too much time in a source, skim it. Skimming — reading just enough to get a general idea of what a source is about — can tell you a great deal in a minimal amount of time. Skimming is an important first step in reading a source critically.

Skimming helps you understand how a source is organized, which can help you more quickly assess its usefulness and relevance. If the source uses a familiar organizational pattern, you'll find it easier to locate key information.

You can also learn a great deal about the content of a source through skimming.

Skimming is most effective when you approach your sources with your writing situation and specific questions in mind. Before you skim a source, write a

Working with Sources

CHECKLIST FOR SKIMMING SOURCES

- ✔ Identify the type of document — for example, book, magazine article, opinion column, scholarly journal article, personal Web site, blog entry.
- ✔ Check the title.
- ✔ Look at the table of contents, if one is provided.
- ✔ Read the abstract, if one is provided, or the introduction.
- ✔ Check major headings and subheadings.
- ✔ Read the titles or captions of any figures and tables.
- ✔ Look for pull quotes (quotations or brief passages pulled out into the margins or set somewhere on the page in larger type).
- ✔ Scan the first sentences and last sentences of paragraphs for key information.
- ✔ Check the works cited list, if one is provided.

list of questions about the source in your research log. As you skim, add questions to your list. When you're finished, write answers to your questions. Your questions might include the following:

- What is the main point of this source?
- What additional points are offered to support the main point?
- What evidence is offered to support the points?
- Who is it written for?
- Why was it written?

My Research Project

USE QUESTIONS TO GUIDE CRITICAL READING

Before you read a source, generate a list of questions about it. As you read, keep those questions in mind and ask additional questions. After you've read the source, use this activity to keep track of the answers to your questions.

In your research log, create a table like the one shown here. For each source, write the name of the source and questions you would like to answer as you read the source. After you read the source, write your responses to your questions in the appropriate column.

SOURCE	
Question 1:	Response:
Question 2:	Response:
Question 3:	Response:
Question 4:	Response:

You can print or download this activity at **bedfordresearcher.com**. Click on Activities > Use Questions to Guide Your Critical Reading.

● Second Pass: Read Actively

After you've skimmed the source and identified promising sections, read those sections actively—highlighting or underlining key passages, making notes in the margin, or recording observations in your research log. You should read either the entire source or at least enough to know that you don't need to read any more.

● Third Pass: Reread Important Passages

If you decide that a source is valuable—or if you still have questions about the source—reread passages that you've identified as important. Again, read actively, continuing to note your reactions and ideas as you read. Rereading key passages in this way can help you gain a better understanding of the source, which can make a tremendous difference as you begin writing.

> **QUICK REFERENCE**

Reading Critically

✔ Draft a preliminary thesis statement. (p. 111)

✔ Read with an attitude, keeping in mind the following: your research question and preliminary thesis statement, your purpose, your readers' needs and interests, the context in which your project will be read, your requirements and limitations, and your opportunities. (p. 113)

✔ Mark and annotate your sources. (p. 116)

✔ Identify primary and secondary sources, main and supporting points, evidence, new and hard-to-understand information, and similarities and differences among sources. (p. 118)

✔ Read the source multiple times, first skimming, then reading actively, then rereading important passages. (p. 121)

9

Evaluating Sources

> **Key Questions**
>
> **9a. What factors should I use to evaluate a source?   124**
> Evaluate relevance
> Evaluate evidence
> Evaluate the author
> Evaluate the publisher
> Evaluate timeliness
> Evaluate comprehensiveness
>
> **9b. Should I evaluate all types of sources in the
> same way?   128**
> Evaluate the relevance and credibility of electronic sources
> Evaluate the relevance and accuracy of field sources

At the beginning of a research project, you'll most likely make quick judgments
about your sources. Skimming an article, book, or Web site might be enough to
tell you that spending more time with the source would be wasted effort. At this
point in your writing process, you will begin to evaluate each of the sources
you've collected to determine how well it meets your needs as a research writer
and how reliably it presents arguments, ideas, and information.

9a

What factors should I use to evaluate a source?

Evaluating a source means examining its relevance, evidence, author, publisher,
timeliness, and comprehensiveness.

Evaluate Relevance

Relevance is the extent to which a source provides information you can use in
your research writing project. The most important questions you should ask to
determine the relevance of a source are about your purpose and audience.

> ### ? WHAT'S MY PURPOSE?
>
> Determine if the information in a source will help you accomplish your purpose. In the course of your research, you might find a number of information-filled sources. If the information is not relevant, however, it won't help you fulfill your purpose. For example, an analysis of the printing features in word processing programs might contain accurate and up-to-date information, but if you're writing about the best laser and inkjet printers for college students, this source won't be of much use to you.

Determine if the information in a source will help you address your readers' needs and interests. The information in a source should be useful to your readers. You might be tempted to include a beautifully worded quotation, but if your readers won't see how it contributes to your document, don't use it. Your readers will expect information that meets their needs. If they want to read about printers for personal computers, for instance, pass up sources that focus only on high-capacity office printers.

Evaluate Evidence

Evidence is information offered to support a point. An argument in favor of charging local sales tax on Web-based purchases might use statistics as evidence: It could calculate the revenue a town of fifty thousand might lose if 5 percent of its citizens made fifteen online purchases in a given year. Statistics, facts, expert opinions, and anecdotes (accounts of the experiences of people involved with or affected by an issue) are among the many types of evidence you'll find. As a research writer, you can evaluate not only the kind of information offered to support points made in a source but also the quality, amount, and appropriateness of that evidence. Ask the following questions about each source:

- **Is enough evidence offered?** A lack of evidence might indicate fundamental flaws in the author's argument.
- **Is the right kind of evidence offered?** More evidence isn't always better evidence. As you evaluate a source, ask yourself whether the evidence is appropriate for the points being made. Ask as well whether more than one type of evidence is being used. Many sources rely far too heavily on a single type, such as personal experience or anecdotal evidence.
- **Is the evidence used fairly?** If statistics are offered as evidence, ask yourself whether they are interpreted fairly or presented clearly. If a quotation is used to support a point, try to determine whether it is used appropriately.
- **Is the evidence convincing?** There are several signs that an argument isn't convincing. Among the most important are the absence of reasonable alternative interpretations of the evidence, questionable or inappropriate use of evidence, and evidence that seems to contradict points made elsewhere in the source. In addition, ask yourself whether the author mentions and

attempts to refute opposing viewpoints or evidence. If the author hasn't done so, his or her argument might not be strong.

- **Is the source of the evidence provided?** Knowing the origins of evidence used in a source can make a significant difference in your evaluation of it. For example, if a source quotes a political poll but doesn't indicate which organization conducted the poll, you won't be able to determine the reliability of that evidence.

Evaluate the Author

In addition to relevance and evidence, you can evaluate a source based on who wrote it. Take for example two editorials published in your local newspaper that make similar arguments and offer similar evidence. One is written by a 14-year-old middle school student, the other by a U.S. senator. You would certainly favor an editorial written by the senator if the subject was U.S. foreign policy. If the subject was student perceptions about drug abuse prevention in schools, however, you might value the middle schooler's opinion more highly.

The importance of authorship as an evaluation criterion varies from source to source. In some cases, including many Web sites, you won't even know who the author is. In other cases, such as signed opinion columns in a newspaper or magazine, your evaluation could be affected by knowing that the author is politically conservative, liberal, or moderate. Similarly, you might find it useful to know that a message published on a Web discussion forum was written by someone who is recognized as an expert in the field.

Ask the following questions about the author of a source:

- **Is the author knowledgeable about the topic?** It can be difficult to judge an author because expertise can be gained in many ways. An author might be an acknowledged expert in a field; he or she might be a reporter who has written extensively about a topic; or he or she might be recounting first-hand experiences. Then again, an author might have little or no experience with a topic beyond a desire to say something about it. How can you tell the difference? Look for a description of the author in the source. If none is provided, the source might give a URL for the author's home page, and you can check out the credentials there. Or perhaps you can locate information about the author on the Web or in a biographical reference such as *Who's Who.*

- **What is the author's affiliation?** Knowing the institution, agency, or organization that employs the author or the political party or organizations to which the author belongs can help you evaluate the assumptions that inform a source.

- **How do the author's biases affect the arguments, ideas, and information in the source?** We all have a bias—a set of interests that shapes our perceptions of a topic. As you evaluate a source, consider the extent to which the author's biases affect the presentation of arguments, ideas, and information in the source. To uncover an author's biases, try to learn more about his or her affiliations. You might infer a bias, for instance, if you learn that an author writes frequently about gun control regulations and works for the National Firearms Association.

Evaluate the Publisher

A publisher is a person or group that prints or produces the documents written by authors. Publishers provide access to print or electronic sources, including books, newspapers, journals, Web sites, sound and video files, and databases. Some documents—such as messages posted to newsgroups or sources obtained through field research—have no publisher.

You can make informed judgments about publishers in much the same way that you can evaluate authors. Ask the following questions about the publisher of a source:

- **How can I locate information about the publisher?**   If a publisher is listed in a print document, search for information about the publisher on the Web. You can often tell whether a publisher is reputable by looking at the types of material it publishes. If you are viewing a document on the Web, search for a link to the site's home page.

- **How do the publisher's biases affect the arguments, ideas, and information in the source?**   Like authors, publishers have biases. Unlike authors, they often advertise them. Many publishers have a mission statement on their Web sites, while others present information on their Web pages that can help you figure out their bias. You might already know a fair amount about the biases of a publisher, particularly if the publisher is a major newspaper or magazine, such as the *New York Times* (regarded as liberal) or the *Wall Street Journal* (regarded as conservative). If the publisher is a scholarly or professional journal, you can often gain an understanding of its biases by looking over the contents of several issues or by reading a few of its articles.

Evaluate Timeliness

The importance of timeliness—when a source was published—varies according to your writing situation. If your research project would benefit from sources that have recently been published, then evaluate recent sources more favorably than dated ones. If you're writing an article on the use of superconducting materials in new mass transportation projects, you probably won't want to spend a lot of time with articles published in 1968. On the other hand, if you're writing about the 1968 presidential contest between Hubert Humphrey and Richard Nixon, sources published during that time period will take on greater importance.

Print sources usually list a publication date; but it can be more difficult to tell when Web sources were created. When in doubt, back up undated information found on the Web with a dated source.

Evaluate Comprehensiveness

Comprehensiveness is the extent to which a source provides a complete and balanced view of a topic. Like timeliness, the importance of comprehensiveness

III Working with Sources

CHECKLIST FOR EVALUATING SOURCES

✔ **Determine whether the source is relevant.** Will the source help you accomplish your purposes and address your readers' needs and interests?

✔ **Determine whether the source provides evidence and uses it appropriately.** Is enough evidence of the right kind offered? Is evidence used fairly, is it convincing, and is its source provided?

✔ **Learn about the author of the source.** Ask whether the author is knowledgeable. Try to determine the author's affiliation and consider how the author's biases affect the arguments, ideas, and information in the source.

✔ **Learn about the publisher of the source.** Try to locate information about the publisher, and reflect on how the publisher's biases affect the arguments, ideas, and information in the source.

✔ **Think about the timeliness of the source** and its impact on and relevance to your project.

✔ **Consider the comprehensiveness of the source** and its impact on and relevance to your project.

---

varies according to the demands of your writing situation. If you are working on a narrowly focused project, such as the role played by shifts in Pacific Ocean currents on snowfall patterns in Colorado in the winter of 2005, you might not find this evaluation criterion as useful as the others. However, comprehensiveness can be a guide if you need to provide a complete and balanced treatment of a general topic, such as the potential effects of global climate change on agricultural production in North America, or if you are still learning as much as you can about your topic.

My Research Project

USE THE BEDFORD BIBLIOGRAPHER TO EVALUATE SOURCES

If you've been using the **Bedford Bibliographer** at **bedfordresearcher.com** to keep track of bibliographic information for your sources, you can evaluate your sources. Click on the Evaluation tab to evaluate a source.

9b

Should I evaluate all types of sources in the same way?

You can apply the general evaluative criteria discussed in section 9a to most types of sources. However, two sets of sources—electronic and field sources—can pose challenges during evaluation. The following discussion highlights additional factors to keep in mind as you evaluate electronic and field sources.

Evaluate the Relevance and Credibility of Electronic Sources

Because anyone can create a Web site, start a blog, or post a message to a newsgroup, email list, or Web discussion forum, approach these sources with more caution than you would reserve for print sources such as books and journal articles, which are typically published only after a lengthy editorial review process.

Web Sites and Blogs   To assess the relevance and credibility of a Web site or a blog, examine its domain (.edu, .com, and so on) and look for information about the site (often available through an About This Site or Site Information page). The following tutorial provides information about evaluating Web sites.

Newsgroups, Email Lists, and Discussion Forums   To assess the relevance and credibility of a message on a newsgroup, email list, or Web discussion forum, check for a "signature" at the end of the message and try to locate a Frequently Asked Questions (FAQ) list. A signature can provide information about the sender, such as a professional title, and the URL for a personal home page where you can learn more about the author. An FAQ can tell you about the purpose of a newsgroup, email list, or discussion forum; whether messages are moderated (reviewed prior to posting); and whether membership is open to all or restricted to a particular group.

> Learn more at **bedfordresearcher.com**. Click on Guides > How to Research Newsgroups, Mailing Lists, and Web Discussion Forums.

Evaluate the Relevance and Accuracy of Field Sources

With some adjustment, most of the criteria discussed in this chapter can be applied to field sources such as interviews, correspondence, observations, and surveys. Relevance and the accuracy of the information you collect deserve additional attention. Ask the following questions as you evaluate information collected through field research:

- Are the questions you asked in an interview, a survey, or correspondence still relevant to your research project?
- Is the information you collected in an observation still relevant? Are your observation notes as complete as you had hoped they would be?
- Are the individuals you interviewed or corresponded with as qualified and knowledgeable as you expected?
- Were questions in interviews, surveys, and correspondence answered fully and honestly?
- Did survey respondents have adequate time to complete the survey? Did they appear to believe their privacy would be respected?

TUTORIAL

How do I evaluate a Web site?

Because people can publish Web sites without going through a rigorous review process, you'll want to evaluate Web sources carefully. Evaluate a Web site by learning about its author, publisher, purpose, publication date, use of evidence, relevance, timeliness, and credibility.

1 Check the domain (e.g., .edu, .gov, .com) to learn about the site's purpose and publisher:

.biz, .com, .coop:	business	**.mil**:	military
.edu:	higher education	**.gov**:	government
.org:	nonprofit organization	**.pro**:	professional
.net:	network organization	**.name**:	personal

2 Check the title bar, page header, and page titles to learn about the site's relevance (p. 124) and publisher (p. 127).

3 Search for information — on the site or through a separate Web search — about the author (p. 126) or publisher (p. 127), if identified.

4 Check timeliness (p. 127) by looking for publication and modification dates.

5 Read the body text and review illustrations to evaluate relevance (p. 124), evidence (p. 125), and comprehensiveness (p. 127).

6 Check page footers for information about the publisher and author. Look for About or Contact links.

Review another example and evaluate your Web sources at **bedfordresearcher.com**. Click on Tutorials.

My Research Project

USE EVALUATION TO TRIM A WORKING BIBLIOGRAPHY

Use your evaluations to determine which sources should be added to or removed from your working bibliography. Add any new sources you think will be useful. If you decide that a source is no longer relevant to your project, remove it from your working bibliography. However, don't throw the source away. There's always a chance that you'll decide you need it later. Instead of putting it in the trash, put it in a category named "irrelevant," or move it into a new bibliography named "other sources" or "unused sources."

You can use the **Bedford Bibliographer** at **bedfordresearcher.com** to evaluate sources on the criteria defined in this chapter, enter publication information, create annotations, save text from electronic sources, and generate a bibliography in MLA, APA, *Chicago,* or CSE format.

> ### QUICK REFERENCE

Evaluating Your Sources

✔ Evaluate the relevance, evidence, author, publisher, timeliness, and comprehensiveness of *all* your sources. (p. 124)

✔ Evaluate Web sources for relevance and credibility. (p. 130)

✔ Evaluate field research for relevance and accuracy. (p. 130)

III Working with Sources

10

Taking Notes

> **Key Questions**

Taking notes allows you to focus more closely on what your sources tell you about your topic and how each source can help you answer your research question. By studying a source and noting the key points it makes, you'll gain a clearer understanding of the source. Careful note taking also helps you avoid plagiarism and lays the foundation for drafting your document. For these reasons, note taking is one of the most important research writing skills.

10a

How can I record my notes?

Some research writers take notes by hand, on note cards, on photocopies of sources, in a notebook, on loose sheets of paper, on the transcript of an interview, or on correspondence. Other researchers choose to take notes electronically, in a word processing program, in a database program, in a bibliographic citation program such as EndNote or Reference Manager, in email messages, or in a blog.

Your notes will be most useful if you take them systematically and consistently. For example, instead of taking some notes on Post-it Notes, some on note cards, and the rest in a word processing file, take all of your notes in one form. A consistent note-taking system will make it easier to find information later and will reduce the time and effort you'll need when you organize your ideas and draft your document.

10b

What methods can I use to take notes?

Notes—in the form of direct quotations, paraphrases, and summaries—provide you with a record of your reactions to your sources. Notes can also include comparisons among sources and your thoughts about how to use them later in your document.

? WHAT'S MY PURPOSE?

Review your purpose in your research log. As you take notes, remember that they should reflect your purpose for working on a project and provide direction for quoting, paraphrasing, and summarizing information. Keeping your purpose as a writer in mind should help you avoid wasting time taking notes that won't be useful to you later.

Quote Directly

A direct quotation is an exact copy of words found in a source. When you quote directly in your notes, you should enclose the passage in quotation marks, identify the source, and list the number of the page (or paragraph, if you are using a digital source that does not indicate page numbers) where the quotation can be found. Proofread what you have written to make sure it matches the original source exactly—including wording, punctuation, and spelling.

You should take direct-quotation notes when

- a passage in a source features an idea that you want to argue for or against
- a passage in a source provides a clear and concise statement that would enhance your project document
- you want to use an authority's or expert's exact words
- you want to use the exact words of someone who has firsthand experience with the issue you are researching

Be sure to place quotation marks around a quoted passage when you take a note. If you don't use quotation marks, you might later think the passage is a paraphrase or summary and unintentionally plagiarize it when you draft your document. To learn more about avoiding plagiarism, see Chapter 14.

Modifying a Direct Quotation Using an Ellipsis   When only part of a passage relates to your project, you might want to quote only that part in your notes. To indicate that you have changed a quotation by deleting words, use three spaced periods, called an ellipsis (. . .). If you don't use an ellipsis, your readers will assume that a quotation you are presenting is identical to the text found in the source.

Original Passage

Anderson is convinced that this is the right way to do it because he's seen all of the ways that aren't. A girls' basketball coach for more than two decades, he'd already experienced firsthand all that modern youth sports had to offer. It wasn't pretty: Screaming, red-faced parents who shuffle their children from program to program because Junior or Jane doesn't get enough court time. Elite squads that serve as showcases for a few superstar players trying to attract the attention of a Division 1 program. Eight-year-old prima donnas factory-installed with a sense of entitlement simply because they know their way around a ball and a pair of high-tops.

Source: Eric Dexheimer, "Nothing to Lose," retrieved from http://www.westword.com/issues/2004-05-13/news/sports_print.html, paragraph 15.

Quotation Modified Correctly Using an Ellipsis

"Anderson is convinced that this is the right way to do it because he's seen all of the ways that aren't. A girls' basketball coach for more than two decades, he'd already experienced firsthand all that modern youth sports had to offer. . . . Screaming, red-faced parents who shuffle their children from program to program because Junior or Jane doesn't get enough court time. Elite squads that serve as showcases for a few superstar players. . . . Eight-year-old prima donnas . . . with a sense of entitlement simply because they know their way around a ball and a pair of high-tops" (paragraph 15).

Four periods indicate the deletion of a full sentence or more.

Three periods indicate material deleted from *within* a sentence.

Modifying a Direct Quotation Using Brackets   To modify a direct quotation by changing or adding words, use brackets: [ ]. If you don't use brackets when you change or add words, readers will assume the quotation you are presenting is identical to the text found in the source.

The words added in brackets clarify "them," which refers to a noun in an earlier sentence.

Quotation Modified Correctly Using Brackets

"At many magazines, editors have a hand in fashioning them [the advertisements]" (paragraph 37).

III Working with Sources

Remember that even if you use brackets and ellipses, you might substantially change the meaning of a text by adding, changing, or deleting words in a direct quotation. Check your notes against original passages to be sure you aren't misrepresenting the source.

Modifying Quotations Using "Sic"   If a passage you are quoting contains a misspelled word or an incorrect fact, use the word "sic" in brackets to indicate that the error occurred in the original passage. If you don't use "sic," your readers will think that the mistake is yours.

Quotation Modified Correctly Using "Sic"

> *"Bill Clinten's [sic] last year in office was beset with nearly as many problems as any of his first seven years" (Richards 22).*

Avoiding Unintentional Plagiarism When Quoting from Sources   In many cases of unintentional plagiarism (see p. 192), a writer doesn't use quotation marks in a note and then uses the information in a document, forgetting that the material is a direct quotation. The solution to this problem is simple: Take careful notes by using the following checklist. Be aware, however, that mistakes can happen, particularly if you are taking notes in a hurry. As you draft your document, remember to look for notes that differ from your usual style of writing. More often than not, if a note doesn't sound like your own writing, it isn't.

CHECKLIST FOR QUOTING

To quote accurately when taking notes, follow these guidelines:

☑ Identify the author, title, and the page or paragraph where the passage can be found.

☑ Avoid unintentional plagiarism by using quotation marks.

☑ Use ellipses, brackets, and "sic" as necessary.

☑ Check your note against the original passage to be sure you aren't introducing errors or misrepresenting the source.

● **Paraphrase**

If you restate a passage from a source in your own words, you are paraphrasing the source. Typically, a paraphrase is roughly as long as the original passage. You can use paraphrases to illustrate or support points you make in your document or to refer to ideas with which you disagree. Even though you are using your own words when you paraphrase, you must still cite the source because the paraphrase presents ideas and information that are not your own.

One of the most common problems with using source material is paraphrasing too closely—that is, making such minor changes to the words of a source that your paraphrase remains nearly identical to the original passage. To avoid plagiarizing unintentionally by paraphrasing too closely, focus on understanding the key ideas in the passage and then restate them in your own words.

The following examples of paraphrasing are drawn from featured writer Patrick Crossland's research writing project.

Original Passage

> "High school grades and test scores are not the only factors considered by colleges and universities in the admissions process. Other factors that influence college admissions decisions include high school rank, being an athlete, alumni connection, extracurricular activities, special talents, and other personal characteristics of applicants."
>
> Source: William H. Gray III, "In the Best Interest of America, Affirmative Action Is a Must," p. 144.

Appropriate Paraphrase

> William H. Gray III notes that, in addition to high school grades and standardized test scores, most colleges and universities make admissions decisions based on an applicant's participation in sports, involvement in extracurricular activities, personal qualities, talents, relations to alumni, and class rank (144).

Preserves the meaning of the original passage without replicating sentence structure and wording

Inappropriate Paraphrase

Does not differ sufficiently from original; uses the same sentence structure and changes only some key words

> William H. Gray III notes that high school grades and test scores are not the only issues weighed by colleges and universities during college admissions decisions. Other factors that influence those decisions are high school rank, participating in athletics, connections to alumni, out-of-school activities, unique talents, and other personal qualities of applicants (144).

Inappropriate Paraphrase

Distorts the meaning of the original passage

> William H. Gray III notes that participation in sports and involvement in extracurricular activities are among the most important factors affecting college admissions decisions (144).

TUTORIAL

How do I paraphrase a source?

Paraphrasing a source involves restating the ideas and information in a passage in your own words. Use different words and sentence structure to help ensure that your paraphrase isn't too close to the original passage.

① Select the passage you want to paraphrase.

Original Passage: Why do athletes risk chronic debilitating diseases and death by taking steroids? Because these drugs work. In very short order, they pack on pounds of muscle and increase strength dramatically. Weight training while using steroids maximizes your gains.

Source: Kendrick, C. (2004). Seduced by steroids. Pearson Education. Retrieved October 1, 2004, from http://www.familyeducation.com/article/0,1120,20-691,00.html.

② Identify relevant information and ideas in the passage.

Why do athletes risk chronic debilitating diseases and death by taking steroids? Because these drugs work. In very short order, they pack on pounds of muscle and increase strength dramatically. Weight training while using steroids maximizes your gains.

③ Draft a paraphrase that identifies the source and includes the information.

Kendrick (2004) asks why athletes use steroids, which can lead to serious illness and death. He responds to his own question by noting that steroids increase muscle mass and strength and are particularly effective when used with weight training.

④ Revise the paraphrase so that it uses wording and sentence structure that differs from the original passage.

Kendrick (2004) notes that, despite longterm and potentially lethal health risks, athletes use steroids because, in combination with weight training, they can dramatically increase strength and muscle mass.

Review another example and work on creating your own paraphrases at **bedfordresearcher.com**. Click on Tutorials.

III Working with Sources

Avoiding Unintentional Plagiarism When Paraphrasing Sources   Begin a paraphrase with "In other words." This strategy reminds you that it's important to do more than simply rephrase the passage. You might also want to set the original source aside while you paraphrase so that you won't be tempted to copy sentences directly from it. After you've completed your paraphrase, check it for accuracy.

CHECKLIST FOR PARAPHRASING

To paraphrase, follow these guidelines:

✔ Be sure that you understand the passage by reading it and the surrounding text carefully.

✔ Restate the passage in your own words. Make sure that you do more than simply change a few key words.

✔ Avoid unintentional plagiarism by comparing the original passage with your paraphrase. Make sure that you've conveyed the meaning of the passage but that the wording and sentence structure differ from those in the original passage.

✔ Note the author, title, and the page or paragraph where the passage can be found.

Summarize

A summary is a concise statement of information in a source. Research writers often summarize an entire source, but they can also summarize lengthy passages. Write summaries to capture the overall argument and information in a source. Keep in mind that summaries must include a citation of the source.

Here is an original passage from a source one might consult while researching television addiction. A note containing a summary of the passage, which appeared in *Scientific American* (February 2002), follows the original.

Original Passage

What is more surprising is that the sense of relaxation ends when the set is turned off, but the feelings of passivity and lowered alertness continue. Survey participants commonly reflect that television has somehow absorbed or sucked out their energy, leaving them depleted. They say they have more difficulty concentrating after viewing than before. In contrast, they rarely indicate such difficulty after reading. After playing sports or engaging in hobbies, people report improvements in mood. After watching TV, people's moods are about the same or worse than before.

Source: Robert Kubey and Mihaly Csikszentmihalyi, "Television Addiction," p. 76

Appropriate Summary

Kubey and Csikszentmihalyi, "Television Addiction," p. 76

Although watching television may relax a viewer, studies have shown it does little to improve a viewer's alertness, energy level, or mood.
(summary)

Problems can arise when a writer fails to summarize ideas and instead either creates a close paraphrase or writes a patchwork paraphrase that is little more than a series of passages copied from the source. The following examples of paraphrasing are drawn from Patrick Crossland's research writing project.

Original Passages from the Source's Introduction

A primary tenet of American society revolves around access to positions of influence and equality of opportunity. Educational attainment provides the central vehicle through which upward mobility can occur. . . . This study examines patterns of attendance at four-year and selective four-year colleges across students from single- and two-parent families. In particular, we examine whether these students differ in their choice of colleges to which they apply, are admitted, and which they attend. . . . Differences in access might arise from two possible sources. First, disrupted and intact families may differ in the resources they can bring to bear to prepare their children for college. Second, the impact of these resources on college choices of children from disrupted and intact families may differ. Our results suggest that although both influences are present, differences in the levels of resources account for the largest proportion of the difference in the college choices between children from disrupted and intact families.

Source: Dean Lillard and Jennifer Gerner, "Getting to the Ivy League: How Family Composition Affects College Choice," p. 709.

Inappropriate Summary

Lillard and Gerner, "Getting to the Ivy League," p. 709

The highlighted passages are paraphrased too closely.

Lillard and Gerner argue that higher education provides the primary means through which upward mobility occurs in the United States. They studied patterns of attendance at four-year and selective four-year colleges across college applicants from single- and two-parent families, focusing in

> *particular on differences in decisions about which college to apply to, admissions decision, and colleges attended. They found that differences in the financial and educational resources accounted for the primary difference in college choices between children from single- and two-parent families. (summary)*

Appropriate Summary

> The summary gives a broad overview of the article's argument and avoids close paraphrases of key points.

> *Lillard and Gerner, "Getting to the Ivy League," p. 709*
>
> *In the article "Getting to the Ivy League: How Family Composition Affects College Choice," Dean Lillard and Jennifer Gerner stress that a student's ability to obtain loans, his or her likelihood of getting financial aid, and family support all affect college admissions choices. Students who grow up in poor families or weak school districts are at a disadvantage compared to students from affluent families and schools, and may not be given the resources they need to help them with the college application process. (summary)*

Avoiding Unintentional Plagiarism When Summarizing a Source. Remind yourself to summarize, rather than mirror the language and sentence structure of the source, by beginning your summary with "The author argues that" or "The author found that." You might want to set the original source aside while you write your summary so that you won't be tempted to copy sentences directly from it. After you've completed your summary, check it for accuracy.

CHECKLIST FOR SUMMARIZING

To summarize, follow these guidelines:

- ✔ Be sure that you understand the source by reading it carefully.
- ✔ Summarize main and supporting points in your own words. Make sure that you do more than string together a series of close paraphrases of key passages.
- ✔ Check for unintentional plagiarism by comparing the original source with your summary.
- ✔ Note the author, title, and, if you are summarizing only part of a source, the page or paragraphs where the information can be found.

● Compare Sources

Your notes can indicate connections among your sources by identifying relationships among ideas, information, and arguments. Paying attention to your sources as a group — not just to individual sources — helps you gain a more complete understanding of your issue. It also can be useful when you begin planning and organizing your document.

Featured writer Maria Sanchez-Traynor reviewed her notes and identified connections she saw between what she'd observed in the classroom and what she'd learned from her interviews with student Marcos DaSilva. In her observation notes, Maria added a comparison note: "This ties in with Marcos's quote."

● Start Planning Your Document

Planning notes are directions to yourself about how you might use a source in your project document, how you might organize the document, or ideas you should remember later. Maria Sanchez-Traynor wrote planning notes—such as, "How will this tie in? Possible lead?"—as she prepared to write her feature article.

My Research Project

TAKE NOTES

Take notes and save them in your research log. Be careful to avoid plagiarizing your sources as you quote, paraphrase, and summarize them.

> **QUICK REFERENCE**

Taking Notes

✔ Decide how you will record your notes; then take notes systematically and consistently.   (p. 133)

✔ Take notes that quote sources directly.   (p. 133)

✔ Take notes that paraphrase passages in sources.   (p. 135)

✔ Take notes that summarize sources.   (p. 138)

✔ Write notes that compare the arguments, ideas, and information in sources.   (p. 140)

✔ Write notes that help you plan your document.   (p. 141)

III Working with Sources

The Bedford Researcher

I	Joining the Conversation
II	Collecting Information
III	Working with Sources
IV	**Writing Your Document**
V	Documenting Sources

PART IV

Writing Your Document

After you read critically, evaluate, and take notes on your sources, you'll have a better understanding of your issue. In the chapters that follow, you'll learn how to use your new knowledge to create a well-written, well-designed document.

143

11

Organizing and Outlining

> **Key Questions**
>
> **11a. How should I organize my arguments, ideas, and information? 145**
> Review your notes and refine your preliminary thesis statement
> Identify organizational patterns in your sources
> Label, group, cluster, or map arguments, ideas, and information
>
> **11b. What kind of outline should I create? 151**
> Create an informal outline
> Create a formal outline

As you shift your attention away from collecting and working with sources and toward crafting your own contribution to the conversation about your issue, you'll begin the process of drafting your project document. That process begins with organizing and outlining.

11a

How should I organize my arguments, ideas, and information?

To organize the arguments, ideas, and information you've collected and worked with, review your notes and refine your preliminary thesis statement. Then identify organizational patterns in your sources, and use labeling, grouping, clustering, or mapping to help you determine how you'll organize your project document.

ORGANIZING YOUR ARGUMENTS, IDEAS, AND INFORMATION

Step 1   Review your notes and refine your preliminary thesis statement

Step 2   Identify organizational patterns in your sources

Step 3   Label, group, cluster, or map arguments, ideas, and information

---

● Step 1: Review Your Notes and Refine Your Preliminary Thesis Statement

To begin organizing your document, read quickly through your notes to gain an overall sense of the arguments, ideas, and information in your sources. You'll probably come to realize that you've gained a more complete understanding of your issue — an understanding that might affect your purpose and role as a writer and, by extension, your preliminary thesis statement. Use the following questions to determine whether you should refine your preliminary thesis statement:

- After collecting and working with your sources, have you found it necessary to alter your argument or approach?

- Have your purposes — the reasons you are working on this project — changed since you started your project?

- Has the role you are adopting changed? Are you informing your readers? Reporting the results of an investigation? Entertaining them? Arguing with them? Will you adopt multiple roles?

My Research Project

REFINE YOUR PRELIMINARY THESIS STATEMENT

In your research log, examine and, if appropriate, improve your preliminary thesis statement using the questions listed above.

You can print or download this activity at **bedfordresearcher.com**. Click on Activities > Develop and Refine Your Thesis Statement.

● Step 2: Identify Organizational Patterns in Your Sources

Reviewing your notes will help you gain an overall sense of the arguments, ideas, and information in the sources you've collected, read, and evaluated. Use this review to identify organizational patterns used by your sources. You might, for example, find that the majority of the sources you've collected attempt to offer a solution to a problem. Or you might find that most of your sources argue the strengths and weaknesses of a specific policy.

If you can identify a common organizational pattern among your sources, keep it in mind as you begin to organize your project document. Your contribution to the conversation about your issue is likely to be more effective if it's consistent with other sources involved in the conversation. Common organizational patterns include:

- **Chronological.** Arguments, ideas, and information are organized according to the sequence in which events occur over time. For example, sources might focus attention on a sequence of events in a recent election.

- **Cause/Effect.** Sources are organized according to factors that lead to (cause) an outcome (effect). For example, sources might identify the reasons behind a recent strike by grocery store employees.

- **Pro/Con.** Ideas and information are organized to favor one side of an argument. Sources might argue, for example, in favor of legislation calling for increased reliance on wind power.

- **Multiple Perspectives.** Sources arrange arguments, ideas, and information according to a range of perspectives about an issue. Sources using this organizing principle frequently provide an analysis supporting one perspective. For example, sources addressing the use of alternative energy might argue in favor of one form of power, such as tidal or solar power.

- **Comparison/Contrast.** Sources identify similarities and differences among the arguments, ideas, and information relevant to an issue. A source offering an analysis of a specific policy initiative, such as raising the voting age, might attempt to pull together the arguments made by several sources arguing against change.

- **Strengths/Weaknesses.** Sources contrast the strengths and weaknesses of one or more arguments about an issue, such as increasing federal funding for higher education by instituting a national lottery. Sources using this organizing principle typically make an argument that one argument is superior to the others.

- **Problem/Solution.** Sources define a problem and discuss the appropriateness of one or more solutions to the problem. If multiple solutions are proposed, an argument is usually made for the appropriateness of one solution.

? WHAT'S MY PURPOSE?

Your choice of organizing pattern will depend not only on the nature of the conversation about your issue, but also on your purpose and the role or roles you adopt as a writer:

- If you're investigating an issue as an *inquirer,* you might choose cause/effect to ask, "What causes something to happen?" For example, featured writer

⬇

WHAT'S MY PURPOSE? (continued)

Patrick Crossland asked about the factors affecting college admissions choices.

● If you're adopting the role of *reporter* or *interpreter,* you might select chronology, cause/effect, or comparison/contrast. You might be suggesting, as featured writer Pete Jacquez did in his analysis of alternative energy policies in the United States, a likely outcome (or effect) of a particular set of events (or causes).

● If you're adopting the role of *advocate,* you might opt for an organizing principle that is well suited to argumentation, such as pro/con or strengths/weaknesses.

Step 3: Label, Group, Cluster, or Map Arguments, Ideas, and Information

Strategies such as labeling, grouping, clustering, and mapping will help you explore the relationships among the arguments, ideas, and information you've recorded in your notes. These strategies will also help you later as you develop an outline of your document.

Labeling Notes   Labeling can help you understand at a glance how and where you will use each note. For example, you might label all of the notes that you want to use in your introduction with "Introduction," those that you plan to use to define a concept with the name of that concept, and so on. If you have taken electronic notes, as featured writer Pete Jacquez did, you have a number of options (see Figure 11.1). Once

 Read about the student writers discussed in this chapter at **bedfordresearcher.com**. Click on Featured Writers.

Economic Issues ——— [Label at the top of a note in a word processing file]

Chasteen, Stephanie. (2004). Who Owns Wind? *Science and Spirit 15*(1), 12-15.

Focuses on the economic aspects, particularly motivations and market potential, of implementing wind power.

Key quotes:

"Technological advancements and federal tax credits have made wind energy potentially profitable, landing it on the radar screen of private developers and utilities" (p. 12).

"On a dollar-for-dollar basis, wind is cost-competitive with the soaring prices of natural gas. It's still more expensive than nuclear and coal power, but studies suggest that when all costs (such as health care for coal miners stricken by black lung disease or federal subsidies of nuclear power) are taken into account, wind energy is actually cheaper" (p. 13).

FIGURE 11.1   Labeling Electronic Notes and Sources

you've labeled your notes and sources, you can organize them into groups or order them according to the outline you will create.

Grouping Notes   Grouping involves categorizing your notes. Paper-based notes (even copies of the sources themselves) can be placed in related piles or file folders; notes in word processing files or a personal digital assistant can be saved into larger files or placed in electronic folders; items in Bookmarks or Favorites lists can be sorted by category (see Figure 11.2).

Clustering and Mapping   Clustering and mapping allow you to develop a visual overview of the arguments, ideas, and information in your notes. They can also be used to develop your own arguments and ideas for your project document.

Clustering is similar to grouping—it shows related arguments, ideas, and information as clusters, or networks, of related material—but it allows you to illustrate these relationships more easily than grouping. You can try clustering as you begin to explore your topic, as you brainstorm to come up with ideas, and now, as you begin to explore relationships among the material you've collected. By putting the most important ideas closest to the center of the cluster and the less important points farther out, your cluster can show how key ideas or supporting points might relate to a main idea.

While clustering is based on a grouping principle, mapping focuses on sequences of arguments, ideas, and information. You can use mapping to understand the relationship among arguments, ideas, or events. For example, you might use mapping to create a timeline or to show how an argument builds on one idea after another. This use of mapping is particularly effective for organizing a document. The following tutorial shows a map that featured writer Alexis Alvarez created to organize her thoughts about key arguments and ideas in her argumentative essay about steroid use among adolescent girls.

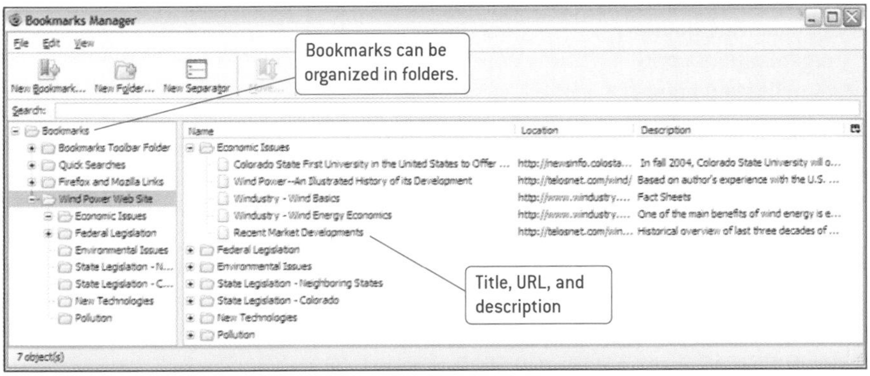

FIGURE 11.2   Grouping Electronic Notes and Sources

TUTORIAL

How can I map my argument?

Before you begin to draft your argument, you can use mapping to arrange information and ideas that support your preliminary thesis statement.

1 List your preliminary thesis statement.

> **Preliminary Thesis Statement:** *Steroid use by adolescent girls involved in competitive sports should be addressed by educating athletes, parents, and coaches about health consequences and emphasizing fair play.*
>
> **Problem**
>
> <u>Situation:</u> *Girls in sports are as likely as boys to use steroids.*
> —*Use CDC report (2004) and Mundell (2004) for stats.*
> —*Use "Girls and Steroids" (1998) and Manning (2002) to show growth in steroid use among girl athletes.*

2 Review your notes to identify key points supporting your thesis statement.

> <u>Causes:</u> *Involvement in sports*

3 Choose organizational patterns (see p. 146). Here the writer discusses the problem and solutions, and the pros and cons of girls' involvement in sports.

> *Positive aspects*
> ➤ *Physical & psychological health*
> ➤ *Positive sense of identity*
> *Good relationships with friends & family*
> *Good school performance*
> *(Support: Kane & Larkin, 1997; interviews with Juan Orozco and Melissa Alvarez)*
>
> *Negative aspects*
> ➤ *Physical (Graham, 1999)*
> ➤ *Psychological (Davies & Armstrong, 1989)*
> *Social (Brown & Banta, 1988; Orozco; Alvarez; Dexheimer, 2004)*
> *Athletic burnout (Davies & Armstrong, Alvarez, Drug Week)*

4 Following your organizational pattern, list key points as general headings.

> **Solutions**
>
> <u>Girls</u>
> *Learn about effects of steroids (Yiannakis & Melnick)*
> *Resist pressure*
>
> <u>Coaches & Parents</u>
> *Learn about effects of steroids*
> *Earn trust of athletes*
> *Maintain perspective (Orozco, Alvarez)*

5 List supporting ideas and information below each heading.

Review another example and work on mapping your own argument at **bedfordresearcher.com**. Click on <u>Tutorials</u>.

My Research Project

CLUSTERING

Clustering can help you organize arguments, ideas, and information. To create a cluster:

1. In the middle of a sheet of paper, or in the center of an electronic document (word processing file or graphics file), list your preliminary thesis statement.

2. Review your notes to identify broad categories of ideas and information that are related to your preliminary thesis statement and list them near it. Think about the importance and relevance of related ideas and information, and draw lines and circles to show the relationships among ideas and information and your preliminary thesis statement.

3. Next to the broad categories you identified in step 2, list related ideas and information. In turn, draw lines and circles to show their relationships.

4. Repeat the process until you've organized all your information and ideas.

You can print or download this activity at **bedfordresearcher.com**. Click on <u>Activities</u> > <u>Clustering</u>.

11b

What kind of outline should I create?

An outline represents the sequence in which your argument, ideas, and information will appear in your document. Outlines are not intended to replace your notes. Instead, an outline refers you to the more detailed information contained in your notes and sources. Your outline acts as a guide to the structure of your project document, while your notes help you to develop the sections within the document. It's best, then, to create your outline after you have reviewed your notes and chosen an organizational pattern for your document.

Create an Informal Outline

Informal outlines can take many forms: a brief list of words, a series of short phrases, or even a series of sentences. You can use informal outlines to remind yourself of key points to address in your document or of notes you should refer to when you begin drafting. Featured writer Jenna Alberter, who wrote a research essay about images of women in seventeenth-century Dutch art, created the following informal outline. In her outline, each item represents a section she planned to include in her essay (see Figure 11.3).

Patrick Crossland wrote the following "thumbnail outline," a type of informal outline, as he worked on his research essay about college admissions decisions. Patrick identified the major sections he would include in his research essay

1. *Introduction*
2. *Role of women in Dutch society*
3. *Jacob Cats's important book* Houwelick *(or Marriage)*
4. *Overview of women's stages of life (with examples from seventeenth-century literature and art)*
5. *Young women and courtship*
6. *Women as wives and mothers*
7. *Elderly women and widows*
8. *Conclusion*

FIGURE 11.3 Jenna Alberter's Informal Outline

and noted which sources he would use to provide background information and to support his argument (see Figure 11.4).

Create a Formal Outline

A formal outline provides a complete and accurate list of the points you want to address in your document. Formal outlines use Arabic numerals, letters, and Roman

Intro

Present problem; offer an introductory look at the question of who's getting into college and what the factors are that affect this. Introduce the various admittance issues to be examined.

Section 1

Examine the notion of competition through the "Caleb" analogy. Look at the college application process through the perspective of a game (therefore beating the competitors). Present the tier system and analogy by Miller.

Section 2

Look at the issue of race, the history of the problem, and the introduction of equal opportunity policies. Present the Krauthammer view of who it hurts or helps (is it fair in that sense?).

Section 3

Discuss family situations and their relation to the ability to succeed in higher education. Use Lillard and Gerner source covering the issues of family makeup.

Section 4

Examine the role that gender plays in getting accepted and succeeding in college. Look at issues of equality of the sexes.

Section 5

Look at mental/physical capabilities and their relation to college success. Discuss a change in curricula to suit people of all different mental capabilities.

Conclusion

FIGURE 11.4 Patrick Crossland's Thumbnail Outline

numerals to indicate the hierarchy of information. An alternative approach, common in business and the sciences, uses numbering with decimal points:

```
        I.                                          1.
             A.                                          1.1
                  1.                                          1.1.1
                  2.                                          1.1.2
             B.                                          1.2
                  1.                                          1.2.1
                  2.                                          1.2.2
        II.                                         2.
```

Writers use formal outlines to identify the hierarchy of arguments, ideas, and information. You can create a formal outline to identify

- your preliminary thesis statement
- the key points you want to make in your document
- the sequence in which those points should be presented
- support for your points
- the notes and sources you should refer to as you work on your document

The most common types of formal outlines are topical outlines and sentence outlines.

Topical Outlines Topical outlines present the topics and subtopics you plan to include in your research document as a series of words and phrases. Items at the same level of importance should be phrased in parallel grammatical form.

In her topical outline for her research essay on steroid use among adolescent girls, Alexis Alvarez includes her preliminary thesis statement, suggests the key points she wants to make in her document, maps out the support for her points, and uses a conventional system of numbers and letters (see Figure 11.5).

> Learn how to use bullets, numbering, and indentation to create outlines at **bedfordresearcher.com**. Click on Guides > How to Use Your Word Processor.

Sentence Outlines Sentence outlines use complete sentences to identify the points you want to cover (see Figure 11.6). Sentence outlines typically serve two purposes:

1. They begin the process of converting an outline into a draft of your document.
2. They help you assess the structure of a document that you have already written.

When you've created your outline, ask whether it can serve as a blueprint for the first draft of your document. Taking the time to create an effective outline now will reduce the time needed to write your first draft later.

IV Writing Your Document

Preliminary thesis statement: Steroid use by adolescent girls involved in competitive sports should be addressed by educating athletes, parents, and coaches about health consequences and emphasizing fair play.

I. **Female Participation in Competitive Athletics**
  A. Short history and current trends
  B. Understanding the female athlete
II. **Positive Impact of Competitive Athletics**
  A. Physiological
    1. Reduced risk of obesity and heart disease
    2. Increased immune functioning and prevention of certain cancers
    3. Improved flexibility, strength, and aerobic power
  B. Psychological
    1. Improved self-esteem
    2. Enhanced mental health
    3. Effective in reducing symptoms of stress, anxiety, and depression
  C. Sociological
    1. Expansion of social boundaries
    2. Teaches responsibility, discipline, and determination
    3. Educational asset
III. **Negative Impact of Competitive Athletics**
  A. Physiological
    1. Overtraining
    2. Eating disorders
    3. Exercise-induced amenorrhea and osteoporosis
  B. Psychological
    1. Unrealistic personal expectations
    2. Loss of self-confidence and emotional trauma
    3. Increased stress and anxiety
  C. Sociological
    1. Pressure to win at any cost
    2. Pressure to attain an unrealistic body
IV. **Repercussions of Negative Impact**
  A. Burnout
    1. Causes
    2. Consequences
  B. Drug use
    1. Causes
    2. Consequences
V. **Avoiding the Pitfalls in Competitive Athletics**
  A. Parents
    1. Supporting your athlete in every situation
    2. Awareness
    3. Communication
  B. Coaches
    1. Looking beyond triumph and defeat
    2. Knowing your players
  C. Athletes
    1. Believing in yourself
    2. Balancing life and competitive athletics

FIGURE 11.5   Alexis Alvarez's Topical Outline

Preliminary thesis statement: Steroid use by adolescent girls involved in competitive sports should be addressed by educating athletes, parents, and coaches about health consequences and emphasizing fair play.

I. Society has been concerned with the use of performance-enhancing drugs among younger male athletes, but many don't know that these drugs are also used by younger female athletes.

    A. Women began participating in sports in the mid-19th century, although participation was not encouraged until recently. Millions of girls are involved in a wide range of physical activities and are participating in school-sponsored sports.

    B. In response to pressures of competitive sports, girls' steroid use has increased and younger and younger girls are taking steroids.

II. Sports can benefit a girl's growth and development physiologically as well as psychologically and sociologically.

    A. Participation in sports has a wide range of positive physiological effects on adolescent girls.

        1. Studies have shown that participation in sports can reduce the risk of obesity and heart disease.

        2. Studies have shown that participation in sports appear to increase immune functioning and prevent certain cancers.

        3. Participation in sports has also been linked to improved flexibility, strength, and aerobic power.

FIGURE 11.6   Part of Alexis Alvarez's Sentence Outline

My Research Project

CREATE AND REVIEW YOUR OUTLINE

In your word processing program or in your research log, create an outline:

- If your word processing program has an outlining tool, use it to create a formal outline. In Microsoft Word, use the VIEW > OUTLINE menu command to view your document in outline mode. Use the PROMOTE and DEMOTE buttons on the outlining toolbar to set the levels for entries in your outline. Use the COLLAPSE and EXPAND buttons to hide and show parts of your outline.

- Review your outline by asking yourself the following questions: Does my outline provide an effective organization for my document? Have I covered all of my key points? Have I addressed my key points in sufficient detail? Do any sections seem out of order?

You can print or download this activity at **bedfordresearcher.com**. Click on Activities > Create and Review Your Outline.

IV Writing Your Document

> **QUICK REFERENCE**

Organizing and Outlining

✔ Review your notes.   (p. 146)

✔ Refine your preliminary thesis statement.   (p. 146)

✔ Identify organizational patterns used in your sources.   (p. 146)

✔ Label, group, cluster, or map the arguments, ideas, and information you've collected.   (p. 148)

✔ Develop an informal outline.   (p. 151)

✔ Create a formal outline.   (p. 152)

Part IV
Writing Your Document

11 Organizing and Outlining

> 12 **Drafting**

13 Integrating Sources

14 Avoiding Plagiarism

15 Revising and Editing

16 Designing

12

Drafting

> **Key Questions**

If you're new to research writing, you might be surprised at how long it's taken to get to the chapter about writing your document. If you are an experienced research writer, you know that you've been writing it all along. Research writing isn't so much the act of putting words to paper or screen as it is the process of identifying and learning about an issue, reflecting on what you've learned, and contributing to the conversation about your issue.

12a

How can I develop my thesis statement?

Up to this point, your research question and your preliminary thesis statement have helped focus your efforts to learn about an issue and decide how best to contribute to a conversation about it. Now it's time to develop a thesis statement that answers your research question in a definitive manner.

At a minimum, your thesis statement should present a clear answer to your research question. If you've asked, for example, about the causes of a problem, then your thesis statement should identify those causes. If you've asked what the best solution to a problem might be, your thesis statement should identify that solution.

Sample Research Question:

What is the cause of the decline in the population of brown trout in the state's rivers?

Sample Thesis Statement:

The decline in the population of brown trout in the state's rivers is a result of disease introduced by rainbow trout grown in the state's fish hatcheries.

In addition to answering your research question, your thesis statement can invite your readers to learn something new, suggest that they change their attitudes or beliefs, or argue that they should take action of some kind.

Sample Research Question:

How can we eliminate disease in brown trout in the state's rivers?

Sample Thesis Statement 1:

State fish hatcheries must take steps to eliminate disease in the rainbow trout they release into state streams.

Sample Thesis Statement 2:

Citizens should contact their state legislators and ask them to direct state fish hatcheries to eliminate disease in the rainbow trout released into state streams.

Table 12.1 presents the featured writers' movements from research question to preliminary thesis statement to thesis statement. Note how each thesis statement answers its research question and either directs readers' attention to one aspect of the conversation, encourages them to change their attitudes or beliefs, or urges them to take action of some kind.

> Read about the student writers discussed in this chapter at **bedfordresearcher. com**. Click on Featured Writers.

Developing an effective thesis statement involves four steps.

TABLE 12.1 THE FEATURED WRITERS' MOVEMENT FROM RESEARCH QUESTION TO THESIS STATEMENT

FEATURED WRITER	RESEARCH QUESTION	PRELIMINARY THESIS STATEMENT	THESIS STATEMENT
Jenna Alberter	What was the relationship between seventeenth-century Dutch paintings of women and the culture in which they were created?	Seventeenth-century Dutch paintings reflected society's expectations of women and helped women understand their roles in society.	Dutch Baroque genre paintings did not simply reflect the reality surrounding them; they also helped shape that reality.
Alexis Alvarez	What are the effects of competitive sports on adolescent girls?	Steroid use by adolescent girls involved in competitive sports should be addressed by educating athletes, parents, and coaches about health consequences and emphasizing fair play.	Although competitive sports can provide young female athletes with many benefits, they can also have negative effects, the worst of which is the increasing use of performance-enhancing drugs.
Patrick Crossland	What cultural, academic, and regional factors affect college admissions decisions?	Factors affecting college admissions decisions include race, gender, and intellectual ability.	Getting into college is like entering a contest in which each applicant is pitted against thousands of others.
Kevin Fahey	How is Nick Adams characterized by Ernest Hemingway?	Nick Adams is a flawed character with whom readers can identify.	By portraying Nick Adams as befuddled, intimidated, and even self-serving, Hemingway gives us a hero with whom most readers can identify.
Pete Jacquez	What strategies, if any, should Coloradoans use to encourage local, state, and federal governments to increase U.S. use of wind-generated electrical power?	Coloradoans should encourage local, state, and federal governments to increase reliance on wind-generated electrical power through a mix of tax incentives and reduced regulation.	Coloradoans should lead a national movement toward increased use of wind power.
Maria Sanchez-Traynor	How is English taught to foreign-language speakers at the Intensive English Program?	Teachers use immersion techniques and explain the theory of the English language to help students at the IEP learn to speak and write English.	Moffie and her colleagues at the Intensive English Program (IEP) at Colorado State University use a variety of motivational strategies to teach English to non-native speakers.

DEVELOPING AN EFFECTIVE THESIS STATEMENT

Step 1	Identify key words in your research question and your preliminary thesis statement
Step 2	Review your purpose and roles
Step 3	Consider your readers' needs and interests
Step 4	Focus your thesis statement

Step 1: Identify Key Words in Your Research Question and Your Preliminary Thesis Statement

Your thesis statement is an answer to your research question. You can begin to develop that answer by identifying key words and phrases in your research question and preliminary thesis statement and using these words and phrases to craft your thesis statement. Consider the following example:

Research Question:

What is the *cause of recent declines* in the *state's brown trout population?*

Preliminary Thesis Statement:

Disease linked to *hatchery-raised rainbow trout* seems to be *causing the decline.*

Thesis Statement:

The Department of Natural Resources should *determine whether the recent decline of brown trout populations in state* streams is *caused by disease* spread by *rainbow trout released from state fish hatcheries.*

Step 2: Review Your Purpose and Role

Make sure your thesis statement fits the purpose of your research writing project. Your thesis statement should also be consistent with the role (or roles) you've adopted as a research writer. Featured writer Kevin Fahey, for example, wanted to analyze Ernest Hemingway's characterization of Nick Adams. His thesis statement, "By portraying Nick Adams as befuddled, intimidated, and even self-serving, Hemingway gives us a hero with whom most readers can identify," answered the research question, "How is Nick Adams characterized by Ernest Hemingway?" His thesis statement was consistent with his purpose (to conduct a literary analysis) and his role (interpreter).

Step 3: Consider Your Readers' Needs and Interests

A thesis statement should invite your readers to learn something new, change their attitudes or beliefs about a topic, or take action of some kind. Featured writer Patrick Crossland could assume that his readers—classmates in his composition class—had experienced the college admissions process. He knew, however, that they might not understand fully the factors that affect admissions decisions. Most important, if any of his classmates were thinking of transferring to another school, they might need to be aware of those factors. Patrick wrote a thesis statement that addressed the nature of the admissions process—a process he characterized as a contest.

> Getting into college is like entering a contest in which each applicant is pitted against thousands of others.

Step 4: Focus Your Thesis Statement

A broad thesis statement does not encourage your readers to learn anything new, to change their attitudes or beliefs, or to take action. The following thesis statement is too broad:

Broad Thesis Statement:
We should protect the health of state wildlife.

There's no conversation to be had about this topic because few people would argue with such a statement. A more focused thesis statement would define what should be done and who should do it.

Focused Thesis Statement:
The state's Department of Natural Resources should place a moratorium on the release of rainbow trout from state fish hatcheries until they are no longer a danger to the wild brown trout population.

My Research Project

DEVELOP AND REFINE YOUR THESIS STATEMENT
In your research log, complete the following activity to draft your thesis statement.

1. My research question:
2. My preliminary thesis statement:
3. My purpose for writing:
4. I want my thesis statement to reflect the following needs and interests of my readers:
5. I want my readers to do one or more of the following:
   - learn about . . .
   - change their attitudes or beliefs about . . .
   - take the following action:
6. The most important words and phrases in my research question:
7. The most important words and phrases in my preliminary thesis statement:

8. Building on my research question and preliminary thesis statement, my thesis statement is:

9. I can narrow the scope of my thesis statement by rephrasing it:

You can print or download this activity at **bedfordresearcher.com**. Click on Activities > Develop and Refine Your Thesis Statement.

12b

How can I use my outline to draft my document?

Your outline provides a framework you can use to draft your document. Your outline likely includes your plans for

- the points you will include in your document
- the order in which you will make your points
- the amount of space you plan to devote to each point

? WHAT'S MY PURPOSE?

Review your purpose and your outline. Check whether you have organized your points in a way that will allow you to achieve your purpose and whether you are addressing the needs and interests of your readers.

If you have listed information about the sources you will use to support your points, you can check whether you are

- providing enough evidence to support your points
- relying too heavily on a limited number of sources
- relying too heavily on support from sources that favor one side of the conversation

As you prepare to draft your document, you might find it necessary to reorganize your ideas to achieve your purpose.

If you created an informal outline, it can be the skeleton of your document, and you can now begin fleshing out sections. Translate a bulleted list of items, for instance, into a series of brief sentences, or write paragraphs based on the key points in the outline. If you created a formal outline, such as a topical outline or a sentence outline, you can use each main point in the outline as a topic sentence for a paragraph. Form supporting sentences from the subpoints under each main point.

If your outline contains references to specific notes or sources, make sure that you use those notes in your draft. Take advantage of the time you spent thinking about which sources are most appropriate for a particular section of your document.

As you work on your document, you might find it necessary to reorganize your ideas. Think of your outline as a flexible guide rather than a rigid blueprint.

12c

How can I draft my introduction?

All readers expect documents to include some sort of introduction. Whether they are reading a home page on a Web site or an opening paragraph in a research report, readers want to learn quickly what a document is about. As you begin to draft, think about how you can help your readers swiftly and easily understand what your document is about. In addition, ask how your readers might react to different types of introductions.

You can introduce your document using one of several strategies.

State the Topic. Tell your readers what your issue is, what conversation you are focusing on, and what your document will tell them about it. Featured writer Jenna Alberter began her introduction with the following direct statement:

> Artists and their artwork do not exist in a vacuum. The images artists create help shape and in turn are shaped by the society and culture in which they are created. The artists and artworks in the Dutch Baroque period are no exception.

Read Jenna Alberter's research paper on p. 266.

Define Your Argument. If your research document presents an argument, use your introduction to get right to your main point—the point you are trying to persuade your readers to accept. In other words, lead with a thesis statement, as in the following introduction:

> While the private tragedies of its central characters have public implications, William Shakespeare's *Julius Caesar* is more about personal struggles than political ambition. It is easy to see the play as one whose focus is the political action of public events. The title character, after all, is at the height of political power. However, the interior lives of Julius Caesar, Marcus Brutus, and their wives offer a more engaging storyline. Shakespeare alternates between public and private scenes throughout the play to emphasize the conflict between duties of the Roman citizenry and the feelings and needs of the individual, but it is the "private mind and heart of the individual" (Edwards 105) that the reader is compelled to examine.

Define a Problem. If your research has led you to propose a solution to a problem, you might begin your document by defining the problem. Featured writer Alexis Alvarez used this strategy to introduce her essay:

Almost daily, headlines and newscasters tell us about athletes' use of performance-enhancing drugs. Indeed, stories of such drug use seem to increase each year, with investigations of possible steroid use by college football players, by major league baseball players, and even by Olympic gold medalists. It is easy to gain the impression that many adult athletes, particularly males, may be using drugs in order to improve their performance and physical appearance. What may be surprising and even shocking to most of us, however, is that these drugs, especially anabolic steroids, are increasingly used by adolescent athletes and that girls are just as likely as boys to be users.

Read Alexis Alvarez's research paper on p. 292.

Ask a Question.   Asking a question invites your readers to become participants in the conversation. At the end of her introduction, Alexis Alvarez encouraged her readers to take an interest in the problem of steroid use by adolescent female athletes by asking a question:

> What role is competitive sports playing in this dangerous trend? Why are some girls feeling the need to ingest performance-enhancing drugs?

Tell a Story.   Everyone loves a story, assuming it's told well and has a point. Patrick Crossland began his research project with a story about his brother Caleb, a high school student and a star athlete who was applying to colleges and universities:

> Caleb is a junior in high school. Last night his mom attended his varsity wrestling match, cheering him on as he once again defeated his competitors. On the way home, they discussed his busy schedule, in which he balances both schoolwork and a job at his father's company. Caleb manages to get good grades in his classes while at the same time he learns a trade in the woodworking industry. . . .

Read Patrick Crossland's research paper on p. 320.

Provide a Historical Account.   Historical accounts can help your readers understand the origins of a situation and how the situation has changed over time. A Web site focusing on relations between the People's Republic of China and Taiwan used this historical account:

> On February 21, 2000, the People's Republic of China (PRC) shocked the world with its release of the white paper "The One-China Principle and the Taiwan Issue." In this 18-page document, the Chinese government outlined its case that, in keeping with the "One China" principle to which the United States and Taiwan had allegedly agreed, Taiwan is the rightful property of the People's Republic of China, and revealed that it intended to use force if Taiwan did not move to reunite with the mainland.

Lead with a Quotation.   A quotation allows your readers to learn about the issue from someone who knows it well or has been affected by it. Featured writer Maria Sanchez-Traynor used the following quotation to introduce her feature article about the Intensive English Program at Colorado State University:

> Read Maria Sanchez-Traynor's article at **bedfordresearcher.com**. Click on Featured Writers.

Attached to Heather Moffie's copy of the syllabus for her intermediate grammar class is a note reading, "Emphasize that you're here to help them—benefit comes from participation."

12d

How can I support my points?

Using sources to support your points is the essence of research writing. Whether you are making your main point or a supporting point, readers will expect evidence to back it up. Depending on the point you want to make, some types of evidence might be more effective than others. The key is how your readers will react to the support you provide. In some cases, for example, statistical evidence might lend better support for a point than a quotation. The following are some of the most effective ways to support your points.

Direct Quotation   Quotations from experts or authorities can lend weight to your argument, and quotations from people who have been affected by an issue can provide concrete evidence of the impact of the issue. Patrick Crossland used a quotation from an admissions expert to support his point about the competitiveness of the college admissions process:

> Duke University Director of Undergraduate Admissions Christoph Guttentag uses a baseball analogy in describing how students advance in the admission process. "Think of it as a baseball game. Everybody gets [his] time at bat. The quality of [students'] academic work that we can measure through test scores and analysis of high school courses gets about 10 percent of the applicants to third base, 50 percent to second base, and about 30 percent to first base. And 10 percent strike out" (qtd. in "College Admissions").

Statistical and Other Numerical Evidence   Much of the support you'll use in your document is textual, typically presented in the form of quotations, paraphrases, and summaries. But your topic may lend itself to numerical evidence. Alexis Alvarez used statistical evidence throughout her essay:

> In May 2004, the Centers for Disease Control and Prevention (CDC) published its latest figures on self-reported drug use among young people in grades 9 through 12. The CDC study, "Youth Risk Surveillance Study—December 2003," found that 6.1% of its survey participants reported using steroids at least once, up from 2.2% in 1993. The report also showed that use of steroids appears to be increasing among younger girls: While only 3.3% of twelfth-grade girls reported using steroids, 7.3% of ninth-grade girls reported using them.

Example   It's often better to *show* with an example than to *tell* with a general description. Examples provide concrete evidence in your document. Kevin Fahey used an example to illustrate a point in his essay about Hemingway's depiction of his character Nick Adams:

"The End of Something," one of the only stories in which Hemingway depicts Nick alone with a female companion for an extended scene (Flora 55), provides a convincing portrayal of Nick as the Everyman. As the story opens, Nick and his girlfriend row to a beach on Horton's Bay, a once-bustling mill town that is now deserted. Hemingway's description of the town's demise heralds catastrophe for the couple's relationship. While the two fish, Marjorie asks Nick what has been bothering him. Revealing his lack of self-understanding, Nick replies, "'I don't know. . . . It isn't fun any more. . . . I don't know, Marge. I don't know what to say'" (Hemingway 204).

> Read Kevin Fahey's research paper at **bedfordresearcher.com**. Click on Featured Writers.

Definition   Definitions explain what something is, how a process works, or what you mean by a statement. Maria Sanchez-Traynor used a definition to explain a teaching strategy:

> Instead, they use a strategy called "immersion" to teach their classes. The goal is to immerse, or surround, the participants with the English language. Immersion means that all classes, no matter their level, are taught solely in English.

Qualification   You can use qualifications to make your meaning more precise and reduce the possibility that your readers might misunderstand your point. Qualifications allow you to narrow the scope of a statement. In the conclusion of her research paper, Jenna Alberter used a qualification to clarify the relationship between painting and culture in seventeenth-century Dutch society:

> Because of their faithful depiction of the world and their painstaking attention to detail, seventeenth-century Dutch paintings of domestic scenes can be called realistic. However, it is important to remember that these images do not always simply depict the people and their world exactly as they were. Instead, these works served multiple purposes—to spread and promote ideas about domestic virtue, to instruct viewers about women's roles, and, finally, to entertain viewers (Franits, *Paragons* 9).

Amplification   Amplification expands the scope of your point. Patrick Crossland used amplification to broaden his discussion of the criteria used in college admissions decisions:

> And it's not just the grades that matter—admissions staff also look at the *kind* of courses students are taking.

Analogy   One of the most common ways to support a point is to describe similarities between one thing and another. You've encountered analogies throughout this book. Here's another: "Drafting a research document is similar to cooking. Without the proper tools, ingredients, and knowledge, the document won't turn out as well as you'd like."

Association   If you remember the advertising slogan "I want to be like Mike," you're already familiar with association. Through association you can support a point by connecting it with something or someone else. When you support your argument using a quotation from an expert, you're using a form of association. It's as if you're saying, "Look, this intelligent person agrees with me."

Contrast   Contrasts are similar to association, but in reverse. You can use contrasts to show that something is not like something else.

Illustration   Visual elements can help your readers understand your points more clearly. In print documents, illustrations are usually photos, drawings, or charts. Electronic documents can also include video, audio, and animations. Jenna Alberter included photographs of the paintings she discussed in her essay about images of women in seventeenth-century Dutch art.

You can read more about using information from sources in Chapter 13, Integrating Sources.

How can I make sure my document is well organized?

In addition to expecting that you'll support your points, readers expect you to organize your document in a sensible way that allows them to understand it easily. Fortunately, you've already spent time organizing your arguments, ideas, and information. It's also likely that you've continued to refine your organization as you've prepared to draft your document.

A well-organized document allows a reader to anticipate—or predict—what will come next, which helps readers understand your goals more easily. The test of good organization is whether your readers can move smoothly through your document without wondering, "Where did that come from?" As you draft, check whether your document is organized consistently and predictably. You might find the following techniques useful.

Provide a Map.   The most direct way of signaling the organization of your document is to provide a map in your introduction. You might write something like "This report will cover three approaches to treating cancer of the bladder: chemotherapy, a combination of chemotherapy and radiation, and surgical removal of the organ."

Use a Table of Contents, a Home Page, or a Menu.   Tables of contents, home pages, and menus are similar to maps. If you are writing a print document, decide whether your document is long enough to justify using a table of contents. If you are writing an electronic document such as a Web site, you can lay out the key elements of your document on a home page. Similarly, you can add a menu on the side, top, or bottom of your pages that readers can see as they work through your site. Featured writer Pete Jacquez provided a menu on every page of his site (see Figure 12.1).

Read Pete Jacquez's Web site at **bedfordresearcher.com.** Click on Featured Writers.

FIGURE 12.1   Menu on Pete Jacquez's Web Site
The menu helps readers understand the organization of the site and move to pages within it.

Learn More
Fossil Fuel Economics
Fossil Fuel & the Environment
Wind Power Economics
Wind Power & the Environment
Bibliography
Related Links

Take Action
Local Efforts
State-Wide Efforts
National Efforts

About This Site
Written by Pedro Jacquez
References

Use Headings and Subheadings. You can help your readers keep their place in your document by using headings and subheadings. Your formatting should distinguish between headings (major sections) and subheadings (subsections).

Provide Forecasts and Cross-References. Forecasts prepare your readers for a shift in your document, such as the boundary between one section and the next. A forecast at the end of a major section might say, "In the next section, you can read about . . ." Cross-references tell your readers that they can find related information in another section of the document or let them know that a particular issue will be addressed in greater detail elsewhere. On a Web site, forecasts and cross-references might take the form of small images, flags, or statements such as "Continue to next section" or "Follow this link for more information."

12f

How can I make my document more readable?

Even a thoughtful, well-researched document will be ineffective if it's difficult to read. As you draft your document, give attention to paragraphing and paragraph structure, transitions between sentences and paragraphs, tone and style, and economy. These issues are discussed briefly in this section and more fully in Chapter 15, Revising and Editing.

Use Effective Paragraphing and Paragraph Structure

Each of your paragraphs should focus on a single idea. Paragraphs often have a topic sentence in which the writer makes an assertion or observation or asks a question. The rest of the sentences in the paragraph develop—or flesh out—the topic. Your readers will also expect you to present your paragraphs in a coherent and sensible order. As you draft, keep in mind the logic of your argument or discussion.

Create Effective Transitions

Good writers provide clear directions to their readers in the form of a transition between sections and paragraphs. Effective transitions smooth readers' movement from one idea to another. Some transitions might be sentences, such as "A sudden job loss creates not only a financial burden but a psychological one as well." Others come in the form of headings and subheadings, which explicitly signal a change in topic. Still others are signal words or phrases, such as *however, on the other hand, in addition,* and *first.*

Use Appropriate and Consistent Tone and Style

In many cases, readers and writers never meet, so your document might be the only point of contact between you and your readers. As a result, your readers will judge you and what you have to say based not only on what you say but on how you say it. Ensure that your readers will react to you positively by paying attention to the following:

- **Word Choice.** Make sure that your readers understand your words, and use technical language appropriate for your audience. How will your readers react to slang? Also ask yourself whether they will find your words too stiff and formal.
- **Sentence Length and Complexity.** A sentence that is too complex will make your readers work overtime to figure out what it means. Can a complicated concept be more simply stated?
- **Variety.** A steady stream of sentences written in exactly the same way will have the same effect as a lecture delivered in a monotone. Vary your sentence length and structure.

Strive for Economy

An effective document says enough to meet the writer's goals, and no more. As you draft your document, ask yourself whether you've written enough to make your point. Then ask whether you could make your point more economically without compromising your ability to meet your goals.

Create an Effective Design

As you write your document, pay attention to its design. Using a readable body font that is clearly different from the font used for headings and subheadings, for example, can improve readability significantly. Similarly, breaking out information using bulleted and numbered lists, providing descriptive page headers or footers, and integrating illustrations effectively into your text can greatly enhance readability. You can read more about design in Chapter 16, Designing.

12g

How can I draft my conclusion?

Your conclusion provides an opportunity to reinforce your message. It offers one last chance to achieve your purposes as a writer and to share your final thoughts about the issue with your readers.

You've probably read conclusions that simply summarize the document. These summaries can be effective, especially when the document has presented complex concepts. A conclusion can do more, though, than simply summarize your points. It can also give your readers an incentive to continue thinking about what they've read, to take action about the issue, or to read more about it.

As you draft, think about what you want to accomplish. You can choose from a range of strategies to draft an effective conclusion.

Summarize Your Argument.   Sum up the argument you've made in your document. Jenna Alberter concluded her analysis of the relationship between society and painting in seventeenth-century Holland by using this technique.

> Because of their faithful depiction of the world and their painstaking attention to detail, seventeenth-century Dutch paintings of domestic scenes can be called realistic. However, it is important to remember that these images do not always simply depict the people and their world exactly as they were. Instead, these works served multiple purposes—to spread and promote ideas about domestic virtue, to instruct viewers about women's roles, and, finally, to entertain viewers (Franits, *Paragons* 9). Just as in the art of every culture in history, the art of the Dutch Baroque period was both a mirror of the world in which it was created and a shaper of that world.

Offer Additional Analysis.   Extend your analysis of the issue by supplying additional insights. In his Web site about wind-generated electrical power, Pete Jacquez concluded his discussion of wind power and the environment by linking wind power to the production of hydrogen gas.

> Another promising area—in terms of wind power's contribution to clean energy—is the role it can play in a "hydrogen economy." Because hydrogen gas, when burned, does not produce carbon dioxide (its only emission is water vapor), some legislators and environmentalists are looking to hydrogen as a replacement for fossil fuels. Generating hydrogen gas, however, requires power, and a number of plans to generate it rely on coal-powered plants. Wind-power advocates argue, instead, that wind turbines can supply the power needed to produce hydrogen gas. Recent government studies support this approach ("Wind Power Facts," 2004).

Speculate about the Future.   Reflect on what might happen next. An essay about younger voters, for example, might speculate on the consequences of their historically low turnout and what will be required to increase it.

> While a repeal of voting rights for 18- to 21-year-olds might be unlikely, other effects will certainly be felt: younger people's interests will not be properly evaluated,

and the "cycle of mutual neglect" will continue. Clearly, the demographic group of 18- to 24-year-olds in America has shown less of an interest in participating in the political process than everyone else. This will remain true until younger voters feel they have trustworthy sources of information as well as candidates to choose from whom they feel listen to them. Finally, they must understand the importance of their vote, and why it is not just a right, but a civic duty.

Close with a Quotation. Select a quotation that does one of the following:

- sums up the points you've made in your document
- points to the future of the issue
- suggests a solution to a problem
- illustrates what you would like to see happen
- makes a further observation about the issue

Maria Sanchez-Traynor used a quotation from a former student to underscore her main point about the dedicated teaching available from the Intensive English Program at Colorado State University.

> Former student Munehito Endo says he is still benefiting from the IEP: "Whenever I have a problem they still help me out, even though I'm not in the program anymore." Students enrolled in the Intensive English Program benefit from the energy and methodology of the program's teachers — teachers who are truly "here to help."

Close with a Story. Tell a story about the issue you've discussed in your document. The story might suggest a potential solution to the problem, offer hope about a desired outcome, or illustrate what might happen if a desired outcome isn't realized. Patrick Crossland continued the story he used to introduce his research paper.

> Thus, in the midst of Caleb Crossland's busy schedule, he applies to various colleges he wants to attend. He continues to get good grades, studies for the SAT, and stays involved in extracurricular activities. He researches schools and plans to apply early. And with the support of his family, Caleb should have an edge over the many other students competing against him for a spot at the nation's top colleges.

Link to Your Introduction. This technique is sometimes called a "bookends" approach because it positions your introduction and conclusion as related ends of your document. The basic idea is to turn your conclusion into an extension of your introduction.

- If your introduction used a quotation, end with a related quotation or respond to the quotation.
- If your introduction used a story, extend that story or retell it with a different ending.
- If your introduction asked a question, answer the question, restate the question, or ask a new question.

IV Writing Your Document

- If your introduction defined a problem, provide a solution to the problem, restate the problem, or suggest that readers need to move on to a new problem.

12h

How should I document my sources?

You should document your sources in the body of your document and at the end of it—in a works cited or references list. Documenting sources acknowledges the contributions of the writers whose work you've used in your project. Documenting sources also helps your readers locate the sources you cited. For a fuller discussion of why you should document sources, see Chapter 17. For guidelines on the MLA, APA, *Chicago,* and CSE documentation systems, see Chapters 18 to 21.

> **QUICK REFERENCE**
>
> *Drafting*
> ✔ Develop your thesis statement.   (p. 158)
> ✔ Use your outline to begin drafting your document.   (p. 162)
> ✔ Draft your introduction.   (p. 163)
> ✔ Support your points.   (p. 165)
> ✔ Use an appropriate organizational pattern.   (p. 167)
> ✔ Make sure your draft is readable by paying attention to your paragraphs, transitions, tone, style, economy, and design.   (p. 168)
> ✔ Draft your conclusion.   (p. 170)
> ✔ Document your sources.   (p. 172)

IV Writing Your Document

13

Integrating Sources

Key Questions

As you draft your document, remember the range of strategies you can use to support your points, convey your ideas, and illustrate positions taken by other authors. This chapter discusses how you can use source information to meet the needs of your writing situation and addresses the primary techniques for integrating source information into your document: quotation, paraphrase, and summary. It also looks at techniques for working with numeric information, images, audio, and video.

Much of the information in this chapter is based on MLA style. See Chapter 18 for more on MLA style and Chapters 19 to 21 for guidelines on APA, *Chicago*, and CSE styles.

13a

How can I use source information to accomplish my purposes as a writer?

Information from your sources can help you introduce your arguments and ideas, contrast the arguments and ideas of other authors with your own, provide evidence for your arguments, define concepts, illustrate processes, clarify statements, and set a mood.

Introduce an Idea or Argument.   You can use a quotation, paraphrase, or summary to introduce an idea or argument to your readers:

Quotation Used to Introduce an Idea

"When I came around the corner, a black bear was standing in the middle of the trail," said Joan Gibson, an avid hiker. "We stared at each other for a moment, wondering who would make the first move. Then the bear looked off to the right and shambled up the mountain. I guess I wasn't worth the trouble."

Joan Gibson's story, like those of most hikers who encounter bears in the woods, ends happily. But the growing encroachment of . . .

Paraphrase Used to Introduce an Idea

A *New York Times* article recently reported that human-bear encounters in Yosemite National Park, which had been on the decline during most of the last decade, had more than doubled in the past year (Spiegel, A4). Although no humans have been injured and only one incident resulted in a decision to destroy a bear, park officials point to the uptick in encounters as a warning sign that . . .

Your choice of a quotation or paraphrase will frame the argument you want to make, calling your readers' attention to a specific aspect of the argument and laying the groundwork for a specific type of response to the issue you are addressing in your document. Think about how the following quotation leads readers to view a public debate about education reform as a battle between reformers and an entrenched teachers union:

"The teachers union has balked at even the most reasonable proposals for school reform," said Mary Sweeney, press secretary for Save Our Schools, which has sponsored a referendum on the November ballot calling for funding for their voucher plan. "We believe the November election will send a wake-up call about the need to rethink their obstructionist behaviors."

If Sweeney and supporters of Referendum D are successful, the educational landscape in . . .

In contrast, note how the following quotation frames the debate as a question of how best to spend scarce education funds:

"In the past decade, state and local funding of public education in real dollars has declined by 7.2 percent," said Jeffrey Allister, state chair of the governor's Special

Commission on Education Reform. "Referendum D, if passed, would further erode that funding by shifting state dollars to private schools."

As the state considers the merits of Referendum D, which would institute the first statewide voucher program in the United States, opponents of the measure have . . .

? WHAT'S MY PURPOSE?

As you draft your document, ask how you can use information from your sources to accomplish your purposes as a writer and to address the needs and interests of your readers. Consider how quotations, paraphrases, summaries, and various types of illustrations (such as images, tables, charts, and graphs) from your sources can lead your readers to see the issue you are addressing in terms that are most favorable to your purposes. Your careful selection of information from your sources can allow you to present arguments that might be more pointed than you might want to make on your own. Calling opponents of a proposal "balky" and "obstructionists," for example, might signal your biases too strongly. Quoting someone who uses those terms, however, allows you to get the point across without undermining an otherwise even and balanced tone.

Contrast Ideas or Arguments.　When you want to indicate that disagreement exists on an issue, you can use source information to contrast and convey the nature and intensity of the disagreements. The following example uses partial quotations (see p. 178) to highlight differences in proposed solutions to a problem:

> Solutions to the state's higher education funding shortfall range from traditional approaches, such as raising taxes, to more radical solutions, among them privatizing state colleges and universities. Advocates of increased taxes, such as Page Richards of the Higher Education Coalition, argue that declines in state funding of higher education "must be reversed immediately or we will find ourselves in a situation where we are closing rural community colleges and only the wealthiest among us will have access to the best education" (A4). Those in favor of privatizing higher education suggest, however, that free market approaches will ultimately bring about "a fairer situation in which the poor, many of whom have no interest in higher education, are no longer asked to subsidize higher and higher faculty salaries and larger football stadiums" (Pieters, 23).

Base your choices about how to contrast ideas and arguments on the clarity and conciseness of your sources and on the effects you hope to achieve. If you want to express complex ideas as concisely as possible, you might use paraphrase and summary. If you want to convey the emotional qualities of an author's position on an issue, use quotations.

Provide Evidence for Your Argument.　Arguments that consist of a series of unsupported assertions amount to little more than a request for a reader's trust. Even when the writer is eminently trustworthy, most readers find such arguments easy to dismiss. In contrast, providing evidence to support your assertions increases the likelihood that your readers will accept your argument. Note the differences between the following passages:

Unsupported Assertion:

Given a choice between two products of comparable quality, reputation, and cost, American consumers are far more likely to purchase goods that use environmentally friendly packaging. Encouraging the use of such packaging is a good idea for America.

Supported Assertion:

Given a choice between two products of comparable quality, reputation, and cost, American consumers are far more likely to purchase goods that use environmentally friendly packaging. A recent study by the High Plains Research Institute found that the shelf life of several biodegradable plastics not only exceeded the shelf life of the products they were used to package, but also cost less to produce (Chen and Lohann). In addition, a study by the Consumer Products Institute found that, when made aware that products were packaged in environmentally friendly materials, consumers were more likely to buy those products.

Similarly, visual sources can lend support to an assertion. An assertion about the unintended consequences of military action, for example, might be accompanied by a photograph of a war-torn street or a wounded child.

Align Your Argument with an Authority.   Aligning an argument with an authority shows your readers that your points are supported by a leader in that area—such as a subject matter expert, a scientist, a politician, or a religious figure—and that you are not alone in your convictions. Essentially, this technique allows you to borrow the credibility and status of someone who has compiled a strong record of accomplishment. Start by making an assertion and follow it with supporting information from a source, such as a quotation, paraphrase, or source summary:

Although voice recognition appears to be a promising technology, challenges associated with vocabulary, homonyms, and accents have slowed its widespread implementation. "The computer right now can do a very good job of voice recognition," said Bill Gates, co-founder and chairman of Microsoft Corporation. "Demonstrations are good but whenever you get it out and start working with it, it has a hard time, particularly if you are working with a very large vocabulary. It certainly will re-define the way we think of the machines when we have that voice input" (Gates, par. 42).

Define a Concept, Illustrate a Process, or Clarify a Statement.   Writers commonly turn to information from sources to define concepts, illustrate processes, or clarify statements when the information is clearer and more concise than what they might write themselves. You might define a concept by quoting or paraphrasing a dictionary or encyclopedia, or use an illustration to help readers understand a complex process, such as the steps involved in cellular respiration.

Writers also use information from sources to clarify their statements. A writer might amplify a statement by providing examples from sources or qualify a statement by noting that it applies only to specific situations and then use a quotation or paraphrase from a source to back that up:

Studies have found connections between weight loss and coffee intake. This doesn't mean that drinking a couple of cups of coffee each day leads to weight loss. However, three recent studies reported that individuals who increased their coffee intake from fewer than three cups to more than eight cups of coffee per day experienced weight losses of up to 7 percent over a two month period (Chang, Johnson and Salazar, Neiman). "It may be that increased caffeine intake led to a higher metabolic level, which in turn led to weight loss," noted John Chang, a senior researcher at the Centers for Disease Control. "Or it might be that drinking so much coffee depressed participants' appetites" (232).

Set a Mood.   You can also choose quotations and illustrations with an eye toward establishing an overall mood for your readers. The emotional impact of images of a celebration at a sporting event, an expression of grief at a funeral, or a calming mountain vista can lead your readers to react in specific ways to your document. Similarly, a striking quote, such as "The screams of pain coming out of that room will stay with me as long as I live," can evoke a specific mood among your readers.

13b

How can I integrate quotations?

A well-chosen quotation can have a powerful impact on your readers' perception of your argument and on the overall quality of your document. Quotations can also add a sense of immediacy by bringing in the voice of someone who has been affected by an issue or lend a sense of authority to your argument by conveying the words of an expert. Quotations can range in form from brief, partial quotations to extended, block quotations. As you integrate quotations into your document, remember to

- decide on partial, complete, or block quotations and blend them smoothly into your text
- acknowledge the source of the quotation in a way that clearly differentiates the quotation from your own ideas
- provide a context for the quotations that demonstrates their relevance
- modify quotations accurately and fairly
- punctuate each quotation properly

Use Partial, Complete, and Block Quotations

Quotations can be parts of sentences (partial), whole sentences (complete), or long passages (block). When you choose one type of quotation over another, keep in mind

- the length of the passage
- the complexity of the ideas and information in the passage
- the obligation to convey ideas and information fairly

IV Writing Your Document

Partial Quotations   Partial quotations can be a single word, phrase, or most of a sentence. They are often used to convey a well-turned phrase or to complete a sentence using important words from a source, as in the following example.

> However, there are those who, according to William H. Gray III, "contend that preferences based upon race are illegal and unfair" (2).

Complete Quotations   Complete quotations are typically one or more complete sentences and are most often used when the meaning of the passage cannot be conveyed adequately by a few well-chosen words, as in the following example.

> Westermann describes the work of Vermeer and de Hooch in this way: "Their paintings invite contemplation of domestic virtue, of the quiet and harmonious household prescribed by Cats and others" (124).

Since the source of the quotation is identified in a signal phrase ("Westermann describes . . ."), only the page number appears in the citation, following MLA guidelines (see p. 241). In contrast, when quotations from a personal interview are used, no page numbers appear:

> "Many students who come in at the intermediate level often have studied English for ten years," Gough says. "However, their grammar is textbook-based and often-times leaves few options to speak or hear the language."

Block Quotations   Block quotations are extended quotations (usually more than four typed lines) that are set off in a block from the rest of the text. In general, use a colon to introduce the quotation, indent the entire quotation one inch (or ten spaces) from the left margin, and include source information according to the documentation system you are using (such as MLA, APA, *Chicago,* or CSE). Since the blocked text indicates to your readers that you are quoting directly, you do not need to include quotation marks:

> In the article "In the Best Interest of America, Affirmative Action in Higher Education Is a Must," William H. Gray III states:

> High school achievement and test scores are considered to be very important criteria in the admissions process by most of the four-year public degree-granting colleges and universities. Nonetheless, high school grades and test scores are not the only factors considered by colleges and universities in the admissions process. Other factors that influence college admissions decisions include high school rank, being an athlete, alumni connections, extracurricular activities, special talents, and other peronal characteristics of applicants. (para. 5)

> *Quotation marks are not used in block quotations.*

> *Paragraph number provided for an online source.*

● Identify the Sources of Your Quotations

You should identify the source of a quotation for three reasons. First, it fulfills your obligation to document your sources. Second, it allows you (and your readers) to distinguish between your ideas and those of your sources. Third, it can help you strengthen your overall argument by calling attention to the qualifications or experiences of the person you are quoting. The following quotation is introduced in a way that clearly indicates who made the statement and what his qualifications are:

| Source of the quotation is identified as an authority. | In *Paragons of Virtue,* art historian Wayne Franits calls attention to this distinction between the ideal and the real, noting "[Both] art and literature present an exemplary image, a topos that does not necessarily reflect the actual situation of young women in seventeenth-century Dutch culture" (25). | Square brackets indicate an altered quotation. |

Research writers who use MLA or APA documentation format include citations—or acknowledgments of source information—within the text of their document. These citations, in turn, refer readers to a list of works cited or a list of references at the end of the document. Both systems use a combination of signal phrases and parenthetical information to refer to sources. Note the following examples:

MLA Style:

Ann Gill argues, "Education reform is the best solution for fixing our public schools" (22).

"Education reform is the best solution for fixing our public schools" (Gill 22).

> MLA-style in-text citations include the author's name and exact page reference.

APA Style:

Ann Gill (2001) has argued, "Education reform is the best solution for fixing our public schools" (p. 22).

"Education reform is the best solution for fixing our public schools" (Gill, 2001, p. 22).

> APA-style in-text citations include the author's name, publication date, and exact page reference.

Provide a Context for Your Quotations

Skilled research writers know the importance of providing a context for the quotations they include in their documents. It's not enough to simply put text within two quotation marks and move on. Readers can be confused by "orphan quotations"—quotations that are inserted into a paragraph without any introduction or context.

To introduce a quotation effectively, give sufficient background information about the source of your quotation and use signal phrases or colons to integrate the quotation into your document. Doing so gives your reader a frame for understanding how you are using the source information.

| Description of the debate. | Many refute the idea that computer use is as damaging to children as television viewing. According to child development expert Jennifer Doyon, "Even a preschooler can benefit from simple computer activities, which by their very | Signal phrase identifies speaker as an expert. |

nature promote interactivity in a way that television shows cannot" (qtd. in Reid 89).

> Writer follows MLA style; "qtd. in" indicates the expert's words are quoted in the article by Kathleen Reid.

You'll also want to vary your attributions—the introduction or context that credits the source of the information or ideas. As you do, be aware of the way that attributions can convey important shades of meaning—for example, the difference between saying that someone "alleged" something and someone "confirmed" something.

Some Common Attributions:

according to	claimed	expressed	reported
acknowledged	commented	inquired	said
affirmed	confirmed	interpreted	stated
alleged	declared	mused	suggested
asserted	denied	noted	thought
assumed	described	observed	wondered
asked	disputed	pointed out	wrote
believed	emphasized	remarked	

Modify Quotations

You can modify quotations to fit your draft. It is acceptable, for example, to delete unnecessary words or to change the tense of a word in a partial quotation so that it fits your sentence. Keep in mind, however, that research writers have an obligation to quote their sources accurately and fairly. You should indicate when you have added or deleted words, and you should not modify quotations in a way that distorts their meaning. The most useful strategies writers can use to modify quotations include

- using ellipses (. . .) to indicate deleted words (see p. 133)
- using brackets [ ] to clarify meaning (see p. 134)
- using "sic" to note errors in a source (see p. 135)

Punctuate Quotations

The rules for punctuating quotations are as follows:

- Use double quotation marks (" ") around partial or complete quotations. Do not use quotation marks for block quotations.
- Use single quotation marks (' ') to indicate quoted material within a quotation:

  "We pragmatically identify the current cross-Strait relations as a 'special state-to-state relationship.'"

- In most cases, place punctuation marks such as commas, periods, question marks, and exclamation points inside quotation marks:

  Dawn Smith asked an important question: "Do college students understand the importance of voting?"

- Place colons and semicolons outside quotation marks:

  Many young voters consider themselves "too busy to vote"; they say that voting takes too much time and effort.

- Do not put a punctuation mark that ends your own sentence inside quotation marks if doing so will alter the meaning of the original text:

  But what can be gained from following the committee's recommendation that the state should "avoid, without exceptions, any proposed tax hike"?

- When citation information is provided after a quotation, place the punctuation mark (comma, period, semicolon, colon, or question mark) after the parenthetical citation. In a block quotation, place the end punctuation before the parenthesis.

  "Preliminary reports have been consistent," Yates notes. "Without immediate changes to current practices, we will deplete known supplies by mid-century" (335).

- Use three spaced periods (ellipsis) to indicate an omission within a sentence.

  According to critic Joe Robinson, Americans are overworked: "Ask Americans how things are really going and you'll hear stories of . . . fifty- and sixty-hour weeks with no letup in sight" (467).

- Place a period before the ellipsis to indicate an omission at the end of a sentence:

  The most recent information indicates, says Chen, that "we can expect a significant increase in costs by the end of the century. . . . Those costs, however, should ramp up slowly" (35).

13c

How can I integrate paraphrases?

A paraphrase is a restatement, in your own words, of a passage from a source. Unlike summaries, which are shorter than the text being summarized, paraphrases are about as long as the text on which they are based. Paraphrases can be used to illustrate or support a point you make in your document or to illustrate another author's argument about an issue.

TUTORIAL

How do I integrate a quotation into my draft?

After you select a passage to quote, you'll need to acknowledge the source, punctuate the quotation properly, and provide a context for the information. This example uses MLA style; be sure to follow the guidelines for the documentation style you are using.

1 Locate the passage you want to quote and identify the text you want to include in the quotation.

Original Passage: But there is still a black cloud hovering over this seemingly sunny scenario. Wind turbines remain expensive to build often prohibitively so. On average, it costs about $1 million per megawatt to construct a wind turbine farm, compared to about $600,000 per megawatt for a conventional gas-fired power plant; in the economic calculations of power companies, the fact that wind is free doesn't close the gap.

Source: Fairley, Peter. "Wind Power for Pennies." Technology Review 105.6 (2002): 40–46.

2 Add quotation marks; or, if the quotation is long, set the text in a block (see p. 178). If you modify the passage, use ellipses and brackets appropriately (see p. 181).

"Wind turbines remain expensive to build. . . . On average, it costs about $1 million per megawatt to construct a wind turbine farm, compared to about $600,000 per megawatt for a conventional gas-fired power plant."

3 Identify the source of the quotation and the location, such as the page number. Give the author's qualifications in an author tag if you haven't already done so for this source in your document.

In his article "Wind Power for Pennies," *IEEE Spectrum* contributing editor Peter Fairley notes, "Wind turbines remain expensive to build. . . . On average, it costs about $1 million per megawatt to construct a wind turbine farm, compared to $600,000 per megawatt for a conventional gas-fired power plant." (40).

4 Make sure that you've punctuated the quotation properly.

5 Avoid orphan quotations. Provide context for your quotation by introducing it and relating it to your argument.

At this point, some still argue that the price of wind power is too steep. In his article "Wind Power for Pennies," Peter Fairely notes, "Wind turbines remain expensive to build. . . . On average, it costs about $1 million per megawatt to construct a wind turbine farm, compared to $600,000 per megawatt for a conventional gas-fired power plant." (40). These differences in cost are then passed on to the consumer in the form of higher energy costs for wind-generated electricity.

Review another example and work on quoting your own sources at **bedfordresearcher.com**. Click on Tutorials.

Your notes are likely to include a number of paraphrases of arguments, ideas, and information from your sources. To integrate these paraphrases into your document, follow these steps:

1. Make sure your paraphrase is an accurate and fair representation of the source. Since most paraphrasing errors occur when writers misread a source, reread the source to double-check the accuracy and fairness of your paraphrase.

2. Revise the paraphrase so that it fits the context and tone of your document.

3. Use signal phrases to ensure a smooth transition from your ideas to the ideas found in the source.

4. Identify the sources of your paraphrases according to the documentation system you are using.

In the following example, note how featured writer Jenna Alberter lets her reader know where her statement ends and where the support for her statement, in the form of a paraphrase, begins:

During the seventeenth century, the concept of domesticity appears to have been very important in all levels of Dutch society; literally hundreds of surviving paintings reflect this theme. Such paintings depict members of every class and occupation, and according to Wayne Franits, a specialist in seventeenth-century Dutch art, they served the dual purpose of both entertaining and instructing the viewer. They invite the viewer to inspect and enjoy their vivid details, but also to contemplate the values and ideals they represented ("Domesticity" 13).

> Jenna's idea.

> Signal phrase marks transition from Jenna's idea to source ideas.

> Source of paraphrase cited per MLA style. Jenna cited two sources by Franits in her paper, so she added a shortened source title.

13d

How can I integrate summaries?

A summary is a concise statement, written in your own words, of information found in a source (see p. 138 to learn about summarizing entire sources and lengthy passages within a source). When you integrate a summary into your draft,

- review the source to make sure your summary is an accurate and fair representation of the ideas in the original source
- properly identify the source

You can summarize an entire source, ideas and information within a particular source, or a group of sources.

IV Writing Your Document

Summarize an Entire Source

Research writers frequently summarize an entire work. In some cases, the summary might occupy one or more paragraphs or be integrated into a discussion contained in one or more paragraphs. In other cases, the summary might be as brief as a single sentence.

Jenna Alberter provided a lengthy summary of *Houwelyck,* a seventeenth-century treatise on marriage. Jenna spread her summary across three paragraphs, interspersing it with interpretive comments. The focus of these three paragraphs, as a result, is not simply a summary of the book, but also Jenna's reflections on its meaning and implications:

> Perhaps the most well-known and influential work of literature of this type is Jacob Cats's book *Houwelyck,* or *Marriage.* Published in 1625, this was a comprehensive reference book for women of all ages, but especially young women, regarding matters of marriage and family. Although many other similar books were being published in the Netherlands and England during this period, Cats's work is perhaps the most extensive; it even contained an alphabetical index for quick reference (Franits, "Paragons" 5).
>
> *Houwelyck,* which by mid-century had sold over 50,000 copies, making it a "bestseller" for its time, contained instruction for women on the proper behavior for the six stages of life: Maiden, Sweetheart, Bride, Housewife, Mother and Widow. It is particularly telling that these stages of life were defined in reference to the roles of men. Although Cats's book specifically addressed women, it had implications for men as well (Westermann 119). According to Cats, by laying out the roles and duties of the woman, his book "encompasses also the masculine counter-duties" (qtd. in Westermann 119).
>
> The title page of the first edition of Cats's work provides a good overview of the typical depiction of the ideal role for a woman at this time. Designed by Adriaen van de Venne, *Stages of Life* (fig. 1) depicts several figural groups arranged on a hill. It shows life as a large hill, with marriage as its pinnacle, and then heading down toward widowhood and death (Westermann 120). This depiction seems to have been reflective of the typical views of a woman: her goal in life should be to provide a man with a good, proper wife, and once that duty has been fulfilled, there is little for her to do but dutifully wait for death to come.

Source cited using MLA style.

The main point of the book.

Shift from summary to interpretation.

Source of quote about the book.

Additional information about the book and writer's interpretation.

In contrast, Jenna offered a much briefer, "nutshell" summary of a related source:

> Another example of the theme of courtship in literature is Jan Soet's work *Maagden-Baak,* or *Maiden's Beacon,* published in 1642, which deals with this theme in even greater detail than Cats's book.

Summarize Specific Ideas and Information from a Source

You can also use summaries to convey key information or ideas from a source. In his research essay, featured writer Patrick Crossland summarized a section of a book about college admissions. His summary is highlighted in the following passage:

> Bill Paul, author of *Getting In: Inside the College Admissions Process,* a book that tells the stories of several students applying to an elite Ivy League institution, shares three suggestions for students who want to get into a college. Paul bases these suggestions on his discussions with Fred Hargadon, who in 1995 was dean of admissions at Princeton. Hargadon suggested that the best way students can enhance their chances for acceptance into the college of their choice is to read widely, learn to speak a second language, and engage in activities that interest and excite them and that also help them develop their confidence and creativity (238–49).

> [Summary is introduced with the author, title, and specific source of the ideas.]

> [Per MLA style, exact pages are cited.]

Summarize a Group of Sources

In addition to summarizing a single source, research writers often summarize groups of sources. It's not unusual, for instance, to encounter in research documents phrases such as "Numerous authors have argued . . ." or "The research in this area seems to indicate that . . ." Such collective summaries allow you to establish a point briefly and with authority. They are effective particularly at the beginning of a document, when you are establishing a foundation for your argument, and can serve as a transitional device when you move from one major section of the document to another.

When you are summarizing a group of sources, separate the citations with a semicolon. MLA guidelines require including author and page information, as in the following example:

> Several critics have argued that the Hemingway code hero is not always male (Graulich 217; Sherman 78; Watters 33).

APA guidelines require including author and date information, as in the following example:

> The benefits of early detection of breast cancer have been well documented (Page, 1999; Richards, 2000; Vincent, 2002).

13e

How can I integrate numerical information?

If it suits the issue you are addressing, you might use numerical information, such as statistics, in your document. You can present this information within sentences, or you might use tables, charts, or graphs, as featured writer Pete

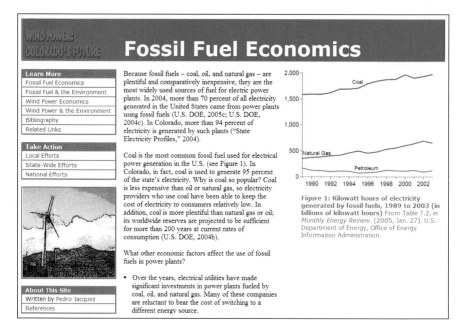

FIGURE 13.1   Chart on Pete Jacquez's Web Site

Jacquez did on his Web site about wind power (see Figure 13.1). Keep in mind that you still need to accurately and fairly present the numerical information in your document and clearly identify the source of the information, just as you would for textual information. For more information about using tables, charts, and graphs, see p. 221.

13f

How can I integrate images, audio, and video?

Including images in your print document and images, audio, or video files in your electronic document can enhance its effectiveness. Use caution, however, when taking images and audio or video from other sources. Simply copying a photograph into your document might be a form of plagiarism. The same is true of audio and video files. Jenna Alberter carefully documented the sources of the images she used in her research essay. Since she was writing an academic paper—rather than a document intended for publication and wide distribution—she did not seek permission to use them. (In contrast, the publisher of this book sought and received permission to publish those images.)

If you are creating an electronic document, the following approach is usually best:

- Make a link between your document and a document that contains an image, sound clip, or video clip—rather than simply copying the image and placing it in your document.

- If it isn't possible or appropriate to create a link to another document, you should contact the owner of the image, sound clip, or video clip for permission to use it.

- If you cannot contact the owner, review the fair use guidelines discussed on page 190 for guidance about using the material.

As you've done for the other sources you cite in your document, make sure you fairly present the information and identify its author or creator.

> **QUICK REFERENCE**

Integrating Sources

✔ Use source information to accomplish your purposes.   (p. 174)

✔ Integrate quotations appropriately.   (p. 177)

✔ Integrate paraphrases appropriately.   (p. 181)

✔ Integrate summaries appropriately.   (p. 183)

✔ Integrate numerical information appropriately.   (p. 185)

✔ Integrate images, audio, and video appropriately.   (p. 186)

IV Writing Your Document

14

Avoiding Plagiarism

> **Key Questions**
>
> **14a. What is plagiarism?**   189
>
> **14b. What are research ethics?**   189
>
> **14c. What is common knowledge?**   190
>
> **14d. What is fair use and when should I ask permission to use a source?**   190
>
> **14e. How can I avoid plagiarism?**   192
> Quote, paraphrase, and summarize accurately and appropriately
> Distinguish between your ideas and ideas in your sources
> Identify sources in your document
>
> **14f. How can I avoid plagiarism during group work?**   194

Few writers intentionally try to pass off the work of others as their own. However, deadlines and other pressures can lead writers to take notes poorly and cite sources improperly. In addition, easy access to documents through the Web and full-text databases has made it all too easy to copy and paste work from other writers without acknowledging its source.

For additional help, consult the St. Martin's Tutorial on Avoiding Plagiarism at **bedfordstmartins.com/ plagiarismtutorial**.

Failing to cite your sources can lead to serious problems. Your readers will not be able to determine which ideas and information in your text are your own or which are drawn from your sources. If they suspect you are failing to acknowledge your sources, they are likely to doubt your credibility and suspect your competence, and they might even stop reading your document. More seriously, submitting academic work that does not include proper identification of sources might result in failure in a course or some other disciplinary action.

14a

What is plagiarism?

Plagiarism is a form of intellectual dishonesty. It involves either unintentionally using someone else's work without properly acknowledging where the ideas or information came from (the most common form of plagiarism) or intentionally copying someone else's work and passing it off as your own (the most serious form of plagiarism).

Plagiarism is based on the notion of "copyright," or ownership of a document or idea. Like a patent, which protects an invention, a copyright protects an author's investment of time and energy in the creation of a document. Essentially, it assures authors that, when they create a document, someone else won't be able to steal ideas from it and profit from that theft without penalty.

In most cases, plagiarism is unintentional, and most cases of unintentional plagiarism result from taking poor notes or failing to use notes properly. You are plagiarizing if you

- quote a passage in a note but neglect to include quotation marks and then later insert the quotation into your document without remembering that it is a direct quotation.
- include a paraphrase that differs so slightly from the original passage that it might as well be a direct quotation.
- don't clearly distinguish between your ideas and ideas that come from your sources.
- neglect to list the source of a paraphrase, quotation, or summary in your text or in your works cited list.

14b

What are research ethics?

Research ethics are based on the notion that writing—and in particular research writing—is an honest exchange of arguments, ideas, and information among writers and readers who share an interest in an issue. As a research writer, you'll want to behave honestly and ethically. In general, you should

- acknowledge the sources of the arguments, ideas, and information used in your document. By doing so, you show respect for the work that others have done before you.
- accurately and fairly represent the arguments, ideas, and information—to ensure that you do not misrepresent that work to your readers.

- provide citation information for your sources. These citations help your readers understand how you have drawn your conclusions and where they can locate those sources should they want to consult them.

These three rules are the essence of research ethics. If your readers suspect that you have acted unethically, they will question the accuracy and credibility of the arguments, ideas, and information in your document. Ultimately, failing to act ethically—even when the failure is unintentional—can reflect poorly on you and your document.

14c

What is common knowledge?

Although crediting other authors for their work is important, you almost certainly won't need to document every fact and idea used in your document, because some of the information you'll use falls under the category of common knowledge. Common knowledge is information that is widely known, such as the fact that the Declaration of Independence was signed in 1776. Or it might be the kind of knowledge that people working in a particular field, such as petroleum engineering, use on a regular basis.

If you're relatively new to your topic, it can be difficult to determine whether information in a source is common knowledge. As you explore your topic, however, you will begin to identify what is generally known. For instance, if three or more sources use the same information without citing its source, you can assume that the information is common knowledge. If those sources use the information and cite the source, however, make sure you cite it as well.

14d

What is fair use and when should I ask permission to use a source?

The concept of fair use deals with how much of a source you can borrow or quote. According to Section 107 of the Copyright Act of 1976—the fair use provision, available at www.copyright.gov/title17/—writers can use copyrighted materials for purposes of "criticism, comment, news reporting, teaching (including multiple copies for classroom use), scholarship, or research." In other words, you generally don't need to seek permission to make brief quotations from a source or to summarize or paraphrase a source. However, if you are making an extended quotation—a quotation that is more than 10 percent of a source—or if you are quoting from a poem or song, you should seek permission to do so. You should also ask permission to use multimedia sources, such as images, audio, or video. Alternatively, you can link to these sources from your electronic document—unless the site specifically asks that you not link to content on their site. Always be sure that linking is allowed. Remember as well that in all cases you must still cite the source of the material you use.

If you seek permission to use a source, explain why and how you want to use it. Many authors and publishers allow academic use of their work but frown on commercial uses. When you contact an author or publisher, send a permission agreement that includes your name and contact information, the source you wish to use, the purpose for which you will use the source, and the time during which it will be used (see Figure 14.1).

Dear Ms. Jackson:

I am a student and am completing a research project for my writing class, English Composition 200, at Colorado State University. The research project **A** will be used only for educational purposes and will be distributed only to my instructor and members of my class for a period of three weeks during April and May of this year.

B I would like to include in my project the following image, which is displayed on your site at www.westernliving.org/images/2302a.jpg, and would greatly appreciate your permission to do so:

If you are able to grant me the requested permission, please respond to this **C** email message. My deadline for completing my project is April 22nd. I appreciate your quick response.

If you are not the copyright holder or do not have authority to grant this request, I would appreciate any information you can provide concerning the current copyright holder.

Thank you for considering this request.

Sincerely,

Glenn Choi **D**

GlennChoi@students.colostate.edu

(970) 555–1515

FIGURE 14.1 Sample Permission Request

A *Or ". . . on the Web at www.myschool.edu."*

B Insert or describe passage or image. For example: *paragraphs 3 through 5 of the article,* a thumbnail of the image, the URL of a document or image on the Web.

C *Or ". . . sign the enclosed copy of this letter and return it to me."*

D Provide contact information, such as name, address, email address, phone number, fax number.

Tip: If you contact an author or publisher by mail, include a self-addressed, stamped envelope. It will save the author or publisher the cost of responding by mail, indicates that you are serious, and, perhaps most important, shows good manners.

14e

How can I avoid plagiarism?

Because plagiarized material will often differ in style, tone, and word choice from the rest of your document, your readers are likely to notice these differences and wonder whether you've plagiarized the material—or, if not, why you've written a document that's so difficult to read. If your readers react negatively, it's unlikely that your document will be successful.

You can avoid plagiarism by

- quoting, paraphrasing, and summarizing accurately and appropriately
- distinguishing between your ideas and ideas in your sources
- identifying sources in your document

Quote, Paraphrase, and Summarize Accurately and Appropriately

Unintentional plagiarism occurs most often when a writer takes poor notes and then uses the information from the note in a document. Notes might contain direct quotations that are not surrounded with quotation marks, paraphrases that differ in only minor ways from the original passage, and summaries that contain original passages from a source. Taking careful notes is the first—and arguably the most important—step in avoiding unintentional plagiarism. For guidance on taking careful notes, see Chapter 10.

Unintentional plagiarism can also occur during drafting. As you draft, keep in mind the following:

- Place quotation marks around any direct quotations, use ellipses and brackets appropriately (see p. 133), and identify the source and the page number (if any) of the quotation.
- Make sure paraphrases differ significantly in word choice and sentence structure from the passage being paraphrased, and identify the source and page number from which you took the paraphrase.
- Make sure summaries are not just a series of passages or close paraphrases copied from the source.
- Look for notes that differ from your usual style of writing. More often than not, if a note doesn't sound like your own writing, it isn't.

IV Writing Your Document

Distinguish between Your Ideas and Ideas in Your Sources

Failing to distinguish between your ideas and ideas drawn from your sources can lead readers to think other writers' ideas are yours. Examine how featured writer Maria Sanchez-Traynor might have failed to distinguish her ideas from those of Heather Moffie, a teacher Maria interviewed for an article about the Intensive English Program at Colorado State University.

Failing to Credit Ideas to a Source:

Moffie has turned to different resources, including texts and other teachers, to help her understand what may be difficult for students. It is helpful to learn a different language at the same time as teaching one in order to understand what students are going through.

Because the second sentence fails to identify Heather Moffie as the person who told Maria about the advantages of learning a foreign language while teaching students English, the passage implies that the idea is Maria's rather than Heather's.

In contrast, Maria actually included the following passage in her article.

Giving Credit to the Source:

Moffie says she has turned to different resources, including texts and other teachers, to help her understand what may be difficult for her students. She also says that when she learns a different language at the same time as she teaches one, it helps her understand what her students are going through—or, as she puts it, "what it's like to be a learner."

To distinguish between your ideas and those obtained through your sources, use signal phrases—phrases that alert your readers to the source of the ideas or information you are using. As you take notes and draft your document, use the name of an author or the title of the source you're drawing from each time you introduce ideas from a source.

Examples of Signal Phrases:

According to Scott McPherson . . .
Jill Bedard writes . . .
Tom Huckin reports . . .
Kate Kiefer observes . . .
Bob Phelps suggests . . .
In the words of Chris Napolitano . . .
As Ellen Page tells it . . .
Reid Vincent indicates . . .
Jessica Richards calls our attention to . . .

You can learn more about using signal phrases to attribute quotations, paraphrases, and summaries in Chapter 13.

Identify Sources in Your Document

Writers sometimes neglect to identify the sources from which they have drawn their information. You should include a complete citation for each source you refer to in your document. The citation should appear in the text of the document (as an in-text citation, footnote, or endnote) or in a works cited list, references list, or bibliography.

In the following MLA-style examples, the writer includes parenthetical citations that refer readers to a list of works cited at the end of the document. Note that MLA style allows for a combination of signal phrases and parenthetical information to refer to sources.

> Vincent Page argues, "We must explore emerging energy technologies before we reach a peak oil crisis" (322).

> "We must explore emerging energy technologies before we reach a peak oil crisis" (Page 322).

MLA-style in-text citations include the author's name and exact page reference.

If you are using MLA format, be sure to cite page or paragraph numbers for paraphrased and summarized information as well as for direct quotations. The following paraphrase of Vincent Page's comments about energy needs includes the page number of the original passage in parentheses.

> Vincent Page argues that we need to investigate new energy technologies now, instead of while we are facing a critical oil shortage (22).

To learn more about identifying sources in your document, see pp. 178–179 in Chapter 13. To learn how to document sources using the MLA, APA, *Chicago*, and CSE documentation systems, see Chapters 17 to 21.

14f

How can I avoid plagiarism during group work?

Peer review and other collaborative activities raise important questions about plagiarism:

- If another writer suggests changes to your document and you subsequently incorporate them into your document, are you plagiarizing?
- What if those suggestions significantly change your document?
- If you work with a group of writers on a project, do you need to identify the parts that each of you wrote?
- Is it ethical to list yourself as a coauthor if another writer does most of the work on a collaborative writing project?

The answers to these questions will vary from situation to situation. In general, it's appropriate to use comments from reviewers in your document without citing them. If a reviewer's comments are particularly helpful, acknowledge his or her contributions in your document; writers often thank reviewers in a footnote or endnote or in an acknowledgments section. It is usually appropriate to list coauthors on a collaboratively written document without individually identifying the text that was written by each coauthor, although some instructors ask that individual contributions be noted in the document or on a cover page.

If you are uncertain about what is appropriate, ask your instructor.

> **QUICK REFERENCE**

Avoiding Plagiarism

✔ Understand plagiarism.   (p. 189)

✔ Understand research ethics.   (p. 189)

✔ Understand the concept of common knowledge.   (p. 190)

✔ Understand the concept of fair use and, if necessary, seek permission to use sources.   (p. 190)

✔ Check your quotations, paraphrases, and summaries to ensure that they are accurate and appropriate.   (p. 192)

✔ Distinguish your ideas from those of your sources.   (p. 193)

✔ Make sure you've acknowledged your sources in your text and in a works-cited list, references list, or bibliography.   (p. 194)

✔ Understand how to avoid plagiarism during group work and collaborative projects.   (p. 194)

IV Writing Your Document

15

Revising and Editing

> **Key Questions**

When writers revise and edit, they evaluate the effectiveness of their drafts and, if necessary, work to improve them. Although the two processes are related, they focus on different aspects of a document. To revise is to assess how well a document responds to a specific writing situation, makes an argument, presents its points, and uses evidence. To edit is to evaluate and improve the expression—at the sentence and word levels—of the argument, ideas, and information in the document.

15a

What should I focus on as I revise my document?

Revising involves rethinking and re-envisioning your document. It focuses on such big-picture issues as whether the document you've drafted is appropriate for your writing situation, whether your argument is sound and well supported, and whether you've organized and presented your arguments, ideas, and information clearly and effectively.

REVISING WITH A FOCUS

Step 1	Consider your writing situation
Step 2	Consider your argument and ideas
Step 3	Consider your use and integration of source information
Step 4	Consider the structure and organization of your document

Step 1: Consider Your Writing Situation

As you revise, ask whether your document helps you achieve your purposes.

WHAT'S MY PURPOSE?

Review your purpose in your research log. If your assignment directed you to inform readers about a particular subject, see whether you've provided appropriate information, whether you've given enough information, and whether that information is presented clearly. If your purpose is to convince readers in some way, ask whether you have presented your argument clearly and effectively.

Review as well your readers' needs, interests, values, beliefs, and knowledge of the issue. It's useful during revision to imagine how your readers will react to your document by asking questions such as these:

- Will my readers trust what I have to say? How can I establish my credibility?

- Will my readers have other ideas about how to address this issue? How can I convince them that they should believe what I say?

- Will my readers find my evidence appropriate and accurate? Is my selection of evidence consistent with their values and beliefs?

Finally, identify your requirements, limitations, and opportunities. Ask yourself whether you've met the specific requirements of the assignment, such as length and number of sources. Evaluate your efforts to work around limitations, such as lack of access to information. Think about whether you've taken full advantage of your opportunities and any new ones that have come your way.

Step 2: Consider Your Argument and Ideas

As you revise, ask how well you are conveying your argument and ideas to your readers. First, check the clarity of your thesis statement. Is it phrased in a way that is compatible with the needs and interests of your readers? Second, ask whether the argument and ideas in your document help your readers understand and accept your thesis statement. As you make this assessment, keep in mind your roles—such as advocate, reporter, interpreter, or inquirer (see p. 33):

- If you are writing an argument, ask whether you have made a clear overall point, given supporting points, and provided evidence for your points.
- If you are writing to inform, ensure that the level of detail you've provided is consistent with your readers' knowledge of the issue. If necessary, clearly define key concepts and ideas.
- If you are writing to interpret or analyze, review the clarity and accuracy of your interpretations and check that you've provided appropriate and sufficient background information to help your readers follow your reasoning.
- If you are writing to inquire, ask whether you've clearly explained the issue and your reasons for investigating it. Also reflect on whether you have clearly and accurately conveyed what you learned about the issue.

Step 3: Consider Your Use and Integration of Source Information

Think about how you've used source information in your document. First, review the amount of support you've provided for your points and the appropriateness of that support for your purpose and readers. Then, if you are arguing about an issue, determine whether you've identified and addressed reasonable opposing viewpoints.

It's also important that you integrate your sources effectively into your document and acknowledge them according to the documentation system you are following. Ensure that you have cited all your sources and that you've clearly distinguished between your ideas and those of other writers. Review your works cited or reference list for completeness and accuracy. Remember that improper documentation can reduce your document's effectiveness and your credibility.

Step 4: Consider the Structure and Organization of Your Document

Your readers should be able to locate information and ideas easily. As you read your introduction, ask whether it clearly and concisely conveys your main point and whether it helps your readers anticipate the structure and organization of your document. Reflect on the appropriateness of your organizing pattern (see p. 145) for your purpose and readers. If you've used headings and subheadings, evaluate their effectiveness.

IV Writing Your Document

TUTORIAL

How do I review my use of source information as I revise and edit?

1 Identify passages where you are using ideas or information from a source. Scan your document looking for:

- direct quotations
- paraphrases
- summaries
- information from field sources
- images
- ideas that are not common knowledge (see p. 190)

2 Check to be sure that the sources of ideas and information are acknowledged and that the citation information (page numbers, author, date, etc.) satisfies the requirements of your documentation system. In this example, the writer is using APA style.

> The tendency to develop an eating disorder, such as anorexia or bulimia, is a third possible effect. Although young women may develop eating disorders for a variety of reasons, Graham (1999) noted, "[D]isordered eating is high among female athletes competing in sports where leanness and/or a specific weight are considered important for either performance or appearance" (p. 74). Being slim and trim may be the goal of many adolescent-female athletes, but when they seek that goal by means of an eating disorder, they hinder their athletic performance. A calorie deficit actually decreases immune function, reduces aerobic capacity, decreases msucle mass and strength, and causes low energy and fatigue (Graham, 1999, p. 75).

3 Check to be sure that the source is listed in the works cited list, bibliography, or references list.

Girls and steroids. (1998). *Teacher Magazine 9*(5), 11. Retrieved September 26, 2004, from Academic Search Premier.

Gorman, C. (1998, August 10). Girls on steriods. *Time 152*(6), 93. Retrieved September 26, 2004, from Academic Search Premier.

Graham, J. (1999). *The Athletic Woman's Sourcebook*. New York: Avon Books.

IV Writing Your Document

Review another example and work on reviewing and revising your in-text and end-of-text references to sources at **bedfordresearcher.com**. Click on Tutorials.

Make sure your document is easy to read. Check for effective paragraphing and paragraph structure. If you have a number of small paragraphs, you might combine paragraphs with similar ideas. If you have a number of long paragraphs, break them up and add transitions. Finally, ask whether your conclusion leaves your readers with something to think about. The most effective conclusions typically provide more than a document summary.

15b

What strategies should I use to revise?

As you revise, you can draw on strategies for reviewing and improving your document. These strategies range from saving multiple drafts of your document to assessing its argument and organization to obtaining feedback from others.

STRATEGIES FOR REVISING
Step 1   Save multiple drafts
Step 2   Identify and challenge your argument, ideas, and evidence
Step 3   Scan, outline, and map your document
Step 4   Ask for feedback

● Step 1: Save Multiple Drafts

You might not be happy with every revision you make. To avoid wishing that you hadn't made extensive revisions to a draft of your document, save a new copy of your draft before every major revising session. Name your drafts by number—as in Draft1.doc, Draft2.doc, and so on—or by date, as in Draft-April6.doc and Draft-April10.doc. Or come up with a naming system that works for you. What's important is that you save multiple versions of your drafts in case you don't like the changes you've made.

● Step 2: Identify and Challenge Your Argument, Ideas, and Evidence

As you use the following strategies, keep track of your ideas for revision by writing comments on sticky notes or in the margins of print documents, by using the Comment tool in word processing documents, or by creating a to-do list in your research log.

Strategies for Identifying Your Argument, Ideas, and Evidence   As you revise, highlight your thesis statement, main points, and evidence. If you are working with a printed document, use a highlighter, colored pens or pencils, or sticky notes. If you are working with your document in a word processing program, use the Highlighting tools to mark the text. You might use different colors to highlight your thesis, main points, and evidence. If you are focusing solely on the evidence in your document, use different colors to highlight evidence from different sources (to help you check whether you are relying too heavily on one or two sources) or to differentiate the type of evidence you are using (such as quotations, paraphrases, summaries, and numerical data).

> Learn how to use the Highlighting and Commenting tools in your word processor at **bedfordresearcher** **.com**. Click on Guides > How to Use Your Word Processor.

Strategies for Challenging Your Argument, Ideas, and Evidence   It's easy to agree with an argument that you've developed. Challenge your arguments, ideas, and evidence by using one of the following strategies. Keep track of your challenges by using the Comment tool in your word processor.

- **Put Yourself in Place of Your Readers.**   As you read, pretend that you are one of your readers. Try to imagine a single reader—or, if you're ambitious, a group of readers. Ask questions they might ask. Imagine concerns they might bring to their reading of your document. A reader interested in solving a problem might ask, for example, whether a proposed solution is cost effective, more appropriate than alternative solutions, or has unacceptable side effects. As you revise, take these questions and concerns into account.

- **Play Devil's Advocate.**   A devil's advocate raises reasonable objections to ideas and arguments. As you review your document, identify your key claims and pose reasonable objections to them. Make note of these potential objections and take them into account as you revise.

- **Play the "So What?" Game.**   As you read your document, ask why readers would care about what you are saying. By asking "so what" questions, you can gain a better understanding of what your readers are likely to care about and how they might respond to your arguments and ideas. Make note of your responses to these questions and consider them as you revise.

Step 3: Scan, Outline, and Map Your Document

Use the following strategies to review the structure and organization of your document:

- **Scan Headings and Subheadings.**   If you have used headings and subheadings, they can help you track the overall flow of your argument and ideas. Ask whether the organization they reveal is appropriate for your writing situation and your role as a writer.

- **Scan the First Sentence of Each Paragraph.**   A quick reading of the first sentence in each paragraph can reveal points at which your argument shifts. As you note these shifts, think about whether they are appropriate and effective.

IV Writing Your Document

- **Outline Your Document.** Create a topical or sentence outline of your document (see p. 153) to assess its structure and organization. This strategy, sometimes called a reverse outline, helps you identify the sequence of your points and amount of space you've devoted to each aspect of your document. If you are viewing your document in a word processor, use the Styles tool to assign levels to headings in your document and then view it in outline view.

- **Map Your Document.** On paper or in a graphics program, draw a map of your document. Like an outline, a map can help you identify the organization of your points and the amount of evidence you've used to support them.

As you review the organization and structure of your document, reflect on whether it is appropriate given your purpose, readers, argument, and available information.

Step 4: Ask for Feedback

After spending long hours on a project, you may find it difficult to identify problems your readers might have with your draft. You might read the same paragraph eight times, failing to notice that the evidence you are using to support a point actually contradicts it. Or you might not notice that your document's organization could confuse your readers. You can ask for feedback on your draft from a friend, relative, colleague, or writing center tutor. It's generally a good idea to ask for help from someone who will be frank as well as supportive and to be specific about the kinds of comments you're looking for. Hearing "it's just fine" from a reviewer will not help you to revise.

> **QUICK REFERENCE**

Revising

✔ **Review your research writing situation.** Ask whether your document helps you achieve your purposes, addresses your readers' needs and interests, meets your requirements, effectively works around limitations, and takes advantage of opportunities. (p. 197)

✔ **Evaluate your argument and ideas.** Ask whether your document provides a clear and appropriate thesis statement and whether your argument and ideas support your thesis statement and are consistent with your roles. (p. 198)

✔ **Assess your use and integration of source information.** Ask whether you have offered adequate support for your points, considered reasonable opposing viewpoints, integrated and acknowledged your sources, and distinguished between your work and that of other writers. (p. 198)

✔ **Examine the structure and organization of your document.** Ask whether the introduction is clear and concise, clearly conveys your main point, and helps your readers anticipate the structure of your document. Also think about

↓

> **QUICK REFERENCE** (continued)
>
> whether the organizational structure is easy to follow, paragraphs are easy to read, and transitions are effective. Ask whether the conclusion provides more than a summary of the document.   (p. 198)
>
> ✔ **Use effective revision strategies.** Create multiple drafts to preserve earlier work; review your document to assess its argument and organization; get feedback from other writers.   (p. 200)

15c

What should I focus on as I edit my document?

Editing involves assessing the effectiveness, accuracy, and appropriateness of the words and sentences in a document. Editing focuses on issues such as the accurate and concise expression of ideas and information; the balance between consistency and variety; use of nonsexist language; appropriate tone and style; and the proper use of punctuation, spelling, and grammar.

Focus on Accuracy

You'll risk damaging your credibility if you provide inaccurate information in your document. To reduce this risk, do the following:

- **Check Your Facts and Figures.**   Your readers might think you're deliberately misleading them if you fail to provide accurate information. As you edit, return to your original sources or your notes to check any facts and figures.
- **Check Every Quotation.**   Return to your original sources or consult your notes to ensure that you have quoted each source exactly. Make sure that you have noted any changes to a quotation with an ellipsis or brackets, and make sure that those changes haven't altered the original meaning of the passage.
- **Check the Spelling of Every Name.**   Don't rely on electronic spelling checkers, which provide the correct spelling for only the most common or prominent names.

Focus on Economy

Editing for economy involves reducing the number of words needed to express an idea or convey information to your readers. The following techniques are often helpful:

- **Remove Unnecessary Modifiers.**   Unnecessary modifiers are words that provide little or no additional information to a reader, such as *fine, many, somewhat, great, quite, sort of, lots, really,* and *very.*

- **Remove Unnecessary Introductory Phrases such as *there are* and *it is*.**   Sentences beginning with *there are* and similar phrases allow you to emphasize a point, as in "There are a number of reasons to use *there are* at the beginning of a sentence." However, you can often recast such sentences more concisely by simply stating the point, as in "You can use *there are* at the beginning of a sentence for several reasons." Keep your eye out for phrases such as *there are, there is, these have, these are, here are, here is, it has been reported that, it has been said that,* and so on.

- **Eliminate Stock Phrases.**   Search your document for phrases that you can replace with single words, such as the following:

Stock Phrase	Alternative
at that point in time	then
at this point in time	now
at the present time	now
by means of	by
in order to	to
in the event that	if

Editing for economy generally makes it easier for your readers to understand your meaning. However, you should use care when you edit for economy; your readers still need to understand the point you are trying to make.

Focus on Consistency

Editing your project document for consistency helps you present information in a uniform way. Use the following techniques to edit for consistency:

- **Treat Concepts Consistently.**   Review your document for consistent treatment of concepts, information, ideas, definitions, and anecdotes.

- **Use Numbers Consistently.**   Check the documentation system you are using for its guidelines on the treatment of numbers. You might find that you should spell out the numbers zero through ten and use Arabic numerals for numbers larger than ten.

- **Treat Your Sources Consistently.**   Avoid referring to some sources using first names and to others using honorifics, such as *Dr., Mr.,* or *Ms.* Also check that you have cited your sources appropriately for the documentation style you are using, such as MLA or APA. Review each reference for consistent presentation of names, page numbers, and publication dates.

- **Format Your Document Consistently.**   Avoid any inconsistencies in your use of fonts, headings and subheadings, and tables and figures.

Focus on Avoiding Sexist Language

As you draft your document, avoid using sexist language, language that stereotypes men or women. For instance, although it is technically correct to use male pronouns, such as *he, him,* and *his* when the gender of a noun is unspecified, many readers find this usage unacceptable. The simplest way to eliminate sexist language is to revise your sentences so that generic references, such as *the writer,* are plural, such as *writers,* as in the following example:

Sexist Language:

Today, the research writer finds at least half of his source information on the Web.

Nonsexist Language:

Today, research writers find at least half of their source information on the Web.

Focus on Tone and Style

Your readers will judge you—and what you have to say—not only on what you say but on how you say it. Use the following techniques as you edit for tone and style:

- **Use Appropriate Words.**   Make sure that your language is suitable for your audience. If you are writing a technical report, your language will be much different than if you are writing a feature article for a magazine.
- **Rewrite Complex Sentences.**   A sentence can be grammatically correct yet incomprehensible. A sentence that is too complex will make your readers work overtime to figure out what it means.
- **Vary Your Sentence Length and Structure.**   A steady stream of sentences written in exactly the same way will have the same effect as a lecture delivered in a monotone. Best bet: add some variety to the length and structure of your sentences.

Focus on Spelling, Grammar, and Punctuation

Poor spelling doesn't necessarily affect your ability to get your point across— in most cases readers will understand even the most atrociously spelled document—but it does affect what your readers think of you. Ignore enough spelling errors in your document and you'll erode their confidence in your ability to present information or make an argument. The same goes for grammar and punctuation. If you haven't made sure that subjects and verbs agree and that sentences all end with the appropriate punctuation, a reader might not trust that you have presented your facts correctly.

IV Writing Your Document

15d

What strategies should I use to edit?

Thorough editing involves making several passes through your document to ensure that you've addressed accuracy, economy, and consistency; sexist language; tone and style; and spelling, grammar, and punctuation. Editing strategies include reading, searching, and marking your text; using word processing tools to check spelling and grammar; and obtaining feedback on your document.

Before you begin to edit, remember that editing focuses on the words and sentences in your document, not on its overall structure or ideas. If you're uncertain about whether you've organized your document as effectively as possible or whether you've provided enough support for your argument, deal with those issues first. In the same way that you wouldn't start painting a house until you've finished building the walls, hold off on editing until you're confident that you're finished revising.

STRATEGIES FOR EDITING

Step 1	Read your document carefully
Step 2	Mark and search your document
Step 3	Use spelling and grammar tools
Step 4	Ask for feedback

Step 1: Read Your Document Carefully

As you've worked on your document, you've become quite familiar with it. As a result, it can be easy to read what you meant to write instead of what you actually wrote. Use the following strategies to read carefully:

- **Set Your Document Aside before You Edit.**   If time permits, allow a day or two to pass before you begin editing your document. Taking time off between revising and editing can help you see your writing with new eyes.

- **Pause between Sentences for a Quick Check.**   Avoid getting caught up in the flow of your document—where the meaning takes precedence over the structure and expression of your sentences—by stopping after each sentence. Slowing down can help you identify problems with your text.

- **Read Aloud.**   Reading your document aloud can help you find problems that might not be apparent when it's read silently.

- **Read in Reverse Order.**   To check for problems with individual sentences, start at the end of your document and read the last sentence first, then work backward through the document. To check for problems at the word level, read each word starting with the last one in the document. Disrupting the normal flow of your document can alert you to problems that might not stand out when it is read normally.

Step 2: Mark and Search Your Document

Use the following marking and searching strategies to edit for accuracy, consistency, and use of sexist language.

Mark Your Document.   As you read, use a highlighting pen or the Highlighting tool in your word processor to mark errors or information that should be double-checked. Consider using different colors to highlight specific types of problems, such as sexist language or inconsistent use of formal titles.

Use the Find and Replace Tools.   Use your word processor to edit concepts, names, numbers, and titles for consistency and accuracy. Once you've identified a word or phrase that you'd like to check or change, you can search for it throughout your document. If you are referring to sources using a parenthetical style, such as MLA or APA, use the Find tool to search for an opening paren-thesis. If you discover that you've consistently misspelled a word or name, use the Replace tool to correct it throughout your document.

Use the Split Window Tool.   Some word processors allow you to split your window so that you can view different parts of your document at the same time. Use this tool to ensure that you are referring to a concept in the same way throughout your document or to check for consistent uses of fonts, headings, subhead-ings, illustrations, and tables.

> Learn how to use the Highlighting, Search and Replace, and Split Window tools in your word processor at **bedfordresearcher.com**. Click on Guides > How to Use Your Word Processor.

Step 3: Use Spelling and Grammar Tools

Most word processors provide tools to check spelling, grammar, punctuation, and style. Used with an awareness of their limitations, these tools can significantly re-duce the effort required to edit a document. Spelling checkers have two primary limitations. First, they can't identify words that are spelled correctly but misused — such as *to/two/too, their/they're/there,* and *advice/advise.* Second, spelling checkers are ineffective when they run into a word they don't recognize, such as proper names, technical and scientific terms, and unusual words. To compound this prob-lem, spelling checkers often suggest replacement words. If you take the advice, you'll end up with a paper full of incorrect words and misspelled names.

The main limitation of grammar, punctuation, and style checkers is inac-curate advice. Although much of the advice they offer is sound, a significant proportion is not. If you are confident about your knowledge of grammar, punc-tuation, and style, you can use the grammar and style-checking tools in your word processor to identify potential problem areas in your document. You'll find that these tools can point out problems you might have overlooked, such as a subject-verb disagreement that occurred when you revised a sentence. However, if you don't have a strong knowledge of grammar, punc-tuation, and style, you can easily be misled by inaccu-rate advice.

> Learn how to use the spelling, grammar, and style tools in your word pro-cessor at **bedfordresearcher.com**. Click on Guides > How to Use Your Word Processor.

If you have any doubts about advice from your spelling checker, consult an up-to-date dictionary. If you have concerns about the suggestions you receive from your grammar, punctuation, and style checker, consult a good handbook.

IV Writing Your Document

Step 4: Ask for Feedback

One of the biggest challenges writers face is reading a draft of their own work as a reader rather than as the writer. Because you know what you're trying to say, you'll find it easy to understand your draft. And because you've read and reread your document so many times, you're likely to overlook errors in spelling, punctuation, and grammar. After you've edited your document, ask a friend, relative, or classmate to proofread it and to make note of any problems.

> **QUICK REFERENCE**
>
> *Editing*
> ✔ **Ensure your document is accurate.** Check facts and figures, quotations, and spelling of names. (p. 203)
> ✔ **Strive for economy.** Remove unnecessary modifiers (*very, really, somewhat*), eliminate unnecessary introductory phrases (*there are, it is*), and avoid use of stock phrases (*at the present time, in order to*). (p. 203)
> ✔ **Ensure that your document is consistent.** Use concepts, numbers, and source information consistently. Check your document for consistent use of formatting and design. (p. 204)
> ✔ **Remove sexist language from your document.** (p. 204)
> ✔ **Use appropriate tone and style.** Use appropriate words, rewrite overly complex sentences, and vary sentence length and structure. (p. 205)
> ✔ **Check for correct spelling, grammar, and punctuation.** Use your word processor's spelling, grammar, punctuation, and style tools; consult a handbook and dictionary; and ask someone to proofread your draft. (p. 205)

16

Designing

> Key Questions

The growing sophistication of word processing and Web editing programs along with access to high-quality color printers have given writers a great deal of control over the design of their documents. Your design decisions, from choosing fonts to formatting tables to selecting appropriate illustrations, will play a critical role in how your readers understand and react to your document. Those decisions will be shaped by your understanding of design principles and elements as well as the conventions of typical research documents.

16a

How can I use design effectively?

Although the most important factor in the success of your writing project is the ability to express your ideas and arguments clearly, you should also think about how the design of your document can help you achieve your purpose and affect your readers.

● Understand Design Principles

Before you begin formatting text and inserting illustrations, consider how the document design principles of *balance, emphasis, placement, repetition,* and *consistency* can help you accomplish your goals as a writer. Keep the following design principles in mind:

Balance   the vertical and horizontal alignment of elements on your pages (see Figure 16.1). Symmetrical designs create a sense of rest and stability and tend to lead the reader's eye to focus on a particular part of a document. In contrast, asymmetrical—or unbalanced—designs suggest movement and guide readers' eyes across the page.

Emphasis   the placement and formatting of elements, such as headings and subheadings, so they catch your readers' attention. You can emphasize an element in a document by using a color or font that distinguishes it from other elements, by placing a border around it and adding a shaded background, or by using an illustration, such as a photograph, drawing, or graph (see p. 220).

Placement   the location of elements on your pages. Placing elements next to or near each other suggests that they are related. Illustrations, for example, are usually placed near the passages in which they are mentioned.

Repetition   the use of elements, such as headers and footers, navigation menus, and page numbers, across the pages in your document. As readers move

FIGURE 16.1   Symmetrical (left) and Asymmetrical (right) Layouts

from page to page, they tend to expect navigation elements, such as page numbers, to appear in the same place. In addition, repeated elements, such as a logo or Web navigation menu, help establish a sense of identity across the pages in your document.

Consistency   the extent to which you format and place text and illustrations in the same way throughout your document. Treating each design element—such as illustrations, headings, and footnotes—consistently will help your readers recognize the different roles played by the elements in your document and, by extension, help them locate the information they seek. A consistent design can also convey a sense of competence and professionalism to your readers, increasing their confidence in the quality and credibility of your document.

Also keep two other principles in mind: moderation and simplicity. An overly complex design can work against the effectiveness of a document by obscuring important ideas and information. Using design elements moderately to create simple yet effective designs is the best approach.

Design for a Purpose

A well-designed document presents your arguments, ideas, and information in a manner that helps you accomplish your purposes. Your purposes, as a result, should inform your design decisions.

? **WHAT'S MY PURPOSE?**

In your research log, review your purpose to determine if you might use design to achieve the following goals:

- **Setting a Tone.** One of the most powerful tools writers have for accomplishing their purpose is establishing an emotional context for their readers. Drawing on the design principles of balance and placement, you can set a tone by using a particular color scheme, such as bright, cheerful hues, or by selecting photographs or drawings with a strong emotional impact.

- **Helping Readers Understand a Point.** You might use the design principles of emphasis and placement to introduce and help readers understand your points. Headings or pull quotes can call your readers' attention to important ideas and information. To introduce a main point, you might use a contrasting font or color to signal the importance of the information. To highlight a definition or example, you might use borders or place the passage in a pull quote. You can also help readers understand a point by using illustrations.

- **Convincing Readers to Accept a Point.** The key to convincing readers is providing them with appropriate, relevant evidence. Drawing on the principles of emphasis and placement, you can use illustrations, marginal glosses, pull quotes, and bulleted lists to call attention to that evidence.

- **Clarifying Complex Concepts.** Sometimes a picture really is worth a thousand words. Rather than attempting to explain a complex concept using text alone, use

↓

WHAT'S MY PURPOSE? (continued)

an illustration. A well-chosen, well-placed photograph, flow chart, diagram, or table can define a complex concept such as photosynthesis in far less space, and in many cases far more effectively, than a long passage of text. You can also clarify the key elements of a complex concept with bulleted and numbered lists.

● Design for Your Readers

A well-designed document helps readers understand the organization of the document, locate information and ideas, and recognize the function of parts of the document. It is also easy on your readers' eyes: Readers working with a well-designed document will not have to strain to read the text or discern illustrations. Use document design to do the following:

Help Readers Understand the Organization of a Document.   You can use headings and subheadings to signal the content of each part of the document. If you do, keep in mind the design principles of emphasis and consistency: Format your headings in a consistent manner that helps them stand out from other parts of the document (see Figure 16.2).

Help Readers Locate Information and Ideas.   Many longer print documents use tables of contents and indexes to help readers locate information and ideas.

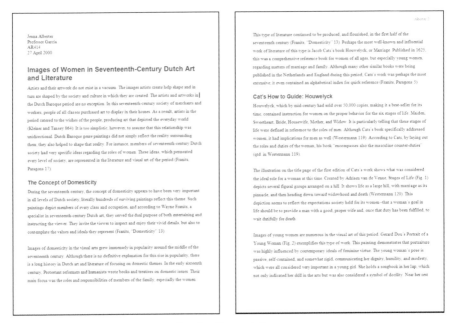

FIGURE 16.2   Headings and Subheadings in a Research Essay
Use of a contrasting font and color helps readers understand the document's organization.

Web sites typically provide a mix of menus and navigation headers and footers to help readers move around the site. When these navigation aids are integrated into pages, they are often distinguished from the surrounding text by the use of bordered or shaded boxes or through the use of contrasting fonts.

Help Readers Recognize the Function of Parts of a Document.   If you include passages that differ from the main text of your document, such as sidebars and "For More Information" sections, help readers to understand their function by designing them to stand out visually. Using emphasis, for example, you might format a sidebar in an article with a shaded or colored box. Similarly, you might format a list of related readings or Web links in a contrasting font or color.

16b

What design elements can I use?

Understanding the range of design elements at your disposal will enable you to decide which of these options to use as you design your document. These elements include fonts, line spacing, and alignment; page layout strategies; navigation aids; color, shading, borders, and rules; and illustrations.

Use Fonts, Line Spacing, and Alignment

Font, line spacing, and alignment choices are the most common design decisions made by writers. They are also among the most important, since poor choices can make a document difficult to read.

Fonts   Fonts are a complete set of type of a particular size and typeface, such as 12-point Times New Roman or 12-point Helvetica. Important concepts related to fonts are illustrated below.

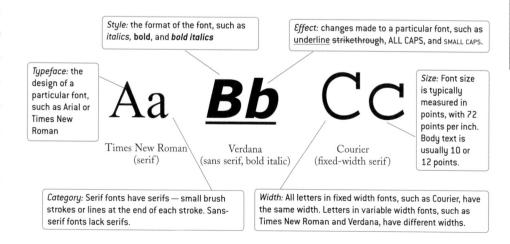

Style: the format of the font, such as *italics*, **bold**, and ***bold italics***

Effect: changes made to a particular font, such as underline ~~strikethrough~~, ALL CAPS, and SMALL CAPS.

Typeface: the design of a particular font, such as Arial or Times New Roman

Times New Roman (serif)

Verdana (sans serif, bold italic)

Courier (fixed-width serif)

Size: Font size is typically measured in points, with 72 points per inch. Body text is usually 10 or 12 points.

Category: Serif fonts have serifs — small brush strokes or lines at the end of each stroke. Sans-serif fonts lack serifs.

Width: All letters in fixed width fonts, such as Courier, have the same width. Letters in variable width fonts, such as Times New Roman and Verdana, have different widths.

IV Writing Your Document

GUIDELINES FOR FONTS

To increase the readability of your document, keep the following guidelines in mind:

✔ **Select fonts that are easy to read.** The reason certain fonts are used as the default in word processors, such as Microsoft Word, is that they are easy to read. Times New Roman, for instance, is much easier to read than KEYPUNCH.

✔ **Select fonts that complement each other.** A serif body font, such as Times New Roman, Century Schoolbook, or Garamond, works well with a sans-serif heading font, such as Arial, Helvetica, or Lucida Sans. If you prefer to use a sans-serif font for body text, try using a serif font for headings.

✔ **Avoid using too many fonts, styles, and effects.** Don't go overboard with fonts. Generally, use no more than four different fonts in a document. Choosing typefaces, styles, and effects at random or because they are interesting can make a document difficult to read or confuse readers about the purpose or function of some passages of text.

Line Spacing   Line spacing refers to the amount of space between lines of text. Spacing can be set precisely, using points (there are 72 points per vertical inch of text), or it can be set relatively, using lines (single-spacing, double-spacing, triple-spacing, and so on). Notice the difference between the following sentences, which have different line spacing:

These are lines of text in 10-point Garamond separated by 12 points of line spacing.

These are lines of text in 10-point Garamond separated by 18 points of line spacing.

When text is crammed together vertically, it is difficult both to read and to insert written comments. Keep this in mind if you are creating a document such as an essay on which someone else might write comments.

Alignment   Alignment refers to the placement of text and illustrations (such as photos and drawings) on the page. You can select four types of alignment: left, right, centered, and justified. Left-aligned text, which has a straight left margin and a "ragged right" margin, is typically the easiest to read. In contrast, justified text (text aligned on both the right and left) offers an attractive, finished look to a document, and can be effective in documents that use columns. Be aware,

Learn more about formatting fonts, line spacing, and alignment at **bedfordresearcher.com**. Click on Guides > How to Use Your Word Processor or How to Write for the Web.

however, that justified text can slow down the reader because it can produce irregular spacing between words (called "rivers"). In addition, it often results in hyphenated words, which can also slow the reading process. Finally, because word processing software does not always hyphenate words properly, readers might find themselves puzzling over hyphens in unexpected places.

Use Page Layout Strategies

Page layout is the placement of text, illustrations, and other objects on a page or screen. Successful page layout draws on a number of design elements, including white space, margins, columns, headers and footers, page numbers, headings, lists, captions, marginal glosses and pull quotes, and sidebars.

White Space   White space—literally, empty space—frames and separates elements on a page. You place more white space, for example, above a major heading than below it to show that the heading is related to the text below. In essays, white space plays an additional role: It provides space for instructor comments.

Margins   Margins are the white space between the edge of the page or screen (top, bottom, right, and left) and text or graphics in your document. In most word processors and desktop publishing programs, you can set the margins using menu commands or the ruler.

Columns   Essays are typically formatted in a single column, while newspaper and magazine articles—and, to a growing extent, articles published on the Web—are often formatted in columns. Columns can improve the readability of a document by limiting the physical movement of an eye across the page (see Figure 16.3).

Headers, Footers, and Page Numbers   Headers, footers, and page numbers— text that appears at the top or bottom of the page, set apart from the main text— serve several functions in print and digital documents. They help readers find their way through a document; they can provide information such as the title of the document, its publication date, and its author; and they can help to frame a page visually (see Figure 16.3).

Headings and Subheadings   Headings and subheadings identify sections and subsections to your readers, allowing them to more easily locate information in your document. They also serve as transitions between sections. Effective headings and subheadings are formatted in a manner that distinguishes among different levels: Bigger, bolder fonts are typically used for headings, and successively smaller fonts are used for subheadings (see Figure 16.2 on p. 212). Headings and subheadings should also be phrased consistently, for example as a set of questions or a series of statements.

Numbered and Bulleted Lists   A numbered or bulleted list displays brief passages of related information using numbers or symbols (usually round "bullets"). The surrounding white space draws the eye to the list, highlighting the information for your readers, while the brief content in each entry can make concepts or processes easier to understand. Use numbered lists when sequence is important—such as when you are asking readers to carry out activities in a certain order or when you are explaining a series of events. Use bulleted lists when the items are of roughly equal importance. For example, in your resumé, your accomplishments can be highlighted in bulleted lists below each job listing. Note the difference in these lists:

Numbered List

How to fly:
1. Watch a bird
2. Be the bird
3. Flap your arms briskly
4. Leave the ground
5. Stay off the ground

Bulleted List

Accomplishments:
- Increased sales by 17 percent over previous year
- Led development of new marketing plan
- Identified new sales prospects

Captions   Captions describe or explain an illustration, such as a photograph or chart. They are usually placed below the illustration. The first word in a caption should always be capitalized, and punctuation is needed at the end of a caption if it is a complete sentence. A caption should be distinguished from the text of your document by its font. If the body text uses a regular serif type face, for example, a caption might use an italic sans-serif font (see Figure 16.3).

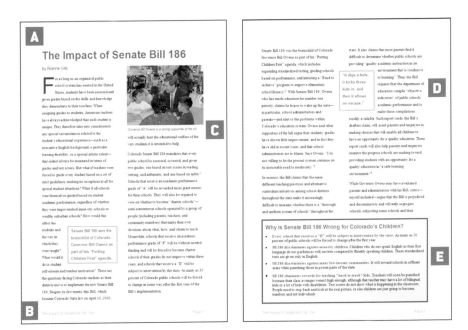

FIGURE 16.3   An Academic Essay Formatted in Two Columns

A Columns limit the movement of the eye across the page, enhance readability, and help frame other elements on the page.

B A footer and page number are given on each page.

C A photo caption set in a font different from the body font.

D A pull quote uses contrasting font, color, and border.

E Sidebar using a border, color background, contrasting font, and color

Marginal Glosses and Pull Quotes   Marginal glosses are brief notes in a margin that explain or expand on text in the body of the document. Authors use them to define an unfamiliar term or concept, to identify sources of information, to comment on a key point, or to refer the reader to related material. Well-designed marginal glosses usually use a font that differs from that used for the body text—often a smaller font in boldface or a contrasting color.

Pull quotes highlight a passage of text—frequently a quotation made by a key figure discussed in the document—by copying it from the main body of the text and surrounding it with a border or white space and often displaying it in a larger font and different color (see Figure 16.3 on p. 216).

You can add pull quotes and marginal glosses to your document in most word processing programs by creating a text box and formatting it so that it appears in the margin or is wrapped by body text.

Sidebars   Sidebars are brief discussions of information related to but not a central part of your document. Sidebars simplify the task of integrating related or supporting information into the body of the article by setting that information off in a clearly defined area. The academic essay illustrated in Figure 16.3 (p. 216) contains a sidebar on the bottom of the second page. Sidebars can be created in most word processing programs by using text boxes and formatting the text box so that body text wraps around it or breaks before and after it. You can use the borders and shading tools in your word processor to distinguish your sidebar from the body text of the article.

Examples: Alternative Page Layouts   Your choices about page layout can affect the readability and attractiveness of your document. Inadequate line spacing, for example, creates the appearance of dense, crowded text—perhaps so crowded that the words on the page will be difficult to make out. Figures 16.4, 16.5, and 16.6, which depict the opening page of an informative article about the Intensive English Program at Colorado State University, illustrate the effects of alternative decisions about page layout.

> Learn more about creating effective page layouts at **bedfordresearcher.com**. Click on Guides > How to Use Your Word Processor or How to Write for the Web.

Use Color, Shading, Borders, and Rules

Color, shading, borders, and rules (lines running horizontally or vertically on a page) are important, but frequently underused, design elements. Writers are starting to give these elements a greater role in their documents because of the growing sophistication of the tools used to format these elements, the ease of distributing digital documents, and the decreasing cost of printing documents in color. In addition to increasing the overall attractiveness of your document, color, shading, borders, and rules can call attention to important information, help readers understand the organization of your document, help readers recognize the function of specific passages of text, and signal transitions between sections.

FIGURE 16.4   Crowded Page Design. Crowded page with little white space is less readable than the examples in Figures 16.5 and 16.6.

A Tight margins contribute to the crowded feeling.

B Line spacing is 11 points, making text difficult to read.

C Body text is fully justified and in one column, causing uneven spacing between words and extremely long lines of text.

D No extra space between paragraphs.

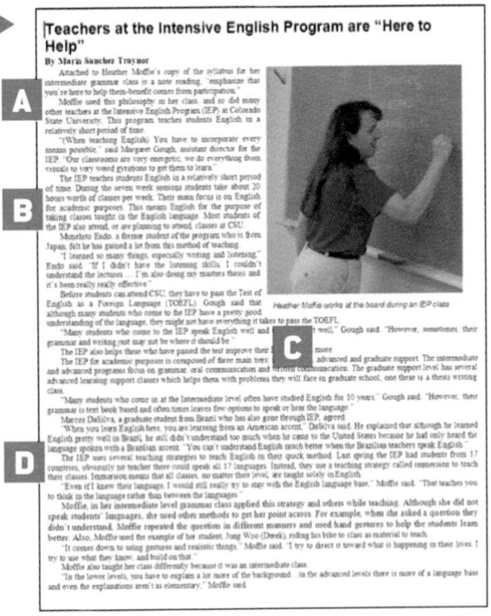

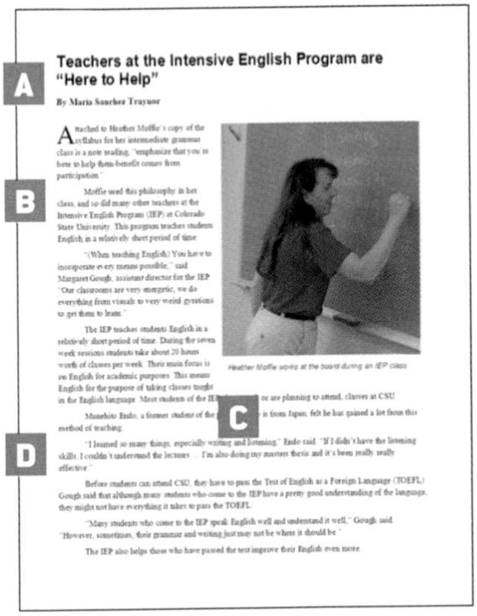

FIGURE 16.5   Open, More Readable Page Design. More white space in layout increases readability.

A Ample margins

B Line spacing is a reader-friendly 15 points.

C Body text is left justified and in a single column.

D Six points of extra space between paragraphs.

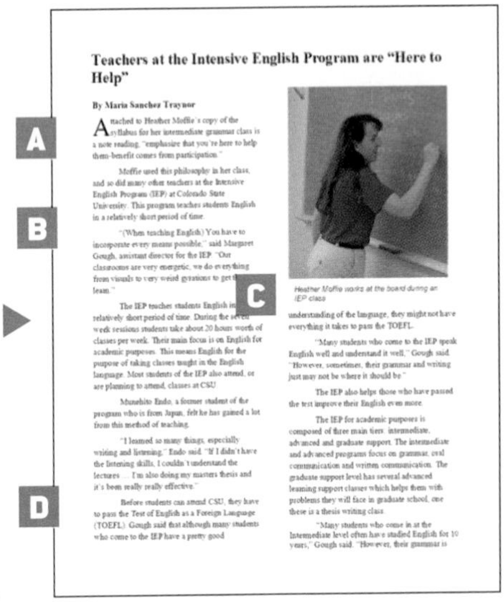

FIGURE 16.6   Open, More Readable Page Design Using Columns. Two-column layout increases the amount of white space on the page.

A Ample margins.

B Line spacing is a reader-friendly 15 points.

C Body text is left justified and in two columns. Photograph is reduced in size to fit the column width.

D Six points of extra space between paragraphs.

IV Writing Your Document

GUIDELINES FOR LAYING OUT PAGES

Consider the following guidelines as you create your page layouts:

- ✔ **Create a common look across your pages.** Giving a similar appearance to the pages in your document will help your readers more easily identify the locations of recurring elements, such as page headers and footers and Web navigation menus.

- ✔ **Provide appropriate margins.** Think about how you and your readers will use your document. If you are writing an academic essay, leave plenty of room for classmates and instructors to write marginal comments. If you are planning to bind your document, leave enough space for the binding.

- ✔ **Use white space to call attention to important elements on the page.** White space can be used to identify the beginning of major sections and to emphasize key ideas and information. Add extra space before major headings and use white space to set off illustrations, pull quotes, and marginal glosses.

- ✔ **Provide sufficient line spacing to make text readable.** Compressed lines of text are difficult to read. Keep your readers with you by providing enough space between lines to ease the reading process.

- ✔ **Use numbered and bulleted lists to chunk and call attention to information.** Lists direct your readers to key information in a compact, easy-to-read form.

- ✔ **Use font size, styles, and effects to clearly distinguish headings and levels of subheadings.** Using bigger, bolder fonts for headings and successively smaller fonts for subheadings will help your readers recognize the beginning of major sections and the presence of subsections in your document.

- ✔ **Phrase your headings consistently.** Use similar grammatical constructions — such as a set of questions or a series of statements — for your headings and subheadings.

- ✔ **Avoid wide columns of text.** The physical act of moving your eyes across long lines of text makes a document more difficult to read. Consider narrower columns on Web pages and in magazine and newspaper articles.

- ✔ **Enhance readability by using left-justified body text.** Most academic essays, for example, are easier to read when they are left justified and ragged on the right.

- ✔ **Signal the functions of text by varying its format and color.** Use text formatting to distinguish captions, headings, block quotes, pull quotes, and sidebars from the body text of your pages.

Calling Attention to Important Information   Used appropriately, color can increase the attractiveness of a document and call attention to specific parts of it. Similarly, a combination of borders and shading can subtly yet clearly emphasize an illustration, such as a table or chart, or an important passage of text, by distinguishing it from the surrounding body text (see the sidebar in Figure 16.3 on p. 216).

Signaling the Organization of a Document   Color can also be used to help readers understand how a document is organized. In a longer print document, such as a report, a manual, or a book, a header or footer might be formatted with a color different from that of the text. Headings and subheadings in that section might also be formatted in that color, further signaling to readers which section they are viewing. On a Web site, a similar color-coding effect might be created by formatting pages in each section with the same background color. Those colors could be shown in a navigation side menu displayed on every page in the site, helping readers recognize which section they are currently viewing.

Signaling the Function of Text   Color, borders, shading, and rules can also provide visual cues about the function of passages of text. A colored or shaded background might indicate that a passage of text is a sidebar (see Figure 16.3, p. 216). Color could be used to differentiate captions and pull quotes from body text (also in Figure 16.3), and shading might be used to show that a heading or footer is not part of the body text. Rules can be placed above and below pull quotes to differentiate them from other text on a page or screen.

Signaling Transitions   Rules can indicate the beginning and end of sections of a document or separate text that serves one function from text that serves another, such as when a rule appears above information about an author at the end of an article. To format horizontal rules in Microsoft Word, use the FORMAT > BORDERS AND SHADING menu command and click on the Horizontal Line button in the borders and shading dialog box. To format vertical rules in Microsoft Word, use the Line, Line Color, and Line Style buttons on the drawing toolbar.

> Learn more about formatting color, borders, shading, and rules at **bedfordresearcher.com**. Click on Guides > How to Use Your Word Processor or How to Write for the Web.

● Use Illustrations

Illustrations—charts, graphs, tables, photographs and other images, animations, audio clips, and video clips—can expand on or demonstrate points made in the text of your document. They can also reduce the text needed to make a point, help readers better understand your points, and increase the visual appeal of your document.

Photographs and Other Images   Photographs and other images, such as drawings, paintings, and sketches, are frequently used to set a mood, emphasize a point, or demonstrate a point more fully than is possible with text alone. Although readers seldom appreciate the repetition of key points in the text of your document, they welcome well-designed and helpful illustrations that complement descriptions in your text. For example, if you were writing about different kinds of wildflowers, the illustration shown in Figure 16.7 would complement a description of the flower. Most word processors, desktop publishing programs, and Web editing programs allow you to place digitized images directly into a document.

FIGURE 16.7   A drawing could illustrate a description given in the text.

GUIDELINES FOR USING COLOR, SHADING, BORDERS, AND RULES

As you work with color, shading, borders, and rules, keep the following guidelines in mind:

✔ **Understand the effects of color.** Color can have surprisingly different effects on readers. Some effects are physical. Bright yellow, for example, can tire your readers' eyes. Other effects are emotional — and are often linked to readers' cultural backgrounds. In many cultures, green is regarded as soothing because it is associated with nature and growth. Red, in contrast, is associated in a number of cultures with danger. As a result, it tends to attract attention. As you work with color, consider both the physical and emotional effects your choices are likely to have on your readers.

✔ **Use color, shading, borders, and rules consistently.** Use the same colors for top-level headings throughout your document, another color for lower-level headings, and so on. Use the same borders and shading for sidebars. Use rules consistently in pull quotes, headers, and footers. Don't mix and match.

✔ **Make sure you have sufficient contrast between colors and shades.** For instance, avoid using light colors or shades on white or light-colored backgrounds, and avoid darker shades on dark-colored backgrounds.

✔ **Restrain yourself.** Avoid using more than three colors on a page, unless you are using a photograph or work of art. Be cautious, as well, about using multiple styles of rules or borders in a document.

Charts and Graphs Charts and graphs represent information visually. They are used to make a point more succinctly than is possible with text alone or to present complex information in a compact and more accessible form. Often, a well-designed chart or graph can take the place of several paragraphs of explanatory text. A pie chart, for instance, might illustrate the results of a survey, as is shown in Figure 16.8. Charts and graphs can be created within many spreadsheet and word processing programs.

Tables Tables provide categorical lists of information. Like charts and graphs, they can express a point more succinctly than is possible with text alone and can

IV Writing Your Document

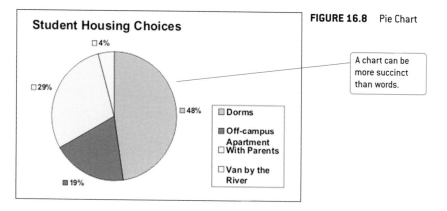

FIGURE 16.8   Pie Chart

A chart can be more succinct than words.

TUTORIAL

How do I insert and format an image?

You can insert and format images of all kinds (photographs, drawings, animations) in Microsoft Word by following these steps.

1 Place your cursor at the point in your document where you want to insert the image.

2 Choose the INSERT > PICTURE command from the main menu.

3 Choose which type of image you wish to insert.

4 Locate or scan the image you want to insert.

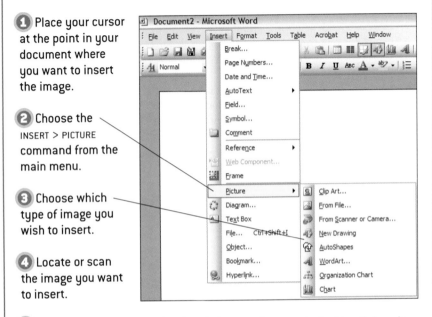

5 To format an image that is already in your document, double-click on it. The Format Picture dialog box that opens will allow you to format the size and layout of the image.

Review another example and learn more about working with images at **bedfordresearcher.com**. Click on Tutorials.

present complex information in a compact form. Tables are frequently used to illustrate contrasts between groups, relationships between variables (such as income, educational attainment, and voting preferences), or change over time (such as growth in population during the past century).

Other Digital Illustrations Digital publications allow you to include a wider range of illustrations, including audio, video, and animations that bring sound and movement to your document. However, there are drawbacks to the use of audio, video, and animation in digital documents. Depending on a computer's capability and the speed with which it connects to the Internet, audio and video illustrations can increase the time it takes readers to view your document. Also, animations might distract your readers from the information you want them to read.

> Learn more about working with illustrations at **bedfordresearcher.com**. Click on <u>Guides</u> > <u>How to Use Your Word Processor</u> or <u>How to Write for the Web</u>.

GUIDELINES FOR USING ILLUSTRATIONS

Remember the following guidelines as you work with illustrations:

- ✔ **Use an illustration for a purpose.** Illustrations are best used when they serve a clear function in your document. Avoid including illustrations simply because you think they might make your document "look better."

- ✔ **Place illustrations near the text they illustrate.** In general, place illustrations as close as possible to the point where they are mentioned in the text. If they are not explicitly mentioned (as is often the case with photographs), place them at a point where they will seem most relevant to the information and ideas being discussed.

- ✔ **Include a title or caption that identifies or explains the illustration.** The documentation style you are using, such as MLA or APA, will usually offer advice on the placement and format of titles and captions. In general, documentation systems suggest that you distinguish between tables and figures (which are all other illustrations), number tables and figures in the order in which they appear in the document, and use compound numbering of tables and figures in longer documents (for example, the second table in Chapter 5 would be labeled "Table 5.2"). Consult the documentation system you are using for specific guidelines on illustrations.

16c

How should I design my document?

Readers familiar with particular genres—or types—of documents, such as academic essays, newspaper columns, informative Web sites, and feature articles, expect documents in a genre to share a particular look and feel. Newspaper articles, for example, are typically laid out in narrow columns of text and are often accompanied by captioned photographs. As you design your document, consider the typical design characteristics associated with the type of document you've chosen.

Understand the Design Conventions of Academic Essays

The design of academic essays is neither flashy nor complex. Their most obvious design features—wide margins, readable fonts, and double-spaced lines—are intended to help their intended audience, typically instructors and classmates, read and review them. These features are influenced by the manuscript preparation guidelines provided by professional organizations such as the Modern Language Association (MLA). The goal of these guidelines is to simplify the task of editing a manuscript and preparing it for its transformation into a book or an article in a journal. Because the writing assignments given by most college instructors have focused on the written expression of the information and ideas in an essay, academic essays have tended to use images sparingly, if at all, and to make limited use of design elements such as color, shading, borders, and rules. With the recent changes in word processing technology, however, writers of academic essays are beginning to take advantage of these design elements. Keep in mind that some instructors prefer that design elements be kept to a minimum in essays. If you are uncertain about your instructor's preferences, ask for guidance.

The pages in Figures 16.9 through 16.12 are from an essay written by college freshman Gaele Lopez for his composition class. They reflect his awareness of his instructor's expectations about line spacing, margins, documentation system, page numbers, and a title page.

For another sample essay formatted in MLA style, see page 266. For a sample essay formatted in APA style, see page 292. For a sample essay formatted in *Chicago* style, see page 320.

CHECKLIST FOR DESIGNING ACADEMIC ESSAYS

✔ Cover page with title, name, and course information

✔ Readable body font (example: 12-point Times New Roman)

✔ Double-spaced lines

✔ Wide margins, one inch or larger

✔ Consistent use of assigned documentation system

✔ Headers and footers in a readable font distinct from body font

✔ If used, headings and subheadings formatted in fonts and colors that distinguish them from the body text and show relative importance of heading levels

✔ If used, illustrations labeled and placed either within the text near relevant passages or in an appendix, according to instructor's preferences

FIGURE 16.9 Cover Page for an Academic Essay

Cover page provides title, author, information about the course, and date the essay was turned in.

A larger, boldface font distinguishes title from other information on the page.

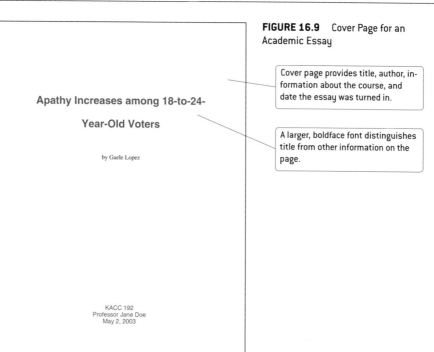

Apathy Increases among 18-to-24-Year-Old Voters

by Gaele Lopez

KACC 192
Professor Jane Doe
May 2, 2003

FIGURE 16.10 First Page of an Academic Essay

A header with writer's last name and page number is repeated at the top of each page.

Title is repeated on first page of essay in a larger, colored, sans-serif font that distinguishes it from the body text.

Body text is set in a serif font, which is more readable than most sans-serif fonts.

All body text is formatted consistently.

One-inch margins and double-spaced lines provide space for the teacher to write comments.

A chart appears near its mention in the text, supporting claims made there. Notice how text is wrapped around the chart.

Lopez 2

Apathy Increases among 18- to 24-Year-Old Voters

Since 1972, when 18-year-olds gained the right to vote, voter turnout among America's youth has been on the decline. In 1972, at the height of the Vietnam War, more than 55 percent of Americans under the age of 25 turned out in the presidential election. By 1996, that turnout had declined to 32 percent. In the incredibly tight 2000 elections, only 38 percent of younger voters cast their votes.

In contrast to older voters, Americans who are 25 or younger are not only less likely to vote, but also are less likely to be registered to vote (see Figure 1). Analysts suggest that this general

Figure 1: Voter registration rates by age group

pattern of declining participation in elections by younger Americans can be attributed to causes ranging from a lack of investment in our system of government to a sense that our political leaders are not addressing issues relevant to youth to a conscious protest of government policies. Regardless of the causes, however, experts on U.S. government agree that the overall pattern of declining voter turnout should be cause for concern among voters – young and old alike.

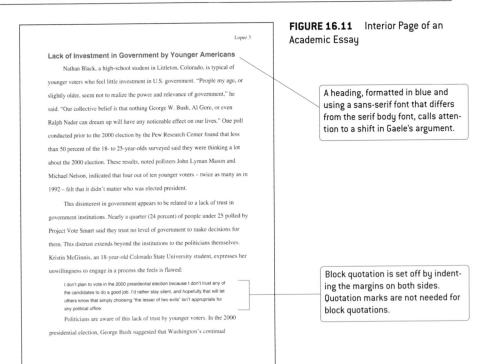

FIGURE 16.11 Interior Page of an Academic Essay

Lopez 3

Lack of Investment in Government by Younger Americans

Nathan Black, a high-school student in Littleton, Colorado, is typical of younger voters who feel little investment in U.S. government. "People my age, or slightly older, seem not to realize the power and relevance of government," he said. "Our collective belief is that nothing George W. Bush, Al Gore, or even Ralph Nader can dream up will have any noticeable effect on our lives." One poll conducted prior to the 2000 election by the Pew Research Center found that less than 50 percent of the 18- to 25-year-olds surveyed said they were thinking a lot about the 2000 election. These results, noted pollsters John Lyman Mason and Michael Nelson, indicated that four out of ten younger voters – twice as many as in 1992 – felt that it didn't matter who was elected president.

This disinterest in government appears to be related to a lack of trust in government institutions. Nearly a quarter (24 percent) of people under 25 polled by Project Vote Smart said they trust no level of government to make decisions for them. This distrust extends beyond the institutions to the politicians themselves. Kristin McGinnis, an 18-year-old Colorado State University student, expresses her unwillingness to engage in a process she feels is flawed:

> I don't plan to vote in the 2000 presidential election because I don't trust any of the candidates to do a good job. I'd rather stay silent, and hopefully that will let others know that simply choosing "the lesser of two evils" isn't appropriate for any political office.

Politicians are aware of this lack of trust by younger voters. In the 2000 presidential election, George Bush suggested that Washington's continual

A heading, formatted in blue and using a sans-serif font that differs from the serif body font, calls attention to a shift in Gaele's argument.

Block quotation is set off by indenting the margins on both sides. Quotation marks are not needed for block quotations.

FIGURE 16.12 Works Cited Page of an Academic Essay

Reference page is titled "Works Cited" per MLA style.

MLA format is used to cite sources. Entries are double-spaced and have a hanging indent.

Lopez 7

Works Cited

Black, Nathan. "Why Vote? Answer: Why Not!" Originally published in *The Denver Post*, 1 Oct. 2000. 1 Dec. 2002 <http://www.geocities.com/ SoHo/Exhibit/6197/voting.htm>.

Gedney, Ryan. Personal interview. 22 Oct. 2002.

The Institute of Politics at Harvard University. *Attitudes toward Politics and Public Service: A National Survey of College Undergraduates*. Cambridge: The Institute of Politics at Harvard University, 2000. 3–16.

Jackson, Bernice Powell. "Must Find New Ways to Encourage Voters." 2 Dec. 2002. 2 Feb. 2003 <http://www.sacobserver.com/government/commentary/ 121002/encourage_voters.htm>.

Magnarelli, Margaret. "Young Voter Apathy: Will America's Youth Go to the Polls?" 1 Dec. 2002 <http://www.govspot.com/features/youngvoterapathy .htm>.

Mason, John Lyman, and Michael Nelson. "Selling Students on the Elections of 2000." Originally published in *The Chronicle of Higher Education*. 22 Sept. 2000. 29 Nov. 2002 <http://www.sos.state.ga.us/sac/18_24_articles.htm>.

Mayfield, Kendra. "Getting Out the Gen Y Vote." 27 Oct. 2000. 1 Dec. 2002 <http://www.wired.com/news/print/0,1294,39601,00.html>.

McGinnis, Kristin. Personal interview. 23 Oct. 2002.

"Project Vote Smart National Survey on Youth and Civic Engagement Completed." Project Vote Smart. 14 Sept. 1999. 9 Oct. 2002 <http://www.votesmart.org/youthsurvey.phtm>.

Rock the Vote. "How Can You Rock the Vote?" 1999. 1 Dec. 2002 <http://www.rockthevote.org/howcanyou.html>.

Torp, Pat. Personal interview. 24 Oct. 2002.

Understand the Design Conventions of Other Types of Documents

You might present your research writing in an article, multimedia presentation, or Web site. If so, you'll want to recognize how the differences among genres will influence the design decisions you will make as an author.

Articles   The design of articles varies far more than the design of academic essays. Depending on the type of publication in which they appear, such as newspapers, magazines, Web sites, and newsletters, among others, articles might use headings and subheadings, columns, sidebars, pull quotes, and illustrations. Writers of articles need to consider several factors that affect design: the overall design of the publication in which they hope to place their article, the audience the publication addresses, the subjects typically written about in the publication, and the style used by other articles in the publication.

The article in Figures 16.13 and 16.14 was written by Christian Rangunton for the University of Texas at Arlington student newspaper, *The Shorthorn*. It

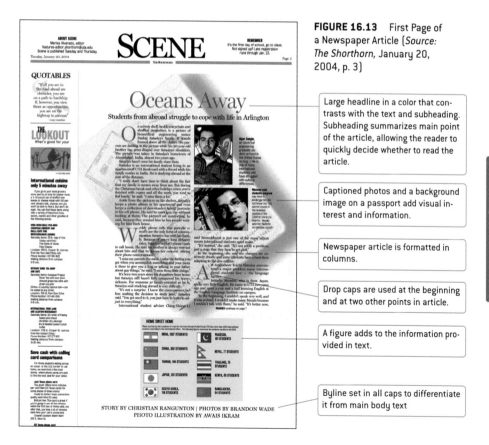

FIGURE 16.13   First Page of a Newspaper Article (*Source: The Shorthorn*, January 20, 2004, p. 3)

Large headline in a color that contrasts with the text and subheading. Subheading summarizes main point of the article, allowing the reader to quickly decide whether to read the article.

Captioned photos and a background image on a passport add visual interest and information.

Newspaper article is formatted in columns.

Drop caps are used at the beginning and at two other points in article.

A figure adds to the information provided in text.

Byline set in all caps to differentiate it from main body text

IV Writing Your Document

> ## CHECKLIST FOR DESIGNING ARTICLES
>
> ✔ Column layout appropriate for target publication
>
> ✔ Line spacing typically single-space
>
> ✔ Readable body font (example: 10-point Times New Roman)
>
> ✔ Appropriate use of color and borders, shading, and rules
>
> ✔ Heading and subheadings formatted in font and colors that distinguish them from body text and show relative importance of heading levels
>
> ✔ Illustrations labeled and placed near relevant passages
>
> ✔ Optional elements: sidebars, pull quotes, and marginal glosses

draws heavily on visual elements to set a mood, call attention to key points, and convey information.

Multimedia Presentations   Multimedia presentations—sometimes referred to as PowerPoint presentations because they are so often created using Microsoft PowerPoint—consist of a series of slides that contain text and illustrations. Most multimedia presentations are designed to enhance the words of a speaker. When multimedia presentations are distributed as stand-alone documents, as is the case when they are presented on a Web site or distributed on CD or DVD, summaries of the speaker's words are sometimes provided through notes attached to each slide.

A brief headline and "continued from . . ." phrase indicate that the article began on a previous page.

The author's name and e-mail address appear at the end of the article, allowing readers with questions or reactions to contact the author.

IV Writing Your Document

Changes

continued from page 1

but I still have trouble with it sometimes.

Although he still speaks in broken English - sometimes pausing in the middle of sentences to root out the right words - Shimizu has come a long way and learned to express himself more freely.

Now, Shimizu said, language isn't as big a problem as cooking.

Although he has fallen in love with cheeseburgers, Shimizu said he misses food from home.

"I'll usually go to the grocery store or the Asian markets around town for groceries and ingredients," he said. "I don't know how to cook very well, but I use books and Web sites to learn."

When Ugur Zengin, an electrical engineering graduate student, arrived last fall, he was startled at the cultural differences. His friends took him to a local restaurant shortly after his arrival where they ordered him an omelet. The

Turkey native said he couldn't eat the omelet because the taste was so alien to him.

"I never leave food on my plate," he said. "I was very hungry, but I just couldn't finish the food."

It's been almost three years since Prashanti Bhamididati, an electrical engineering graduate student, came to the campus. He said it's impossible for somebody from another place to fully be comfortable in the states.

"The first six months were really bad," he said. "We come from a different place. It's expected, but it's kind of hard."

Posters and Indian books stacked on his desks, help him cope. A miniature temple constructed from a FedEx delivery box hangs on his wall with figurines of Hindu gods placed inside. It's a helpful reminder of where he's from, Bhamididati said. He added that the international student population — over 4,000 according to the University's International Office — helps him adapt to the environment while sustaining his roots.

"It's great that there is such a

great international student population here at UTA. They can relate with me and share the same emotions we have about being away from home," he said. "It makes me more comfortable to be around them."

There's no set method to curing the culture shock, Li said. She said that students have to give themselves time to adapt to the environment. Her department offers orientations for incoming students every semester. The orientations consist of tips on topics from dealing with culture shock to managing immigration information.

"We can prepare them, but we can't force them to feel comfortable," Li said. "It's a learning process that takes time."

Because Arlington doesn't have a stable public transportation system, international students are also finding it hard to get around. Electrical engineering senior Kunal Barawkar is without a car and frustrated.

"In India, there was a good transportation system. You could hop on a bus and go anywhere

you wanted to go," he said. "Arlington is so big, and everything is so spaced out."

During his first weeks, Barawkar was restricted to the vicinities around campus. He said it felt somewhat imprisoning.

"I didn't know what to do," he said. "I really had nothing to do except roam around the apartment, watch television or surf the Internet."

The limited city transportation creates an extended list of problems for international students. What others consider effortless errands are laborious to Barawkar and his counterparts.

Barawkar said he wishes he could spend more of his free time at the mall or movie theater, but the absence of a vehicle has restricted his leisure to television.

"It takes about an hour trip to walk to the movies and back. That's too long of a walk," he said. "It's not worth it."

Groceries are a hassle for him and his three roommates because of the lack of transportation. During his first attempt at grocery shopping, Barawkar and

his roommates hopped aboard the Mav Mover shuttle bus to get to Wal-Mart. On their way home, they found out the closest the shuttle bus could drop them off was two streets before their apartment complex. They trekked a couple of blocks to their apartment, the four clenching handfuls of grocery bags that slowly slipped from their grasps. It was a very bad idea, Barawkar said.

The Cornerstone, along with numerous campus organizations, helps international students by offering them 'grocery trips'. They also organize free coffee house nights and events where international students can practice their English and hang out.

Until Barawkar saves enough money to purchase a car, he said he depends on grocery trips and carpools to get him places. He doesn't know if he'll ever be able to buy a car because he can't find a job, he said.

Barawkar has applied to the campus bookstore, computer labs and dining services but has only been called back to one interview.

"Trying to find a job here is extremely competitive because there are so many international students who are applying," he said.

Bhamididati graduated last December and was forced to let go of his job at Nedderman Hall because on-campus jobs are reserved for students. He said there are very few jobs back in India, so he's hoping to find a job in the states, but due to policy, only has a year to do so. He says he'll go back to India if he doesn't find a job but that all the hardships he's dealt with were worthwhile in the end.

"We came here for the education system, the exposure and the experience. The experience is useful and very rewarding," he said. "All of us are here for a purpose. We want to make a career for ourselves so we can support ourselves and our families, even if it means putting up with all the adjustments and sacrificing time away from our close ones."

CHRISTIAN RAGGENTON
crr3758@exchange.uta.edu

FIGURE 16.14   Second Page of a Newspaper Article in Narrow Columns (*Source: The Shorthorn*, January 20, 2004, p. 7)

Page designs range from simple combinations of titles and lists to complex pages that incorporate illustrations and heavily formatted text. Presenters can highlight information through colors, fonts, tables, and an expanded range of illustrations, such as audio and video clips, animation, and links to online documents. Because many presentations are viewed on a computer or projection screen by a live audience, it is important to use legible fonts and illustrations.

Figures 16.15 through 16.18 show a selection of slides from a multimedia presentation about the impact of Senate Bill 186, a law passed by the Colorado state legislature to reform public education in the state. Note the use of color, headings and subheadings, bulleted lists, and illustrations to clearly convey information about the impact of the bill.

FIGURE 16.15   Opening Slide of a Multimedia Presentation

Title, set in easy-to-read sans-serif font, contrasts with the background and clearly presents the topic.

The illustration focuses on children and evokes Colorado.

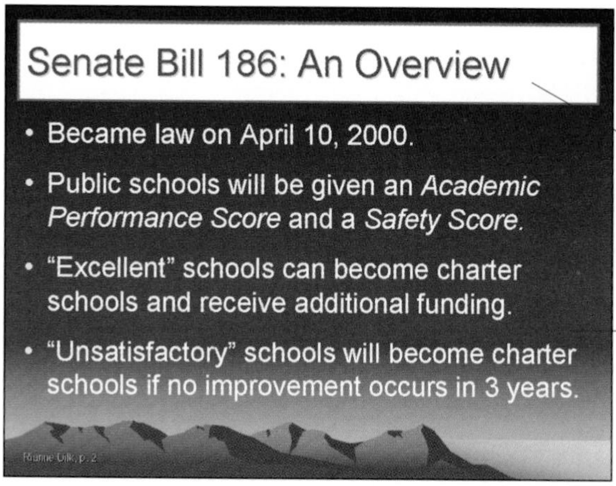

FIGURE 16.16   Introductory Slide of a Multimedia Presentation

Slide titles are brief yet informative. Title in sans-serif font is reversed against light-colored bordered box, catching the eye.

A bulleted list and text formatting (bold, contrasting color, larger font) highlight key points and provide an overview of the bill.

IV Writing Your Document

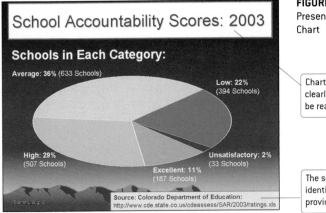

FIGURE 16.17   Multimedia Presentation Slide Using a Pie Chart

Chart showing 2003 scores is clearly labeled using a font that can be read from a distance.

The source of the chart's data is identified, and a live Web link is provided.

FIGURE 16.18   Final Slide of a Multimedia Presentation

The final slide provides links to related Web sites and uses a photograph that focuses once again on Colorado's children. The Web links can be clicked to open the site in a browser.

CHECKLIST FOR DESIGNING MULTIMEDIA PRESENTATIONS

☑ Title page clear, uncluttered, and includes title of presentation

☑ Introductory pages provide clear overview of main points of presentation

☑ Overall design consistent across pages (placement of titles and text; use of fonts, colors, rules, illustrations)

☑ Readable heading font (example: 36-point Helvetica)

☑ Readable body font (example: 24-point Helvetica)

☑ Appropriate use of color

☑ Information presented in brief, readable chunks, using bulleted and numbered lists when appropriate

☑ Illustrations — especially charts, graphs, tables, and video — are easy to view at a distance

☑ If used, transitions between slides (dissolves, page flips) are not distracting

☑ If used, sound is audible and not distracting

Web Sites Web sites consist of linked pages, typically organized through a home page and navigational devices such as menus, tables of contents, indexes, and site maps. The main pages of Web sites usually provide broad overviews of the topic, and reduced pages add detailed information. Designs used for Web sites are growing more similar to those found in magazines, with a heavy use of images and other illustrations. Information is highlighted though colors, borders, shading, rules, fonts, tables, and an expanded range of digital illustrations.

Web sites pose intriguing design challenges to writers. In addition to many of the design elements that are used in print documents, you also must choose from the expanded range of design options for publishing online, such as selecting an organizational structure for a site, selecting navigation tools, and using digital illustrations. Most important, you must have some familiarity with the range of Web sites you can create, such as informative Web sites, articles for Web-based journals, magazines, and newspapers, business Web sites, personal home pages, and blogs, to name only a few of the types of sites that can now be found on the Web.

> Learn more about creating and designing Web sites at **bedfordresearcher.com**. Click on Guides > How to Write for the Web.

Figures 16.19 through 16.21 show pages from featured writer Pete Jacquez's Web site about wind-generated electrical power.

FIGURE 16.19 Web Site Home Page

A A large heading identifies the issue addressed by the site.

B A side menu provides links to pages on the site.

C A photograph illustrates a key point raised in the body text.

D Caption is set off from body text with a different font (Verdana) and contrasting color.

E Body text is formatted in a 12-point serif font that is easy to read.

F Site information is provided. A list of references cited in the site is available.

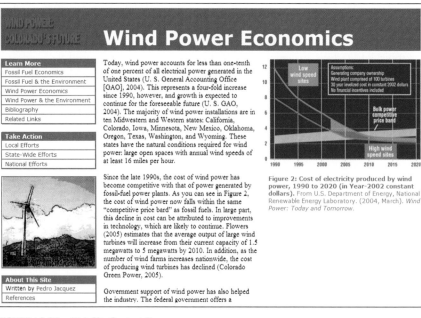

FIGURE 16.20   Web Site Content Page

A A link to the home page is provided on all other pages.

B Headings are formatted in a large sans-serif font that contrasts with the body text.

C The side menu appears in the same place on each page of the site.

D A chart provides information about wind power economics.

E The figure title is followed by source information.

F Extra space after each paragraph helps differentiate one from another.

CHECKLIST FOR DESIGNING WEB SITES

✔ Organizational structure is consistent with the purpose of the site and the needs and expectations of readers

✔ Home page provides links to main pages on the site

✔ Home page and main pages offer navigation tools appropriate for readers of the site

✔ Overall design is consistent across the site (placement of titles, text, and navigation tools; use of fonts, colors, rules, and illustrations)

✔ Information is presented in brief, readable chunks, using bulleted and numbered lists whenever possible

✔ Body font is readable (example: 12-point Times New Roman)

✔ Heading and subheadings are formatted in fonts and colors that distinguish them from body text and show relative importance of heading levels

✔ Informational flags are used to help readers understand links and images

☑ Appropriate use of color

☑ Illustrations are placed near the passages to which they refer

☑ Images are kept as small (in kilobytes) as possible, while being clear and easy to see

☑ Contact information and other relevant information are included and easy to locate

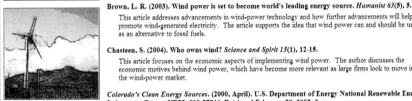

WIND POWER:
COLORADO'S FUTURE

Wind Power Bibliography

Learn More
Fossil Fuel Economics
Fossil Fuel & the Environment
Wind Power Economics
Wind Power & the Environment
Bibliography
Related Links

Take Action
Local Efforts
State-Wide Efforts
National Efforts

About This Site
Written by Pedro Jacquez
References

Aabakken, J. (2004, June). *Power technologies data book 2003 edition.* Golden, CO: National Renewable Energy Laboratory. Retrieved February 20, 2005, from http://www.nrel.gov/docs/fy04osti/36347.pdf

This report, commissioned by the U.S. Department of Energy, provides a comprehensive listing of data on energy use in the United States.

Bisbee, D. W. (2004). NEPA review of offshore wind farms. *Boston College Environmental Affairs Law Review 31*(2), 349-385.

This review focuses on offshore wind farms and their efficiency at producing electricity. The article notes that offshore wind farms can sometimes be inconsistent in their output of electrical power due to variable winds. The article speculates about whether this inconsistency makes offshore wind farms less viable as an alternative to fossil fuel plants.

Brown, L. R. (2003). Wind power is set to become world's leading energy source. *Humanist 63*(5), 5.

This article addresses advancements in wind-power technology and how further advancements will help promote wind-generated electricity. The article supports the idea that wind power can and should be used as an alternative to fossil fuels.

Chasteen, S. (2004). Who owns wind? *Science and Spirit 15*(1), 12-15.

This article focuses on the economic aspects of implementing wind power. The author discusses the economic motives behind wind power, which have become more relevant as large firms look to move into the wind-power market.

Colorado's Clean Energy Sources. (2000, April). U.S. Department of Energy National Renewable Energy Laboratory Report NREL-810-27846. Retrieved February 20, 2005, from http://www.eere.energy.gov/state_energy_program/pdfs/coloradochoices.pdf,

This booklet, available as a PDF file, provides information about environmentally sound energy choices, green power, and environmentally friendly transportation options.

FIGURE 16.21 Annotated Bibliography Web Page

🅰 An annotated bibliography provides information for visitors to the site.

🅱 Source citations are formatted in APA style, with a hanging indent, as Pete's instructor required.

🅲 Links to other documents are signaled by a contrasting blue color.

🅳 Citations are distinguished from annotations with bold font.

🅴 Annotations — brief descriptions of each source — are indented and formatted in normal text.

> **QUICK REFERENCE**

Designing

✔ Understand the design principles of balance, emphasis, placement, repetition, and consistency.   (p. 210)

✔ Design to achieve your purposes.   (p. 211)

✔ Design to address your readers' needs and interests.   (p. 212)

✔ Use design elements — such as, fonts, line spacing, alignment, page layout, color, borders, shading, rules, and illustrations — effectively and appropriately to increase the legibility and readability of your document.   (p. 213)

✔ Follow the design conventions of the type of document you are creating, such as an academic essay (p. 224), an article (p. 227), a multimedia presentation (p. 228), or a Web site (p. 231).

The Bedford Researcher

I	Joining the Conversation
II	Collecting Information
III	Working with Sources
IV	Writing Your Document
V	**Documenting Sources**

PART V

Documenting Sources

As you complete your work on your research project, you can turn your attention fully to the task of citing and documenting your sources. This section of *The Bedford Researcher* discusses reasons to document your sources and describes four major documentation systems: MLA, APA, *Chicago,* and CSE.

17

Understanding Documentation Systems

> **Key Questions**
>
> **17a. What is a documentation system and which one should I use?   237**
>
> **17b. How should I document my sources?   238**

Research writers document their sources to avoid plagiarism, give credit to others who have written about an issue, and create a record of their work that others can follow and build upon. These reasons illustrate the concept of writing as participation in a community of writers and readers. By documenting your sources, you show that you are aware that other writers have contributed to the conversation about your issue and that you respect them enough to acknowledge their contributions. In turn, you expect that writers who read your document will cite your work.

? WHAT'S MY PURPOSE?

Documenting your sources can help you achieve your purposes as a writer, such as establishing your authority and persuading your readers. If your readers find that you haven't documented your sources, they'll suspect that you're careless, or decide that you're dishonest. In either case, they won't trust what you have to say.

17a

What is a documentation system and which one should I use?

Many professional organizations and publications have developed their own rules for formatting documents and citing sources. As a result, writers in many disciplines know how to cite their sources clearly and consistently, and their readers know what to expect. For example, imagine that a psychologist is writing an article for the *Journal of Counseling Psychology*. The writer is likely to know that submissions to the journal go through a rigorous review for substance and style before being accepted for publication. Among its expectations, the journal requires that writers use the documentation system created by the American Psychological Association (APA). Given the high level of competition for space in the journal, the writer knows that even if the article is substantive and compelling it will not be accepted for publication if it does not use APA style appropriately. After ensuring the article is clearly written and well argued, the writer double-checks the article to ensure it follows the formatting and source citation guidelines specified by the APA documentation system.

Several of the documentation systems most commonly used in the various academic disciplines are covered in this book:

- **MLA** This style, from the Modern Language Association (MLA), is used primarily in the humanities—English, philosophy, linguistics, languages, and so on. See Chapter 18.

- **APA** This style, from the American Psychological Association, is used mainly in the social sciences—psychology, sociology, anthropology, political science, economics, education, and so on. See Chapter 19.

- *Chicago* Developed by the University of Chicago Press, this style is used primarily in history, journalism, and the humanities. See Chapter 20.

- **CSE** This style, from the Council of Science Editors (formerly the Council of Biology Editors), is used mainly in the physical and life sciences—chemistry, geology, biology, botany, and so on—and in mathematics. See Chapter 21.

Your choice of documentation system will be guided by the discipline or field within which you are writing and by any requirements associated with your research writing project. If your project has been assigned to you, ask the person who assigned it or someone who has written a similar document which documentation system you should use. If you are working on a project for a writing class, your instructor will most likely tell you which documentation system to follow.

If you don't have access to advice about which documentation system is best for your project, consider the discipline in which you are writing. In engineering and business, for example, a wide range of documentation styles are used, with most of these specific to scholarly journals or specializations within the discipline.

17b

How should I document my sources?

How you document sources will depend on your writing situation. Most often, you will

1. provide a reference to your source within the text
2. provide a complete set of citations, or formal acknowledgments, for your sources in a works cited or reference list

The specific format of your in-text citations will depend on the documentation system you use. If you use MLA or APA style, you'll cite—or formally acknowledge—information in the text using parentheses and add a list of sources to the end of your document. If you use the *Chicago* notes style, you'll acknowledge your sources in footnotes or endnotes and supply a bibliography at the end of your document. If you use the CSE citation-sequence style, you will number the citations in your text and list your sources in the order in which they are referenced. If you write an electronic document that cites other online sources, you might simply link to your sources. Table 17.1 presents examples of in-text citations and works cited or reference list entries for each of these major documentation styles.

As Table 17.1 shows, although each style differs from the others, especially in the handling of in-text citation, they share a number of similarities. With the

TABLE 17.1 EXAMPLES OF IN-TEXT CITATIONS AND BIBLIOGRAPHIC ENTRIES FOR MAJOR DOCUMENTATION STYLES		
STYLE	IN-TEXT CITATION	WORKS CITED OR REFERENCE LIST ENTRY
MLA Style	Although Cats's book specifically addressed women, it had implications for men as well (Westermann 119).	Westermann, Mariët. A Worldly Art: The Dutch Republic, 1585–1718. London: Calmann, 1996.
APA Style	Although Cats's book specifically addressed women, it had implications for men as well (Westermann, 1996).	Westermann, M. (1996). *A worldly art: The Dutch republic, 1585–1718.* London: Calmann.
Chicago Style: Notes System	Although Cats's book specifically addressed women, it had implications for men as well.[3]	3. Mariët Westermann, *A Worldly Art: The Dutch Republic, 1585–1718* (London: Calmann, 1996), 119. Westermann, Mariët. *A Worldly Art: The Dutch Republic, 1585–1718.* London: Calmann, 1966. *Note: The citation is placed in a footnote or endnote, and again in the bibliography.*
CSE Style: Citation-Sequence System	Although Cats's book specifically addressed women, it had implications for men as well.[3]	3. Westermann M. A worldly art: The Dutch republic, 1585–1718. London: Calmann; 1996. 192 p. *Note: Numbered citations are placed in the reference list in the order they appear in the text.*
Web Style	Westermann notes that, although Cats's book specifically addressed women, it had implications for men as well.	Many Web documents will link directly to a cited work, as shown here. Or they may use a style such as MLA, APA, *Chicago,* or CSE.

exception of Web style, key publication information is usually provided in a works cited list, reference list, or bibliography. These lists appear at the end of the document and include the following information about each source:

- author(s) and/or editor(s)
- title
- publication date
- publisher and city of publication (for books)
- periodical name, volume, issue, and page numbers (for articles)
- URL and access date (for online publications)

Each documentation system creates an association between citations in the text of a document and the works cited page.

My Research Project

REVIEW YOUR WORKING BIBLIOGRAPHY

Start by reviewing the source citations in your working bibliography. Make sure that you've used the appropriate documentation system and entered sufficient source information to fully document your sources. If you have used the **Bedford Bibliographer** tool at **bedfordresearcher.com**, you can select from several documentation systems, including MLA, APA, *Chicago,* and CSE.

> ## QUICK REFERENCE

Understanding Documentation Systems

✔ Choose an appropriate documentation system.   (p. 237)

✔ Document your sources in your text and, depending on the documentation system, create a works cited list, reference list, or bibliography. Review your sources for accuracy and completeness.   (p. 238)

∨ Documenting Sources

Part V
Documenting Sources

18

Using MLA Style

Key Questions

18a. How do I cite sources within the text of my document? 244

18b. How do I prepare the list of works cited? 247

Modern Language Association (MLA) style, used primarily in the humanities, emphasizes the authors of a source and the pages on which information is located in the source. Writers who use the MLA documentation system cite, or formally acknowledge, source information within their text using parentheses, and they provide a list of sources in a works cited list at the end of their document. For more information about MLA style, consult the *MLA Handbook for Writers of Research Papers,* Sixth Edition. Information about the MLA Handbook can also be found at www.mla.org.

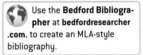
Use the **Bedford Bibliographer** at **bedfordresearcher .com.** to create an MLA-style bibliography.

To see featured writer Jenna Alberter's research essay, formatted in MLA style, turn to page 266.

ENTRIES IN YOUR WORKS CITED LIST

18a

How do I cite sources within the text of my document?

MLA style uses parentheses for in-text citations to acknowledge the use of another author's words, facts, and ideas. When you refer to a source within your text, place the author's last name and specific page number(s)—if the source is paginated—within parentheses. Your reader then can go to the works cited list at the end of your document and find a full citation there.

1. Basic Format for Direct Quotation   Often you will want to name the author of a source within your sentence rather than in a parenthetical citation. By doing so, you create a context for the material (words, facts, or ideas) that you are including and indicate where the information from the author begins. When you are using a direct quotation from a source and have named the author in your sentence, place only the page number in parentheses after the quotation. The period follows the parentheses.

> Allen asserts that "the abundance of caution is born of a hard lesson: 10 years ago, one patient died and another suffered irreversible heart damage at the Dana-Farber because the staff wasn't cautious enough" (A1).

When you have not mentioned the author in your sentence, you must place the author's name and the page number in parentheses after the quotation.

> Hospitals often need a highly publicized incident to prompt the "abundance of caution" that Dana-Farber adopted after their "hard lesson" of 1994 (Allen A1).

When you are using a block (or extended) quotation, the parenthetical citation comes after the final punctuation and a single space.

If you continue to refer to a single source for several sentences in a row within one paragraph—and without intervening references to another source—you may reserve your reference to the end of the paragraph. However, be sure to include all of the relevant page numbers.

2. Basic Format for a Summary or Paraphrase   When you are summarizing or paraphrasing information gained from a source, you are still required to cite the source. If you name the author in your sentence, place only the page number in parentheses after the paraphrase or summary. Punctuation marks follow the parentheses. When you have not mentioned the author in your sentence, you must place the author's name and the page number in parentheses after the quotation.

> Allen suggests that the staff's new procedures are a reaction to Dana-Farber's highly publicized accidental patient death in 1994 (A1).

Dana-Farber realized how deadly this lack of caution could be when a patient died accidentally in 1994 (Allen A1).

3. Entire Source   If you are referring to an entire source rather than to a specific page or pages, you will not need a parenthetical citation.

The explorations of race in ZZ Packer's <u>Drinking Coffee Elsewhere</u> can be linked thematically to the treatment of immigrants in Lahiri's work.

4. Corporate or Group Author   Cite the corporation or group as you would an individual author. You may use abbreviations for the source in subsequent references if you add the abbreviation in parentheses at the first mention of the name.

The Brown University Office of Financial Aid (BUOFA) has adopted a policy that first-year students will not be expected to work as part of their financial aid package (12). BUOFA will award these students a one-time grant to help compensate for the income lost by not working (14).

5. Unknown Author   If you are citing a source that has no known author, such as the article "Censorship in the United States: 1620–2000," use a brief version of the title in the parenthetical citation.

Even in the United States, despite its First Amendment freedoms, censorship has a long history ("Censorship" 22).

6. Two or More Works by the Same Author   For references to authors with more than one work in your works cited list, insert a short version of the title between author and page number, separating the author and the title with a comma.

(Ishiguro, <u>Unconsoled</u> 146)

(Ishiguro, <u>Remains</u> 77)

7. Two or More Authors with the Same Last Name   Include the first initial and last name in the parenthetical citations.

(G. Martin 354)

(F. Martin 169)

8. Two or Three Authors   Include the last name of each author in your citation.

Casting physically attractive actors wins points with film audiences: "Primitive as the association between outward strength and moral force may be, it has its undeniable appeal" (Clarke, Johnson, and Evans 228).

9. Four or More Authors   Use only the last name of the first author and the abbreviation "et al." (Latin for "and others"). Note that there is no comma between the author's name and "et al."

> (Barnes et al. 44)

10. Literary Work   Along with the page number(s), give other identifying information, such as a chapter, scene, or line number, that will help readers find the passage.

> The sense of social claustrophobia is never as palpable in The Age of Innocence as when Newland realizes that all of New York society has conspired to cover up what it believes to be an affair between him and Madame Olenska (Wharton 339; ch. 33).

11. Work in an Anthology   Cite the author of the work, not the editor of the anthology. (See also #34 on p. 251.)

> In "Beneath the Deep, Slow Motion," Leo says, "The Chinese call anger a weary bird with no place to roost" (Barkley 163).

12. Sacred Text   Give the name of the edition you are using along with the chapter and verse (or their equivalent).

> He should consider that "Where no counsel is, the people fall: but in the multitude of counselors there is safety" (King James Bible, Prov. 11.14).

> In the Qu'ran, sinners are said to be blind to their sins ("The Cow" 2.7).

13. Two or More Works   Use a semicolon to separate entries.

> Forethought is key in survival, whether it involves remembering extra water on a safari trail or gathering food for a long winter in ancient times (Wither and Hosking 4; Estes and Otte 2).

14. Source Quoted in Another Source   Ideally, you will be able to find the primary, or original, source for material used in your research project document. If you quote or paraphrase a secondary source — a source that contains information about a primary source — use the abbreviation "qtd. in" (for "quoted in") when you cite the source.

> President Leonid Kuchma insisted that "we cannot in any instance allow the disintegration or division of Ukraine" (qtd. in Lisova A1).

15. Print Source without Page Numbers   If no page numbers are provided, list only the author's name in parentheses.

Although his work has been influenced by many graphic artists, it remains essentially text-based (Fitzgerald).

16. Electronic or Nonprint Source Give a page, section, paragraph, or screen number, if numbered, in the parenthetical citation.

Clinton believes his greatest legacy is that he improved the lives of ordinary Americans (Beatty, par. 2).

18b

How do I prepare the list of works cited?

MLA-style research documents include a reference list titled "Works Cited," which begins on a new page at the end of the document. If you wish to acknowledge sources that you read but did not cite in your text, you may title the list "Works Consulted" and include them. The list is alphabetized by author. If the author's name is unknown, alphabetize using the title of the source. To cite more than one work by the same author, use the author's name in the first entry. Thereafter, use three hyphens followed by a period in place of the author's name; list the entries alphabetically by title. All entries in the list are double-spaced, with no extra space between entries. Entries are formatted with a hanging indent: The first line of an entry is flush with the left margin and subsequent lines are indented one-half inch or five spaces.

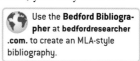

Use the **Bedford Bibliographer** at **bedfordresearcher .com.** to create an MLA-style bibliography.

In longer documents, a list of works cited may be given at the end of each chapter or section. In electronic documents that use links, such as a Web site, the list of works cited is often a separate page to which other pages are linked. To see a works cited list in MLA style, see p. 273.

Books, Conference Proceedings, and Dissertations

17. One Author

Robinson, Marilynne. Gilead: A Novel. New York: Farrar, 2004.

18. Two or Three Authors List all the authors in the same order as on the title page, last name first for only the first author listed. Use commas to separate authors' names.

Hill, Gina, and Gregg Hill. On the Run: A Mafia Childhood. New York: Warner, 2004.

Jowett, Garth S., Ian C. Jarvie, and Kathryn H. Fuller. Children and the Movies: Media Influence and the Payne Fund Controversy. Cambridge: Cambridge UP, 1996.

MLA

V Documenting Sources

19. Four or More Authors   Provide the first author's name (last name first) followed by a comma, and then the abbreviation "et al." (Latin for "and others").

> Hudson, Renaldo, et al. Lockdown Prison Heart. Lincoln: iUniverse,
> 2004.

20. Corporate or Group Author   Write out the full name of the corporation or group, and cite the name as you would an author. This name is often also the name of the publisher.

> National Geographic. National Geographic Atlas of the World. 8th ed.
> Washington: Natl. Geographic, 2004.

21. Unknown Author   When no author is listed on the title or copyright page, begin the entry with the title of the work. Alphabetize the entry by the first word of the title other than *A, An,* or *The.*

> International Yearbook of Industrial Statistics 2004. Northampton: Elgar,
> 2004.

22. Two or More Books by the Same Author   List the entries alphabetically by title.

> Nussbaum, Martha C. Hiding from Humanity: Disgust, Shame, and the
> Law. Princeton: Princeton UP, 2004.
>
> ---. Upheavals of Thought: The Intelligence of Emotions. Cambridge:
> Cambridge UP, 2003.

23. Editor(s)   Use the abbreviateion "ed." or "eds."

> Peterson, Joseph H., ed. The Lesser Key of Solomon. York: Weiser, 2001.

24. Translated Book   List the author first and then the title, followed by the name of the translator and publication information.

> Saari, Salli. A Bolt from the Blue: Coping with Disasters and Acute
> Traumas. Trans. Annira Silver. Philadelphia: Kingsley, 2005.

25. Book in a Language Other Than English   You may give a translation of the book's title in brackets.

> Márquez, Gabriel García. Vivir para contarla [Living to Tell the Tale]. New
> York: Knopf, 2002.

26. Edition Other Than the First   Include the number of the edition and the abbreviation "ed." after the title.

TUTORIAL

How do I cite books using MLA style?

LITERATURE, PSYCHOANALYSIS, RACE, AND GENDER

THE FEMINIST DIFFERENCE

BARBARA JOHNSON

When citing a book, use the information from the title page and the copyright page (on the reverse side of the title page), not from the book's cover or a library catalog. Consult pages 247–52 for additional models for citing books.

A
Johnson, Barbara. **B** The Feminist Difference: Literature, Psychoanalysis,

C Race, and Gender. **D** Cambridge: **E** Harvard UP, 1998.

A **The author.** Give the last name first, followed by a comma, the first name, and the middle initial (if given). Don't include titles such as MD, PhD, or Sir; include suffixes after the name and a comma (O'Driscoll, Gerald P., Jr.). End with a period.

B **The title.** Give the full title; include the subtitle (if any), preceded by a colon. Underline or (if your instructor permits) italicize the title and subtitle; capitalize all major words. End with a period.

C **The city of publication.** If more than one city is given, use the first one listed. For a city that may be unfamiliar to your readers or confused with another city, add an abbreviation of the state, country, or province (Birmingham, Eng.). Insert a colon.

D **The publisher.** Give a shortened version of the publisher's name (Harper for HarperCollins Publishers; Harcourt for Harcourt Brace; Oxford UP for Oxford University Press). Do not include the words *Press, Publisher,* and *Inc.* Follow with a comma.

E **The year of publication.** If more than one copyright date is given, use the most recent one. Use n.d. if no date is given. End with a period.

Use the **Bedford Bibliographer** at **bedfordresearcher.com** to create a works cited list formatted in MLA style.

MLA

V Documenting Sources

> Simpson, J. A., and Edmund S. Weiner. The Oxford English Dictionary.
> 2nd ed. New York: Oxford UP, 1989.

27. Multivolume Work Include the total number of volumes and the abbreviation "vols." after the title.

> Eisenstadt, S. N. Comparative Civilizations and Multiple Modernities.
> 2 vols. Leiden: Brill, 2003.

If you have used only one of the volumes in your document, include the volume number after the title. List the total number of volumes after the publication information.

> Gibbon, Edward. The Decline and Fall of the Roman Empire. Vol. 1. New
> York: Everyman, 1993. 3 vols.

28. Book in a Series If a series is named on the title page, include that name just before the publication information. Include the series number after a period. If the word "Series" is part of the series name, use the abbreviation "Ser."

> Passaro, Maria C. Representation of Women in Medieval and Renaissance
> Texts. Studies in Renaissance Lit. Ser. 27. Lewiston: Mellen, 2005.

29. Republished Book Indicate the original date of publication after the title.

> Ellison, Ralph. The Invisible Man. 1947. New York: Random, 1995.

30. Book with a Title within the Title

> Rutledge, Fleming. The Battle for Middle-Earth: Tolkien's Divine Design
> in The Lord of the Rings. Grand Rapids: Eerdmans, 2004.

31. Author with an Editor Include the name of the editor (first name first) after the title.

> Wilde, Oscar. De Profundis and Other Writings. Ed. Colin Tobin. New York:
> Penguin, 2004.

32. Anthology To cite an anthology of essays, stories, or poems or a collection of articles, list the editor or editors first (as on the title page), followed by the abbreviation "ed." or "eds."

> Keyser, Elizabeth Lennox, John Daniel Stahl, and Bettina L. Hanlon, eds.
> Anthology of Children's Literature. New York: Oxford UP, 2005.

33. Foreword, Introduction, Preface, or Afterword Begin with the author of the part you are citing and the name of that part. Continue with the title of the work and its author (first name first), following "By." At the end of the entry, list the inclusive page numbers on which the part of the book appears.

> Knox, Bernard. Introduction. The Iliad. By Homer. Trans. Robert Fagles. New York: Penguin, 1990. 3-64.

If the author of the foreword or other part is also the author of the work, use only the last name after "By."

> Morrison, Toni. Afterword. The Bluest Eye. By Morrison. New York: Plume-Penguin, 1994. 209-16.

If the foreword or other part has a title, include the title in quotation marks between the author and the name of the part.

> Gates, Henry Louis, Jr. "Toni Morrison (1931-)." Preface. Toni Morrison: Critical Perspectives Past and Present. Ed. Gates and K. A. Appiah. New York: Amistad, 1993. ix-xiii.

34. Chapter in an Edited Book or Selection in an Anthology Begin your citation with the author and the title of the chapter or selection. Follow this with the title of the anthology or collection, the abbreviation "Ed" (meaning "Edited by"), and names of the editors (first name first) as well as publication information. At the end of your entry, give the inclusive page numbers for the selection or chapter.

> Barkley, Brad. "Beneath the Deep, Slow Motion." New Stories from the South: The Year's Best, 2002. Ed. Shannon Ravenel. Chapel Hill: Algonquin, 2002. 158-82.

35. Two or More Works from One Anthology To avoid repeating the same information about the anthology several times, include the anthology itself in your list of works cited.

> Intrator, Sam M., and Megan Scribner, eds. Teaching with Fire: Poetry That Sustains the Courage to Teach. San Francisco: Jossey, 2003.

In the entries for individual selections or chapters, cross-reference the anthology by giving the editor's name and the page numbers on which the selection appears.

> Dickinson, Emily. "The Chariot." Intrator and Scribner, 10-12.

36. Screenplay

> Kaufman, Charlie. Eternal Sunshine of the Spotless Mind: The Shooting Script. New York: Newmarket, 2004.

MLA

∨ Documenting Sources

37. Published Proceedings of a Conference   Provide information as you would for a book, adding information about the conference sponsors, date(s), and place before the publication data.

> Caspian Studies Program Staff. US-Russian Relations: Implications for the Caspian Region (Conference Report). Caspian Studies Program, 11 July 2001, Harvard U. Cambridge: Caspian Studies Program, 2004.

38. Paper Published in Proceedings of a Conference   Treat a selection from conference proceedings as you would a selection in an edited collection.

> Norris, Pippa. "E-campaigning and E-voting." Conference on Political Communications in the Twenty-first Century, January 2004, St. Margaret's Coll., U. of Otago, NZ. Otago: St. Margaret's Coll., 2004: 173-99.

39. Sacred Text   Include the title of the version as it appears on the title page. If the title does not identify the version, place that information directly after the title.

> Dhammapada: The Way of Truth. Trans. Sangharakshita. New York: Barnes, 2004.

40. Published Dissertation or Thesis   Cite as you would a book, but include information specific to the dissertation, such as the school and, if relevant, the University Microfilms International (UMI) order number.

> Huls, Simone. Disrobing the White Wizard: A Postcolonial Examination of Race and Culture in Harry Potter. Diss. U of Alabama in Huntsville, 2004. Ann Arbor: UMI, 2004. 1420069.

41. Unpublished Dissertation or Thesis   Place the title of the thesis or dissertation in quotation marks and add information about the type of dissertation, the school, and the date.

> Fitzgerald, Ryan T. "Reinterpreting Raymond Carver: A Look at Carver's Stories in Light of Gordon Lish." MA thesis. Brown U, 1999.

42. Abstract of a Dissertation or Thesis   Treat an abstract as you would an article in a journal. First give the information for the dissertation. Then add the source, abbreviated either *DA* or *DAI* (for *Dissertation Abstracts* or *Dissertation Abstracts International*), volume number, year (in parentheses), and page number.

> Chantharothai, Sasitorn. "Transforming Self, Family, and Community: Women in the Novels of Anne Tyler, Toni Morrison, and Amy Tan." Diss. Indiana U of Pennsylvania, 2004. DAI 64 (2004): 2489.

Sources in Journals, Magazines, and Newspapers

43. Article in a Journal Paginated by Volume. Most journals continue pagination for an entire year, beginning again at page 1 only in the first volume of the next year. After the journal title, list the volume number, year of publication in parentheses, a colon, and inclusive page numbers.

> Greer, Allan. "Natives and Nationalism: The Americanization of
>   Kateri Tekakwitha." The Catholic Historical Review. 90 (2004):
>   260-72.

44. Article in a Journal Paginated by Issue Some journals begin at page 1 for every issue. After the volume number, add a period and the issue number, with no space.

> Kriegel, Leonard. "Synagogues." The American Scholar 69.4 (2000):
>   61-75.

45. Article that Skips Pages Give only the first page number and a plus sign (+), with no space between.

> Dominus, Susan. "Growing Up with Mom and Mom." New York Times
>   Magazine 24 Oct. 2004: 69+.

46. Article with a Quotation in the Title Enclose the quotation in single quotation marks within the article title, which is enclosed in double quotation marks.

> Nachumi, Nora. "'I Am Elizabeth Bennet': Defining One's Self through
>   Austen's Third Novel." Pedagogy 4 (2004): 119-24.

47. Article in a Monthly or Bimonthly Magazine After the author's name and title of the article, list the title of the magazine, the date (use abbreviations for all months except May, June, and July), and the inclusive pages.

> Oppenheim, Noah. "Big Important Book of the Month." Esquire Dec.
>   2004: 58.

48. Article in a Weekly or Biweekly Magazine Give the exact date of publication, inverted.

> Flanagan, Caitlin. "What Teachers Want." New Yorker 6 Dec. 2004:
>   64-68.

49. Article in a Daily Newspaper If the title of the newspaper begins with *The,* omit the word. If the newspaper is not a national newspaper (such as the *Wall Street Journal, Christian Science Monitor,* or *Chronicle of Higher Education*) or the

TUTORIAL

How do I cite articles from periodicals using MLA style?

Periodicals include journals, magazines, and newspapers. This page gives an example of a citation for a print journal article. Models for citing articles from magazines and newspapers are on pages 253–57. If you need to cite a periodical article you accessed electronically, follow the guidelines below and see also page 260.

A **B**

Morgan, David. "Spirit and Medium: The Video Art of Bill Viola."

C **D** **E** **F**

Image: A Journal of the Arts & Religion 26 (2000): 29-39.

A **The author.** Give the last name first, followed by a comma, the first name, and the middle initial (if given). Omit titles such as MD, PhD, or Sir; include suffixes after the name and a comma (O'Driscoll, Gerald P., Jr.). End with a period.

B **The article title.** Give the full title; include the subtitle (if any), preceded by a colon. Enclose the title and subtitle in quotation marks, and capitalize all major words. Place a period inside the closing quotation mark.

C **The periodical title.** Underline or (if your instructor permits) italicize the periodical title; exclude any initial *A, An,* or *The;* capitalize all major words.

D **The volume number and issue number.** For journals, give the volume number; if each issue starts with page 1, include a period (no space) and then the issue number as well.

E **The date of publication.** For journals, give the year in parentheses, followed by a colon. For monthly magazines, don't use parentheses; give the month and year. For weekly magazines and newspapers, don't use parentheses; give the day, month, and year (in that order). Abbreviate the names of all months except May, June, and July.

F **Inclusive page number(s).** For numbers 100 and above, give only the last two digits and any other preceding digits if different from the first number (22-28, 402-10, 1437-45, 592-603). Include section letters for newspapers, if relevant. End with a period.

Use the **Bedford Bibliographer** at **bedfordresearcher.com** to create a works cited list formatted in MLA style.

city of publication is not part of its title, give the name of the city in square brackets [Salem, OR] after the title. List the date in inverted order and, if the masthead indicates that the paper has more than one edition, give this information after the date ("natl. ed.," "late ed."). Follow with a colon and a space, and end with the page numbers (use the section letter before the page number if the newspaper uses letters to designate sections). If the article does not appear on consecutive pages, write only the first page number and a plus sign (+), with no space between.

> Gottlieb, Jeff. "4 Hearts, 1 Marriage." <u>Los Angeles Times</u> 1 Dec. 2004: A1+.

50. Unsigned Article in a Newspaper or Magazine Begin with the title of the article. Alphabetize by the first word other than *A, An,* or *The*.

> "The Must List." <u>Entertainment Weekly</u> 19 Nov. 2004: 59.

51. Editorial in a Newspaper Include the word "Editorial" after the title.

> "Speed Bumps." Editorial. <u>Boston Globe</u> 14 Apr. 2005: A14.

52. Letter to the Editor Include the word "Letter" after the author.

> Videll, John. Letter. "Pheasant Hunting." <u>Chicago Tribune</u> 20 Nov. 2004, final ed.: 28.

53. Review After the author and title of the review, include the words "Rev. of," followed by the title of the work under review; a comma; the word "by" (for a book) or "dir." (for a play or film); and the name of the author or director. Continue with publication information for the review.

> Dirda, Michael. "Richard Wilbur's <u>Collected Poems</u>." Rev. of <u>Collected Poems: 1943-2004</u>, by Richard Wilbur. <u>Washington Post</u> 28 Nov. 2004: BW15.

54. Published Interview Begin with the person interviewed. If the published interview has a title, give it in quotation marks. If not, write the word "Interview" (no quotation marks or underline). If an interviewer is identified and relevant to your project, give that name next. Then supply the publication data.

> Chilcoat, Joanna, Robin DeJesus, and Daniel Letterle. "Roundtable: The Cast of <u>Camp</u>." Interview with Jamie Malanowski. <u>Entertainment Weekly</u> 27 Feb. 2004: 53+.

55. Special Issue Include the words "Spec. issue of" before the regular title of the periodical. End with the total number of pages in the issue.

> Baur, Michael, ed. <u>Person, Soul, and Immortality</u>. Spec. issue of <u>American Catholic Philosophical Quarterly</u> 75 (2001): 287.

Print Reference Works

56. Encyclopedia, Dictionary, Thesaurus, Handbook, or Almanac Cite as you would a book (see p. 247).

57. Entry in an Encyclopedia, Dictionary, Thesaurus, Handbook, or Almanac In many cases, the entries and articles in reference works are unsigned. Therefore, begin your citation with the title of the entry in quotation marks, followed by a period. Give the title of the reference work, underlined, and the edition and year of publication. Include the editor's name if the reference work is not well known. If the work is arranged alphabetically, you may omit the volume and page numbers.

> "Aargau." Columbia Encyclopedia. 6th ed., 2000.

If you cite a specific definition, include that information after the title of the entry, adding the abbreviation "Def." and the number of the definition.

> "Abatement." Def. 2. Webster's Third New International Dictionary. 2002.

If a reference work is not well known (perhaps because it includes highly specialized information), provide all of the bibliographic information.

> Porter, Roy. "Great Chain of Being." The Harper Dictionary of Modern
> Thought. Ed. Alan Bullock and Stephen Trombley. Rev. ed. New York:
> Harper, 1988.

58. Map or Chart Generally, treat a map or chart as you would a book without authors. Give its title (underlined), the word "Map" or "Chart," and publication information. For a map in an atlas, give the map title followed by publication information for the atlas and page numbers for the map. If the creator of the map or chart is listed, use his or her name as you would an author's name.

> Nevada. Map. Chicago: Rand, 2002.

> "The Middle East from 1945." Map. Hammond Atlas of the 20th Century.
> Maplewood: Hammond, 1996. 135.

59. Government Publications In most cases, cite the government agency as the author. If there is a named author, editor, or compiler, provide that name after the title. Use the abbreviations "Dept." for department, "Cong." for Congress, "S." for Senate, "H." or "HR" for House of Representatives, "Res." for resolution, "Rept." for report, "Doc." for document, and "GPO" for Government Printing Office.

> United States. Dept. of Educ. Office of Educ. Research and Improvement.
> Natl. Center for Educ. Statistics. Literacy behind Prison Walls:
> Profiles of the Prison Population from the National Adult Literacy
> Survey. By Karl O. Haigler et al. Washington: GPO, 1994.

Commonwealth of Massachusetts. Dept. of Educ. Requirements for the
    Participation of Students with Disabilities in MCAS: Spring 2005
    Update. Malden: Massachusetts Dept. of Education, 2004.

If you are citing from the *Congressional Record,* the entry is simply *Cong. Rec.* followed by the date, a colon, and the page numbers.

60. Pamphlet   Format the entry as you would for a book (see p. 247).

Lincoln, Abraham. Abraham Lincoln on Prohibition. New York: Prohibi-
    tion Educ. League of New York County, 1926.

Field Sources

61. Personal Interview   Place the name of the person interviewed first, words to indicate how the interview was conducted ("Personal interview," "Telephone interview," or "E-mail interview"), and the date.

Tomar, Stephen. Personal interview. 25 Feb. 2004.

62. Unpublished Letter   If written to you, give the writer's name, the words "Letter to the author" (no quotation marks or underline), and the date the letter was written.

Wayden, Rose. Letter to the author. 1 May 2004.

If the letter was written to someone else, give that name rather than "the author."

63. Lecture or Public Address   Give the speaker's name and the title of the lecture (if there is one) or the form ("Lecture," "Panel discussion," "Reading"). If the lecture was part of a meeting or convention, identify that event. Conclude with the event data, including venue, city, and date.

Livesey, Margot. Reading. Harvard Book Store, Cambridge. 12 Nov. 2004.

Media Sources

64. Film or Video Recording   Generally begin with the title of the film or recording (underlined). Always supply the name of the director (following the abbreviation "Dir."), the distributor, and the year of original release. You may also insert other relevant information, such as the names of performers or screenplay writers, before the distributor.

House of Flying Daggers. Dir. Yimou Zang. Perf. Ziyi Zhang. Sony Pictures
    Classics, 2004.

If you wish to emphasize an individual's role in the film or movie, such as the director or screenplay writer, you may list that name first.

Olivier, Laurence, dir. and perf. Hamlet. Paramount, 1948.

MLA

V Documenting Sources

For media other than film (such as videotape and DVD), identify the medium before the distributor.

> Notorious. Dir. Alfred Hitchcock. Perf. Cary Grant and Ingrid Bergman.
>   1946. DVD. Anchor Bay Entertainment, 1999.

65. Television Program Include the title of the program (underlined), the network, the station's call letters and city (if any), and the date on which you watched the program. If there are relevant persons to name (such as an author, director, host, narrator, or actor), include that information after the title. If the program has named episodes or segments, list those in quotation marks. If the program is part of a series, include that information before the network.

> "Deep Water." Deadwood. HBO. 3 Dec. 2004.

66. Radio Program   Cite as you would a television program.

> Talk of the Nation. Host Neal Conan. Natl. Public Radio. KOAC, Corvallis.
>   24 Jan. 2005.

67. Radio or Television Interview   Provide the name of the person interviewed and the title of the interview. If there is no title, write "Interview" and, if relevant, the name of the interviewer. Then provide the name of the program, the network, the call letters of the station, the city, and the date.

> Bush, Laura. Interview with Campbell Brown. The Today Show. NBC.
>   WHDH, Boston. 20 Jan. 2005.

68. Sound Recording   Begin with the name of the person whose work you want to highlight: the composer, the conductor, or the performer. Next list the title, followed by names of other artists (composer, conductor, performers), with abbreviations indicating their roles. The recording information includes the manufacturer and the date. If the recording is not a compact disc, identify its form (such as Audiocassette, Audiotape, LP, or MP3) before the recording data.

> Mozart, Wolfgang Amadeus. The Symphonies: Salzburg 1772-1773. Acad.
>   of Ancient Music. Cond. Jaap Schroeder and Christopher Hogwood.
>   LP. Decca, 1979.

If you wish to cite a particular track on the recording, give its performer and title (in quotation marks) and then proceed with the information about the recording. For live recordings, include the date of the performance between the title and the recording data.

Redding, Otis. "Mr. Pitiful." The Very Best of Otis Redding. 1964.
    Atlantic, 1992.

69. Musical Composition   Give the composer and title. Underline the title unless it identifies the composition by form ("symphony," "suite"), number ("op. 39," "K. 231"), or key ("E flat").

Brahms, Johannes. Walzer für Klavier zu Vier Händen. op. 39. 1865. Munich: Henle, 1955.

If you are referring to a published score, provide publication data as you would for a book. Insert the date of composition between the title and the publication information.

Sondheim, Stephen. A Little Night Music. 1973. New York: Warner, 1997.

70. Live Performance   Generally, begin with the title of the performance (underlined). Then give the author and director; the major performers; and theater, city, and date.

Pygmalion. By George Bernard Shaw. Dir. Marc S. Miller. Cambridge Family YMCA Theater, Cambridge. 10 Dec. 2004.

71. Work of Art   Give the name of the artist, the title of the work (underlined), the date of completion, and the name of the collection, museum or owner, and the city.

Guston, Philip. The Deluge. 1969. Museum of Fine Arts, Boston.

72. Advertisement   Provide the name of the product, service, or organization being advertised, followed by the word "Advertisement." Then provide the usual publication information.

Napster. Advertisement. Entertainment Weekly 19 Nov. 2004: 83.

73. Cartoon   Treat a cartoon like an article in a newspaper or magazine. Give the cartoonist's name, the title of the cartoon if there is one (in quotation marks), the word "Cartoon," and the publication data for the source.

Chast, Roz. "Someone Is Out There Watching." Cartoon. New Yorker 10 Jan. 2005: 64.

● **Electronic Sources**

74. Article from an Online Database or Subscription Service.   Cite it as you would a print article, then give the name of the database, subscription service, and library, access date, and brief URL for the database. (See also p. 260.)

How do I cite articles from databases using MLA style?

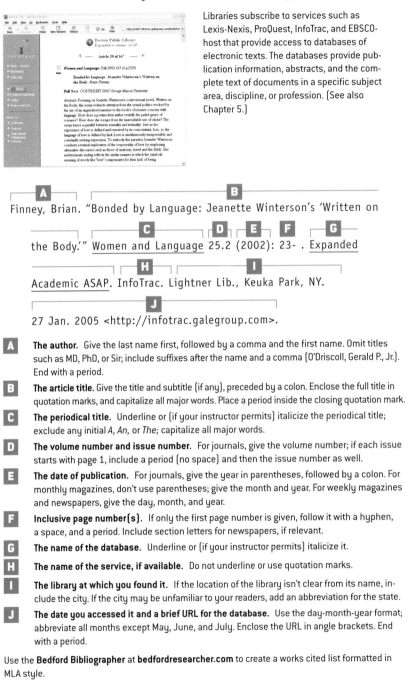

Libraries subscribe to services such as Lexis-Nexis, ProQuest, InfoTrac, and EBSCO-host that provide access to databases of electronic texts. The databases provide publication information, abstracts, and the complete text of documents in a specific subject area, discipline, or profession. (See also Chapter 5.)

A **B**

Finney, Brian. "Bonded by Language: Jeanette Winterson's 'Written on

C **D** **E** **F** **G**

the Body.'" Women and Language 25.2 (2002): 23- . Expanded

H **I**

Academic ASAP. InfoTrac. Lightner Lib., Keuka Park, NY.

J

27 Jan. 2005 <http://infotrac.galegroup.com>.

A **The author.** Give the last name first, followed by a comma and the first name. Omit titles such as MD, PhD, or Sir; include suffixes after the name and a comma (O'Driscoll, Gerald P., Jr.). End with a period.

B **The article title.** Give the title and subtitle (if any), preceded by a colon. Enclose the full title in quotation marks, and capitalize all major words. Place a period inside the closing quotation mark.

C **The periodical title.** Underline or (if your instructor permits) italicize the periodical title; exclude any initial *A, An,* or *The;* capitalize all major words.

D **The volume number and issue number.** For journals, give the volume number; if each issue starts with page 1, include a period (no space) and then the issue number as well.

E **The date of publication.** For journals, give the year in parentheses, followed by a colon. For monthly magazines, don't use parentheses; give the month and year. For weekly magazines and newspapers, give the day, month, and year.

F **Inclusive page number(s).** If only the first page number is given, follow it with a hyphen, a space, and a period. Include section letters for newspapers, if relevant.

G **The name of the database.** Underline or (if your instructor permits) italicize it.

H **The name of the service, if available.** Do not underline or use quotation marks.

I **The library at which you found it.** If the location of the library isn't clear from its name, include the city. If the city may be unfamiliar to your readers, add an abbreviation for the state.

J **The date you accessed it and a brief URL for the database.** Use the day-month-year format; abbreviate all months except May, June, and July. Enclose the URL in angle brackets. End with a period.

Use the **Bedford Bibliographer** at **bedfordresearcher.com** to create a works cited list formatted in MLA style.

Granastein, Lisa. "Comfort Food." Mediaweek 27 May 2002: 32- .
Academic Search Premier. EBSCOhost. Emerson Coll. Lib., Boston.
6 Mar. 2005 <http://web.epnet.com/>.

75. Abstract from an Online Database   Provide the publication information for the source, followed by the word "Abstract," information about the database, the library from which you accessed it, the date you accessed it, and the URL.

Foy, Nathalie. "'Our Unfixed Vision': The Undermining of Vision in Contemporary Canadian Fiction." Diss. U of Toronto, 2004. DAI 65 (2004): 1789. Abstract. UMI Proquest. Boston Public Lib., MA. 11 Nov. 2004 <http://wwwlib.umi.com/dissertations/fullcit/NQ91716>.

76. Entire Web Site.   Provide publication information followed by the access date and the URL in angle brackets. Place a period after the final angle bracket.

Miller, Jack. America's Most Literate Cities. 29 Nov. 2004. U of Wisconsin-Whitewater. 1 Dec. 2004. <http://www.uww.edu/npa/cities/overview.html>.

77. Work from a Professional or Commercial Web Site   Include the author (if available), the title of the document, and the title of the Web site, followed by the date of publication or last update, the sponsoring organization, the access date, and the URL. (See also p. 263.)

Pikulski, Jack. "Expert Q & A: Turning Kids into Lifelong Readers." PBS Parents. 2004. PBS. 8 Feb. 2005 <http://www.pbs.org/parents/experts/archive/pikulski.html>.

78. Academic Course or Department Web Site   For a course page, give the name of the instructor, the course title, a description such as "Course home page," the course dates, the department, the institution, the access date, and the URL. For a department page, give the department name, a description, the institution, and the access information.

Grove, Allen. English 220: Deviance and the British Novel. Course home page. Spring 1999. English Div., Alfred U. 10 Feb. 2005 <http://las.alfred.edu/~egl/grove/spring99/egl220/directory.html>.

English and Technical Communication. Dept. home page. U of Missouri-Rolla. 22 Mar. 2005 <http://english.umr.edu/>.

79. Work from a Personal Web Site   If the site has no title, give a description such as "Home page."

Siegel, Kristi. Home page. 12 Aug. 2003. 25 Jan. 2005 <http://
www.kristisiegel.com/>.

80. Message Posted to a Newsgroup, Electronic Mailing List, or Online Discussion Forum   Cite the name of the person who posted the message; the title (from the subject line, in quotation marks); the phrase "Online posting"; the date of the message; the name of the newsgroup, list, or forum; the access date; and the URL.

Wilder, Andrea. "Dyslexia." Online posting. 17 Nov. 2004. Learning
Disabilities Discussion List. 21 Feb. 2005 <http://www.nifl.gov/
lincs/discussions/nifl-ld/learning_disabilities.html>.

81. Entire Blog   To cite an entire Weblog, give the author (if available), the title, the description "Weblog," the date of publication or last update, the sponsoring organization (if any), the access date, and the URL.

Green, Tyler. Modern Art Notes. Weblog. 3 May 2005. ArtsJournal.com.
7 June 2005 <http://www.artsjournal.com/man/>.

82. Entry or Comment on a Blog   To cite an entry or a comment on a Weblog, give the author of the entry or comment (if available), the title of the entry or comment in quotation marks, the description "Weblog entry" or "Comment on a Weblog entry," the title of the blog (underlined), the date the material was posted, the sponsoring organization (if any), the access date, and the URL.

Allbritton, Christopher. "Our Hearts and Conscience." Weblog entry.
Back to Iraq 3.0. 19 Apr. 2005. 7 June 2005 <http://
www.back-to-iraq.com/archives/2005_04.php>.

83. Email message   Cite the sender of the message; the title (from the subject line, in quotation marks); a phrase indicating the recipient of the message; and the date of the message.

Shaw, Melissa. "Critique of 'Anna's Ordinary Blues.'" E-mail to the author.
19 Aug. 2005.

Eduardo, Juan. "Brainstorming for Essay." E-mail to Micah Thomson. 24
Apr. 2004.

84. Online Book   Cite an online book as you would a print book; then give the access date and the URL (see also #17 on p. 247).

Spence, Lewis. Legends and Romances of Brittany. New York: Stokes,
1917. 13 Apr. 2005 <http://www.sacred-texts.com/neu/celt/lrb/>.

TUTORIAL

How do I cite works from Web sites using MLA style?

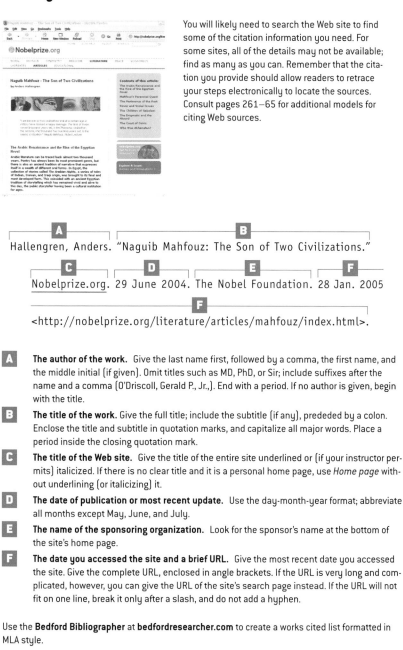

You will likely need to search the Web site to find some of the citation information you need. For some sites, all of the details may not be available; find as many as you can. Remember that the citation you provide should allow readers to retrace your steps electronically to locate the sources. Consult pages 261–65 for additional models for citing Web sources.

A **B**
Hallengren, Anders. "Naguib Mahfouz: The Son of Two Civilizations."
C **D** **E** **F**
Nobelprize.org. 29 June 2004. The Nobel Foundation. 28 Jan. 2005
F
<http://nobelprize.org/literature/articles/mahfouz/index.html>.

A **The author of the work.** Give the last name first, followed by a comma, the first name, and the middle initial (if given). Omit titles such as MD, PhD, or Sir; include suffixes after the name and a comma (O'Driscoll, Gerald P., Jr.,). End with a period. If no author is given, begin with the title.

B **The title of the work.** Give the full title; include the subtitle (if any), prededed by a colon. Enclose the title and subtitle in quotation marks, and capitalize all major words. Place a period inside the closing quotation mark.

C **The title of the Web site.** Give the title of the entire site underlined or (if your instructor permits) italicized. If there is no clear title and it is a personal home page, use *Home page* without underlining (or italicizing) it.

D **The date of publication or most recent update.** Use the day-month-year format; abbreviate all months except May, June, and July.

E **The name of the sponsoring organization.** Look for the sponsor's name at the bottom of the site's home page.

F **The date you accessed the site and a brief URL.** Give the most recent date you accessed the site. Give the complete URL, enclosed in angle brackets. If the URL is very long and complicated, however, you can give the URL of the site's search page instead. If the URL will not fit on one line, break it only after a slash, and do not add a hyphen.

Use the **Bedford Bibliographer** at **bedfordresearcher.com** to create a works cited list formatted in MLA style.

85. Article in an Online Periodical   Provide information as you would for a print periodical, adding the date of access and the URL (see also #43 on p. 253).

> Clark, Kelly. "The Job Openings and Labor Turnover Survey: What Initial
>   Data Show." Monthly Labor Review Online 127 (2004). 1 Dec. 2004
>   <http://stats.bls.gov/opub/mlr/2004/11/art2full.pdf>.

86. Online Poem   Cite an online poem as you would a print poem, followed by the name of the site, the sponsoring organization (if any), the date of electronic publication, the access date, and the URL.

> Chang, Victoria. "To Want." Circle. Carbondale: Southern Illinois UP,
>   2005. Verse Daily. 18 Jan. 2005. 11 May 2005 <http://
>   www.versedaily.org/2005/towant.shtml>.

87. Online Editorial or Letter to the Editor   Include "Letter" or "Editorial" after the title (if any) (see also #51 and #52 on p. 255).

> Ivey, Gilbert F. "Criticisms of Water Policies Are All Wet." Letter.
>   LATimes.com. 26 Jan. 2005. 27 Jan. 2005 <http://
>   www.latimes.com/>.

88. Online Review   (See also #53 on p. 255.)

> O'Donnell, Tobin. "Hope Amid Clouds of Suffering." Rev. of The
>   Painting, by Nina Schuyler. San Francisco Chronicle 24 Oct. 2004.
>   27 Oct. 2004 <http://sfgate.com/cgi-bin/article.cgi?f=/c/a/2004/
>   10/24/RVGOH9A2S51.DTL>.

89. Entry in an Online Reference Work   (See also #57 on p. 256.)

> "Nihilism." Encyclopaedia Britannica Online. 2005. Encyclopaedia
>   Britannica. 31 Mar. 2005 <http://www.britannica.com>.

90. Online Film or Art Clip   (See also #64 on p. 257.)

> Sax, Geoffrey, dir. White Noise. 2004. 23 Oct. 2004 <http://
>   www.apple.com/trailers/universal/white_noise/>.

91. Online Work of Art   (See also #71 on p. 259.)

> Yazzolino, Brad. Memaloose. 2002. Lewis and Clark 200 Years Later.
>   24 Oct. 2004 <http://www.lc200.com/artwork4.html>.

92. Online Map or Chart (See also #58 on p. 256.)

"Portland by Bicycle." Map. City of Portland Office of Transportation.
24 Oct. 2004 <http://www.trans.ci.portland.or.us/Bicycles/images/
MapFinal.gif>.

93. Online Advertisement Give the item or organization being advertised followed by the word "Advertisement." (See also #72 on p. 259.)

Lingo. Advertisement. New York Times on the Web 25 Jan. 2005.
<http://www.nytimes.com/>.

94. Other Online Sources For other online sources, adapt the guidelines to the medium. Include as much information as necessary for your readers to easily find your source. The examples below are for a radio program available in an online archive, and an online archive of oral-history interviews.

"The Sanctity of Marriage." This American Life. Host Ira Glass.
WBEZ, Chicago. 26 Mar. 2004. 8 June 2005 <http://
www.thisamericanlife.org/>.

Crowe, Michael. MP3. 27 Jan. 2005 <http://www.storycorps.net/listen/>.

95. CD-ROM Treat a CD-ROM as you would a book, noting "CD-ROM" after the title.

Stein, Mark. Black British Literature: Novels of Transformation. CD-ROM.
Columbus: Ohio State UP, 2004.

96. Multidisc CD-ROM Either give the total number of discs or, if you used only one of the discs, give the number of that disc.

Rosenzweig, Roy, et al. Who Built America? From the Great War of 1914
to the Dawn of the Atomic Age in 1946. CD-ROM. Disc 1. New York:
Worth, 2001.

97. Computer Software or Video Game Cite computer software as you would a book. Provide additional information about the medium on which it is distributed and the version.

Grand Theft Auto: San Andreas. CD-ROM. New York: Rockstar Games,
2004.

MLA

v Documenting Sources

MLA-style Research Essay

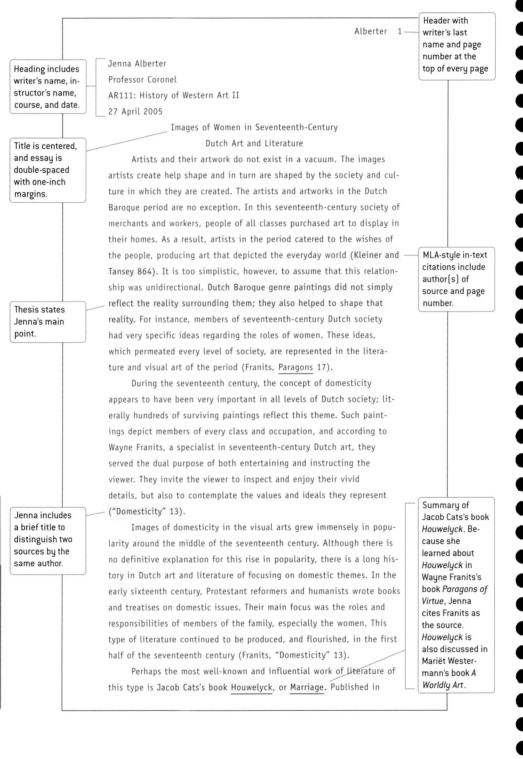

Alberter   1

Jenna Alberter

Professor Coronel

AR111: History of Western Art II

27 April 2005

Images of Women in Seventeenth-Century

Dutch Art and Literature

Artists and their artwork do not exist in a vacuum. The images artists create help shape and in turn are shaped by the society and culture in which they are created. The artists and artworks in the Dutch Baroque period are no exception. In this seventeenth-century society of merchants and workers, people of all classes purchased art to display in their homes. As a result, artists in the period catered to the wishes of the people, producing art that depicted the everyday world (Kleiner and Tansey 864). It is too simplistic, however, to assume that this relationship was unidirectional. Dutch Baroque genre paintings did not simply reflect the reality surrounding them; they also helped to shape that reality. For instance, members of seventeenth-century Dutch society had very specific ideas regarding the roles of women. These ideas, which permeated every level of society, are represented in the literature and visual art of the period (Franits, Paragons 17).

During the seventeenth century, the concept of domesticity appears to have been very important in all levels of Dutch society; literally hundreds of surviving paintings reflect this theme. Such paintings depict members of every class and occupation, and according to Wayne Franits, a specialist in seventeenth-century Dutch art, they served the dual purpose of both entertaining and instructing the viewer. They invite the viewer to inspect and enjoy their vivid details, but also to contemplate the values and ideals they represent ("Domesticity" 13).

Images of domesticity in the visual arts grew immensely in popularity around the middle of the seventeenth century. Although there is no definitive explanation for this rise in popularity, there is a long history in Dutch art and literature of focusing on domestic themes. In the early sixteenth century, Protestant reformers and humanists wrote books and treatises on domestic issues. Their main focus was the roles and responsibilities of members of the family, especially the women. This type of literature continued to be produced, and flourished, in the first half of the seventeenth century (Franits, "Domesticity" 13).

Perhaps the most well-known and influential work of literature of this type is Jacob Cats's book Houwelyck, or Marriage. Published in

---

Callout annotations:

Heading includes writer's name, instructor's name, course, and date.

Title is centered, and essay is double-spaced with one-inch margins.

Thesis states Jenna's main point.

Jenna includes a brief title to distinguish two sources by the same author.

Header with writer's last name and page number at the top of every page

MLA-style in-text citations include author(s) of source and page number.

Summary of Jacob Cats's book Houwelyck. Because she learned about Houwelyck in Wayne Franits's book Paragons of Virtue, Jenna cites Franits as the source. Houwelyck is also discussed in Mariët Westermann's book A Worldly Art.

MLA

V Documenting Sources

Alberter   2

1625, this was a comprehensive reference book for women of all ages, but especially young women, regarding matters of marriage and family. Although many other similar books were being published in the Netherlands and England during this period, Cats's work was perhaps the most extensive; it even contained an alphabetical index for quick reference (Franits, Paragons 5).

Houwelyck, which by mid-century had sold over 50,000 copies, making it a best-seller for its time, contained instruction for women on the proper behavior for the six stages of life: Maiden, Sweetheart, Bride, Housewife, Mother, and Widow. It is particularly telling that these stages of life were defined in reference to the roles of men. Although Cats's book specifically addressed women, it had implications for men as well (Westermann 119). According to Cats, by laying out the roles and duties of the woman, his book "encompasses also the masculine counter-duties" (qtd. in Westermann 119).

> Cats's six stages of life are used as the organizing principle for the research essay.

> Jenna cites an indirect source: words quoted in another source.

The illustration on the title page of the first edition of Cats's work shows what was considered the ideal role for a woman at this time. Created by Adriaen van de Venne, Stages of Life (Fig. 1) depicts several figural groups arranged on a hill. It shows life as a large hill, with marriage as its pinnacle, and then heading down toward widowhood and death (Westermann 120). This depiction seems to reflect the expectations society held for its women--that a woman's goal in life should be to provide a man with a good, proper wife and, once that duty has been fulfilled, to wait dutifully for death.

> Reference to an illustration found later in the text.

Images of young women are numerous in the visual art of this period. Gerard Dou's Portrait of a Young Woman (Fig. 2) exemplifies this

FIG. 1   Pieter de Jode after Adriaen van de Venne, Stages of Life, engraved frontispiece to Jacob Cats's Houwelyck (Marriage), 1625, private collection (Westermann 120).

> Illustration caption includes figure number and source information.

Alberter   3

type of work. This painting demonstrates that portraiture was highly influenced by contemporary ideals of feminine virtue. The young woman's pose is passive, self-contained, and somewhat rigid, communicating her dignity, humility, and modesty, which were all considered very important in a young girl. She holds a songbook in her lap, which not only indicated her skill in the arts but was also considered a symbol of docility. Near her rest two additional books, one of which is a Bible. Besides the obvious reference to the importance of piety, these items also were indicative of the practical value of literacy. Young women were brought up with the sole purpose of becoming wives and mothers, and the ability to read was crucial for the management of an efficient household (Franits, Paragons 19).

Another common element in images of young women is needlework, such as in Nicolaes Maes's Young Girl Sewing. This theme was meant to represent ideals of docility, domesticity, and diligence, all highly prized virtues in future wives. In addition, proper training of young women was considered very important, and activities such as sewing and lace making were thought to prevent laziness and prepare young women for their future as wives and mothers (Franits, Paragons 21). According to scholar Mariët Westermann, women would also sometimes sell their cloth, yarn, and lace to bring extra income into the households. Occasionally, women who sold their goods would form guilds of workers, although this was rare in the male-dominated guild system of the time (125).

The young women in such pieces are beautifully rendered. Elegant and refined, they are obviously of the middle or upper classes; their clothes are made of expensive, luxurious cloth and their beautiful,

> Effective transition between paragraphs creates coherence.

> Jenna names the author of the source in her text sentence. She cites her source even when paraphrasing.

FIG. 2   Gerard Dou, Portrait of a Young Woman, oil on panel, date unknown, private collection (Franits, Paragons 20).

braided hair is laced with shiny, smooth ribbon. Their skin looks like porcelain, smooth and clear. While these images were designed and painted to look very realistic, it is important to remember that, like the literature of the time, they represented an ideal, not necessarily the reality. In Paragons of Virtue, art historian Wayne Franits calls attention to this distinction between the ideal and the real, noting, "[Both] art and literature present an exemplary image, a topos that does not necessarily reflect the actual situation of young women in seventeenth-century Dutch culture" (25).

> Brackets indicate a modified quotation.

In the large number of paintings depicting young women, probably commissioned by their parents, another popular theme is that of courtship. These works, such as Jacob van Loo's Wooing, are often an appreciation or celebration of love and romance but also serve to instruct about expected and appropriate behavior of young women in such situations.

Contemporary literature of this period also concerns courtship. In Houwelyck, for example, Cats discusses the "rules" and etiquette of courtship as well as the virtues a young woman should possess in order to acquire a good husband (Franits, Paragons 18). Cats argues that women should show only limited initiative in the relationship; for the most part, they should follow the lead of the suitor. Women should meet with suitors only in the safe confines of their own homes, under the watchful eye of their parents. They should avoid the use of very showy clothing or jewelry to attract men; instead, they should utilize the "jewels" of humility, modesty, piety, and so forth. And of course, the decision regarding the choice of spouse is ultimately left to the parents (Franits, Paragons 34).

Jan Soet's work Maagden-Baak, or Maiden's Beacon, published in 1642, deals with the courtship theme in even greater detail than Cats's book. The frontispiece to Soet's book depicts several young women standing on the shore, where they have been watching a ship coming into harbor. They have turned to look at a veiled figure, thought to be an allegory for Chastity. The metaphor is that women, like the ship in the drawing, must endure the storms and dangers of courtship before they can enter the secure harbor of marriage. To accomplish this, women must have the guidance of a beacon, in this case Soet's book (Franits, Paragons 33).

Once the maiden navigated the perilous seas of courtship, she could enter into the safety and security of marriage and motherhood, where she found for herself a very rigid, prescribed role. The marriage portraiture of Johannes Verspronck illuminates the status of men and women in their roles in marriage. In Portrait of a Man and Portrait of a Woman (Figs. 3 and 4), Verspronck provides visual cues to the

> Transitional sentence carries readers from one idea to the next.

Alberter   5

FIG. 3   Johannes Verspronck, Portrait of a Man, oil on canvas, 1641, Rijksmuseum Twenthe, Enschede (Westermann 132).

FIG. 4   Johannes Verspronck, Portrait of a Woman, oil on canvas, 1640, Rijksmuseum Twenthe, Enschede (Westermann 132).

differences between the roles of husband and wife. The separate portraits are meant to hang side by side, the partners turned toward each other. Though nearly identical composition may suggest equality, the woman's pose is conservative and self-contained, while the man's is bold and engaging. He has pulled off his glove, as if preparing to greet the viewer; in contrast, the woman waits, quietly and expectantly, to be approached. In the same way, shadows play on the man's face, creating depth, while the woman's face is smoothed by soft, direct light. Such visual cues reinforce the social and cultural norms and expectations of husbands and wives (Westermann 133).

Both men and women had prescribed roles and responsibilities in the home and community. The workplace, usually separate from the home, was generally the domain of the husband, especially in upper- and middle-class families. Women, in contrast, spent most of their time in the private, domestic space of the home. A wife's main duties were to help her husband, care for the children, run the household, and supervise the servants (Franits, Paragons 64).

Alberter   6

Two well-known Dutch Baroque painters, Johannes Vermeer and Pieter de Hooch, specialized in painting scenes from everyday life (Russell). Much of their work depicts the interiors of typical middle- and upper-class Dutch homes as quiet, serene, orderly domestic spaces. De Hooch's Woman and Child in an Interior reflects such a space, where the woman is adept at her role as wife and mother and runs the household efficiently. In these works, the man is often absent, as the home is not considered his domain (Alpers 95). Westermann describes the work of Vermeer and de Hooch in this way: "Their paintings invite contemplation of domestic virtue, of the quiet and harmonious household prescribed by Cats and others" (124).

These pervasive ideas about gender status and roles were reinforced by theological views of the time. Protestant and humanist philosophers wrote extensively about domestic life, outlining specific roles and duties for each member of the family, focusing much of their attention on the wife and mother. Marriage was considered to be a natural and honorable state instituted by God; the primary goal was companionship, not procreation. (Indeed, children were often viewed as the inevitable danger of married life, rather than its purpose.) Wives, like Eve, were meant to act as helpmates for their husbands. In short, marriage was "viewed as a covenantal alliance between spouses who agreed to fulfill particular obligations appropriate to their sex" (Franits, Paragons 66-67).

A surprisingly large number of Dutch Baroque paintings depict images of the elderly, especially as compared with work in other European countries at the time. Dutch authors of the Baroque period also often explored themes of aging and widowhood. The final chapter in Cats's Houwelyck discusses these topics at length and in a very sensitive and moving manner. The chapter is divided into two sections. The first focuses on issues of the fleeting nature of human existence and the need for the elderly to turn away from worldly matters and toward the spiritual realm; the second section provides practical advice and instruction for widows regarding their roles and behavior (Franits, Paragons 161). Many authors, including Cats, argued that growing older and deteriorating physically could have positive consequences as well. They believed that aging forced elderly people to turn their minds to death and the afterlife. Older people were thought to possess prized virtues such as moderation and simplicity and therefore would be favored by God and looked upon with compassion. Because of this spiritual wisdom, it was thought that aging allowed a person to contemplate death without fear (Franits, Paragons 163-64).

Artists dealt with this idea of spirituality perhaps with even greater frequency than authors. Gerard Dou's The Prayer of the Spinner

Effective transition between paragraphs builds coherence.

MLA

V Documenting Sources

Alberter   7

(Fig. 5) is one of many paintings of the time depicting this theme. Dou's subject is rendered with little individuality; rather, she is meant to represent an ideal, an image of appropriate conduct for a widow or elderly woman. Her heavy garments and pious disposition are typical of this type of painting. Dou also included several symbolic elements that seventeenth-century viewers would have immediately understood: the spinning wheel and sewing basket representing domestic virtue and the burned-out candle signifying the transitory nature of life (Franits, Paragons 171).

Widows of this time were expected to do more than live simple, pious lives. Authors, philosophers, and artists of the time also encouraged elderly women to be virtuous role models for young women and girls. Artists such as Gerard ter Borch were known to place young and elderly women side by side. Such works probably served to instruct older women to act as guides and teachers to their younger family members.

Because of their faithful depiction of the world and their painstaking attention to detail, seventeenth-century Dutch paintings of domestic scenes can be called realistic. However, it is important to remember that these images do not always simply depict the people and their world exactly as they were. Instead, these works served multiple purposes—to spread and promote ideas about domestic virtue, to instruct viewers about women's roles, and, finally, to entertain viewers (Franits, Paragons 9). Just as in the art of every culture in history, the art of the Dutch Baroque period was both a mirror of the world in which it was created and a shaper of that world.

> Conclusion reinforces Jenna's thesis statement.

FIG. 5   Gerard Dou, The Prayer of the Spinner, oil on panel, date unknown, Alta Pinakothek, Munich (Franits, Paragons 171).

MLA

∨ Documenting Sources

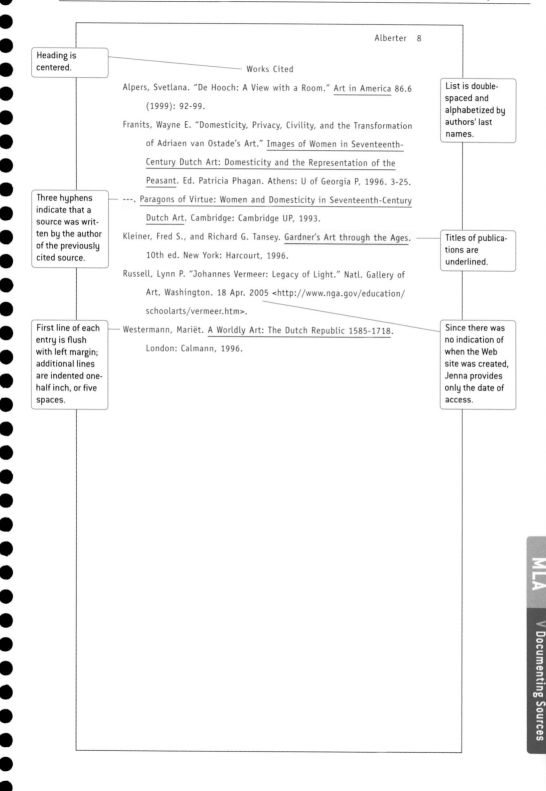

Alberter 8

Heading is centered.

Works Cited

Alpers, Svetlana. "De Hooch: A View with a Room." Art in America 86.6 (1999): 92-99.

Franits, Wayne E. "Domesticity, Privacy, Civility, and the Transformation of Adriaen van Ostade's Art." Images of Women in Seventeenth-Century Dutch Art: Domesticity and the Representation of the Peasant. Ed. Patricia Phagan. Athens: U of Georgia P, 1996. 3-25.

---. Paragons of Virtue: Women and Domesticity in Seventeenth-Century Dutch Art. Cambridge: Cambridge UP, 1993.

Kleiner, Fred S., and Richard G. Tansey. Gardner's Art through the Ages. 10th ed. New York: Harcourt, 1996.

Russell, Lynn P. "Johannes Vermeer: Legacy of Light." Natl. Gallery of Art, Washington. 18 Apr. 2005 <http://www.nga.gov/education/schoolarts/vermeer.htm>.

Westermann, Mariët. A Worldly Art: The Dutch Republic 1585-1718. London: Calmann, 1996.

List is double-spaced and alphabetized by authors' last names.

Three hyphens indicate that a source was written by the author of the previously cited source.

Titles of publications are underlined.

First line of each entry is flush with left margin; additional lines are indented one-half inch, or five spaces.

Since there was no indication of when the Web site was created, Jenna provides only the date of access.

Part V
Documenting Sources

17 Understanding
    Documentation Systems
18 Using MLA Style
19 **Using APA Style**
20 Using *Chicago* Style
21 Using CSE Style

19

Using APA Style

> **Key Questions**
>
> **19a. How do I cite sources within the text of my document?   276**
>
> **19b. How do I prepare the reference list?   279**

American Psychological Association (APA) style, used primarily in the social sciences and in some of the natural sciences, emphasizes the author(s) and publication date of a source. Writers who use the APA documentation system cite, or formally acknowledge, information within their text using parentheses and provide a list of sources, called a reference list, at the end of their document. For more information about APA style, consult the *Publication Manual of the American Psychological Association,* Fifth Edition, and *Mastering APA Style: Student's Workbook and Training Guide.* Information about these publications can be found on the APA Web site at www.apa.org.

Use the **Bedford Bibliographer** at **bedfordresearcher .com** to create an APA-style bibliography.

To see featured writer Alexis Alvarez's research essay, formatted in APA style, turn to page 292.

CITATIONS WITHIN YOUR TEXT

1. Basic format for direct quotation   276
2. Basic format for summary or paraphrase   277
3. Two authors   277
4. Three, four, or five authors   277
5. More than five authors   277
6. Corporate or group author   278
7. Unknown author   278
8. Two or more works   278
9. Source quoted in another source   278
10. Source with no page numbers   278
11. Two or more authors with the same last name   279
12. Email and other personal communication   279
13. Web site or document from a Web site   279

ENTRIES IN YOUR REFERENCE LIST

19a

How do I cite sources within the text of my document?

APA uses an author-date form of in-text citation to acknowledge the use of another writer's words, facts, or ideas. When you refer to a source, insert a parenthetical note that gives the author's last name and the year of the publication, separated by a comma. Even when your reference list includes the day or month of publication, the in-text citation should include only the year. For a quotation, the citation in parentheses also includes the page(s) on which the quotation can be found, if the source has page numbers. Note that APA style requires using the past tense or present perfect tense to introduce the material you are citing: *Renfrew argued* or *Renfrew has argued*.

1. Basic Format for Direct Quotation   When you are using a direct quotation from a source and have named the author in your sentence, place the publication date in parentheses directly after the author's last name. Include the page number (with "p." for page) in parentheses after the quotation.

> Kirby (2004) found that indeed "the seven African American men suggest that their economic status is associated with the structural context of rural Caswell County, which perpetuates social deprivation" (p. 1).

If you are using a direct quotation from a source and have not mentioned the author's name in your sentence, place the author's last name, the publication date, and the page number in parentheses:

> (Oakley, 1992, p. viii).

2. Basic Format for Summary or Paraphrase When you are summarizing or paraphrasing, place the author's last name and date either in the sentence or in parentheses at the end of the sentence. Include a page or chapter reference if it would help readers find the original material in a longer work.

> Kirby (2004) found that the policy makers for the Caswell County local government were not receptive to the needs of the African American men in her study (p. 4).

> Recent studies have suggested that local government fails to serve African Americans' needs adequately (Kirby, 2004, p. 4).

3. Two Authors List the last names of both authors in every mention in the text. If you mention the authors' names in a sentence, use the word "and" to separate the last names, as shown in the first example. If you place the authors' names in the parenthetical citation, use an ampersand (&) to separate the last names, as shown in the second example.

> Inman and George (2004) have suggested that kids often vocalize their belief that voting is important while they are still unable to name the governor or a congressperson from their state.

> Politics enters the worldview of children at a very young age, surprisingly even in the form of taunting if a candidate's or official's child is a classmate (Inman & George, 2004).

4. Three, Four, or Five Authors In parentheses, name all the authors the first time you cite the source, using an ampersand (&) before the last author's name. In subsequent references to the source, use the last name of the first author followed by the abbreviation "et al." (Latin for "and others").

> Although studies have shown that the behavior of peers and family members affects the development of eating disorders in children, no clear patterns have been established (Phares, Steinberg, & Thompson, 2004). Even more troublesome, hardly any data exist to document the differences between young girls and young boys in their development of eating disorders (Phares et al., 2004).

5. More Than Five Authors In all references to the source, give the first author's last name followed by "et al."

> Boyle et al. (2004) theorized that children were affected not only by the level of parenting but also by the difference between the level of parenting a child receives in comparison to siblings in the household.

APA

V Documenting Sources

6. Corporate or Group Author In general, cite the full name of the corporation or group the first time it is mentioned in your text. If you add an abbreviation for the group in square brackets the first time you cite the source, you can use the abbreviation in subsequent citations.

> With older patients, the line between physical illness and emotional problems may be difficult to identify (American Psychological Association [APA], 2004). However, care for many of older adults' problems will require the same skills that practitioners employ for other patients (APA, 2004).

7. Unknown Author Sources with unknown authors are listed by title in the list of references. In your in-text citation, shorten the title as much as possible without introducing confusion. Add quotation marks to article titles, and italicize book titles.

> Recent scientific discoveries continue to inflame the evolution-creationism debate ("Fossil," 2005).

If a source identifies its author as "Anonymous," use that word to cite the author of the source.

> The rise in water levels along the Missouri River has been referred to as a national crisis (Anonymous, 2001).

8. Two or More Works List the sources in alphabetical order and separate them with semicolons. If you are referring to two or more sources by the same author, order those sources chronologically.

> A subject's confidence, whether justified or inflated, can have a significant impact on his or her ability to identify facial features of others from memory (Semmler, Brewer, & Wells, 2004; Weber & Brewer, 2003).

9. Source Quoted in Another Source Ideally, you will be able to find the primary, or original, source for material used in your research project document. If you quote or paraphrase a secondary source — a source that contains information about a primary source — mention the primary source and indicate that it was cited in the secondary source.

> Kwansman et al. (1995) has shown that few physicians refer children with ADHD to mental health professionals for treatment (as cited in Dawkins, 2004, p. 15).

10. Source with No Page Numbers Many Web sources lack stable page numbers. In such cases, indicate the paragraph number or section heading in which the cited passage exists.

Richards (2004) suggested that cognitive behavioral therapy has been proven to be the most consistently reliable treatment for anxiety disorders (para. 4).

11. Two or More Authors with the Same Last Name Use the authors' initials in each citation.

While L. N. Miller (2003) emphasized the logical basis for criminal profiling, the insights of E. C. Miller (2003) into society's assumptions about female criminality provide an easy example of potential flaws in profiling.

12. Email and Other Personal Communication Give the first initial(s) and last name of the person with whom you corresponded, the words "personal communication," and the date. Don't include personal communication in your reference list.

(A. L. Chan, personal communication, October 9, 2005)

B. E. Hassan (personal communication, February 12, 2005)

13. Web Site or Document from a Web Site For an entire Web site, give the URL in parentheses in your text and don't include it in your reference list. To cite a quotation from a Web site, give the page number or paragraph number and include the source in your reference list.

Wisniewski (2004) has shown that many students need "direct instruction rather than just unfettered exploration in order to learn" (para. 5).

19b

How do I prepare the reference list?

The reference list contains publication information for all sources that you have cited within your document, with two exceptions. Entire Web sites and personal communication—such as correspondence, email messages, and interviews—are cited only in the text of the document.

Begin the list on a new page at the end of the document and center the title "References" at the top. Organize the list alphabetically by author; if the source is an organization, alphabetize the source by the name of the organization. All of the entries should be double-spaced with no extra space between entries. Entries are formatted with a hanging indent: The first line of an entry is flush with the left margin and subsequent lines are indented one-half inch or five spaces.

In longer documents, a reference list could be given at the end of each chapter or section. In electronic documents that use links, such as Web sites, the reference list is often a separate page to which other pages are linked. To see a reference list in APA style, see p. 300.

Books, Conference Proceedings, and Dissertations

14. One Author

> Roese, N. J. (2005). *If only: How to turn regret into opportunity.* New York: Broadway Books.

15. Two or More Authors
List the authors in the same order as the title page does, each with last name first. Use commas to separate authors and use an ampersand (&) before the final author's name. List every author up to six; for a work with more than six authors, give the first six names followed by "et al." (Latin for "and others").

> Girdano, D. A., Dusek, D. E., & Everly, G. S. (2005). *Controlling stress and tension.* San Francisco: Pearson/Benjamin Cummings.

16. Corporate or Group Author
Write out the full name of a corporate or group author. If the corporation is also the publisher, use "Author" for the publisher's name.

> American Psychological Association. (2005). *Concise rules of APA style.* Washington, DC: Author.

17. Unknown Author
When there is no author listed on the title or copyright page, begin the entry with the title of the work. Alphabetize the entry by the first significant word of the title (not including *A, An,* or *The*).

> *Heroes and helpers: A supplement to childcraft.* (2003). Chicago: World Book.

18. Two or More Works by the Same Author(s)
Give the author's name in each entry and list the works in chronological order.

> Coles, Robert. (1990). *The call of stories: Teaching and the moral imagination.* Boston: Mariner Books.

> Coles, Robert. (2001). *Lives of moral leadership: Men and women who have made a difference.* New York: Random House.

19. Translated Book
List the author first followed by the year of publication, the title, and the translator (in parentheses, identified by the word "Trans."). Place the original date of the work's publication at the end of the entry.

TUTORIAL

How do I cite books using APA style?

When citing a book, use the information from the title page and the copyright page (on the reverse side of the title page), not from the book's cover or a library catalog. Consult pages 280–84 for additional models for citing books.

THE
DANGEROUS
RISE OF
THE SUV
KEITH
BRADSHER

HIGH AND MIGHTY

A **B** **C**

Bradsher, K. (2003). *High and mighty: The dangerous rise of the SUV.*

D **E**

New York: Public Affairs Books.

A **The author.** Give the last name first, followed by a comma and initials for first and middle names. Separate initials with a space (Leakey, R. E.). Separate the names of multiple authors with commas; use an ampersand (&) before the final author's name.

B **The year of publication.** Put the most recent copyright year in parentheses, and end with a period (outside the parentheses).

C **The title.** Give the full title; include the subtitle (if any), preceded by a colon. Italicize the title and subtitle, capitalizing only the first word of the title, the first word of the subtitle, and any proper nouns or proper adjectives. End with a period.

D **The city of publication.** If more than one city is given, use the first one listed. For a city that may be unfamiliar to your readers or confused with another city, add an abbreviation of the state, country, or province (Cambridge, Eng.). Insert a colon.

E **The publisher.** Give the publisher's name. Omit words such as *Inc.* and *Co.* Include and do not abbreviate such terms as *University* and *Press.* End with a period.

APA

V Documenting Sources

Use the **Bedford Bibliographer** at **bedfordresearcher.com** to create a references list formatted in APA style.

Schivelbusch, W. (2003). *The culture of defeat: On national trauma, mourning, and recovery* (J. Chase, Trans.). New York: Metropolitan. (Original work published 2001)

20. Republication

R. Havens. (2004). *Wisdom of Milton H. Erickson* (Complete ed.). New York: Crown House Publishing. (Original work published 1985)

21. Book in an Edition Other Than the First   Note the edition ("2nd ed.," "Rev. ed.") after the title.

American Psychiatric Association. (2000). *Diagnostic and statistical manual of mental disorders* (4th ed.). Washington, DC: American Psychiatric Publishing.

22. Multivolume Work   Include the number of volumes in parentheses after the title.

Massarik, F. (Ed.). (1990). *Advances in organization development* (Vols. 1–3). Norwood, NJ: Ablex.

If you have used only one volume in a multivolume work, identify that volume by number and by title.

Hickman, L. A., & Alexander, T. M. (Eds.). (1998). *The essential John Dewey: Vol. 2. Ethics, logic, psychology.* Bloomington: Indiana University Press.

23. Editor   Include "Ed." or "Eds." in parentheses.

Motherwell, L., & Shay, J. J. (Eds.). (2004). *Complex dilemmas in group therapy: Pathways to resolution.* New York: Taylor & Francis.

24. Author with an Editor   Include the editor's name and the word "Ed." in parentheses after the title.

Schulz, S. C. (2005). *Juvenile-onset schizophrenia: Assessment, neurobiology, and treatment* (J. L. Findling, Ed.). Baltimore: Johns Hopkins University Press.

25. Anthology   To cite an entire anthology of essays or collection of articles, list the editor or editors first, followed by the abbreviation "Ed." or "Eds." in parentheses.

Andersen, M. L., & Collins, P. H. (Eds.). (2003). *Race, class, and gender: An anthology.* Belmont, CA: Wadsworth.

26. Chapter in an Edited Book or Selection in an Anthology   Begin the entry with the author, the publication date, and the title of the chapter or selection (not italicized). Follow this with the names of the editors (initials first) and the abbreviation "Ed." or "Eds." in parentheses, the title of the anthology or collection (italicized), inclusive page numbers for the chapter or selection (in parentheses, with abbreviation "pp."), and place and publisher.

> Polster, E. (2004). Sensory functioning in psychotherapy. In I. Macnaughton (Ed.), *Body, breath, & consciousness: A somatics anthology* (pp. 71-78). Berkeley, CA: North Atlantic Books.

27. Foreword, Introduction, Preface, or Afterword   Treat as you would a chapter in a book.

> Vladeck, B. C. (2004). Foreword. In T. E. Gass, *Nobody's home: Candid reflections of a nursing home aide* (pp. ix-xiv). Ithaca, NY: Cornell University Press.

28. Published Proceedings of a Conference   Cite information as you would for a book, capitalizing the name of the conference, meeting, or symposium (if there is one).

> *Constructing and applying objective functions: Proceedings of the Fourth International Conference on Econometric Decision Models, Constructing and Applying Objective Functions.* (2002). Transcript of proceedings sponsored by University of Hagen and held in Haus Nordhelle, August 28-31, 2000. New York: Springer.

29. Paper Published in the Proceedings of a Conference   Treat a conference paper as you would a selection from an edited collection.

> Paul, C. (2004). Morphology and computation. In *From animals to animats 8: Proceedings of the Eighth International Conference on the Simulation of Adaptive Behavior* (pp. 33-38). Los Angeles, California, July 13-17, 2004. Cambridge, MA: MIT Press.

30. Sacred Text   Treat as you would a book (see p. 280).

> *The Holy Bible: Illuminated family edition.* (2004). San Diego, CA: Thunder Bay Press.

31. Published Dissertation or Thesis   Give the author, date, and title before giving information about the college or university that granted the degree. Follow with the *Dissertation Abstracts International* information obtained from University Microfilms International (UMI).

> Leon, S. C. (2004). Examining congruence in implicit and self-attributed motives: Does the unconscious really become conscious? (Doctoral dissertation, Adelphi University, 2004). *Dissertation Abstracts International, 65-03B,* 3126976.

32. Unpublished Dissertation or Thesis   Format as you would a book, replacing the publisher information with the phrase "Unpublished doctoral dissertation" or "Unpublished master's thesis," followed by information about the college or university.

> Piccin, T. (2004). *A resource conservation view of the mutual exclusivity effect in children's word learning.* Unpublished master's thesis, Villanova University, Philadelphia.

33. Abstract of a Dissertation or Thesis   Treat an abstract as you would an article in a journal. Follow with the *Dissertation Abstracts International* information obtained from UMI.

> Abuzahara, K. G. (2004). Understanding resilience in Muslim-American immigrant women: An examination of protective processes. *Dissertation Abstracts International 65-03B,* 3119783.

● Sources in Journals, Magazines, and Newspapers

34. Article in a Journal Paginated by Volume   Most journals continue page numbers throughout an entire annual volume, beginning again at page 1 only in the first volume of the next year. After the author and publication year, provide the article title, the journal title, the volume number (italicized), and the inclusive page numbers.

> Lee, D. L., Sohn, N. H., & Park, S. H. (2004). Adolescents' peer-rated mental health, peer-acceptance, and irrational beliefs. *Psychological Reports, 94,* 1144-1149.

35. Article in a Journal Paginated by Issue   Some journals begin at page 1 for every issue. Include the issue number (in parentheses, not italicized) after the volume number.

> Savishinsky, J. (2004). The volunteer and the sannyasin: Archetypes of retirement in America and India. *International Journal of Aging and Human Development, 59*(1), 25-42.

36. Article in a Magazine   The author's name and the publication date are followed by the title of the article, the magazine title (italicized), and the volume number, if any (also italicized). Include all page numbers.

> Hodder, H. F. (2004, November-December). The future of marriage. *Harvard Magazine, 107,* 38-45.

TUTORIAL

How do I cite articles from periodicals using APA style?

Periodicals include journals, magazines, and newspapers. This page gives an example of a citation for a print journal article. Models for citing articles from magazines and newspapers are on pages 284–86. If you need to cite a periodical article you accessed electronically, follow the guidelines below; see also page 290.

Human Rights Quarterly

A Comparative and International Journal of the Social Sciences, Humanities, and Law

Volume 25   Number 4   November 2003
The Johns Hopkins University Press

A **B** **C**

Howe, R. B., & Covel, K. (2003). Child poverty in Canada and the

D **E** **F**

rights of the child. *Human Rights Quarterly, 25,* 1067-1087.

A   **The author.** Give the last name first, followed by a comma and initials for first and middle names. Separate the names of multiple authors with commas; use an ampersand (&) before the final author's name.

B   **The year of publication.** Put the year in parentheses and end with a period (outside the parentheses). For magazines and newspapers, include the month and, if relevant, the day (2005, April 13).

C   **The article title.** Give the full title; include subtitle (if any), preceded by a colon. Do not underline, italicize, or put the title or subtitle in quotes. Capitalize only the first word of the title, the first word of the subtitle, and any proper nouns or proper adjectives. End with a period.

D   **The periodical title.** Italicize the periodical title, and capitalize all major words. Insert a comma.

E   **The volume number and issue number.** For journals, include the volume number, italicized. If each issue starts with page 1, include the issue number in parentheses, not italicized. Insert a comma.

F   **Inclusive page number(s).** Give all of the numbers in full (248-254, not 248-54). For newspapers, include and abbreviation *p.* for page and section letters, if relevant (p. B12). End with a period.

Use the **Bedford Bibliographer** at **bedfordresearcher.com** to create a references list formatted in APA style.

37. Article in a Newspaper   List the author's name and the complete date (year first). Next give the article title followed by the name of the newspaper (italicized). Include all page numbers, preceded by "p." or "pp."

> Carey, B. (2004, December 3). TV time, unlike child care, ranks high in mood study. *The New York Times,* p. A22.

38. Unsigned Article in a Newspaper   Begin with the article title, and alphabetize in the reference list by the first word in the title other than *A, An,* or *The.* Use "p." or "pp." before page numbers.

> Healey rejects study on health care costs. (2004, August 10). *The Boston Globe,* p. B2.

39. Letter to the Editor   Include the words "Letter to the editor" in square brackets after the title of the letter, if any. Note that the page numbers in the example indicate that the letter was printed on nonconsecutive pages.

> San Gabriel, D. (2004, December 3). Not all kids are self-absorbed [Letter to the editor]. *The Boston Globe,* pp. A26, A28.

40. Review   After the title of the review, include the words "Review of the book . . ." or "Review of the film . . ." and so on in brackets, followed by the title of the work reviewed.

> Yagoda, B. (2000, May/June). Coloring public opinion [Review of the book *The black image in the white mind: Media and race in America*]. *The New Leader, 78*(2), 27-28.

When the review is untitled, follow the date with the bracketed information.

> Eisenman, R. (2000). [Review of the book *Brushing back Jim Crow: The integration of minor league baseball in the American South*]. *Multicultural Review, 9*(2), 74.

41. Published Interview   Cite a published interview like a journal article (see p. 284).

> Isaac, D. (September 2004). Thomas Sowell. *The American Enterprise 15*(6), 14-20.

42. Two or More Works by the Same Author in the Same Year   List the works alphabetically and include lowercase letters (*a, b,* etc.) after the dates.

> Chin, G. (2004a). Biotechnology: Targeting morphine. *Science 306,* 1441.
>
> Chin, G. (2004b). Psychology: Crunch time. *Science 306,* 1651.

Print Reference Works

43. Encyclopedia, Dictionary, Thesaurus, Handbook, or Almanac Cite a reference work, such as an encyclopedia or a dictionary, as you would a book (see p. 280).

> *Random House Webster's college thesaurus.* (2005). New York: Random House.

44. Entry in an Encyclopedia, Dictionary, Thesaurus, Handbook, or Almanac Begin your citation with the name of the author or, if the entry is unsigned, the title of the entry. Proceed with the date, the entry title (if not already given), the title of the reference work, the edition number, and the pages. If the contents of the reference work are arranged alphabetically, omit the volume and page numbers.

> Hine, D. C., Brown, E. B., & Terborg-Penn, R. (Eds.). (2004). Mabley, Jackie. In *Black women in America: An historical encyclopedia* (pp. 739-741). New York: Oxford University Press.

45. Government Publication Give the name of the department (or office, agency, or committee) that issued the report as the author. If the document has a report or special file number, place that in parentheses after the title.

> National Clearinghouse on Child Abuse and Neglect Information. (2004). *Child abuse and neglect fatalities: Statistics and interventions.* Washington, DC: U.S. Government Printing Office.

46. Pamphlet Format the entry as you would a book (see p. 280).

> Department of Psychology at Oakland University. (2004). *Majoring in psychology at Oakland University.* Rochester, MI: Author.

Field Sources

47. Personal Interview Treat unpublished interviews as personal communications and include them in your text only (see p. 276). Do not cite personal interviews in your reference list.

48. Letter Cite a personal letter only in the text (see p. 276), not in the reference list.

49. Lecture or Public Address Cite a lecture or public address the same way you would cite an unpublished paper presented at a conference.

> Euben, R. (2004, December 15). Travel, theory, and the search for knowledge: Western and Islamic journeys to "the other shore." Lecture presented at Harvard University, Cambridge, MA.

APA

V Documenting Sources

Media Sources

50. Film or Video Recording   List the director and producer (if available), the date of release, the title followed by "Motion picture" in square brackets, the country where the film was made, and the studio or distributor.

> Anderson, W. (Director). (2004). *The life aquatic with Steve Zissou* [Motion picture]. United States: Touchstone Pictures.

51. Television Program   List the director (if available), the broadcast date, the title followed by "Television broadcast" or "Television series episode" in square brackets, and the producer.

> Lennon, T. (Director) & Angier, J. (Producer). (2004, March 25).
> *Becoming American: The Chinese experience* [Television broadcast].
> Alexandria, VA: Public Broadcasting Service.

52. Radio Program   List the host, the broadcast date, the title followed by "Radio broadcast," or "Radio series episode," in square brackets, and the producer.

> Littlefield, B. [Host]. (2005, February 5). *Only a game* [Radio series episode]. Boston: WBUR.

53. Sound Recording   Name the author of the song; the date; the song title followed by "On" and the recording title in italics; the medium (in square brackets); and the production data.

> DiFranco, A. (2005). Recoil. On *Knuckle down* [CD]. Buffalo, NY:
> Righteous Babe Records.

Electronic Sources

54. Article or Abstract Obtained through a Database   Provide publication information about the source obtained through a database, the date the source was retrieved, and the database in which the information was found. It is not necessary to indicate the format of the database (CD-ROM, network, and so on). If you are referring to an abstract in a database, include the word "Abstract" in square brackets (no quotation marks or italics) following the title of the source.

> Fox, S. (2004, June). Preliminary psychometric testing of the Fox
> Simple Quality-of-Life Scale. *Journal of Neuroscience Nursing 36*(3),
> 157-167. Retrieved July 17, 2004, from InfoTrac database.

> Olsen, F. (1999, October 8). The promise and problems of a new way
> of teaching math [Abstract]. *Chronicle of Higher Education, 46*(7),
> A31-A32, A34. Retrieved July 18, 2000, from ERIC database.

55. Online Article Originally Published in a Print Periodical Publication information is followed by the retrieval date and the URL.

> Wong, W., & Scott, J. D. (2004). Anchored signaling complexes. *Nature Reviews Molecular Cell Biology 5,* 959. Retrieved December 7, 2004, from http://www.nature.com/cgi-taf/DynaPage.taf?file=/nrm/ journal/v5/n12/full/nrm1527_fs.html

56. Article in an Online Periodical Publication information follows the retrieval date and the URL. Since the article was published online, it is unlikely to have page numbers. Note that the journal in the first example provides volume and issue numbers, while the second does not.

> Brent, D. (1997). Rhetorics of the Web: Implications for teachers of literacy. *Kairos: A Journal for Teachers of Writing in Webbed Environments, 2*(1). Retrieved July 18, 2000, from http://english.ttu.edu/ kairos/2.1/features/brent/bridge.html

> Beatty, J. (2004, September 28). Your health insurance is on the ballot. *The Atlantic Unbound.* Retrieved December 4, 2004, from http://www.theatlantic.com/doc/prem/200409u/pp2004-09-28

57. Nonperiodical Web Document For a stand-alone Web source, such as a report or an online brochure, cite as much of the following information as possible: author, publication date, document title, retrieval date, and the URL.

> Grayson, C. E. (2004, October). *What is bipolar depression?* Retrieved December 7, 2004, from http://my.webmd.com/content/article/60/ 67149.htm?z=4249_00000_0000_tn_01

For a chapter or section within a Web document, identify the section as well as the main document.

> Calambokidis, J., Evenson, J., Steiger, G., & Jeffries, S. (1994). Watching gray whales. In *Gray whales of Washington state* (chap. 4). Retrieved February 4, 2005, from http://www.cascadiaresearch.org/ gray/whale7.pdf

For a document within a government agency Web site or other complex site, include the name of the agency or organization before the URL.

> American Psychological Association. (n.d.). *What is APA's Office of International Affairs?* Retrieved December 6, 2004, from the American Psychological Association Web site: http://www.apa.org/ international/

APA

V Documenting Sources

TUTORIAL

How do I cite articles from databases using APA style?

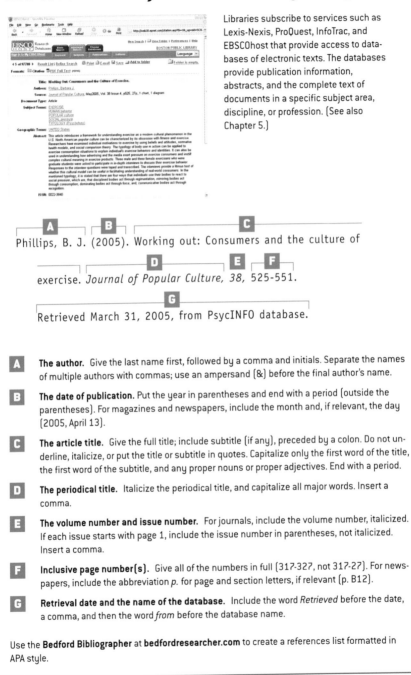

Libraries subscribe to services such as Lexis-Nexis, ProQuest, InfoTrac, and EBSCOhost that provide access to databases of electronic texts. The databases provide publication information, abstracts, and the complete text of documents in a specific subject area, discipline, or profession. (See also Chapter 5.)

A **B** **C**
Phillips, B. J. (2005). Working out: Consumers and the culture of

D **E** **F**
exercise. *Journal of Popular Culture, 38,* 525-551.

G
Retrieved March 31, 2005, from PsycINFO database.

A **The author.** Give the last name first, followed by a comma and initials. Separate the names of multiple authors with commas; use an ampersand (&) before the final author's name.

B **The date of publication.** Put the year in parentheses and end with a period (outside the parentheses). For magazines and newspapers, include the month and, if relevant, the day (2005, April 13).

C **The article title.** Give the full title; include subtitle (if any), preceded by a colon. Do not underline, italicize, or put the title or subtitle in quotes. Capitalize only the first word of the title, the first word of the subtitle, and any proper nouns or proper adjectives. End with a period.

D **The periodical title.** Italicize the periodical title, and capitalize all major words. Insert a comma.

E **The volume number and issue number.** For journals, include the volume number, italicized. If each issue starts with page 1, include the issue number in parentheses, not italicized. Insert a comma.

F **Inclusive page number(s).** Give all of the numbers in full (317-327, not 317-27). For newspapers, include the abbreviation *p.* for page and section letters, if relevant (p. B12).

G **Retrieval date and the name of the database.** Include the word *Retrieved* before the date, a comma, and then the word *from* before the database name.

Use the **Bedford Bibliographer** at **bedfordresearcher.com** to create a references list formatted in APA style.

58. Email Message or Real-Time Communication Because email messages are difficult or impossible for your readers to retrieve, APA does not recommend including them in your reference list. You should treat them as personal communications and cite them parenthetically in your text (see #12 on p. 279).

59. Message Posted to a Newsgroup, Electronic Mailing List, or Online Discussion Forum List the author, posting date, message title, name of the list or forum, and URL, as well as any additional identifying information such as message number.

> Kajayan, M. (2004, April 19). Video on the Armenian genocide
>   [Msg 1]. Message posted to AnthroSussex, archived at http://
>   groups-beta.google.com/group/AnthroSussex?hl=en

60. Entire Blog To cite an entire Weblog, give the author's name (or screen name, if available), the publication date or last update, the title, the retrieval date, and the URL.

> Green, T. (2005 May 3). *Modern art notes.* Retrieved June 7, 2005, from
>   http://www.artsjournal.com/man/

61. Entry or Comment on a Blog To cite an entry or a comment on a Weblog, give the author (or screen name, if available), the date the material was posted, the title of the entry or comment, the title of the blog, and the URL.

> Allbritton, C. (2005 April 19). Our hearts and conscience. Entry on
>   Back to Iraq 3.0 Weblog, at http://www.back-to-iraq.com/
>   archives/2005_04.php

62. Computer Software Sometimes a person is named as having rights to the program, software, or language: in that case, list that person as the author. Otherwise, begin the entry with the name of the program and identify the source in square brackets after the name as "Computer software." Treat the organization that produces the software as the publisher. If you're referring to a specific version that isn't included in the name, put this information last.

> Microsoft Access 2003 [Computer software]. Redmond, CA: Microsoft.

Other Sources

63. General Advice about Other Sources For citing other types of sources, APA suggests that you use as a guide a source type listed in their manual that most closely resembles the type of source you want to cite.

APA-style Research Essay

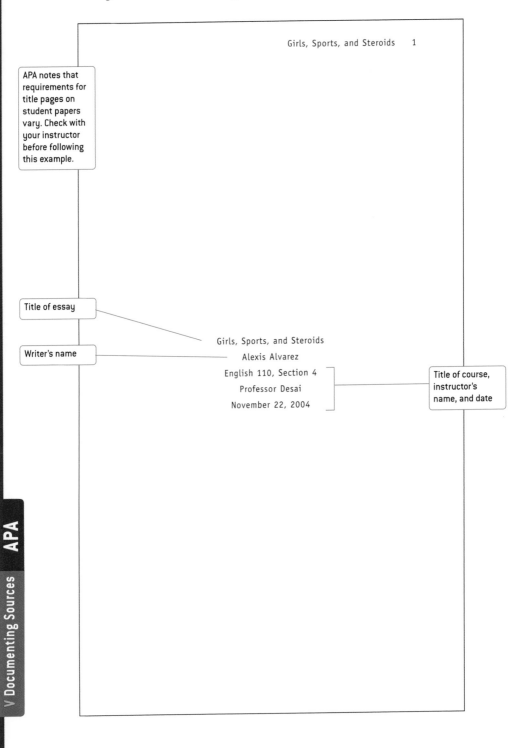

APA notes that requirements for title pages on student papers vary. Check with your instructor before following this example.

Title of essay

Writer's name

Girls, Sports, and Steroids   1

Girls, Sports, and Steroids

Alexis Alvarez

English 110, Section 4

Professor Desai

November 22, 2004

Title of course, instructor's name, and date

Girls, Sports, and Steroids

Almost daily, headlines and newscasters tell us about athletes'
use of performance-enhancing drugs. Indeed, stories of such drug use
seem to increase each year, with investigations of possible steroid use
by college football players, by major league baseball players, and even
by Olympic gold medalists. It is easy to gain the impression that
many adult athletes, particularly males, may be using drugs in order
to improve their performance and physical appearance. What may be
surprising and even shocking to most of us, however, is that these
drugs, especially anabolic steroids, are increasingly used by adolescent athletes and that girls are just as likely as boys to be users.

In May 2004, the Centers for Disease Control and Prevention
(CDC) published its latest figures on self-reported drug use among
young people in grades 9 through 12. The CDC study, "Youth Risk Behavior Surveillance--December 2003," found that 6.1% of its survey
participants reported using steroids at least once, up from 2.2% in
1993. The report also showed that use of steroids appears to be increasing among younger girls: While only 3.3% of 12th-grade girls reported using steroids, 7.3% of 9th-grade girls reported using them.
Moreover, girls might be starting to use steroids at a higher rate than
boys. The CDC study indicated that 9th-grade girls had reported
slightly higher rates of steroid use than boys (7.3% and 6.9% respec-
tively), while 10th-, 11th-, and 12th-grade girls all reported lower
use than boys. Other studies support the conclusion that steroid use
is both widespread and rising quickly among adolescent girls. According to Mundell (2004), experts estimate that as many as a million
high school students have used steroids-- and that a significant
percentage of that group are girls. Moreover, since the late 1990s,
studies have shown that steroid use is increasing among adolescent
girls. In 1998, *Teacher Magazine* reported that steroid use among
high school girls had increased 300% since 1991, from 0.4% of all
high school girls to 1.4% ("Girls and Steroids," 1998). And Manning
(2002) wrote, "A 1999 Youth Risk Behavior Surveillance study by the
Centers for Disease Control and the 2001 Monitoring the Future survey
both show steady growth in steroid use by 8th- to 12th-graders"
(para. 13).

What role are competitive sports playing in this dangerous
trend? Why are some girls feeling the need to ingest performance-
enhancing drugs? Although competitive sports can provide young
female athletes with many benefits, they can also have negative
effects, the worst of which is increasing drug use. Let's look first
at the positives.

Annotations:

Title of essay repeated

Alexis's statement is likely to surprise readers, drawing them into the essay.

Effective use of statistical evidence shows growth of the problem over time.

Source of paraphrased information acknowledged using APA's parenthetical reference system

A source that does not have an author is identified by shortened title and publication year.

Paragraph number given for location of material quoted from an online source

Thesis states Alexis's main point

Girls, Sports, and Steroids   3

Headings, centered throughout, help readers follow the essay's organization

Girls and Sports: The Upside

Title of essay, shortened if necessary, followed by page number.

Millions of girls are now involved in a variety of sports activities, and girls' participation in school athletics and community-based programs continues to increase. As the President's Council on Physical Fitness and Sport (1997) has pointed out, when girls participate in competitive sports, their lives can be affected in a number of positive and interrelated ways. Physical and psychological health, a positive sense of identity, good relationships with friends and family, and improved performance in school all work together to influence a girl's complete growth and development.

Shortened name of the council; it was introduced by its full name the first time it was cited.

According to the President's Council (1997), adolescent girls who exercise regularly can lessen their risks for adult-onset coronary disease and certain cancers. Girls' involvement in sports and exercise also tends to improve immune functioning, posture, strength, flexibility, and heart-lung endurance (President's Council, 1997; Dudley, 1994).

Two sources are cited in one parenthetical citation.

In addition, competitive athletics can enhance mental health by offering adolescent girls positive feelings about body image; tangible experiences of competency, control, and success; improved self-esteem and self-confidence; and a way to reduce anxiety (President's Council, 1997). Juan Orozco, who has coached adolescent females in competitive soccer for nine years, confirmed that making a competitive sports team is a privilege that many girls work toward with determination and longing and that being picked to participate encourages these young athletes to believe in themselves and their abilities (personal communication, September 22, 2004).

Personal communication — an interview — is cited in the text of the document, but not in the reference list.

A final benefit is that sports expand social boundaries and teach many of the personal and social skills girls will need throughout their lives. According to Orozco, through competitive athletics girls learn a crucial lesson in how to interact with, get along with, and depend on athletes from different social and economic groups. In short, they learn to adapt to and enjoy each other's differences. Melissa Alvarez, a 17-year-old athlete who has participated in high school basketball and club soccer, draws a similar conclusion. In an interview, she stated that sports "give you something to work for as an individual and as a team. You learn self-discipline and dedication, which are essential skills to have in life" (personal communication, September 26, 2004). Competitive sports also teach athletes how to cope with failure as well as success. In the best of situations, as Sieghart (2004) noted, athletes are able to assess their achievements realistically, letting neither winning nor losing consume their reality.

An author tag alerts readers that information is taken from a source.

Girls and Sports: The Downside

In spite of the many positive effects of competitive athletics, sports can have a negative impact on girls' bodies and minds, and some girls falter under the pressure to succeed. Overtraining, eating disorders, and exercise-induced amenorrhea (which may result in osteoporosis) are some of the most common negative physical side effects that young female athletes experience; negative psychological and social side effects include increased stress and anxiety and a loss of self-confidence. Let's look at each of these effects.

Negative Physical Side Effects

Overtraining occurs when your body can no longer adapt to increasing workloads--instead of building up, it breaks down. When a young girl overtrains, her body's balance between training and recovery is lost. Because the athlete's body can't recover, her performance stays flat and she cannot improve. Overtraining also makes a young female athlete prone to a variety of physical and psychological ills, such as unusual fatigue, irritability, feelings of apathy, and menstrual irregularities (Graham, 1999).

Another negative effect is amenorrhea, which refers to an atypical inability to menstruate. Graham (1999) pointed out, "in some sports as many as 50% of the athletes who are competitive may suffer from what's known as exercise-induced or athletic amenorrhea" (p. 26). Furthermore, research has shown that when a woman does not menstruate regularly, she loses bone density and becomes more prone to stress fractures (cracks in bones, especially hands and feet) and osteoporosis later in life. Amenorrhea can be caused by inadequate nutrition as well as by overtraining, both of which cause the athlete to burn more calories than she eats. As a result, her body shuts down its reproductive function to conserve energy (Graham, 1999).

The tendency to develop an eating disorder, such as anorexia or bulimia, is a third possible effect. Although young women may develop eating disorders for a variety of reasons, Graham (1999) noted, "Disordered eating is high among female athletes competing in sports where leanness and/or a specific weight are considered important for either performance or appearance" (p. 74). Being slim and trim may be the goal of many adolescent female athletes, but when they seek that goal by means of an eating disorder, they hinder their athletic performance. A calorie deficit actually decreases immune function, reduces aerobic capacity, decreases muscle mass and strength, and causes low energy and fatigue (Graham).

> Page number identifies the location of material quoted from a print source.

Girls, Sports, and Steroids 5

Negative Psychological and Social Effects

Just as a girl's body and mind often benefit from sports, so too are body and mind linked when it comes to those aspects of sports that are not positive. Often, negative physical effects occur because female athletes feel the need to win at any cost and the pressure to attain an unrealistic ideal. They may resort to extremes such as over-training in order to have the "ideal" body or be the "best of the best." When they can't meet these expectations, some girl athletes lose self-confidence and become overly stressed and anxious. In fact, they may see their failures as a serious threat to their self-esteem (Davies & Armstrong, 1989).

Pressures at home, at school, among friends, and from coaches can be daunting as well because young athletes tend to worry about the actions and reactions of the people who make up their social cir-cles (Brown & Branta, 1988). In addition, learning to balance the de-mands of sports, school, family, and fun can be incredibly fatiguing. Juan Orozco recalled that some of the girls he coached were involved in three sports at a time and still had to keep their grades up in order to participate (personal communication, September 22, 2004). Add to these demands the pressure from parents, and real problems can occur. Gary Anderson, a girls' basketball coach for more than two decades, has seen it all: parents who are overly dramatic, teams that serve primarily as stages for a few superstar athletes, and girls who seem "factory-installed with a sense of entitlement simply because they know their way around a ball and a pair of high-tops" (Dexheimer, 2004, para. 15). All of these situations and pressures affect young fe-male athletes and can result in their making some regrettable, if not devastating, choices.

Girls' Reactions: Burnout and Steroids

What happens when these young women decide the pressure is too much? What measures will they take to lighten their load? Some of these athletes simply burn out. They stop participating in competi-tive athletics because the pressure and anxiety make them physically ill. They no longer enjoy competitive sports, but consider them a tor-ment to be endured. In fact, according to Davies and Armstrong (1989), it is not unusual for promising 12-year-olds to abandon the game entirely by the age of 16 and move on to less distressing pas-times. Melissa Alvarez had one such experience while playing high school basketball. The coach put so much pressure on her that her stomach began to ache during games and during practice. The more the coach yelled, the worse she played, but when the coach was absent, her performance improved dramatically and her stomach

Subheadings are set in italic and aligned flush left to differentiate them from higher-level headings.

A partial quotation is integrated into the sentence.

APA

∨ Documenting Sources

Girls, Sports, and Steroids   6

problems disappeared. Eventually, Melissa quit the basketball team because the game had become a burden instead of something she en-
joyed (M. Alvarez, personal communication, September 26, 2004).

An alternative much more dangerous than burnout, however, is
the use of performance-enhancing drugs such as anabolic steroids. A
2003 article in *Drug Week* stated that girls who participate in sports
more than eight hours a week are at considerable risk for taking many
illicit drugs: The higher the level at which athletes compete, the
higher their risk for substance abuse ("Sporting Activities").

> Since the publi-
> cation year is
> given in the
> sentence, it is
> not included in
> the citation.

Teenage girls take steroids for some of the same reasons that
professional athletes do--to increase stamina and strength and to acquire a lean, muscular body. However, girls also take steroids to compete for athletic scholarships ("Girls and Steroids," 1998). According
to Charles Yesalis, a professor of sports science and senior author of a
Penn State report, a lot of young women see steroid use as an investment in their future; athletes can take the hormones for a few months
in high school, qualify for a college scholarship, and then stop taking
the drugs before sophisticated lab tests can spot them (Faigenbaum,
Zaichkowsky, Gardner, & Micheli, 1997). What teenagers don't realize,
though, is that even a few months of steroid use can permanently
damage the heart, trigger liver failure, stunt physical growth, and put
a woman's childbearing ability at risk. Steroids cause muscles to out-
grow and injure the tendons and ligaments that attach them to the
bone (Faigenbaum et al.). As Farnaz Khadem, spokeswoman for the
World Anti-Doping Agency has emphasized, "A lot of these young people have no idea of what this is doing to their bodies. This is a real
health danger" (DeNoon, 2004).

> In APA style, the
> first parentheti-
> cal reference to a
> source with three
> to five authors
> lists all
> authors . . .

> . . . subsequent
> references to the
> source use "et
> al." in place of all
> but the first
> author.

Although health is the most important concern in the issue of
steroid use, it is not the only one. Possessing or selling steroids without a prescription is a crime, so those who are involved in such activities may also endure criminal penalties (Gorman, 1998). Young
women who use steroids are resorting to illegal actions and may eventually be labeled as "criminals," a label that will follow them for the
rest of their lives. Doors to coaching jobs, teaching careers, and many
other occupations may be shut permanently if one has a criminal past.

How Girl Athletes Can Avoid Steroid Use

What can we do to help adolescent female athletes avoid illicit
drug use? How can we help them avoid the pitfalls of competitive athletics? Parents, coaches, and the athletes themselves all play a crucial
role in averting bad choices. First, parents and coaches need to be
aware that performance-enhancing drugs are a problem. Some adults
believe that steroid use is either minimal or nonexistent among

teenagers, but one study concluded that "over half the teens who use steroids start before age 16, sometimes with the encouragement of their parents. . . . Seven percent said they first took 'juice' by age ten" (Dudley, 1994, p. 235).

> An ellipsis indicates that words from the source were not included in the quotation.

Parents need to take the time to know their children and know what their children are doing. Coaches must know their players well enough to be able to identify a child in trouble. When asked what parents and coaches could do to help girl athletes remain healthy and not use drugs or overwork themselves, Juan Orozco offered the following advice:

> An athlete should be happy in her activity of choice, and her parents should encourage her desires to do well. Parents should be involved in her life and let her know that her efforts are valued highly, but they also need to be on the lookout for danger signs--such as unusual weight loss or moodiness. As a coach, I need to know the personalities of my players and get them to trust me, not only as their coach but as their friend--someone they can talk to if they have a problem. (personal communication, September 22, 2004)

> Extended quotation is set off in block style without quotation marks

It is also important for parents and coaches to teach the athletes how to develop a healthy lifestyle and not focus only on winning. If an athlete seems to take her sport too seriously, parents might negotiate with her, encouraging her to balance sports with other endeavors. Some parents and coaches push kids too hard, teaching them to win at any cost. In fact, a number of researchers believe that some parents and coaches are actually purchasing expensive black-market steroids for their young athletes (Kendrick, 2004). As University of Massachusetts researcher Avery Faigenbaum has put it, "I don't know a lot of ten-year-olds who have a couple of hundred dollars--to spend on drugs or anything else" (Kendrick, 2004, para. 8).

Athletes, too, must take responsibility for their own lives. Adolescent girls should try to resist undue pressures imposed by parents, coaches, and society. They must learn about the damage steroids can cause and understand that pursuing an "ideal" body type is not only unrealistic but also unhealthy (Yiannakis & Melnick, 2001). Most of all, young female athletes need to know that they are more important than the competition. No scholarship or medal is worth liver failure or losing the ability to bear children.

The vast majority of excellent athletes do not overtrain, become bulimic, or wind up using steroids. Clearly, they have learned to avoid the pitfalls of competitive athletics. They believe in themselves and their abilities and know how to balance sports and other activities.

APA

V Documenting Sources

Girls, Sports, and Steroids   8

They have learned how to sacrifice and work hard, but not at the expense of their integrity or health. In short, these athletes have not lost sight of the true objective of participating in sports--they know that their success is due to their efforts and not to the effects of a performance-enhancing drug. When asked what she would say to athletes considering steroid use, Melissa Alvarez said:

In the essay's conclusion, Alexis uses a quotation to reinforce her main point.

If you are training and doing your best, you should not have to use steroids. At the end of the day, it is just a game. You should never put your health at risk for anything, or anyone. It should be your top priority. (personal communication, September 26, 2004)

Girls, Sports, and Steroids   9

References

Brown, E. W., & Branta, C. F. (Eds.). (1988). *Competitive sports for children and youth: An overview of issues and research*. Champaign, IL: Human Kinetics.

Centers for Disease Control and Prevention. (2004, May 21). Youth risk behavior surveillance--December 2003. *Morbidity and Mortality Weekly Report 53*(SS-2). Retrieved October 2, 2004, from http://www.cdc.gov/mmwr/PDF/SS/SS5302.pdf

Costello, B. (2004, July 4). Too late? Survey suggests millions of kids could be juicing. *New York Post,* 059. Retrieved October 2, 2004, from http://www.nypost.com/sports/24424.htm

Davies, D., & Armstrong, M. (1989). *Psychological factors in competitive sport*. New York: Falmer Press.

DeNoon, D. (2004, August 4). Steroid use: Hitting closer to home. *WebMD*. Retrieved October 1, 2004, from http://my.webmd.com/content/Article/92/101457.htm

Dexheimer, E. (2004, May). Nothing to lose: The Colorado Impact teaches girls about life--then hoops. *Denver Westword 13*. Retrieved September 26, 2004, from LexisNexis database.

Dudley, W. (Ed.). (1994). *Sports in America: Opposing viewpoints*. San Diego, CA: Greenhaven Press.

Faigenbaum, A. D., Zaichkowsky, L. D., Gardner, D. E., & Micheli, L. J. (1997). Anabolic steroid use by male and female middle school students. *Pediatrics 101*(5), E6. Retrieved September 29, 2004, from http://pediatrics.aappublications.org/cgi/content/full/101/5/e6

Girls and steroids. (1998). *Teacher Magazine 9*(5), 11. Retrieved September 26, 2004, from Academic Search Premier database.

Gorman, C. (1998, August 10). Girls on steroids. *Time 152*(6), 93. Retrieved September 26, 2004, from Academic Search Premier database.

Graham, J. (1999). *The athletic woman's sourcebook*. New York: Avon Books.

Kendrick, C. (2004). Seduced by steroids. Retrieved October 1, 2004, from the FamilyEducation Web site: http://www.familyeducation.com/article/0,1120,20-691,00.html

Manning, A. (2002, July 9). Kids, steroids don't mix. *USA Today* p. 1C. Retrieved September 26, 2004, from http://www.usatoday.com/sports/baseball/stories/2002-07-09-cover-steroids-kids.htm

---

Annotations (left column):

Sources are alphabetized by author's name or, if no author, by title.

First line of each entry starts at left margin; additional lines indented one-half inch, or five spaces

Online article originally published in a print periodical

Book with two authors

Retrieval date and source URL given

Edited book

Online article originally published in a print periodical

Articles from online databases

Nonperiodical Web document

Online article originally published in a print periodical

Annotations (right column):

List of references on a separate page, heading centered

Edited book

Online government report

In book, article, essay, and chapter titles, only the first words, words following a colon or question mark, and proper nouns are capitalized.

Titles of books and journals italicized

Nonperiodical Web site

Article from an online database

Retrieval date and name of database

Book with one author

Tab markings (left margin):

APA

V Documenting Sources

Girls, Sports, and Steroids   10

Mundell, E. J. (2004, May 12). Schools struggle to control steroid use. HealthDay. Retrieved October 1, 2004, from http://www .healthday.com/view.cfm?id=518706

President's Council on Physical Fitness and Sports. (1997, May). *Physical activity and sport in the lives of girls: Physical and mental health dimensions from an interdisciplinary approach.* Washington, DC: Author. Retrieved September 26, 2004, from University of Minnesota, Tucker Center for Research on Girls and Women in Sport Web site: http://education.umn.edu/tuckercenter/pcpfs/ default.html

Sieghart, M. A. (2004, August 27). Competitive sport is harsh and unforgiving. *The Times* of London. Retrieved October 1, 2004, from LexisNexis Academic database.

Sporting activities impact illicit drug use among male and female teenagers. (2003, September 26). *Drug Week,* pp. 16–17.

Yiannakis, A., & Melnick, M. J. (Eds.). (2001). *Contemporary issues in sociology of sport.* Champaign, IL: Human Kinetics.

Article from a database

Magazine article without a named author

Book editors are identified using (Ed.) or (Eds.)

APA

∨ Documenting Sources

20

Using *Chicago* Style

> **Key Questions**
>
> **20a. How do I cite sources within the text of my document?   304**
>
> **20b. How do I format notes and prepare the bibliography?   306**

The documentation style described in *The Chicago Manual of Style: The Essential Guide for Writers, Editors, and Publishers*, Fifteenth Edition, is used in the humanities and in some of the social sciences. The *Manual* recommends two systems, an author-date system similar to the APA system (see Chapter 19) and a notes system. This chapter describes and provides models for the notes system.

> Use the **Bedford Bibliographer** at **bedfordresearcher .com.** to create a *Chicago*-style bibliography.

In the notes system, researchers acknowledge their sources in footnotes or endnotes. Footnotes appear at the bottom of a printed page, whereas endnotes appear at the end of the document. Although a bibliography can be omitted when using the note system (since all relevant publication information is provided in the notes), the manual encourages authors to provide a bibliography or list of works cited in documents where more than a few sources are cited. For more information about this system, consult *The Chicago Manual of Style.* Information about the manual can also be found at www.press.uchicago.edu.

To see featured writer Patrick Crossland's research essay, formatted in *Chicago* style, turn to page 320.

CITATIONS WITHIN YOUR TEXT

NOTES AND ENTRIES IN YOUR BIBLIOGRAPHY OR LIST OF WORKS CITED

20a

How do I cite sources within the text of my document?

Chicago uses footnotes or endnotes. Notes can also be used to expand on points made in the text—that is, notes can contain both citation information and commentary on the text. For electronic documents such as Web sites that consist of multiple "pages" of text, footnotes can take the form of links to notes at the end of a "page" or to pop-up windows that display the notes.

The first time you refer to a source in a note, provide complete publication information for the source. In subsequent references, you need to cite only the author's last name, a shortened version of the title, and the page numbers (if the source has page numbers) to which you refer. Separate the elements with commas and end with a period. *Chicago* style italicizes titles of books and periodicals.

The following examples illustrate the most common ways of citing sources within the text of your document using *Chicago*'s note system.

1. Numbering Notes should be numbered consecutively throughout your work, beginning with 1.

2. Placement of the Note Numbers in the Text Place the number for a note at the end of the sentence containing the reference after punctuation and outside any parentheses. If you are citing the source of material that comes before an em dash (or two hyphens) used to separate parts of a sentence, the note number should precede the dash. Note numbers are set as superscripts.

> Lee and Calandra suggest that the poor organization of online historical documents may impair students' ability to conduct research without guidance.[1]

Tomlinson points out that the erosion of Fiji's culture was accelerated by both British and Indian immigration² — though the two immigrant groups inhabited very different roles and social classes.

3. Placement of Notes You may choose between footnotes, which appear at the bottom of the page containing corresponding note numbers, and endnotes, which appear at the end of the document in a section titled "Notes." Longer works, such as books, typically use endnotes. The choice depends on the expectations of your readers and your preferences. Regardless of placement, notes are numbered consecutively throughout the document. If you use a bibliography, it follows the last page of text or the last page of endnotes.

Model notes for various types of sources appear in section 20b, which begins on p. 306.

4. Including Page Numbers in a Note Use page numbers whenever you refer to a specific page of a source rather than to the source as a whole. The use of page numbers is required for quotations.

> 4. Bill Bryson, *A Short History of Nearly Everything* (New York: Broadway Books, 2003), 10.

5. Cross-Referencing Notes If you are referring to a source identified in a previous note, you can refer to that note instead of repeating the information.

> 5. See note 3 above.

6. Citing the Same Source in Multiple Notes If you refer to the same source in several notes, provide a full citation in the first note. In subsequent notes, provide the author's last name, a brief version of the title, and the page number. If you are referring to the same source cited in the previous note, you can use the Latin abbreviation "ibid." (for *ibidem,* or "in the same place").

> 1. Diarmaid McCulloch, *The Reformation: A History* (New York: Viking, 2004), 16.

> 2. Ibid., 24.

> 6. McCulloch, *Reformation,* 121.

7. Citing a Source Quoted in Another Source

> 7. Jonathan Messerli, *Horace Adams: A Biography* (New York: Knopf, 1972), 16, quoted in Gordon S. Wood, *The Radicalism of the American Revolution* (New York: Vintage Books, 1991), 315.

Chicago

V Documenting Sources

20b

How do I format notes and prepare the bibliography?

The Chicago Manual of Style provides guidelines for formatting notes and entries in a bibliography of works that are relevant to but not necessarily cited within your document. In print documents and linear documents that are distributed electronically (such as a word processing file or a newsgroup post), the bibliography appears at the end of the document. In longer documents, a bibliography could be given at the end of each chapter or section. In electronic documents that use links, such as a Web site, the bibliography is often a separate page to which other pages are linked. To see a bibliography in *Chicago* style, see p. 329.

For notes, include the number of the note, indented and not superscript, followed by these elements:

- author's name (first name first)
- title (followed by the title of the complete work if the source is an article, chapter, or other short work contained in a larger work)
- publisher (for a book) or publication title (for a journal, magazine, or newspaper)
- date
- page(s) being cited

For entries in the bibliography, include these elements:

- author's name (last name first)
- title (followed by the title of the complete work if the source is an article, chapter, or other short work contained in a larger work)
- publisher (for a book) or publication title (for a journal, magazine, or newspaper)
- date
- page(s) (if the source is a shorter work included in a complete work)

Note: For each type of source, a pair of examples is presented in this section: a model note followed by a model bibliographic entry.

● **Books, Conference Proceedings, and Dissertations**

8. One Author Use the basic format described on page 307.

> 8. Robin W. Winks, *Europe, 1890–1945: Crisis and Conflict* (New York: Oxford University Press, 2003), 201.

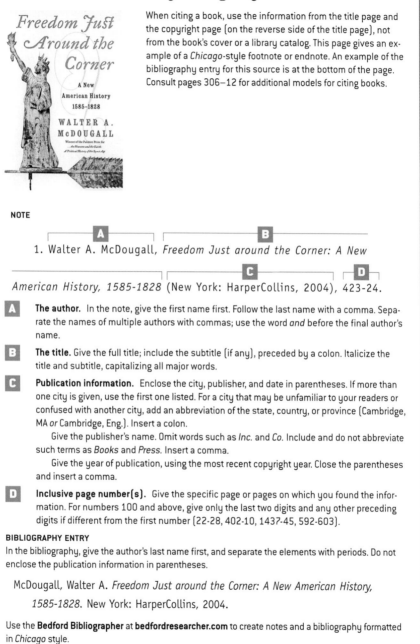

TUTORIAL

How do I cite books using Chicago style?

When citing a book, use the information from the title page and the copyright page (on the reverse side of the title page), not from the book's cover or a library catalog. This page gives an example of a *Chicago*-style footnote or endnote. An example of the bibliography entry for this source is at the bottom of the page. Consult pages 306–12 for additional models for citing books.

Cover text:

Freedom Just Around the Corner

A New American History 1585–1828

WALTER A. McDOUGALL

NOTE

[A] [B]

1. Walter A. McDougall, *Freedom Just around the Corner: A New*

[C] [D]

American History, 1585-1828 (New York: HarperCollins, 2004), 423-24.

A **The author.** In the note, give the first name first. Follow the last name with a comma. Separate the names of multiple authors with commas; use the word *and* before the final author's name.

B **The title.** Give the full title; include the subtitle (if any), preceded by a colon. Italicize the title and subtitle, capitalizing all major words.

C **Publication information.** Enclose the city, publisher, and date in parentheses. If more than one city is given, use the first one listed. For a city that may be unfamiliar to your readers or confused with another city, add an abbreviation of the state, country, or province (Cambridge, MA *or* Cambridge, Eng.). Insert a colon.

Give the publisher's name. Omit words such as *Inc.* and *Co.* Include and do not abbreviate such terms as *Books* and *Press.* Insert a comma.

Give the year of publication, using the most recent copyright year. Close the parentheses and insert a comma.

D **Inclusive page number(s).** Give the specific page or pages on which you found the information. For numbers 100 and above, give only the last two digits and any other preceding digits if different from the first number (22-28, 402-10, 1437-45, 592-603).

BIBLIOGRAPHY ENTRY

In the bibliography, give the author's last name first, and separate the elements with periods. Do not enclose the publication information in parentheses.

McDougall, Walter A. *Freedom Just around the Corner: A New American History, 1585-1828.* New York: HarperCollins, 2004.

Use the **Bedford Bibliographer** at **bedfordresearcher.com** to create notes and a bibliography formatted in *Chicago* style.

Chicago V Documenting Sources

Winks, Robin W. *Europe, 1890-1945: Crisis and Conflict.* New York: Oxford University Press, 2003.

9. Two or Three Authors List the authors in the order on the title page. In a note, list the first name for each author first. In the bibliography, list the first author's last name first and list the first names for each other author first.

9. F. Lee Benns and Mary Elisabeth Seldon, *Europe, 1939 to the Present* (New York: Appleton-Century-Crofts, 1965), 112.

Benns, F. Lee, and Mary Elisabeth Seldon. *Europe, 1939 to the Present.* New York: Appleton-Century-Crofts, 1965.

10. Four or More Authors In a note, give only the first author's name followed by "et al." or "and others." In the bibliography, list the authors as they appear on the title page.

10. Paul S. Boyer and others, *The Oxford Companion to United States History* (New York: Oxford University Press, 2001), 89.

Boyer, Paul S., Melvyn Dubofsky, Eric H. Monkkonen, Ronald L. Numbers, David M. Oshinsky, and Emily S. Rosenberg. *The Oxford Companion to United States History.* New York: Oxford University Press, 2001.

11. Corporate or Group Author Use the corporation or group as the author; it may also be the publisher.

11. National Geographic, *National Geographic Atlas of the World,* 8th ed. (Washington, DC.: National Geographic, 2004), 66.

National Geographic. *National Geographic Atlas of the World.* 8th ed. Washington, DC: National Geographic, 2004.

12. Unknown Author When no author is listed on the title or copyright page, begin the entry with the title of the work. In the bibliography, alphabetize the entry by the first word other than *A, An,* or *The.*

12. *New York Times Guide to Essential Knowledge: A Desk Reference for the Curious Mind* (New York: St. Martin's Press, 2004), 77.

New York Times Guide to Essential Knowledge: A Desk Reference for the Curious Mind. New York: St. Martin's Press, 2004.

13. Translated Book List the author first and the translator after the title. Use the abbreviation "trans." in a note, but spell out "Translated by" in the bibliography.

13. Gilles Deleuze, *Desert Islands and Other Texts, 1953-1974,* trans. Michael Taormina (Los Angeles: Semiotext(e), 2004), 109.

V Documenting Sources Chicago

Deleuze, Gilles. *Desert Islands and Other Texts, 1953-1974.* Translated by
Michael Taormina. Los Angeles: Semiotext(e), 2004.

14. Edition Other Than the First   Give edition information after the title.

14. Roger S. Bagnall and Klaas A. Worp, *Chronological Systems of
Byzantine Egypt,* 2nd ed. (Boston: Brill, 2004), 99.

Bagnall, Roger S., and Klaas A. Worp. *Chronological Systems of
Byzantine Egypt.* 2nd ed. Boston: Brill, 2004.

15. Untitled Volume in a Multivolume Work   In the bibliography, if you have
used all the volumes, give the total number of volumes after the title, using the
abbreviation "vols." ("2 vols." or "4 vols."). If you have used one volume, give
the abbreviation "Vol." and the volume number after the title. In the notes,
give the volume number and page number, separated by a colon, for the specific
location of the information referred to in your text.

15. Frederic Brenner, *Diaspora: Homelands in Exile* (New York:
HarperCollins, 2004), 1:77-87.

Brenner, Frederic. *Diaspora: Homelands in Exile.* Vol. 1. New York:
HarperCollins, 2004.

16. Titled Volume in a Multivolume Work   Give the title of the volume to
which you refer, followed by the volume number and the general title for the entire work.

16. Simone Schwarz-Bart, *Modern African Women,* vol. 3 of *In Praise
of Black Women* (Madison: University of Wisconsin Press, 2004), 46.

Schwarz-Bart, Simone. *Modern African Women.* Vol. 3 of *In Praise of
Black Women.* Madison: University of Wisconsin Press, 2004.

17. Book in a Series   The series name follows the title and is capitalized as a
title but is not italicized. If the series numbers its volumes, include that information as well.

17. John Toland, *The Rising Sun: The Decline and Fall of the Japanese Empire, 1936-1945,* Modern Library War Series (New York: Modern Library, 2003), 211-30.

Toland, John. *The Rising Sun: The Decline and Fall of the Japanese
Empire, 1936-1945.* Modern Library War Series. New York: Modern Library, 2003.

18. Republished Book   Place the original publication date before the publication information for the reprint.

18. Sophocles, *Antigone, Oedipus the King, Electra* (1962; repr., New York: Oxford University Press, 1998), 207-51.

Sophocles. *Antigone, Oedipus the King, Electra.* 1962. Reprint, New York: Oxford University Press, 1998.

19. Author with an Editor   List the author at the beginning of the citation and add the editor's name after the title. In notes, use the abbreviation "ed." before the editor's name. In the bibliography, include the phrase "Edited by" before the editor's name.

19. Margaret Thatcher, *Margaret Thatcher: Complete Public Statements, 1945-1990,* ed. Christopher Collins (London: Gordon & Breach Publishing Group, 1999), 95-99.

Thatcher, Margaret. *Margaret Thatcher: Complete Public Statements, 1945-1990.* Edited by Christopher Collins. London: Gordon & Breach Publishing Group, 1999.

20. Anthology or Collection with an Editor   To cite an entire anthology or collection of articles, give the editor(s) before the title of the collection, adding a comma and the abbreviation "ed." or "eds."

20. Lynn Hawley, ed., *Women's History: An Anthology* (Dubuque, IA: Kendall/Hunt, 2001), 232-37.

Hawley, Lynn, ed. *Women's History: An Anthology.* Dubuque, IA: Kendall/Hunt, 2001.

21. Foreword, Introduction, Preface, or Afterword   Give the name of the writer of the foreword, introduction, preface, or afterword followed by the appropriate phrase ("introduction to," "preface to," and so on) before the title of the book. After the title insert the word "by" and the author's name.

21. Owen Gingerich, foreword to *Ptolemy's Almagest,* by Ptolemy (Princeton, NJ: Princeton University Press, 1998), vii-x.

Gingerich, Owen. Foreword to *Ptolemy's Almagest,* by Ptolemy. vii-x. Princeton, NJ: Princeton University Press, 1998.

22. Chapter in a Book or Selection in an Anthology   Give the author and title (in quotation marks) for the chapter or selection. Then give the title, editor, and publication data for the book or anthology. Give the inclusive page numbers before the publication data in the bibliography.

22. Nancy Hewitt, "Feminist Friends: Agrarian Quakers and the Emergence of Woman's Rights in America," in *U.S. Women in Struggle: A*

Feminist Studies Anthology, ed. Claire Goldberg Moses and Heidi I. Hartmann, 21-41 (Chicago: University of Illinois Press, 1995).

Hewitt, Nancy. "Feminist Friends: Agrarian Quakers and the Emergence of Woman's Rights in America." In *U.S. Women in Struggle: A Feminist Studies Anthology,* edited by Claire Goldberg Moses and Heidi I. Hartmann, 21-41. Chicago: University of Illinois Press, 1995.

23. Published Proceedings of a Conference Provide information as for an anthology or collection with an editor (see also #20 on p. 310).

23. Horst Siebert, ed., *Economic Policy for Aging Societies* (symposia and conference proceedings, Berlin: Springer-Verlag, 2002), 9-26.

Siebert, Horst, ed. *Economic Policy for Aging Societies.* Symposia and conference proceedings. Berlin: Springer-Verlag, 2002.

24. Paper Published in the Proceedings of a Conference Cite as a chapter in an edited book (see also #22 on p. 310).

24. Burt Ramsay, "Hospitality and Translation in Katherine Dunham's 'L'Ag'Ya,'" in *2003 Society of Dance History Scholars Conference Proceedings,* 22-28 (Birmingham, AL: Society of Dance History Scholars, 2003), 23.

Ramsay, Burt. "Hospitality and Translation in Katherine Dunham's 'L'Ag'Ya.'" In *2003 Society of Dance History Scholars Conference Proceedings.* 22-28. Birmingham, AL: Society of Dance History Scholars, 2003.

25. Sacred Text Cite sacred texts within the text of your document. A note should include the book, chapter, and verse, but not a page number.

25. Qur'an, 2:10 (New York: Penguin Classics, 2004).

26. Published Dissertation or Thesis Give the author and title, the phrase "PhD diss." or "master's thesis," followed by information about the institution that granted the degree and the year. Include information from *Dissertation Abstracts International* if appropriate.

26. Mohammed Abdullah Almaraee, *Improving Competencies of Mathematics Teachers' Use of Technology at Colleges of Education in Saudi Arabia* (PhD diss., University of Pittsburgh, 2003), Ann Arbor: UMI, 2004, 3097633, 22.

Almaraee, Mohammed Abdullah. *Improving Competencies of Mathematics Teachers' Use of Technology at Colleges of Education in Saudi Arabia.*

PhD diss., University of Pittsburgh, 2003. Ann Arbor: UMI, 2004. 3097633.

27. Unpublished Dissertation or Thesis   Give the author and title, in quotation marks. Then include the phrase "PhD diss." or "master's thesis," information about the institution that granted the degree, and the date.

27. Michael McCoyer, "Mestizaje Meets the Color Line: Mexicans and Racial Formation in Chicago, East Chicago, and Gary, 1917-1960" (PhD diss., Northwestern University, 2004), 47-59.

McCoyer, Michael. "Mestizaje Meets the Color Line: Mexicans and Racial Formation in Chicago, East Chicago, and Gary, 1917-1960." PhD diss., Northwestern University, 2004.

28. Abstract of a Dissertation or Thesis   Provide information as you would for an article in a journal (see also #29 below). Add information about *Dissertation Abstracts International.*

28. Lisa Booth Brooten, "Global Communications, Local Conceptions: Human Rights and the Politics of Communication among the Burmese Opposition-in-Exile" (PhD diss., Ohio University, 2003), abstract in *Dissertation Abstracts International* 64 (2003): 322.

Brooten, Lisa Booth. "Global Communications, Local Conceptions: Human Rights and the Politics of Communication among the Burmese Opposition-in-Exile." PhD diss., Ohio University, 2003. Abstract in *Dissertation Abstracts International* 64 (2003): 322.

● **Sources in Journals, Magazines, and Newspapers**

29. Article in a Journal   After the journal title, include the volume number, a comma, and the issue number after the abbreviation "no." Then give the year.

29. Marc Bourreau and Pinar Dogan, "Unbundling the Local Loop," *European Economic Review* 49, no. 1 (2005): 179.

Bourreau, Marc, and Pinar Dogan. "Unbundling the Local Loop." *European Economic Review* 49, no. 1 (2005): 173-200.

30. Article in a Monthly Magazine   Magazines are cited by their dates rather than by volume and issue.

30. Sara Solovitch, "The American Dream," *Esquire,* January 2005, 89.

> Solovitch, Sara. "The American Dream." *Esquire,* January 2005, 88-93, 114-18.

31. Article in a Weekly Magazine   Cite like a monthly magazine, but provide the day of publication.

> 31. Caitlin Flanagan, "What Teachers Want," *New Yorker,* December 6, 2004, 66-68.

> Flanagan, Caitlin. "What Teachers Want." *New Yorker,* December 6, 2004, 64-68.

32. Article in a Newspaper   If the name of the newspaper does not include the city, insert the city before the name (and italicize it). If an American city is not well known, name the state as well (in parentheses, abbreviated). Identify newspapers from other countries with the city in parentheses (not italicized) after the name of the newspaper.

> *Eugene* (OR) *Register-Guard*

> *Sunday Times* (London)

If a paper comes out in more than one edition, identify the edition after the date.

> 32. Victoria Burnett, "History Made as Karzai Sworn In: Afghanistan President Opens 'New Chapter,'" *Boston Globe,* December 8, 2004, late edition.

> Burnett, Victoria. "History Made as Karzai Sworn In: Afghanistan President Opens 'New Chapter.'" *Boston Globe,* December 8, 2004, late edition.

33. Unsigned Article in a Newspaper or Magazine   If no author is given, begin with the title of the article.

> 33. "Best-Sellers," *Entertainment Weekly,* November 19, 2004, 89.

> "Best-Sellers." *Entertainment Weekly,* November 19, 2004, 89.

34. Letter to the Editor   Treat as a newspaper article. If no title is provided, place "Letter to the editor" in the title position.

> 34. Kenneth J. Sher, letter to the editor, *New Yorker,* December 6, 2004, 12.

> Sher, Kenneth J. Letter to the Editor. *New Yorker,* December 6, 2004, 12.

35. Review   Give the author of the review, the review title, if any, and then the words "review of" followed by the title and author of the work reviewed.

TUTORIAL

How do I cite articles from periodicals using Chicago *style?*

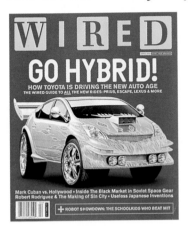

Periodicals include journals, magazines, and newspapers. This page gives an example of a *Chicago*-style footnote or endnote for a print magazine article. (An example of the bibliography entry for this source is at the bottom of the page.) Models for citing articles from journals and newspapers are on pages 312–15. If you need to cite a periodical article you accessed electronically, follow the guidelines below and see also page 319.

NOTE

     2. Lisa Margonelli, "China's Next Cultural Revolution," *Wired,*

April 2005, 108.

A   **The author.** In the note, give the first name first. Follow the last name with a comma. Separate the names of multiple authors with commas; use the word *and* before the final author's name.

B   **The article title.** Give the full title; include the subtitle (if any), preceded by a colon. Put the article title and subtitle in quotes, capitalizing all major words.

C   **The periodical title.** Italicize the periodical title, and capitalize all major words.

D   **The date of publication.** For monthly magazines, give the month and year. For weekly magazines include the day of publication (September 6, 2004). Do not abbreviate the month. Use a comma after the year.

E   **Inclusive page number(s).** Give the specific page or pages on which you found the information. For numbers 100 and above, give only the last two digits and any other preceding digits if different from the first number (22-28, 402-10, 1437-45, 592-603).

BIBLIOGRAPHY ENTRY
In the bibliography, give the author's last name first, separate the elements by periods, and give inclusive pages for the entire article.

    Margonelli, Lisa. "China's Next Cultural Revolution." *Wired,* April 2005, 106-11.

Use the **Bedford Bibliographer** at **bedfordresearcher.com** to create notes and a bibliography formatted in *Chicago* style.

35. Christopher J. Lee, review of *African Words, African Voices: Critical Practices in Oral History,* ed. Luise White, Stephan F. Miescher, and David William Cohen, *Oral History Review* 31, no.1 (2004): 84.

Lee, Christopher J. Review of *African Words, African Voices: Critical Practices in Oral History,* ed. Luise White, Stephan F. Miescher, and David William Cohen. *Oral History Review* 31, no.1 (2004): 83-87.

● Print Reference Works

36. Entry in an Encyclopedia, Dictionary, Thesaurus, Handbook, or Almanac In notes, provide the title of the work (italicized), the edition, the abbreviation "s.v." (for *sub verbo,* or "under the word"), and the title of the entry.

36. *Encyclopaedia Britannica,* s.v. "Lee, Robert E."

Chicago does not recommend including reference works such as encyclopedias or dictionaries in the bibliography.

37. Government Publication In general, give the issuing body, then the title and any other information (such as report numbers) that would help your readers locate the source. Follow with the publication data and the page numbers if relevant. You may abbreviate "Government Printing Office" to GPO.

37. U.S. Senate, Select Committee on Intelligence, *Report of the Select Committee on Intelligence on the U.S. Intelligence Community's Prewar Intelligence Assessments on Iraq* (Washington, DC: GPO, 2004), 59-63.

U.S. Senate. Senate Select Committee on Intelligence. *Report of the Select Committee on Intelligence on the U.S. Intelligence Community's Prewar Intelligence Assessments on Iraq.* Washington, DC: GPO, 2004.

38. Pamphlet, Report, or Brochure Cite it as you would a book (see p. 306).

38. Neil Foley and John R. Chávez, *Teaching Mexican American History* (Baltimore: American Historical Association, 2002).

Foley, Neil, and John R. Chávez. *Teaching Mexican American History.* Baltimore: American Historical Association, 2002.

● Field Sources

39. Personal Interview Give the location and date in a note. Do not include unpublished interviews in the bibliography.

39. Elisabeth Silverman, interview by author, Philadelphia, June 12, 2005.

Chicago

∨ Documenting Sources

40. Letter or Other Personal Communication Do not include personal communications such as letters or phone calls in the bibliography. In a note, give the name of the person with whom you communicated, the form of communication, and the date.

> 40. Meaghan Farrell, conversation with author, September 5, 2005.

> 41. Mary Ann Fitzgerald, letter to author, November 2, 2004.

41. Survey *Chicago* does not specify how to cite unpublished survey results. Cite them in your text as you would personal communication (see #40, above).

42. Observation Note *Chicago* does not specify how to cite observation notes. Cite them in your text as you would personal communication (see #40 above).

43. Lecture or Public Address Provide the title, the nature of the speech (such as lecture or keynote address), the name of the organization sponsoring the meeting or lecture, and the location and date it was given.

> 43. Tess Fredette, "Clues in the Cloth: Tapestries in the Gothic Room" (lecture, Isabella Stewart Gardner Museum, Boston, February 16, 2005).

> Fredette, Tess. "Clues in the Cloth: Tapestries in the Gothic Room." Lecture, Isabella Stewart Gardner Museum, Boston, February 16, 2005.

● Media Sources

44. Film or Video Recording Provide the title first, the medium (film, videocassette, DVD), the name of the director, the company, and the year it was filmed.

> 44. *Star Wars*, videocassette, directed by George Lucas (Beverly Hills: 20th Century Fox, 1977).

> *Star Wars.* Directed by George Lucas. 2 hrs. 1 min., 20th Century Fox. 1977. Videocassette.

45. Television Program *Chicago* does not specify how to cite a television program. Cite as you would a video recording, identifying the medium as "television program" or "television broadcast."

46. Radio Program *Chicago* does not specify how to cite a radio program. Cite as you would a video recording, identifying the medium as "radio program" or "radio broadcast."

47. Sound Recording Give the composer and title of the recording, the performers and conductor, the label, and identifying number.

47. Gustav Mahler, *Symphony no. 10 in F sharp,* Bournemouth Symphony Orchestra, dir. Simon Rattle, compact disc, EMI Classics, 7544062, 1997.

Mahler, Gustav. *Symphony No. 10 in F sharp.* Bournemouth Symphony Orchestra, dir. Simon Rattle. Compact disc. EMI Classics. 7544062. 1997.

Electronic Sources

48. Article from a Database

48. Diane E. Lewis, "Younger Bosses, Older Workers Seek Balance on the Job," *Boston Globe,* January 30, 2005, http://www.lexisnexis.com (accessed April 28, 2005).

Lewis, Diane E. "Younger Bosses, Older Workers Seek Balance on the Job." *Boston Globe,* January 30, 2005. http://www.lexisnexis.com (accessed April 28, 2005).

49. Article in an Electronic Journal

49. Thomas Dublin and Melissa Doak, "Miner's Son, Miners' Photographer: The Life and Work of George Harvan," *Journal for Multimedia History* 3 (2000), http://www.albany.edu/jmmh/ (accessed May 22, 2005).

Dublin, Thomas, and Melissa Doak. "Miner's Son, Miners' Photographer: The Life and Work of George Harvan." *The Journal for Multimedia History* 3 (2000). http://www.albany.edu/jmmh/ (accessed May 22, 2005).

50. Article in an Online Magazine

52. Peter Huber and Mark Mills, "The Art of Energy," *Slate,* February 1, 2005, http://www.slate.com/id/2112806/ (accessed February 5, 2005).

Huber, Peter, and Mark Mills. "The Art of Energy." *Slate,* February 1, 2005. http://www.slate.com/id/2112806/ (accessed February 5, 2005).

51. Nonperiodical Web Site

51. Lenka Vytlacilova, "Women in Medicine," *Czech Feminist Trailblazers,* http://www.pinn.net/~sunshine/czech/medicine.html (accessed December 6, 2004).

Vytlacilova, Lenka. "Women in Medicine." *Czech Feminist Trailblazers.* http://www.pinn.net/~sunshine/czech/medicine.html (accessed December 6, 2004).

52. Online Book

52. Lewis Liebovitch, *The Press and the Modern Presidency: Myths and Mindsets from Kennedy to Election 2000* (Westport, CT: Praeger, 2001), http://www.netlibrary.com/Reader/ (accessed December 9, 2004).

Liebovitch, Lewis. *The Press and the Modern Presidency: Myths and Mindsets from Kennedy to Election 2000.* Westport, CT: Praeger, 2001. http://www.netlibrary.com/Reader/ (accessed December 9, 2004).

53. Entire Blog

53. Tyler Green, *Modern Art Notes,* May 3, 2005, http://www .artsjournal.com/man/ (accessed June 7, 2005).

Green, Tyler. *Modern Art Notes,* May 3, 2005. http://www.artsjournal .com/man/ (accessed June 7, 2005).

54. Entry or Comment on a Blog

54. Christopher Allbritton, "Our Hearts and Conscience," Entry on *Back to Iraq 3.0* Weblog, April 19, 2005, http://www.back-to-iraq.com/ archives/2005_04.php (accessed June 15, 2005).

Allbritton, Christopher. "Our Hearts and Conscience." Entry on *Back to Iraq 3.0* Weblog, April 19, 2005. http://www.back-to-iraq.com/ archives/2005_04.php (accessed June 15, 2005).

55. Email Message   *Chicago* recommends that personal communication, including email, not be included in the bibliography, although it can be cited in your text.

55. Amy Rutenberg, e-mail message to author, January 4, 2005.

TUTORIAL

How do I cite articles from databases using Chicago *style?*

Libraries subscribe to services such as Lexis-Nexis, ProQuest, InfoTrac, and EBSCOhost that provide access to databases of electronic texts. The databases provide publication information, abstracts, and in some cases the complete text of documents in a specific subject area, discipline, or profession. (See also Chapter 5.)

This page gives an example of a *Chicago*-style footnote or endnote for a newspaper article accessed via a database. (An example of the bibliography entry for this source is at the bottom of the page.) To cite journal articles and magazine articles from databases, see also pp. 312–14.

NOTE

> **A**   **B**
> 3. David Abel, "Harvard University to Increase Wages of Its
> **C**   **D**
> Lowest Paid Workers," *Boston Globe,* February 1, 2002,
> **E**   **F**
> http://rdsweb1.rdsinc.com/ (accessed April 1, 2005).

A   **The author.**   In the note, give the first name first. Follow the last name with a comma. Separate the names of multiple authors with commas; use the word *and* before the final author's name.

B   **The article title.**   Give the full title; include the subtitle (if any), preceded by a colon. Put the article title and subtitle in quotes, capitalizing all major words.

C   **The periodical title.**   Italicize the periodical title, and capitalize all major words.

D   **The date of publication.**   Give the month (not abbreviated), day, and year. Insert a comma.

E   **The main URL for the database.**   Give the URL in full; do not use underlining or angle brackets.

F   **The access date (optional).**   You can include the word *accessed* and the date in parentheses.

BIBLIOGRAPHY ENTRY
In the bibliography, give the author's last name first, and separate the elements with periods.

> Abel, David. "Harvard University to Increase Wages of Its Lowest Paid Workers." *Boston Globe,* February 1, 2002. http://rdsweb1.resinc.com/ (accessed April 1, 2005).

Use the **Bedford Bibliographer** at **bedfordresearcher.com** to create notes and a bibliography formatted in *Chicago* style.

Chicago

V Documenting Sources

Chicago-style Research Essay

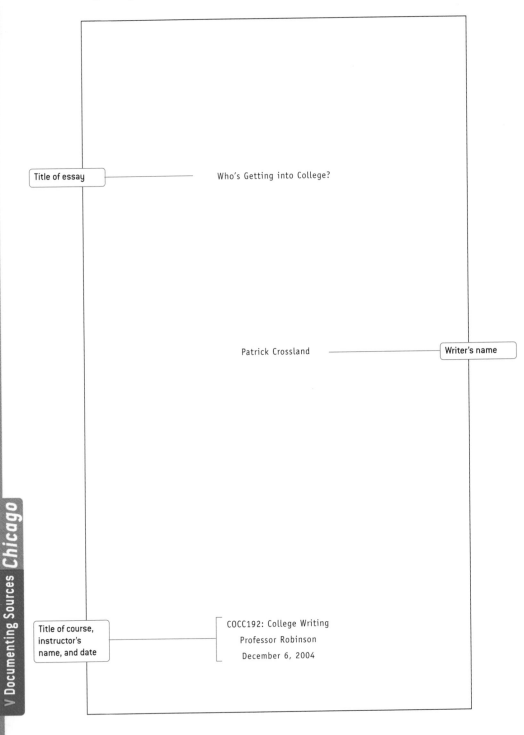

Title of essay

Who's Getting into College?

Patrick Crossland — Writer's name

Title of course, instructor's name, and date

COCC192: College Writing
Professor Robinson
December 6, 2004

Crossland   2

Title of essay
repeated

Who's Getting into College?

Caleb Crossland is a junior in high school. Last night his mom attended his varsity wrestling match, cheering him on as he once again defeated his competitors. On the way home, they discussed his busy schedule, in which he balances both schoolwork and a job at his father's company. Caleb manages to get good grades in his classes while at the same time he learns a trade in the woodworking industry. Both of his parents are proud of him and support him as he accomplishes the various feats of yet another busy day.

As his senior year of high school approaches, Caleb is bombarded with information and applications from various colleges he is interested in attending. However, the more he studies the applications and their requirements, the more he is confused. He knows he wants to go to college, he's just not sure how to best position himself to get into his top choices. As he stares at the many essay questions, he wonders what exactly the colleges are looking for and who is getting in.

What many college applicants like Caleb don't realize is that getting into college is much like entering a contest in which each applicant is pitted against thousands of others. The objective of the college contest is to beat out the other competitors by getting good grades and scoring high on standardized tests, participating in academic or extracurricular activities, and having a particular economic background and race.

Grades and Standardized Test Scores

If you ask high school students what they worry most about in terms of getting into the college of their choice, most will answer their grades and standardized test scores. Indeed, experts agree that a student's intellect is an important admissions decision factor, as colleges tend to admit the students they feel have the greatest potential for academic success. Mary Lee Hoganson, college consultant for Homewood-Flossmoor High School in Flossmoor, Illinois, says that many colleges won't make a decision about a student's admittance until they have received his or her first semester senior grades, and many schools' offers of admission are contingent upon a student's continued high performance over the course of their senior year. According to Hoganson: "[Colleges] expect to see a performance that indicates you are ready for college-level work. . . . (Admissions letters often contain [contingency clauses requiring] continued successful performance.) It is not at all rare for a college to withdraw an offer of admission when grades drop significantly over the course of the senior year."[1]

Margin notes:

First two paragraphs offer an anecdote — a brief story — to draw readers into the text.

Thesis states Patrick's main point

Headings, centered throughout, help readers follow the essay's organization.

Author tag indicates the source of paraphrased information.

Paraphrased information

Brackets and ellipses indicate the quotation has been modified.

Notes are numbered by order of appearance.

And it's not just grades that matter; admissions staff also look
at the kind of courses students are taking. Nadine K. Maxwell, coordinator of guidance services for Fairfax County Public Schools in Fairfax,
Virginia, says that college admissions staff are looking to see whether
a student's high school academic profile "indicates that [he or she
has] the potential for academic success on their campus."[2] Maxwell
says admissions staff take into consideration whether the student has
taken rigorous courses such as AP or honors courses. In addition,
some admissions offices will consider the student's class rank and the
quality of the student's high school as they decide whether to admit
someone.

> A partial quota-
> tion is integrated
> effectively into
> the sentence.

Of course, one of the greatest monsters applicants must slay before they can enter college is taking an entrance exam or standardized
test, such as the SAT and ACT. These tests are used by many colleges
to assess student aptitude and academic capability. According to Joel
Levine and Lawrence May, authors of *Getting In*, entrance exams are an
extremely important part of a student's college application and carry a
great deal of weight. In fact, they claim that a college entrance ex-
amination is "one of the two most significant factors" in getting into
college (the other, unsurprisingly, being high school grades).[3]

However, in recent years, there has been much debate about the
reliance on college entrance exams in assessing student aptitude. Says
Derek Bok, professor at the John F. Kennedy School of Government at
Harvard, the SAT "tells you very, very little about what [students are]
going to contribute to the education of [their] classmates. It tells
you very little about what [students are] going to be able to contribute to society, once [they] leave the college and those are very
important considerations and have been for more than 100 years to
universities."[4] In addition, tests such as the SAT "enhance the performance of those with conventional education and the experiences
and values of American middle-class culture."[5] Thus, these tests do
not accurately measure intelligence or aptitude because they fail to
measure the skills and know-how of students from other cultures.

The good news is that the College Board has addressed the problem and is seeking ways to fix culturally unfair exams, and college admissions staff also have become increasingly aware of these problems;
some schools do not even require such tests for admission. Meanwhile,
according to howstuffworks.com, most colleges no longer have a set
cutoff SAT score.[6] This means that even if an applicant's score is
quite low, he or she may still be accepted. As the site notes, however,
standardized test scores are all relative: "If your SAT score is under
1,000 and you're trying to get into a highly selective school that

> The name of the
> Web site is used
> to identify the
> source.

> Writer's name is followed by the page number.

admits less than one-third of its applicants, you'll have to do some pretty fast talking to qualify."[7] Although a low entrance exam score won't put a student completely out of contention, those with higher scores obviously have a greater chance of getting in.

Academic and Extracurricular Activities

Students' high school academic and extracurricular activities (including their participation in clubs, involvement in sports and community service, and after-school jobs) also have an impact on admissions decisions, as colleges view past success as an indication of future success. By proving that they are at the top of their class in a certain subject or that they excel at a certain sport, students can elevate their chances of being accepted into the college of their choice.

William H. Gray III, president and chief executive officer of the United Negro College Fund, notes that achievements in high school play an important role in the admissions decisions made by most college and universities. According to Gray, factors that affect admissions decisions include participation in sports, involvement in extracurricular activities, applicants' personal qualities, and "special talents" applicants might possess. Duke University director of undergraduate admissions Christoph Guttentag uses a baseball analogy in describing how students advance in the admission process: "Think of it as a baseball game. Everybody gets their time at bat. The quality of [students'] academic work that we can measure (through test scores and analysis of high school courses) gets about 10 percent of the applicants to third base, 50 percent to second base and about 30 percent to first base. And 10 percent strike out."[8] According to Guttentag, students can get closer to "home base" by participating in extracurricular activities.

However, critics claim it is difficult to measure achievements, and so there is no set-in-stone rule regarding how much different colleges value extracurricular activities. Is earning a varsity letter in sports worth more than winning a chess championship? Should a student who has participated in the National Honor Society be rated higher than a student who has designed Web sites professionally? Obviously, it is difficult to assess excellence among such a broad range of activities. However, much of the relevance of an activity will depend on the particular college a student is applying to. For example, if a student wants to attend film school, the admissions department there would most likely value extracurricular activities relating to film higher than it would those relating to, say, basketball (unless the school has a strong basketball team as well). Most admissions experts agree that the bottom line is that students with extracurricular activities are more likely to get into college, as such activities indicate that the student will be well-rounded and have more to offer the college community.

Economic Background

A student's economic background can also affect his or her likelihood of being accepted into a particular college. Although the majority of colleges have what they call a "need-blind" admission policy, meaning that they do not take into account ability to pay as an admission criteria, there are schools that are "need-conscious," and a student's ability to pay will come into play.

In addition, a student's economic background not only plays a role in predicting who gets admitted into college, it helps determine whether a student is likely to apply to college in the first place. In the article "Getting into the Ivy League: How Family Composition Affects College Choice," Dean Lillard and Jennifer Gerner stress that a student's ability to obtain loans, his or her likelihood of getting financial aid, and family support all affect college admissions choices.[9] Students who grow up in poor neighborhoods or weak school districts are at a disadvantage compared with students from affluent neighborhoods and schools and may not be given the resources they need to help them with the college application process. In fact, many in the field of college education are working to determine what should be done to accommodate the needs of applicants whose backgrounds work against their being admitted to college and succeeding thereafter. They are hoping to improve the system of admittance and yet preserve a standard of excellence, ensuring that students who come from low-income backgrounds are reached and addressed in a manner that provides them the same opportunities afforded to students who come from more affluent backgrounds.

Mary Lee Hoganson, college consultant for Homewood-Flossmoor High School, suggests that students find out before they apply to schools whether they are need-blind or need-conscious. She also advises potential applicants to be aware and discerning: "If you need financial assistance, you wouldn't be well-served at a college that couldn't assist you financially."[10]

Race

Another variable in the realm of student background, and often the most controversial, is race. Affirmative action policies that weight a minority's application higher than a nonminority student's application are practiced frequently in admissions processes to ensure that colleges across the nation have a mixed student body. Although they play an important role in determining who gets into college, high

Crossland   6

school grades, test scores, extracurricular activities, and various other attributes get nowhere near as much attention in public discussions and the news media as does the issue of race-based admissions. In his article "In the Best Interest of America, Affirmative Action in Higher Education Is a Must," William H. Gray III states: "At many colleges it is acceptable to use preferences in admissions based on student characteristics such as special talents, geographic origin, and alumni legacy. The most publicized and debated preference, however, is race."[11]

In fact, Gray observes that ever since John F. Kennedy, "[E]very American President has used an Executive Order to attempt to eliminate discrimination by race, color and gender in the federal government and its agencies." Thus, for years the highest executive powers have attempted to deal with race and equality in college admissions.

Proponents of race-based admissions claim it's important to give minority students an advantage when considering their applications, in part to compensate for disadvantages they normally face and in part because by admitting students of different races, the college prepares all its students for the real world. Says Derek Bok:

> If you understand what the purposes of selective universities are, I think you see very quickly why it's fair to put weight on race. One of the purposes is to educate students for an increasingly diverse society by allowing them to study in an environment where they live and work together with different races. . . . To achieve that purpose, you need to make sure you have a diverse student body. The second thing that we're trying to do is to respond to a need which is proclaimed all the time in the outside society for more minority representation among business executives, doctors, lawyers, other professions and positions of influence in the society. . . .
>
> To do that, you've got to have a pool of well-qualified, well-prepared candidates, so universities are trying to get a student body of people who have a contribution to make as leaders and in the different professions in their communities. . . .
>
> Race becomes a relevant consideration because there are exceptional opportunities for minorities, because they're in such short supply, to move into these professions and positions where they are being asked for by society.[12]

However, there are those who, as Gray puts it, "contend that preferences based upon race are illegal and unfair." Charles Krauthammer, author of "Lies, Damn Lies, and Racial Statistics,"

Extended quotation of eight or more lines is set off in block style without quotation marks.

Source of extended quotation is provided in a note.

Chicago

V Documenting Sources

Crossland   7

claims that bright, young minority students who were qualified to attend many schools are "artificially turned into failures by being admitted to high-pressure campuses, where only students with exceptional academic backgrounds can survive."[13] Krauthammer claims that it is important to avoid hurting minorities by sending them into a situation that they are not prepared to deal with.[14]

> Source of paraphrased material is provided in a note.

Although the debate about the fairness of the role of affirmative action in the college admissions process continues, Christoph Guttentag sees the situation in a bit broader terms. He says the most selective schools — those that admit only 30 percent of those who apply — won't admit students "simply to make the school's minority numbers look better. Most schools want students who are going to succeed there. To admit someone who isn't likely to be successful is not good for anybody — not for the university and not for the student."[15] So although race does matter when it comes to admissions, it's not going to guarantee a student a place, nor is it going to necessarily be a factor for exclusion.

> A colon (:) is not used when the quoted text in a quotation is part of the sentence.

Other Factors

Other, somewhat simpler factors affect a student's chance of being accepted into the college of his or her choice. Strong letters of recommendation and a clear, coherent essay can help applicants propel themselves above others. Applying early may also help students get accepted. Nadine K. Maxwell, guidance services coordinator in Fairfax, Virginia, says that students' chances of being admitted can be greater if they apply early, although this varies from school to school and year to year and "may depend upon the applicant pool at the school where [they] are applying."[16] Maxwell advises students to "[d]o your homework first and check to see what percentage of the students in the previous graduating classes at your high school were admitted early decision to a specific college or university. Are you qualified to apply as early decision? If you are, and this is a school you really wish to attend, then apply early decision."[17]

College consultant Mary Lee Hoganson also says that students should let a college know whether it is their first choice, especially if they are placed on the waitlist. She advises further: "Write a letter to the Director of Admission expressing your continuing strong interest and updating the admission office with any new information that reflects well on your ability to contribute to the quality of the freshman class. In addition, you may wish to ask your counselor to make a call on your behalf. Many colleges keep track of these kinds of contacts and students who are enthusiastic and persistent will

Crossland   8

get looked at first. Colleges want to admit students off the waitlist who they believe will accept the offer of admission."[18]

Summarized material from a book follows.

Bill Paul, author of *Getting In: Inside the College Admissions Process,* a book that tells the stories of several students applying to an elite Ivy League institution, shares three suggestions for students who want to get into college. Paul bases these suggestions on his discussions with Fred Hargadon, who in 1995 was dean of admissions at Princeton. Hargadon suggested that the best way students can enhance their chances for acceptance into the college of their choice is to read widely, learn to speak a second language, and engage in activities that interest and excite them and that also help them develop their confidence and creativity.[19] The idea, it seems, is that being an active learner, someone who is creative and enthusiastic about what he or she is doing, is more important than what you do. According to Paul, it might not be important whether you've won a medal in track or a prize for poetry as long as you are engaged with, confident about, and committed to the activity.[20]

The original source of the summarized material is identified.

Finally, just because a student doesn't get into his or her dream school doesn't mean all hope is lost. Most community colleges have academic requirements that include only a high school diploma or GED. If the student earns good grades at the community college level, he or she may be able to transfer to a more competitive and selective college or university later.

Conclusion

Harvard professor Derek Bok describes the college admissions process well: "What you have to ask is [whether] this student — compared with this student and looked at in the context of the class as a whole — is going to contribute more to the learning environment on campus and then has a better chance at making a big contribution to society than some other student."[21]

Patrick returns to the anecdote he used to introduce the essay.

Thus, in the midst of Caleb Crossland's busy schedule, he applies to various colleges he wants to attend. He continues to get good grades, studies for the SAT, and stays involved in extracurricular activities. He researches schools and plans to apply early. And with the support of his family, Caleb should have an edge over the many other students competing against him for a spot at the nation's top colleges.

Chicago

∨ Documenting Sources

Crossland 9

List of notes on a separate page, heading centered

Notes

1. College Board, "Experts Answer Your Application Questions: Get the Inside Scoop on Applying to College," *Collegeboard.com*, http://www.collegeboard.com/article/0,1120,5-26-0-8487,00.html?orig=sec (accessed November 14, 2004).

Entries listed by order of appearance in essay

Nonperiodical Web site

Indicates source of material is the same as that for the previous note

2. Ibid.

Book with two authors

3. Joel Levine and Lawrence May, *Getting In* (New York: Random House, 1972), 116.

4. Derek Bok, interview, *PBS Online*, November 12, 2004, http://www.pbs.org/wgbh/pages/frontline/shows/sats/interviews/bok.html (accessed November 20, 2004).

Interview available on the Web

Abbreviated reference to source identified in note 3.

5. Levine and May, *Getting In*, 118.

6. How Stuff Works, "How College Admission Works," *Howstuffworks.com*, http://people.howstuffworks.com/college-admission.htm (accessed November 5, 2004).

Nonperiodical Web site

7. Ibid.

8. Ibid.

Journal article with two authors

9. Dean Lillard and Jennifer Gerner, "Getting into the Ivy League: How Family Composition Affects College Choice," *Journal of Higher Education* (November-December 1999): 709.

10. College Board, "Experts Answer."

11. William H. Gray III, "In the Best Interest of America, Affirmative Action in Higher Education Is a Must," *The Black Collegian*, February 1, 1999, 144-146, http://www.elibrary.com/education (accessed November 20, 2004).

Magazine article from a database

12. Bok, interview.

Article in a weekly magazine

13. Charles Krauthammer, "Lies, Damn Lies, and Racial Statistics: Figures from All the University of California Campuses Paint Another Picture," *Time*, April 20, 1998, 86.

14. Ibid.

15. "How College Admission Works."

16. College Board, "Experts Answer."

17. Ibid.

18. Ibid.

19. Bill Paul, *Getting In: Inside the College Admissions Process* (Reading, MA: Addison-Wesley, 1995), 238-49.

Book with one author

20. Ibid., 249.

21. Bok, interview.

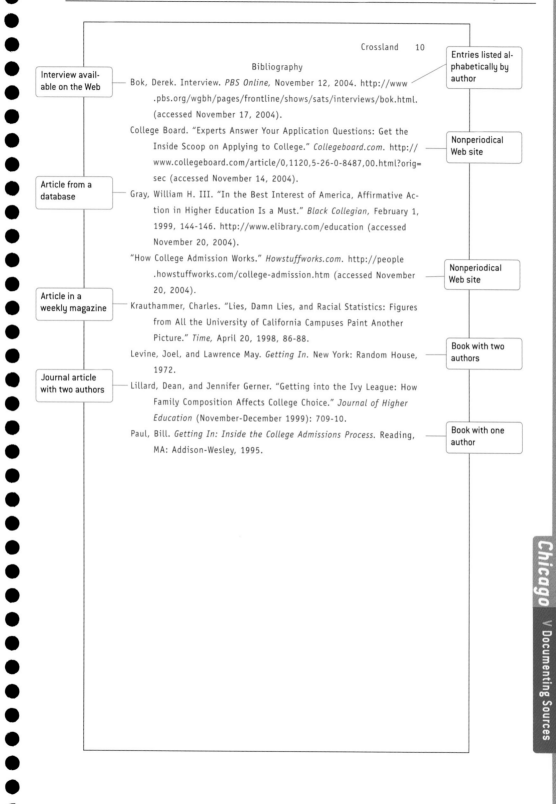

Crossland   10

Entries listed alphabetically by author

Bibliography

Interview available on the Web

Bok, Derek. Interview. *PBS Online,* November 12, 2004. http://www
.pbs.org/wgbh/pages/frontline/shows/sats/interviews/bok.html.
(accessed November 17, 2004).

College Board. "Experts Answer Your Application Questions: Get the
Inside Scoop on Applying to College." *Collegeboard.com.* http://
www.collegeboard.com/article/0,1120,5-26-0-8487,00.html?orig=
sec (accessed November 14, 2004).

Nonperiodical Web site

Article from a database

Gray, William H. III. "In the Best Interest of America, Affirmative Action in Higher Education Is a Must." *Black Collegian,* February 1,
1999, 144-146. http://www.elibrary.com/education (accessed
November 20, 2004).

"How College Admission Works." *Howstuffworks.com.* http://people
.howstuffworks.com/college-admission.htm (accessed November
20, 2004).

Nonperiodical Web site

Article in a weekly magazine

Krauthammer, Charles. "Lies, Damn Lies, and Racial Statistics: Figures
from All the University of California Campuses Paint Another
Picture." *Time,* April 20, 1998, 86-88.

Levine, Joel, and Lawrence May. *Getting In.* New York: Random House,
1972.

Book with two authors

Journal article with two authors

Lillard, Dean, and Jennifer Gerner. "Getting into the Ivy League: How
Family Composition Affects College Choice." *Journal of Higher
Education* (November-December 1999): 709-10.

Paul, Bill. *Getting In: Inside the College Admissions Process.* Reading,
MA: Addison-Wesley, 1995.

Book with one author

Chicago

∨ Documenting Sources

21

Using CSE Style

> **Key Questions**
>
> **21a. How do I cite sources within the text of my document?   332**
>
> **21b. How do I prepare the reference list?   332**

In 2000, the Council of Biology Editors (CBE) changed its name to the Council of Science Editors (CSE) to more accurately reflect its expanding membership. In this book, CSE style is based on the sixth edition of *Scientific Style and Format: The CBE Manual for Authors, Editors, and Publishers* published in 1994 and, for citing Internet sources, the *National Library of Medicine Recommended Formats for Bibliographic Citation Supplement: Internet Formats,* published in July 2001.

> Use the **Bedford Bibliographer** at **bedfordresearcher .com** to create a CSE-style bibliography.

CSE style, used primarily in the physical sciences, life sciences, and mathematics, recommends two systems:

- a citation-sequence system, which lists sources in the reference list according to the order in which they appear in the document
- a name-year system, which is similar to the author-date system used by the APA (see Chapter 19).

This chapter describes and provides models for the citation-sequence system.

For more information on CSE style, visit the Council of Science Editors Web site at www.councilscienceeditors.org.

CITATIONS WITHIN YOUR TEXT

1. Format and placement of the note   332
2. Citing a previously mentioned source   332
3. Citing a source within a source   332

ENTRIES IN YOUR REFERENCE LIST

Books, Conference Proceedings, and Dissertations

4. One author   333
5. Two or more authors   333
6. Corporate or group author   333

21a

How do I cite sources within the text of my document?

The CSE citation-sequence system uses sequential numbers to refer to sources within a document. These numbers, in turn, correspond to numbered entries in the reference list. This approach to citing sources reduces distraction to the reader and saves space within a document.

1. Format and Placement of the Note   Sources are cited using superscript numbers or numbers placed in parentheses. Superscript numbers should be formatted in a font one or two points smaller than the body text:

> The anomalies in the data[3] call the study's methods into question.

> The anomalies in the data (3) call the study's methods into question.

2. Citing a Previously Mentioned Source   Use the first number assigned to a source when citing the source for the second time. In the following examples, the author is referring to sources earlier numbered 3, 9, and 22:

> The outlying data points[3,9,22] seem to suggest a bias in the methodology.

> The outlying data points (3,9,22) seem to suggest a bias in the methodology.

3. Citing a Source within a Source   When referring to a source cited in another source, use the phrase "cited in":

> The results[12(cited in 8)] collected in the first month of the study . . .

> The results (12 cited in 8) collected in the first month of the study . . .

21b

How do I prepare the reference list?

CSE style specifies that you should create a list of works that are cited in your document or that contributed to your thinking about the document. Sources cited should be identified in a section titled "References," while sources that contributed to your thinking should be given in a section titled "Additional References." There are, however, two exceptions: personal communication and oral presentations.

Personal communication, such as correspondence and interviews, is cited only in the text of your document, using the term "unreferenced" to indicate that it is not found in the reference list:

> . . . this disease has proven to be resistant to antibiotics under specific conditions (a 2005 letter from Asterson to me; unreferenced, see "Notes").

Typically, information about personal communication is placed in a "Notes" or "Acknowledgments" section. Similarly, oral presentations at conferences that are not available in any form (such as microform, reference database, conference proceedings, or online) should be cited in the text of your document but not included in your reference list.

The *CBE Manual* does not specify the location of the reference list, deferring instead to the formatting guidelines of individual journals in the sciences. In general, however, the reference list appears at the end of print documents and linear documents that are distributed electronically (such as word processing files or newsgroup posts). In the case of longer documents or documents in which sections of a book (such as chapters) are intended to stand on their own, the reference list might appear at the end of each section or chapter. In electronic documents that use links, such as Web sites, the reference list often is a separate page to which other pages are linked.

To see an example of a CSE-style reference list, turn to page 342.

● Books, Conference Proceedings, and Dissertations

4. One Author   Give the author's last name and first initial with no comma. Next, include the title, capitalizing only the first word and proper nouns, followed by publication information and total number of pages in the book, using the abbreviation "p."

> 4. Pevsner P. Bioinformatics and functional genomics. New York: Wiley-Liss; 2003. 792 p.

5. Two or More Authors   List the authors in the order in which they appear on the title page, each of them last name first. Note that periods are not used after initials. Separate authors with commas.

> 5. Packer L, Ong C, Halliwell B. Herbal and traditional medicine: molecular aspects of health. New York: Dekker; 2004. 941 p.

6. Corporate or Group Author   Identify the organization as the author.

> 6. Global Book Publishing. Flora: plant names. Portland (OR): Timber; 2003. 376 p.

CSE

V Documenting Sources

TUTORIAL

How do I cite books using CSE style?

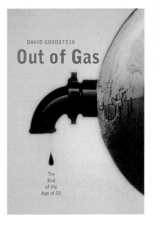

When citing a book, use the information from the title page and the copyright page (on the reverse side of the title page), not from the book's cover or a library catalog. This page gives an example of a citation in the CSE citation-sequence system. Consult pages 333–37 for additional models for citing books.

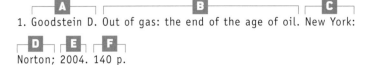

[A] [B] [C]
1. Goodstein D. Out of gas: the end of the age of oil. New York:

[D] [E] [F]
Norton; 2004. 140 p.

[A] **The author.** Give the last name first, followed by initials for first and middle names. Separate the last name and initials with only a space, not a comma. Do not separate initials. Separate the names of multiple authors with commas (Cobb C, Fetterolf ML). End with a period.

[B] **The title.** Give the full title; include the subtitle (if any), preceded by a colon. Capitalize only the first word of the title and proper nouns. Do not underline or italicize the title or subtitle. End with a period.

[C] **The city of publication.** If more than one city is given, use the first one listed. For a city that may be unfamiliar to your readers or confused with another city, add an abbreviation of the state, country, or province in parentheses: Depew (OK). Insert a colon.

[D] **The publisher.** Give the publisher's name. The CBE manual includes guidelines for abbreviating publisher's names. Insert a semicolon.

[E] **The date of publication.** Use the publication date if one is given; otherwise use the copyright date. If a month of publication is given, use that as well (2005 Aug).

[F] **The total number of pages.** Give the total number of pages in the book followed by *p* and a period.

Use the **Bedford Bibliographer** at **bedfordresearcher.com** to create a references list formatted in CSE style.

V Documenting Sources CSE

7. Unknown Author   Begin with the title.

> 7. Atlas of the world. 11th ed. New York: Oxford Univ Pr; 2003. 448 p.

8. Translated Book   Identify the translator after the title, giving last name first.

> 8. Moberg K. The oxytocin factor: tapping the hormone of calm, love, and healing. Francis R, translator. Cambridge (MA): Perseus; 2003. 240 p.

9. Book in an Edition Other Than the First   Note the edition (for instance, "2nd ed" or "New rev ed") after the title and with a separating period.

> 9. Avise J. Molecular markers, natural history, and evolution. 2nd ed. Sunderland (MA): Sinauer; 2004. 684 p.

10. Multivolume Work   Include the total number of volumes if you are making a reference to all volumes in the work, or "volume" followed by the specific volume number followed by the title of that volume (if that volume is separately titled).

> 10. Abd-El-Aziz A, Carraher C, Pittman C, Zeldin M, Sheats J. Macromolecules containing metal and metal-like elements: biomedical applications. Volume 3. New York: Wiley; 2004. 218 p.

11. Authored Book with an Editor   Identify the editor before the publication information.

> 11. Reagan R. Reagan: a life in letters. Skinner KK, Anderson A, Anderson M, editors. New York, Free Pr, 2003. 960 p.

12. Anthology or Collection with an Editor   To cite an anthology of essays or a collection of articles, treat the editor's name as you would an author's name. Identify with the word "editor."

> 12. Brush S, Hall N, editors. Kinetic theory of gases: an anthology of classic papers with historical commentary. London: Imperial Coll Pr; 2003. 661 p.

13. Chapter in an Edited Book or a Work in an Anthology   List the author and title of the section; then include the word "In" followed by a colon, the editor's name (last name first followed by initials) and the word "editor." Include the book title, place, and publisher, and note the inclusive pages of the section rather than the total number of pages in the book.

> 13. Jones R. Polysilanes: formation, bonding and structure. In: Jutzi P, Schubert U, editors. Silicon chemistry: from the atom to extended systems. New York: Wiley; 2003. p 1239-58.

CSE

V Documenting Sources

14. Foreword, Introduction, Preface, or Afterword of a Book   If the part is written by someone other than the author of the book, treat it as you would a chapter in an edited book (see p. 333), but do not identify the author of the book as an "editor."

> 14. Biggs P. Preface. In: Davison F. Marek's disease: an evolving problem. New York: Academic Pr; 2004. p vii-xviii.

15. Chapter of a Book   If you wish to refer to a chapter of a book, identify the chapter of the book after the publication information. Identify the inclusive pages of the chapter.

> 15. Gonzales, L. Deep survival: who lives, who dies, and why. New York: Norton; 2004. Chapter 4, A gorilla in our midst; p 67-79.

16. Published Proceedings of a Conference   List the editors of the proceedings as authors (if there are no editors, write "Anonymous" in brackets). Give the title of the publication and, if different, the name of the conference that produced it; date and place of the conference; publication data; and number of pages.

> 16. Fawcett T, Mishra N, editors. Proceedings of the Twentieth International Conference on Machine Learning; 2003 Aug 21-24; Washington. Menlo Park (CA): Am Assoc for Artificial Intelligence; 2004. 1000 p.

17. Paper Published in the Proceedings of a Conference   Format the citation as you would a chapter in an edited book.

> 17. Garbacz P. The four dimensions of artifacts. In: Dubois D, Welty C, Williams M, editors. Principles of knowledge representation and reasoning: proceedings of the ninth international conference; 2004 June 2-5; Whistler (BC). Menlo Park (CA): Am Assoc for Artificial Intelligence; 2004. p 289-99.

18. Published Dissertation or Thesis   Use the general format for a book, adding the word "dissertation" or "thesis" in square brackets after the title. Treat the institution granting the degree as the publisher. Follow with the phrase "Available from" followed by a colon, followed by the *Dissertation Abstracts International* information.

> 18. Bryan N. Formation and physiological significance of tissue nitrosation/nitrosylation products [dissertation]. Shreveport (LA): Louisiana

State Univ Health Sciences Center; 2004. 128 p. Available from: University Microfilms, Ann Arbor, MI; 3137767.

19. Unpublished Dissertation or Thesis   Use the general format for a book, adding the word "dissertation" or "thesis" in square brackets as a final element of the title. Treat the institution granting the degree as the publisher.

19. Whitley B. Plasminogen activator inhibitor-1 in breast and ovarian cancer invasion [dissertation]. Chapel Hill (NC): Univ North Carolina; 2004. 200 p.

Sources in Journals, Magazines, and Newspapers

20. Article in a Journal Paginated by Volume   If a journal is paginated continuously through a volume, cite only the volume number and then the page numbers. A semicolon separates the year and volume number. There are no spaces between the year, volume number, and page numbers.

20. Paquette L, Seekamp C, Kahane A, Hilmey D, Galluci J. Stereochemical features of Lewis acid-promoted glycosidations involving 4′-spiroannulated DNA building blocks. J Org Chem 2004;69:7442-8.

21. Article in a Journal Paginated by Issue   If a journal begins each issue at page 1, include the issue number (in parentheses) directly following the volume number. As with an article in a journal paginated by volume, there are no spaces between the year, issue number, and page numbers.

21. Dinan F, Yee G. An adventure in stereochemistry: Alice in mirror image land. J Coll Sci Teaching 2004;34(2):25-30.

22. Article in a Weekly Journal   Provide the date (year, month, day) as well as the issue number (in parentheses after the volume number). As with an article in a journal paginated by volume, there are no spaces between the year, issue number, and page numbers.

22. Emery N, Clayton N. The mentality of crows: convergent evolution of intelligence in corvids and apes. Science 2004 Dec 10;306(5703):1903-7.

23. Article in a Magazine   Magazines are not identified by volume; give only the date (year, month, day).

23. Miller K. Juggling two worlds: Richard Jefferson's high-tech plan to feed the poor. Newsweek 2004 Nov 29:36.

CSE

V Documenting Sources

TUTORIAL

How do I cite articles from periodicals using CSE style?

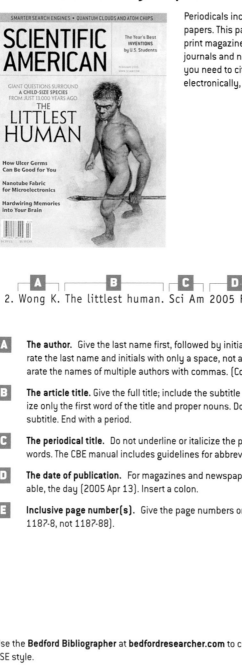

Periodicals include journals, magazines, and newspapers. This page gives an example of a citation for a print magazine article. Models for citing articles from journals and newspapers are on pages 337–39. If you need to cite a periodical article you accessed electronically, see page 340.

2. Wong K. The littlest human. Sci Am 2005 Feb: 55-6.

A   **The author.** Give the last name first, followed by initials for first and middle names. Separate the last name and initials with only a space, not a comma. Do not separate initials. Separate the names of multiple authors with commas. (Cobb C, Fetterolf ML). End with a period.

B   **The article title.** Give the full title; include the subtitle (if any), preceded by a colon. Capitalize only the first word of the title and proper nouns. Do not underline or italicize the title or subtitle. End with a period.

C   **The periodical title.** Do not underline or italicize the periodical title; capitalize all major words. The CBE manual includes guidelines for abbreviating journal titles.

D   **The date of publication.** For magazines and newspapers, include the month and, if available, the day (2005 Apr 13). Insert a colon.

E   **Inclusive page number(s).** Give the page numbers on which the article appears (154-77; 1187-8, not 1187-88).

Use the **Bedford Bibliographer** at **bedfordresearcher.com** to create a references list formatted in CSE style.

24. Article in a Newspaper   Treat newspaper articles as you would magazine articles, identifying their pages by section, page, and column on which they begin (in parentheses).

> 24. Rowland C. Consumer Reports turns focus to prescription drugs. Boston Globe 2004 Dec 10;Sect A:1(col 1).

25. Unsigned Article in a Newspaper   In place of the author's name, write "Anonymous" in brackets.

> 25. [Anonymous]. Healey rejects study on health care costs. Boston Globe 2004 Aug 10;Sect B:2 (col 6).

● Print Reference Works

26. Encyclopedia, Dictionary, Thesaurus, Handbook, or Almanac   Begin with the title of the reference work and information about the edition. Identify the editor, if listed. Provide publisher and publication date.

> 26. The essential dictionary of science. Clark J, editor. New York: Barnes & Noble; 2004.

27. Map or Chart   Use the name of the area in place of an author. Follow with the title, type of map in brackets (such as physical map or demographic map), place of publication and publisher, and a description of the map. If the map is part of a larger document, such as an atlas, provide publication information for the document and the page number(s) of the map.

> 27. South America. Average annual rainfall [climate map]. In: The new comparative world atlas. Maplewood (NJ): Hammond; 1999. p 85. Color.

28. Pamphlet   Format entries as you would for a book (see also #4 on p. 337).

> 28. Case Western Reserve University. Department of Astronomy. Pamphlet on undergraduate studies. Cleveland (OH): Case Western Reserve Univ; 2003. 6 p.

● Media Sources

29. Film or Video Recording   Give the title then the type of medium identified in brackets, followed by individuals listed as authors, editors, performers, conductors, and so on. Identify the producer if different from the publisher. Provide publication information.

> 29. Lions of darkness [videotape]. Joubert D, Joubert B, directors. Washington: National Geographic; 2004.

CSE

V Documenting Sources

30. Television Program CSE style does not provide guidance on citing television programs. Cite as you would a film or video recording.

> 30. Shadow over the sun: a story of eagles [television program].
> Garia M, producer. New York: Thirteen Online; 2003.

31. Radio Program CSE style does not provide guidance on citing radio programs. Cite as you would a film or video recording.

> 31. Thai chicken farms are front line for bird flu fight [radio program].
> Hamilton J, reporter. Washington: National Public Radio; 2004.

32. Sound Recording Cite as you would a film or video recording.

> 32. Requiem [sound recording]. Mozart A, composer. Dresden Staatskapelle, performers. Schreier P, conductor. New York: Philips; 1990.

Field Sources

33. Personal Interview Treat unpublished interviews as personal communication (see p. 333). Cite them in the text only; do not cite them in the reference list.

34. Personal Letter Cite personal letters as personal communication (see p. 333). Cite them in the text only; do not cite them in the reference list.

35. Lecture or Public Address Like an unpublished paper presented at a meeting, lectures or public addresses are treated as personal communication and are cited only in the text (see p. 333).

Electronic Sources

36. Material from Online Database

> 36. Eisner T, Berenbaum M. Chemical ecology: missed opportunities? Science 2002 Mar 1;292(5562):1973. In: Expanded Academic ASAP [database on the Internet]. Farmington Hills (MI): InfoTrac, c2002 [cited 2005 Jan 24]. [about 5 paragraphs]. Available from: http://infotrac.galegroup.com/itw; Article: A84370011.

37. Electronic Book (Monograph) If you must estimate the length, include it in brackets.

> 37. Stokes DE. Pasteur's quadrant: basic science and technological innovation [monograph on the Internet]. Washington: Brookings Inst; 1997 [Cited 2005 Feb 8]. [about 180 p]. Available from: http://brookings.nap.edu/books/0815781776/html/index.html

38. Electronic Journal Article

38. Stark WS, Thomas CF. Microscopy of multiple visual receptor types in Drosophila. Molecular Vision [serial on the Internet]. 2004 Dec 15 [cited 2005 Feb 21];10:943-55. Available from: http://www.molvis.org/molvis/v10/a113/

39. Electronic newspaper article

39. Zuger A. When is a doctor too old? Or too young? NY Times on the Web [Internet]. 2005 Feb 8 [cited 2005 Feb 11]:[about 20 paragraphs]. Available from: http://www.nytimes.com/2005/02/08/health/08essa.htm

40. Web Site

40. Geology & Public Policy [Internet]. Boulder (CO): Geological Society of America; c2005 [updated 2005 Feb 4; cited 2005 Feb 8]. Available from: http://www.geosociety.org/science/govpolicy.htm

41. Government Web Site

41. Colleges and Universities: 2004-05 Influenza Season [Internet]. Atlanta (GA): Centers for Disease Control and Prevention (US); [2005 Jan 27; cited 2005 Feb 16]. Available from: http://www.cdc.gov/flu/school/college.htm

42. Email Message

42. Chin K. Epidemiology essay [electronic mail on the Internet]. Message to: Seth Laffal. 2005 Jan 10, 4:20 pm [cited 2005 Jan 18]. [about 2 screens].

43. Electronic Discussion List Message

43. Quasarano C (Boston University Medical School ceg@bu.edu). Tagging zebrafish. In: BIONET [discussion list on the Internet]. [London; Medical Research Council]; 2004 Apr 05, 11:18 am [cited 2005 Feb 28]. [about 8 lines]. Available from: http://www.bio.net/bionet/mm/zbrafish/2004-April/00512.html

44. Entire Blog

44. Cerminaro A. Life science lawyer: biotechnology and life sciences [blog on the Internet]. 2005 May 5 [cited 2005 Jun 13]. Available from: http://lifesciencelawyer.blogspot.com/

CSE

V Documenting Sources

45. Entry or Comment on a Blog

45. Cerminaro A. Guidelines released for embryonic stem cell research. Life science lawyer: biotechnology and life sciences [blog on the Internet]. 2005 May 5 [cited 2005 Jun 13]. [about 9 paragraphs]. Available from: http://lifesciencelawyer.blogspot.com/2005/05/guidelines-released-for-embryonic-stem

A Reference List in CSE Citation-Sequence Style

> The reference list is titled "References."

REFERENCES

> The reference list is not alphabetical. Sources are numbered and listed in the order in which they appear in the document.

1. Kinzey WG, editor. New world primates: ecology, evolution and behavior. New York: Aldine de Gruyter; 1997. 436 p.

2. Krashen S. Effects of phonemic awareness training on delayed tests of reading. Perceptual and Motor Skills 1999;89:79-82.

3. Burros F, Chen RY. Training in phonemic awareness: three case studies. Perceptual and Motor Skills 1999;89:186-202.

4. Snowdon CT. Is speech special? lessons from new world primates. In: Kinzey WG, editor. New world primates: ecology, evolution and behavior. New York: Aldine de Gruyter; 1997. p 75-93.

5. Tomasello M, Call J. Primate cognition. New York: Oxford Univ Pr; 1997. 517 p.

> Titles of books and periodicals are neither underlined nor italicized. All major words in the titles of periodicals are capitalized. For all other sources, only initial words of the main title and proper nouns and adjectives are capitalized.

APPENDIX

Guide to Resources in the Disciplines

Use this guide as a starting point for finding resources in specific disciplines. A more comprehensive guide containing over one thousand hyperlinked entries can be found at *The Bedford Researcher* Web site at **bedfordresearcher.com**. Each category that follows is organized into three subcategories: print resources, databases, and Web sites.

CONTENTS

GENERAL

Print Resources

Book Review Index. Detroit: Gale, 1965–. Over 100,000 reviews of books, periodicals, and journals.

New York Times Index. New York: New York Times, 1948–. Easy access to all material from the *New York Times*. Abstracts provided of significant news events.

Readers' Guide to Periodical Literature. New York: Wilson, 1900–. Index to English-language periodicals.

Databases

ArticleFirst (OCLC, available through OCLC FirstSearch) Over 12,000 articles from 1990 to the present.

Biography Index (Wilson, available through OCLC FirstSearch) Covers biographical information for books and periodicals for a wide range of subject areas.

Dissertation Abstracts Online (Bell & Howell, available through OCLC FirstSearch) Includes dissertations and theses on a wide range of academic subjects.

Electric Library (Infonautics) Articles on a wide range of subjects. Sources include books, newspapers, magazines, TV/radio transcripts, and pictures.

FactSearch (Pierian, available through OCLC FirstSearch) Emphasis on sources with date-linked and statistical evidence. Includes over 99,000 records on subjects such as economics, the environment, health, political issues, and social issues. Some full-text sources.

Lexis-Nexis Academic Universe Provides sources on legal, medical, news, business, and reference issues. Many entries are full-text sources.

Newspaper Abstracts (Bell & Howell, available through OCLC FirstSearch) Includes all types of newspaper articles, editorials, commentaries, and reviews from over 50 newspapers. Most entries include abstracts.

Periodical Abstracts (Bell & Howell, available through OCLC FirstSearch) Contains abstracts from general and academic publications.

Proquest Provides access to thousands of current periodicals and newspapers. Updated daily and archived to 1986.

Readers' Guide Abstracts (Wilson, available through OCLC FirstSearch) Bibliographic citations of articles from popular magazines from 1983 to the present. Many include abstracts, and listings cover a wide range of topics.

Readers' Guide to Periodical Literature (Wilson, available through SilverPlatter) Electronic equivalent of the print version of the *Readers' Guide to Periodical Literature.*

Web Sites

About.com: www.about.com Boasts depth and breadth, with hundreds of guide sites organized into channels—covers more than 50,000 subjects.

Academic Info: www.academicinfo.net No-nonsense, information-only site provides on-line college-level research material via its subject directory.

EServer.org: eserver.org Clearinghouse of original work and scholarship on a range of topics.

Google Directory: www.google.com/dirhp Extensive directory sponsored by Google. Displays results from the Open Directory project using Google PageRank ratings.

Open Directory: dmoz.org Subject directory managed by volunteer editors—provides organization missing in automated search engines.

Yahoo!: dir.yahoo.com Popular directory directs you to categorized and reviewed indexes to sites. Provides daily updated links to news and topics of interest.

ARTS AND HUMANITIES

GENERAL

Print Resources

The American Humanities Index. Albany: Whitston, 1974–. Indexes English-language humanities journals and periodicals. Limits entries to articles from American publications.

Humanities Index. New York: Wilson, 1974–. Indexes English-language periodicals for all areas of the humanities.

Databases

***Arts and Humanities Citation Index* (Web of Science — Institute for Scientific Information)** A multidisciplinary database that contains sources from 1975 to the present.

***Humanities Abstracts* (Wilson, available through OCLC FirstSearch)** This database includes abstracts of book reviews, original fiction, articles, and play reviews.

Library of Congress Databases and E-resources Contains over 200 databases that include print journals, magazines, books, manuals, and other materials.

Web Sites

***Academic Info's Humanities Directory*: www.academicinfo.net/subhum.html** Humanities section of collegiate-level research searchable by keyword or subject index.

***Open Directory's Arts Directory*: dmoz.org/ Arts/** Contains a varied subject index, including individual links to topics such as body art, animation, and native and tribal arts, in addition to typical categories such as dance and literature.

***Search Engine Guide's Arts Links*: www. searchengineguide.com/pages/Arts/** Subcategorized by architecture, artists, crafts, humanities, performing arts, and photography.

ARCHITECTURE

Print Resources

***Dictionary of Architecture and Construction.* Ed. Cyril M. Harris. 3rd ed. New York: McGraw, 2000.** An alphabetical list of short definitions of architecture terms, people, and events. Includes many illustrations.

Kidder Smith, G. E. *Source Book of American Architecture.* New York: Princeton Architectural, 1996. Includes information and descriptions of over 500 buildings. Also provides historical surveys of the development of American architecture.

Packard, Robert T., and Balthazar Korab. *Encyclopedia of American Architecture.* 2nd ed. New York: McGraw, 1995. Alphabetical list of information on art topics and artists.

Specialized terms are defined, and entries offer further reading suggestions.

Database

***Architecture Database* (British Architectural Library, Royal Institute of British Architects)** Entries include articles, reviews, obituaries, and biographies from 400 periodicals as well as monographs, conference proceedings, exhibition catalogs, and technical literature.

Web Sites

***Cyburbia Directory*: www.cyburbia.org/ directory/** Contains a directory of Internet resources relevant to planning, architecture, urbanism, and growth.

***The Great Buildings Collection*: www. greatbuildings.com** An online multimedia encyclopedia of world architecture that documents buildings and architects from around the world.

ART

Print Resources

***Art Index.* New York: Wilson, 1929–.** Covers both foreign and domestic art publications. Entries are listed by author and subject and cover a wide range of art topics.

***Concise Oxford Dictionary of Art and Artists.* Ed. Ian Chilvers. 2nd ed. Oxford: Oxford UP, 1996.** Covers art from the fifth century B.C. to the present. Includes biographies of notable artists as well as information on topics such as techniques, styles, museums, and galleries.

***Contemporary Artists.* Ed. Joann Cerrito. 4th ed. New York: St. James, 1996.** Biographical profiles of over 800 contemporary artists. Covers painting, sculpture, performance art, graphic arts, and more.

***Dictionary of Art.* Ed. Jane Turner. 34 vols. New York: Grove's Dictionaries, 1996.** Thirty-four volumes of information on general art topics and artists. Entries appear alphabetically. The final volume is a cumulative index.

Databases

***Art Abstracts* (Wilson, available through OCLC FirstSearch)** Covers a range of art subjects including painting, sculpture, photography, film, and folk arts.

Art Index (SilverPlatter) Index includes entries from over 350 journals.

Bibliography of the History of Art (J. Paul Getty Trust and the Centre National de la Recherche Scientifique, available through Research Libraries Group) Covers European and American art. Entries include a citation and an abstract.

Grove Art Online (Oxford) Provides online access to *The Dictionary of Art* (1996, 34 vols.) with ongoing additions of new material and updates to the text, plus extensive image links.

Web Sites

Art Full Text: www.hwwilson.com/databases/artindex.htm Contains full text plus abstracts and indexing for international articles from 1997 to the present.

Open Directory's Arts Directory: dmoz.org/Arts/ Contains a varied subject index, including links to topics such as body art, animation, and native and tribal arts in addition to typical categories such as dance and literature.

World Wide Art Resources: wwar.com/ Access to arts services, artist portfolios, and global arts resources.

World Wide Arts Art History Directory: wwar.com/arthistory/ Contains a varied subject index, including links to topics such as art movements, biographies of noted artists, major artists by century, and artists by nationality.

COMMUNICATIONS

Print Resources

Block, Eleanor S., and James K. Bracken. *Communication and the Mass Media: A Guide to Reference Literature.* Englewood: Libraries Unlimited, 1991. Detailed descriptions of reference sources in the communications and media field. Organized by type of source.

Index to Journals in Communication Studies through 1995. Ed. Ronald J. Matlon. Annandale, VA: National Communication Association, 1997. Provides the tables of contents for twenty-four journals in the field. Also includes an author index and a keyword index.

Web Sites

National Public Radio: www.npr.org Offers audio archives of past shows as well as up-to-the-minute news resources.

Public Broadcasting Service: www.pbs.org Includes news reports, programming information, and daily feature topics.

DRAMA
Print Resources

Cambridge Guide to the Theatre. Ed. Martin Banham. New York: Cambridge UP, 1995. Covers the history and practice of worldwide theater. Thousands of entries are listed alphabetically.

Critical Survey of Drama. Ed. Frank N. Magill. Rev. ed. 7 vols. Pasadena: Salem, 1994. Essays on drama topics organized by author and genre. Final volume is a cumulative index.

Drama Criticism. Ed. Lawrence Trudeau. 9 vols. Detroit: Gale, 1991–. Designed specifically for the beginning student or the average theatergoer. Provides critical essays on authors and their works.

Database

International Index to the Performing Arts (Bell & Howell) Sources covering a wide range of topics within performing arts.

Web Sites

Eserver Drama Collection: www.eserver.org/drama Contains a collection of original plays and screenplays, criticism, and links to other drama sites.

Theater Resources from Artslynx: www.artslynx.org/theatre/ Extensive directory of links for theater.

FILM
Print Resources

International Dictionary of Films and Filmmakers. Ed. Samantha Cook. 5 vols. Detroit: St. James, 1994. Separate volumes for films and filmmakers, actors and actresses, and writers, producers, and artists. Provides a summary, a list of film credits, and suggestions for further reading.

Katz, Ephraim. *The Film Encyclopedia.* 4th
ed. New York: Harper, 2001. Includes nearly
8,000 entries on film topics, with biographical information on actors, directors, producers, screenwriters, and cinematographers.
Provides definitions of industry terminology.

*New York Times Film Reviews. Time-Life
Books.* New York: Garland, 1913–. Over
100,000 reviews of motion pictures. Organized by the date the review appeared in the
New York Times. Provides a name index for
searching by author, director, producer, composer, etc.

Databases

International Film Archive (International
Federation of Film Archives, available through
SilverPlatter) An index of the International
Federation of Film Archives. Also includes
a list of members and a bibliography of
publications.

Movie Review Query Engine Contains over
410,000 movie reviews and links to other film
resources.

Web Sites

American Film Institute: www.afi.com American Film Institute's home site describes the
AFI's founding as a nonprofit organization
and its mission in preserving film heritage.
Lists links to AFI's history of awards, events,
and projects.

ScreenSite: www.screensite.org Provides educators and students with resources to facilitate
the study of film and television.

Yahoo!'s Movies and Film Directory: dir.yahoo.
com/Entertainment/Movies_and_Film/ Links
to everything from classic Hollywood films to
the most recent releases, with an emphasis on
pop culture.

FOREIGN LANGUAGES AND LITERATURES

Print Resource

Campbell, George L. *Concise Compendium
of the World's Languages.* New York: Routledge, 1995. Lists and provides nontechnical
descriptions of over 100 international
languages.

Web Sites

Academic Info's Foreign Language Study Directory: www.academicinfo.net/lang.html Provides main links by language and includes
Sanskrit, Ancient Egyptian, Ancient Near
Eastern, and Australian Indigenous among the
more common choices. Also contains an annotated list of indexes and general directories.

Center for Applied Linguistics Resources:
www.cal.org/resources/ Wide range of resources, including digests from the former
ERIC Clearinghouse on Languages and
Linguistics.

HISTORY

Print Resources

Cambridge Ancient History. Ed. Averil Cameron
and Peter Garnsey. 14 vols. Cambridge: Cambridge UP, 1998. Articles by historians on
chronologically arranged topics covering only
ancient history.

Documents of American History. Ed. Henry
Steele Commager and Milton Cantor. 10th ed.
Englewood Cliffs: Prentice, 1988. Compiles
primary resources from American history, including letters, speeches, memoirs, poetry,
newspaper articles, and sermons.

Encyclopedia of American History. Ed. Richard
B. Morris and Jeffrey B. Morris. 7th ed. New
York: Harper, 1996. Entries are arranged in
chronological order and by subject, with a
separate section of biographies and a basic
chronology of American history.

Encyclopedia of World History. Ed. Patrick K.
O'Brien. New York: George Philip, 2000. Over
6,500 articles on all areas of world history,
arranged alphabetically. Includes a general
chronology of people, dates, and events spanning 17,000 years.

Slavens, Thomas P. *Sources of Information for
Historical Research.* New York: Neal-Schuman,
1994. Bibliographic information for all types
of reference sources including online databases.

Databases

America: History and Life (ABC-Clio) A bibliographic reference to American and Canadian
history.

Historical Abstracts **(ABC-Clio)** Over 500,000 entries on the history of the world, excluding Canada and the United States. Lists sources from 2,000 journals worldwide.

Web Sites

Education Planet History Directory: **www. educationplanet.com/search/Social_Studies/ History/** Directory of links to education-related sites on history.

WWW Virtual Library: History: **vlib.iue.it/ history/** The central catalog of the main network provides direct links to other network sites through its index. Select from main categories and by countries and regions.

Yahoo! History Directory: **dir.yahoo.com/Arts/ Humanities/History/** A comprehensive directory of Web resources on historical topics.

LAW

Print Resources

Burnham, William. *Introduction to the Law and Legal System of the United States.* **St. Paul: West, 1995.** Specifically aimed at those who have not completed law school. Provides an overview of primary topics and methodology in American law. Appendix includes an extensive list of notable cases.

Great American Court Cases. **Ed. Mark Mikula and L. Mpho Mabunda. 4 vols. Detroit: Gale, 1999.** Describes and analyzes over 800 notable court cases, most of which were heard by the U.S. Supreme Court. Provides an overview of each case, a discussion of its importance, and excerpts from judges' opinions.

Databases

Index to Legal Periodicals and Books **(Wilson, available through OCLC FirstSearch and Silver-Platter)** Includes references to journals, yearbooks, reviews, and government publications. Most are from North America and the United Kingdom.

PAIS Archive **(through OCLC Firstsearch)** A retrospective database chronicling global public policy and social issues from the early twentieth century through the 1970s.

Web Sites

CataLaw: **www.catalaw.com/** Lists all major worldwide Internet catalogs of law and government. Site can be searched by legal topics and regional (including international) law as well as for information such as legal directories and law societies.

Internet Legal Resource Guide: **www.ilrg.com/** This categorized index of over 4,000 international sites is edited to include only the most substantive legal resources.

LITERATURE

Print Resources

The Bloomsbury Guide to Women's Literature. **Ed. Claire Buck. New York: Bloomsbury, 1992.** Essays provide a geographical and historical overview of women's literature. Reference section includes alphabetical entries for works, authors, and terms. Some entries include bibliographic information.

Contemporary Literary Criticism. **Ed. Sharon R. Gunton. Detroit: Gale, 1973–.** Criticism and general information on authors of all genres of writing. Each entry includes passages from and reviews of author's work.

Dictionary of Literary Biography. **Detroit: Gale, 1978–.** Covers an enormous range of authors, periods, genres, cultures, and nationalities. Provides personal information, a list of publications, and critical reviews.

Nineteenth-Century Literary Criticism. **Detroit: Gale, 1981–.** Excerpts from criticism on all genres of creative writing. Covers authors who died between 1800 and 1899.

Twentieth-Century Literary Criticism. **Detroit: Gale, 1978–.** Excerpts from criticism on all genres of creative writing. Covers authors who died between 1900 and 1960.

Databases

Contemporary Authors **(Gale)** Biographical and bibliographical references for over 90,000 authors. Covers fiction, nonfiction, poetry, journalism, drama, movies, television, and more.

MLA International Bibliography **(MLA, available through OCLC FirstSearch)** A bibliography of sources in the fields of literature, language, linguistics, and folklore.

Women Writers Online (Brown University Women Writers Project) Full-text editions of works by over 100 English and American women writers. Focuses on authors from 1500 to 1830.

World Authors (Wilson, available through SilverPlatter) Information on over 10,000 authors from a variety of cultures and across genres.

Web Sites

The English Server: eserver.org A niche for literature not always found on the more commercial sites. Offers collections on diverse topics such as design, race, and contemporary art. Hypertext, audio, and video recordings are also available.

Internet Public Library: Literary Criticism: ipl.si.umich.edu/div/litcrit/ Substantive literary research and criticism; solely dedicated to critical and biographical sites about authors and their works.

LitLinks: www.bedfordstmartins.com/litlinks/ Organized alphabetically by author within five genres with annotated links.

Voice of the Shuttle: vos.ucsb.edu/ Humanities Web page directs you to extensive sets of literature links organized by period, nation, subculture, and genre. Includes pages of noteworthy sites.

MUSIC
Print Resources

The Guinness Encyclopedia of Popular Music. **Ed. Colin Larkin. 6 vols. New York: Stockton, 1995.** Articles on titles, composers, musicians, record labels, and more. Includes discographies where appropriate.

Music Article Guide. Philadelphia: Information Services, 1986–. Annotated guide to articles in over 250 American music periodicals. Designed for school and college music educators.

The New Grove Dictionary of Music and Musicians. **Ed. Stanley Sadie. 29 vols. New York: Grove's Dictionaries, 2001.** Articles on musi-

cians and works. Entries for musicians include bibliographies and works. Expansive geographical and historical coverage.

Databases

Grove Music Online **(Oxford)** Comprises the full texts of *The New Grove Dictionary of Music and Musicians, The New Grove Dictionary of Opera,* and *The New Grove Dictionary of Jazz.*

MusicLiterature **(RILM, available through OCLC FirstSearch)** Indexes sources from over 500 scholarly journals, including articles, books, bibliographies, catalogs, conference proceedings, discographies, and more.

Web Sites

Society for Music Theory: **www. societymusictheory.org** Contains a variety of electronic resources for music theory and includes numerous links to other resources.

UCC Resources for Research in Music: **www.music.ucc.ie/wrrm/** Music links organized by period, traditional and popular music, and genre and thematic categories.

Worldwide Internet Music Resources: **www.music.indiana.edu/music_resources/** Indiana University School of Music site offers useful links to students looking for material with an academic approach.

PHILOSOPHY
Print Resources

Bynagle, Hans E. *Philosophy: A Guide to the Reference Literature.* **2nd ed. Englewood: Libraries Unlimited, 1997.** Intended for professionals, teachers, students, and librarians.

Cambridge Dictionary of Philosophy. **Ed. Robert Audi. 2nd ed. Cambridge: Cambridge UP, 1999.** Over 4,000 entries on philosophers and philosophical terminology. Detailed overviews of the subfields of philosophy.

Encyclopedia of Classical Philosophy. **Ed. Donald J. Zeyl. Westport: Greenwood, 1997.** Covers Greek and Roman philosophy and philosophers from the sixth century B.C. to the sixth century A.D.

The Philosopher's Index. Bowling Green, OH: Philosopher's Information Center, 1978–. Indexes over 400 journals and books in the field from 1940 to the present. Organized by subject and author headings.

Databases

Encyclopedia of Philosophy (Routledge) Online version of Routledge *Encyclopedia of Philosophy*.

The Philosopher's Index (SilverPlatter) An index and bibliography of philosophy books and journals.

Web Sites

Internet Encyclopedia of Philosophy: www.iep.utm.edu Provides detailed, scholarly information on key topics and philosophers in all areas of philosophy.

Philosophy in Cyberspace: www-personal.monash.edu.au/~dey/phil/ Divided into five main categories: branches of philosophy, text-related information (such as journals and libraries), organizations, forums, and miscellaneous topics.

RELIGION

Print Resources

The Encyclopedia of Religion. Ed. Mircea Eliade. 16 vols. New York: Macmillan, 1987. An expansive encyclopedia of articles on international religions. Covers historical religious issues as well as contemporary topics. Entries listed alphabetically.

Penguin Dictionary of Religions. Ed. John R. Hinnells. New York: Penguin, 1995. An alphabetical listing of topics and issues concerning religions around the world. Includes a bibliography and index.

World Religions. New York: Macmillan, 1998. Covers religious ideas and the practice of religion worldwide. Provides definitions for important terms.

Database

ATLA Religion (American Theological Library Association, available through OCLC First-Search) An index of publications that spans all religions but emphasizes Western religions.

Web Sites

Academic Info Religion Gateway: www.academicinfo.net/religindex.html An orderly list leading to informative sites covering world religions by country and type. A good place for students to find straightforward historical religious material.

Open Directory's Religion and Spirituality Directory: dmoz.org/Society/Religion_and_Spirituality/ In addition to links by specific religion or spiritual code, the Open Directory also includes a set of links to related areas of interest, such as near-death experiences, reincarnation, opposing views, and religious art and music.

Rutgers University Virtual Religion Index: religion.rutgers.edu/vri This site's list of categorical links is diverse and coherent in its divisions, and the index is efficiently designed to analyze and highlight important content of sites.

WRITING

Print Resources

Encyclopedia of Rhetoric and Composition. Ed. Theresa Enos. New York: Garland, 1996. Over 450 entries on major people, concepts, and applications.

An Introduction to Composition Studies. Ed. Erika Lindemann and Gary Tate. New York: Oxford UP, 1991. A general introduction to the composition field.

Sourcebook on Rhetoric: Key Concepts in Contemporary Rhetoric Studies. James Jasinski. Thousand Oaks: Sage, 2001. A comprehensive introduction to the language of contemporary rhetorical studies.

Database

ERIC (available through OCLC FirstSearch, Cambridge Scientific Abstracts, SilverPlatter, and on the Web at www.eric.ed.gov) Includes over 900,000 annotated references from *Resources in Education and Current Index to Journals in Education.*

Web Sites

CCCC Bibliography of Composition and Rhetoric: www.ibiblio.org/cccc/links.html

A diverse collection of links to works that deal with written communication.

Writing @ CSU Links: writing.colostate.edu/links/ Collection of links to Internet-based writing resources. Includes references for writing across the curriculum as well as topic search sites and tools such as grammar guides, glossaries, and composition tips.

SOCIAL SCIENCES

GENERAL

Print Resources

Social Sciences Citation Index. **Philadelphia: Institute for Scientific Information, 1973–.** Helps determine the largest, most popular, and most used journals in the field.

Social Sciences Index. **New York: Wilson, 1974–.** Covers English-language periodicals. Fields include anthropology, criminal justice, economics, law, political science, psychology, women's studies, and more.

Databases

Social Sciences Abstracts **(Wilson, available through OCLC FirstSearch and SilverPlatter)** Abstracts of articles concerning the social sciences. Includes articles, interviews, biographies, and book reviews.

Social Sciences Citation Index **(Web of Science — Institute for Scientific Information)** Includes references, bibliographic information, some author abstracts, and links to full-text sources.

Social Sciences Index **(Wilson, available through SilverPlatter)** Designed for easy use by students, teachers, and researchers.

Web Sites

Research Resources in Social Science: **www.researchresources.net/** General resources on social sciences. Best suited as a starting point for investigation.

Social Science Information Gateway: **sosig.ac.uk/** Browse or search the database of online resources selected and described by subject experts, or use the Social Science Search Engine. Designed for researchers and

practitioners of the social sciences, business, or the law.

ANTHROPOLOGY

Print Resources

Abstracts in Anthropology. **Ed. Roger W. Moeller and Jay F. Custer. Westport, CT: Greenwood, 1970–.** Entries include bibliographic information and abstracts. Articles on a range of current and significant anthropology topics.

Encyclopedia of Social and Cultural Anthropology. **Ed. Alan Barnard and Jonathan Spencer. New York: Routledge, 1996.** Designed for use by students and teachers. Includes a glossary of terms and suggestions for further reading.

Encyclopedia of World Cultures. **Ed. David Levinson. 10 vols. Boston: G.K. Hall, 1991–.** Intended for a general audience. The volumes are organized alphabetically by geographic area. Also has a glossary of technical terms.

Web Sites

Academic Info's Anthropology Directory: **www.academicinfo.net/anth.html** Social and cultural anthropology, physical and biological anthropology, and links to general organizations, educational resources, and directories on the Web.

Anthro.net: **www.anthro.net/** Choose from 53 anthropology-related topics to reach specific bibliographic references and links to Internet resources.

Open Directory's Anthropology Directory: **dmoz.org/Science/Social_Sciences/Anthropology/** Divides the broad discipline of anthropology into five branches of study. Within each branch, you can browse links in greater detail or search the database with keywords.

ECONOMICS

Print Resources

Index of Economic Articles. **Nashville: American Economic Association, 1886–.** Provides both subject and author indexes.

Journal of Economic Literature. **Nashville: American Economic Association, 1886–.** Articles and book reviews on economic topics. Each article has a bibliography.

Databases

***ABI/Inform* (Bell & Howell, available through OCLC FirstSearch)** Indexes articles from professional publications, scholarly journals, and trade magazines around the world.

***EconLit* (American Economic Association, available through OCLC FirstSearch and Silver-Platter)** Citations for over 400,000 dissertations and articles from 1969 to the present.

Web Sites

***ECONLinks:* www.ncat.edu/ffsimkinss/econlinks.html** Developed to provide students with easy access to basic economic and financial information available on the Web.

***EconoLink:* www.progress.org/econolink/** User-friendly site lets you select from categories: best sites for content, research, and innovation; best sites for journalists, activists, and students; and other economics sites.

EDUCATION

Print Resources

Berry, Dorothea. *A Bibliographic Guide to Educational Research.* 3rd ed. Metuchen: Scarecrow, 1990. An annotated bibliography of sources in the field of education. Title and subject indexes.

***Encyclopedia of Educational Research.* Ed. Marvin Alkin. 6th ed. 4 vols. New York: Macmillan, 1992.** A list of articles on educational research, each with a substantial list of references.

***The Encyclopedia of Higher Education.* Ed. Burton R. Clark and Guy Neave. 4 vols. Oxford: Pergamon, 1992.** A collection of analytical articles on topics in higher education. Articles are arranged by subject and organized alphabetically.

Unger, Harlow G. Encyclopedia of American Education. New York: Facts on File, 1996. Designed for students and all members of the education community. Covers all areas of American education.

Databases

***Education Abstracts* (Wilson, available through OCLC FirstSearch and SilverPlatter)** Covers all education levels from preschool through college and a wide range of education issues.

***Education Full Text* (Wilson, available through SilverPlatter)** Lists sources from 1983 to the present and includes abstracts and full text from August 1994 on.

***Education Index* (Wilson, available through OCLC FirstSearch and SilverPlatter)** Indexes over 450 current periodicals and yearbooks for all levels of education. Topics include critical thinking, teaching methods, curriculum, and legal issues in education.

***ERIC* (available through OCLC FirstSearch, Cambridge Scientific Abstracts, and SilverPlatter, and on the Web at www.eric .ed.gov)** Includes more than 900,000 annotated references from *Resources in Education and Current Index to Journals in Education.*

Web Sites

***About.com's Education Directory:* home.about.com/education/** Information is divided into adult and continuing education, college/university education, and primary and secondary education. Each section contains information for both the student and the educator.

***Education Index:* www.educationindex.com/** Annotated guide provides not only lists of links but summaries of each site. Directory includes topics from pre-K through college as well as continuing education and careers.

***Education World:* www.education-world.com/** Updated daily, this site focuses on current issues in the education field, including technology in the classroom, relevant legislative action, and interviews with educators.

GEOGRAPHY

Print Resources

***Companion Encyclopedia of Geography: The Environment and Humankind.* Ed. Ian Douglas, Richard Huggett, and Mike Robinson. New York: Routledge, 1996.** Articles on geography issues arranged under larger subject headings. Each entry provides a bibliography and suggestions for further reading.

***World Geography.* Ed. Ray Sumner. 8 vols. Pasadena: Salem, 2001.** Provides general information about nations, physical geography, natural resources, human geography, and economic geography for each region.

Database

GEOGRAPHY **(Elsevier, available through SilverPlatter)** An international compilation of journals, books, reports, and theses. Entries have both bibliographic information and abstracts.

Web Sites

GEOSource: **www.library.uu.nl/geosource/** Contains links to Web pages with information in cartography, environmental science and policy, human geography, physical geography, and planning science.

Social Science Internet Gateway Geography Directory: **sosig.ac.uk/geography/** Information is divided by resource type: papers and reports, bibliographic databases, data sources, governmental bodies, news, organizations, journals, and research projects/centers.

GOVERNMENT

Print Resources

Derbyshire, J. Denis, and Ian Derbyshire. *Encyclopedia of World Political Systems.* **2 vols. Armonk: Sharpe, 2000.** Historical information on and explanation of features of governments around the world. Organized geographically and alphabetically. Provides suggestions for further reading and a cumulative index.

Encyclopedia of American Government. **4 vols. Englewood Cliffs: Salem, 1998.** A list of alphabetical articles on all aspects of the U.S. government.

Encyclopedia of the American Constitution. **Ed. Leonard W. Levy and Kenneth L. Karst. 2nd ed. New York: Macmillan, 2000.** Alphabetical listing of articles related specifically to the Constitution. Covers related court cases.

Databases

Congressional Universe **(Lexis-Nexis)** Congressional publications, records of congressional hearings, information on committees and members and on specific bills and laws.

GPO Monthly Catalog **(U.S. Government Printing Office, available through OCLC FirstSearch and SilverPlatter)** Sources include government-issued reports, studies, fact sheets, maps, handbooks, and more. Also provides records of congressional hearings on bills and laws.

PAIS International **(OCLC Public Affairs Information Service, available through OCLC FirstSearch, Cambridge Scientific Abstracts, and SilverPlatter)** More than 400,000 entries including books, periodicals, reports, and government publications.

Web Sites

FedStats: **search.fedstats.gov** This site provides easy access to the statistics and information produced by 70 U.S. federal government agencies.

FedWorld: **www.fedworld.gov** A program of the U.S. Department of Commerce, this site disseminates information made available by the federal government.

FirstGov: **www.firstgov.gov** The official U.S. gateway to all government information. Includes a search tool and directory.

JOURNALISM

Print Resources

Biographical Dictionary of American Journalism. **Ed. Joseph P. McKerns. New York: Greenwood, 1989.** Biographical information on nearly 500 persons important to American journalism.

Cates, Jo A. *Journalism: A Guide to Reference Literature.* **2nd ed. Englewood, CO: Libraries Unlimited, 1997.** Annotated descriptions of over 700 reference sources for journalism.

Ellmore, R. Terry. *NTC's Mass Media Dictionary.* **Lincolnwood, IL: NTC, 1991.** An alphabetical list of over 20,000 definitions of important terms for television, radio, newspapers, film, and magazines.

Database

Gale Database of Publications and Broadcast Media **(Gale Group)** Current information on newspapers, periodicals, radio and television stations, and cable TV companies.

Web Sites

Columbia Journalism Review Journalism Tools: **www.cjr.org/tools/** Provides links to Web resources of use to journalists and journalism students.

JournalismNet: **www.journalismnet.com** This site calls itself "Your investigative guide to Internet research" and has links to numerous global journalistic databases.

Journalism Resources: **bailiwick.lib.uiowa. edu/journalism/** Contains links to news archives, information sources, indexes, media law resources, journalism magazines, and teaching.

Open Directory Journalism Directory: **dmoz. org/News/Media/Journalism/** Includes broadcast journalism, photojournalism, and editorial cartoons as well as issues and education. Featured links are annotated.

POLITICAL SCIENCE

Print Resources

A Bibliography of Contents: Political Science and Government. **Santa Barbara: ABC-CLIO, 1975–.** Indexes current articles from periodicals in political science and related disciplines.

International Political Science Abstracts. **Paris: International Political Science Organization, 1951–.** Includes bibliographical information and abstracts on journal articles in the field.

A New Handbook of Political Science. **Ed. Robert E. Goodin and Hans-Dieter Klingemann. Oxford: Oxford UP, 1996.** Essays that provide an overview of the foundations, history, and current issues of political science. Organized by subdivisions within political science.

Databases

International Political Science Abstracts (**International Political Science Association, available through SilverPlatter**) Indexes and abstracts articles from over 800 journals and yearbooks.

Political Science and Government Abstracts (**Cambridge Scientific Abstracts**) Abstracts

and political science-related sources from 1975 to the present.

Web Sites

Academic Info's Political Science Directory: **www.academicinfo.net/polisci.html** Some regional categorizations include United States, Australia, Great Britain, Canada, China, India, Russia, and Native American. Also contains links to political theory, anarchism, Marxism, communism, socialism, resources, and organizations.

Political Information: **www.politicalinformation. com/** Search policy and political sites, browse links to the latest political news, and skim the latest political headlines.

Politics.com: **www.politics.com** Contains links to the latest polls, nationwide election news, candidate information, media bites, political columns/editorials, and political humor.

PSYCHOLOGY

Print Resources

Biographical Dictionary of Psychology. **Ed. Noel Sheehy, Anthony J. Chapman, and Wendy Conroy. New York: Routledge, 1997.** Biographical information on over 700 notable figures in the field of psychology.

Encyclopedia of Psychology. **Ed. Alan E. Kazdin. 8 vols. Oxford: Oxford UP, 2000.** Over 1,500 articles on psychological concepts, events, figures, and methods.

Handbook of Child Psychology. **Ed. William Damon. 5th ed. 4 vols. New York: Wiley, 1998.** Entries are organized under larger topical headings. Covers wide array of issues and topics in child psychology.

Reed, Jeffery G., and Pam M. Baxter. *Library Use: A Handbook for Psychology.* **2nd ed. Washington: APA, 1992.** Explains how to conduct library research specific to psychology.

Stratton, Peter, and Nicky Hayes. *A Student's Dictionary of Psychology.* **2nd ed. New York: Routledge, 1993.** Alphabetical list of definitions of psychology terminology. Intended specifically for students encountering psychology for the first time.

Databases

PsycARTICLES **(American Psychological Association)** Provides full text of 42 journals published by the APA.

PsycINFO **(APA, available through OCLC First-Search, Cambridge Scientific Abstracts, and SilverPlatter)** Offers references to professional and academic literature in psychology and related disciplines.

Web Sites

Encyclopedia of Psychology: **www.psychology. org** Information is classified by category: paradigms and theory, biological factors, environmental factors, people and history, publications, organizations, and career information.

Psychology Online Resource Central: **www. psych-central.com** Includes links to graduate schools, licensure, online research resources, conventions, and career planning.

Psych Web: **www.psywww.com** Links to scholarly resources, self-help resources, online brochures, careers and academic departments, and an APA style guide.

SOCIAL WORK

Print Resources

Encyclopedia of Social Work. **Ed. Richard L. Edwards and June Gary Hopps. 19th ed. Washington: National Association of Social Workers, 1995.** Alphabetical list of articles on topics in social work and related disciplines.

Ginsberg, Leon. *Social Work Almanac.* **2nd ed. Washington: National Association of Social Workers, 1995.** Facts and statistics on population, children, crime, education, health and mortality, mental health, and the social work profession.

Databases

Social Services Abstracts **(Cambridge Scientific Abstracts)** Over 78,000 bibliographic references on current research in the discipline.

Social Work Abstracts Plus **(National Association of Social Workers, available through SilverPlatter)** Contains over 35,000 records

from social work journals and related fields from 1977 to the present. Includes search aids such as finding word variants.

Web Sites

Grassroots: Social Science Search: **www. andrews.edu/SOWK/grassroots.htm** Information on field work, research, values, and ethics as well as on cultural and ethnic diversity, populations at risk, social welfare policy and service, and social and economic justice.

World Wide Web Resources for Social Workers: **www.nyu.edu/socialwork/wwwrsw/** Provides links to social work resources, including databases and other sources.

SOCIOLOGY

Print Resources

Bart, Pauline, and Linda Frankel. *The Student Sociologist's Handbook.* **4th ed. New York: Random, 1986.** An overview of sociological foundations and methodologies intended specifically for the sociology student. Includes sections on periodicals and reference sources.

A Dictionary of Sociology. **Ed. Gordon Marshall. Oxford: Oxford UP, 1998.** Provides over 2,500 substantial definitions of sociology terms, methods, and brief biographies of key figures.

Johnson, Allan G. *The Blackwell Dictionary of Sociology.* **Cambridge: Blackwell, 1995.** Articles on a wide array of topics in sociology and related fields. A separate section of biographies of key figures.

World of Sociology. **Ed. Joseph M. Palmisano. Detroit: Gale, 2001.** Concise explanations of 1,000 sociological topics, theories, concepts, and organizations. Arranged alphabetically.

Databases

Criminal Justice Abstracts **(Sage, available through SilverPlatter)** A list of sources from international journals, books, dissertations, reports, and unpublished papers.

Sociological Abstracts **(Cambridge Scientific Abstracts, available through SilverPlatter)** Indexes information from over 2,600 journals as well as books, conferences, and dissertations.

Web Sites

Open Directory Sociology Directory: dmoz. org/Science/Social_Sciences/Sociology/ Extensive annotated directory of Web sites related to sociology.

The SocioWeb: www.socioweb.com An independent guide that categorizes information by type: commercial sites, theory, surveys/statistics, university department, writings, journals, and topical research.

TECHNICAL COMMUNICATION

Print Resources

Eisenberg, Anne. *Effective Technical Communication*. 2nd ed. New York: McGraw, 1992. An overview of the background, techniques, and applications of technical communication.

Encyclopedia of Technology and Applied Sciences. 11 vols. New York: Marshall Cavendish, 2000. Articles are arranged alphabetically and written for those without a strong background knowledge.

Web Sites

About.com's Technical Writing Directory: freelancewrite.about.com/od/technicalwriting/ Useful links for technical writers or those in related fields.

Open Directory's Technical Writing Page: dmoz. org/Arts/Writers_Resources/Non-Fiction/ Technical_Writing/ Information divided into businesses, organizations, and software categories as well as an annotated list of links to technical writing sites and resources.

WOMEN'S STUDIES

Print Resources

Andermahr, Sonya, Terry Lovell, and Carol Wolkowitz. *A Concise Glossary of Feminist Theory*. New York: St. Martin's, 1997. Explanations for concepts of feminist theory.

Brownmiller, Sara, and Ruth Dickstein. *An Index to Women's Studies Anthologies*. New York: G.K. Hall, 1994. Indexes over 500 anthologies across disciplines to identify articles related to women's studies.

A Reader's Guide to Women's Studies. Ed. Eleanor B. Amico. Chicago: Fitz Dearborn, 1998. Brief descriptions of books on over 500 topics and people in women's studies.

Women's Studies Encyclopedia. Ed. Helen Tierney. 2nd ed. 2 vols. Westport: Greenwood, 1999. Alphabetically organized articles on a wide array of women's studies issues, people, and events. Focuses mostly on the United States.

Databases

Contemporary Women's Issues (Responsive Database Services, available through OCLC FirstSearch) Indexes books, journals, newsletters, research reports, and fact sheets. Provides information on women from over 150 countries.

Women's Resources International (National Information Services Corporation, available through BiblioLine) Includes bibliographic references for books, essays, and journal articles. Focuses on topics such as women's studies and feminist criticism and theory.

Web Sites

Reading Room: Women's Studies Database: www.mith2.umd.edu/WomensStudies/ ReadingRoom/ A virtual reading room, this site includes a database of selected readings written by or about prominent women and indexes materials according to fiction, nonfiction, history, book reviews, poetry, and academic papers and articles.

Women's Studies/Women's Issues Resource Sites: research.umbc.edu/ffkorenman/wmst/ links.html An annotated list of sites that contain resources and information about women's issues.

NATURAL SCIENCES

GENERAL

Print Resources

The Dictionary of Science. Ed. Peter Lafferty and Julian Rowe. New York: Simon, 1993. Designed for both academic and general readers.

Notable Scientists from 1900 to the Present. **Ed. Brigham Narins. 5 vols. Detroit: Gale, 2001.** Biographical information on 1,600 scientists from all scientific disciplines. Offers selected works by each scientist and suggestions for further reading.

Science and Technology Almanac. **Ed. William Allstetter. Phoenix: Oryx, 1999.** Reports of notable news stories in each discipline as well as facts, figures, and statistics. Also includes sections on people, history, and countries.

Scientific American Desk Reference. **New York: Wiley, 1999.** Each chapter includes an overview, chronology, glossary, biographies, further reading suggestions, and topical articles for a range of disciplines.

Databases

Complete Cambridge Sciences Collection **(Cambridge Scientific Abstracts)** Covers full range of sciences and allows you to narrow your search to include databases for specific scientific disciplines.

Science Citation Index **(Web of Science — Institute for Scientific Information)** Indexes over 5,700 journals that span over 150 scientific disciplines.

ScienceDirect **(Elsevier)** Full-text articles from journals published by Elsevier Science and abstracts from major scientific journals.

Web Sites

Open Directory's Science Directory: **dmoz. org/Science/** A directory of links organized by general scientific fields.

SciCentral: **www.scicentral.com** The latest research news in an extensive list of areas of scientific study, subcategorized as biological, health, physical and chemical, earth and space, engineering sciences, and analytical tools.

SciSeek: **www.sciseek.com** Includes more atypical topics, such as cryptozoology and astroarcheology, in addition to biology, health sciences, etc.

AGRICULTURAL SCIENCES

Print Resources

Biological and Agricultural Index. **New York: Wilson, 1914–.** Indexes over 200 English-language periodicals in the field. Provides a separate listing of citations for book reviews.

Encyclopedia of Agricultural Science. **Ed. Charles J. Arntzen and Allen M. Ritter. 4 vols. San Diego: Academic, 1994.** Intended for both general and academic audiences, with thorough articles on a range of agricultural topics.

Databases

AGRICOLA **(National Agricultural Library of the U.S. Department of Agriculture, available through OCLC FirstSearch and SilverPlatter)** Bibliographic citations for journal articles, monographs, patents, technical reports, and more. Includes worldwide coverage of agriculture issues.

Biological and Agricultural Index **(Wilson, available through OCLC FirstSearch and SilverPlatter)** Citations from a wide range of popular and professional journals. Also includes forestry and ecology.

Web Sites

AgriSurf: **www.agrisurf.com** Over 17,500 sites are organized into 34 main categories such as agritourism, aquaculture, feedlots, soil, organic farming, and education programs. Many sites are commercial or business-related.

National Agricultural Library: **www.nal.usda. gov** Comprehensive topical index to resources selected by the U.S. Department of Agriculture's National Agricultural Library.

ASTRONOMY

Print Resources

Astronomy and Astrophysics Abstracts. **New York: Springer, 1969–.** Abstracts from journals, books, conferences, and more.

The Astronomy and Astrophysics Encyclopedia. **Ed. Stephen P. Maran. New York: Van Nostrand Reinhold, 1992.** Approximately 400 articles on topics covering all areas in astronomy. Intended for a general audience.

Encyclopedia of the Solar System. Ed. Paul R. Weissman, Lucy-Ann McFadden, and Torrence V. Johnson. San Diego: Academic, 1999. Information on all aspects of the solar system, with entries organized around the physical arrangement of the solar system.

Moore, Patrick. *Atlas of the Universe.* Cambridge: Cambridge UP, 1998. Informative articles about the planets, sun, stars, and more. Numerous illustrations, photographs, and charts.

Database

SPIN (American Institute of Physics, available through AIP Online Information Service) Indexes and abstracts current research and publications from major American and Russian journals. Focuses on astronomy and physics.

Web Sites

Astronomy Links: astronomylinks.com Links subjects include articles, news, astronomers and astrophysicists, and terminology. Many of the links are to sites supported by academic institutions or NASA.

AstroWeb: www.stsci.edu/astroweb/astronomy.html An extensive index for space-related Web sites, offering nearly 3,000 resources pooled by individuals at seven educational institutions.

ATHLETICS AND SPORTS SCIENCES

Print Resources

Encyclopedia of Sports Science. Ed. John Zumerchik. 2 vols. New York: Macmillan, 1997. A general reference source of articles on subjects in the sports sciences.

Oxford Handbook of Sports Medicine. Ed. Eugene Sherry and Stephen F. Wilson. Oxford: Oxford UP, 1998. Articles and information in sports sciences and the treatment of sports-related injuries. Offers background and fundamentals of sports medicine.

Physical Education Index. Cape Girardeau, MO: Ben Oak, 1976–. A subject index of domestic and foreign articles in fields such as sports medicine, physical education, physical therapy, and health.

Database

SPORTDiscus (Sport Information Resource Centre, available through OVID) A database of mostly periodical articles. Includes sources from 1949 to the present, some with abstracts.

Web Sites

Scholarly Sports Sites: www.ucalgary.ca/library/ssportsite/ This subject directory brings together Web sites of interest to the serious sports researcher, kinesiology librarian, sport information specialist, and college student or faculty.

WWW Virtual Library Physiology and Biophysics Directory: neocortex.med.cornell.edu/VL-Physio/ Provides links to a wide range of interests, techniques, and publications relevant to contemporary physiology and biophysics as well as physiology and biophysics servers.

BIOLOGY

Print Resources

Becher, Anne. *Biodiversity: A Reference Handbook.* Santa Barbara: ABC-CLIO, 1998. Explores issues surrounding biological diversity. Offers a chronology and biographies of important people in the field.

Biological Abstracts. Philadelphia: BIOSIS, 1926–. Abstracts of articles from journals in the field. Includes author, organism, and subject indexes.

Hine, Robert. *The Facts on File Dictionary of Biology.* 3rd ed. New York: Checkmark, 1999. Almost 3,000 entries for frequently used terminology in the biological sciences.

Information Sources in the Life Sciences. Ed. H. V. Wyatt. 4th ed. London: Bowker-Saur, 1997. Chapters cover types of reference works and specific life science disciplines. Detailed information on a wide variety of sources.

Oxford Dictionary of Biology. 4th ed. Oxford: Oxford UP, 2000. Definitions for key terms, biographies of biologists, and chronologies of important discoveries.

Databases

Biological Abstracts (BIOSIS, available through OVID) References to biological research findings and clinical studies. Most of the citations include abstracts.

Biological and Agricultural Index (Wilson, available through OCLC FirstSearch and Silver-Platter) Citations from a wide range of popular and professional journals. Also includes forestry and ecology.

BIOSIS (BIOSIS, available through OCLC First-Search) Entries include sources from both popular and scholarly publications.

Web Sites

About.com's Biology Directory: biology.about. com Offers extensive topical index divided into a wide range of subject headings, in addition to the latest news releases in the area of biological sciences.

BioNetbook: www.pasteur.fr/recherche/ BNB/bnb-en.html Search by topics in a classified listing, do a word search, combine word and topic searches, or search the site directory.

CHEMISTRY

Print Resources

Chemical Titles. Columbus, OH: Amer. Chemical Soc., 1989–. Entries are organized by keyword and are also in bibliographic form by topic.

Maizell, Robert E. *How to Find Chemical Information.* 3rd ed. New York: Wiley, 1998. An extensive annotated list of chemistry sources, with entries organized by source type.

World of Chemistry. Ed. Robyn V. Young. Detroit: Gale, 2000. Over 1,000 entries providing information on general terms, concepts, and applications of chemistry. Biographical entries on notable figures.

Database

Chemical Abstracts Student Edition (Chemical Abstracts Service, available through OCLC FirstSearch) Indexes over 250 periodicals and over 200,000 dissertations.

Web Site

Academic Info's Chemistry Directory: academicinfo.net/chem.html Geared toward college students and recent college graduates, offering annotated links to topical sites.

ECOLOGY AND ENVIRONMENTAL SCIENCE

Print Resources

The Dictionary of Ecology and Environmental Science. Ed. Henry W. Art. New York: Holt, 1993. Provides numerous cross-references, illustrations, charts, and diagrams for more thorough explanations.

Encyclopedia of Environmental Issues. Ed. Craig W. Allin. 3 vols. Pasadena: Salem, 2000. Alphabetically arranged articles on a wide range of environmental issues.

Encyclopedia of Environmental Science. Ed. David E. Alexander and Rhodes W. Fairbridge. Boston: Kluwer, 1999. Over 300 entries ranging from brief definitions of terms and concepts to longer articles on major topics within environmental science.

Databases

ECODISC (Elsevier, available through SilverPlatter) Includes worldwide research on subjects within ecology and the ecosystem.

Envirofacts (U.S. Environmental Protection Agency) Allows users access to databases maintained by the Environmental Protection Agency.

Environmental Sciences and Pollution Management (Cambridge Scientific Abstracts) Entries focus on topics such as air quality, types of pollution, energy resources, hazardous waste, and water resource issues.

Web Sites

The Ecology WWW Page: pbil.univ-lyon1.fr/ Ecology/Ecology-WWW.html A huge list of links connected to the study of ecology.

The EnviroLink Library: library.envirolink.org A comprehensive resource for individuals and organizations interested in social and environmental change.

Open Directory's Environment Directory:
dmoz.org/Science/Environment/ Provides
links to subdirectories on environmental issues, sciences, organizations, and topics.

FOOD SCIENCES AND NUTRITION

Print Resources

Ensminger, Audrey H., et al. *Concise Encyclopedia of Foods & Nutrition.* **2nd ed. London: CRC, 1995.** Aimed at a general consumer audience.

Food Science and Technology Abstracts. **Reading, UK: International Food Information Service, 1928–.** Covers articles on food sciences, processes, and products. Indexes journals as well as books, patents, conference proceedings, and more.

Frank, Robyn C., and Holly Berry Irving. *The Directory of Food and Nutrition Information.* **2nd ed. Phoenix: Oryx, 1992.** Includes information on professional and academic organizations along with bibliographic information and descriptions of journals, indexes, books, databases, and other sources.

Databases

Food Science and Technology Abstracts **(International Food Information Service, available through SilverPlatter)** A comprehensive database of sources in the food technology, food science, and human nutrition fields from books, journals, reports, theses, conferences, and more.

FOREGE Current Food Legislation **(Leatherhead Food RA, available through SilverPlatter)** Focuses on worldwide legislation of food additives and food standards. Translates complex legal documents into a concise, easy-to-read format.

Web Sites

About.com's Nutrition Directory: **nutrition. about.com** Extensive directory of nutrition resources.

HealthLinks: **healthlinks.washington.edu** Site has a monthly feature news story and provides links to medical journals and to reference, educational, and other health-related sites.

GEOLOGY

Print Resources

A Dictionary of Earth Sciences. **Ed. Ailsa Allaby and Michael Allaby. 2nd ed. Oxford: Oxford UP, 1999.** Over 6,000 definitions of terminology and concepts in geology and related fields.

The Facts on File Dictionary of Earth Science. **Ed. John O.E. Clark and Stella Stiegeler. New York: Checkmark, 2000.** Offers over 3,000 clear and concise explanations of frequently used terminology in earth science.

Geology. **Ed. James A. Woodhead. 2 vols. Pasadena: Salem, 1999.** Over 80 articles, each of which includes an overview of the subject, definitions of relevant terms, a bibliography, and cross-references.

Databases

GEOBASE **(Elsevier, available through OCLC FirstSearch and SilverPlatter)** Over 600,000 entries with abstracts of books, journals, monographs, reports, and more.

GeoRef **(American Geological Institute, available through OCLC FirstSearch and Cambridge Scientific Abstracts)** Over 2 million references to articles, maps, books, conference papers, and theses.

Web Sites

AGIWEB: **www.agiweb.org** The American Geological Institute's home page has links to affiliated sites, such as its magazine *GeoTimes,* its data repository, and information about careers in the geosciences.

Geology.com: **geology.com** Contains a list of geology links organized by topic. Also includes links to an illustrated dictionary of geological terminology, geology journals, and professional organizations.

MATHEMATICS

Print Resources

The Facts on File Dictionary of Mathematics. **Ed. John Daintith and John Clark. 3rd ed. New York: Facts on File, 1999.** Entries span all branches of mathematics and often utilize illustrations and charts.

Peeva, K., et al. *Elsevier's Dictionary of Mathematics.* New York: Elsevier, 2000. A comprehensive compilation of mathematical terminology with over 11,000 definitions.

Weisstein, Eric W. *CRC Concise Encyclopedia of Mathematics.* New York: CRC, 1999. Mathematical definitions, formulas, figures, and references. Aimed at a general audience.

Database

MathSciNet (American Mathematical Society, also available through SilverPlatter as MathSci Database) Combines two print publications (*Math Reviews* and *Current Mathematical Publications*) for reviews of mathematical research and current bibliographic records.

Web Sites

Mathematical Association of America: **www.maa.org** Features math-related articles and news.

Mathematical Atlas: **www.math-atlas.org** Offers the ability to search within the index and a beginner's guide to math subject areas.

MathSearch: **www.maths.usyd.edu.au:8000/ MathSearch.html** A search engine for math-related topics.

MEDICINE AND HEALTH SCIENCES

Print Resources

Best of Health: Demographics of Health Care Consumers. Ithaca: New Strategist, 1998. Explanations and statistics concerning issues in the health care system.

Compact American Medical Dictionary. Boston: Houghton, 1998. A dictionary for the general reader that provides over 10,000 definitions for all types of medical terms.

Information Sources in the Medical Sciences. Ed. L. T. Morton and Shane Godbolt. 4th ed. London: Bowker-Saur, 1992. Descriptions of print, journal, and online sources in all medical fields. Entries are organized by either type of source or branch of medicine.

Miller-Keane Encyclopedia and Dictionary of Medicine, Nursing, and Allied Health. 6th ed. Philadelphia: Saunders, 1997. Entries explain terms, concepts, and practical applications in medicine, nursing, and related fields.

World of Health. Ed. Brigham Narins. Detroit: Gale, 2000. Entries cover a range of issues, principles, and recent developments in the medical sciences and related fields.

Databases

Health and Wellness Information or HealthInfo (Gale Group, also available through OCLC FirstSearch) Draws on over 500 sources to provide records from periodicals, reference books, newsletters, and pamphlets.

MDXHealth (Medical Data Exchange, available through OCLC FirstSearch) Consumer site lists records from magazines, medical journals, medical schools, hospital publications, and bulletins.

MEDLINE (National Library of Medicine, available through OCLC FirstSearch and Cambridge Scientific Abstracts) A general medical database that includes sources in the dentistry and nursing fields.

Web Sites

HealthLinks: **healthlinks.washington.edu** Site has a monthly feature news story and provides links to medical journals and to reference, educational, and other health-related sites.

WWW Virtual Library of Medicine: **londonbridge.ohsu.edu/wwwvl/** Access to government organizations, academic departments, online journals, and independent links. Includes both professional and general-interest sites.

NATURAL RESOURCES

Print Resources

Dunster, Julian, and Katherine Dunster. *Dictionary of Natural Resources Management.* Vancouver: UBC, 1996. Many entries use cross-referencing or illustrations for more thorough explanation.

Environmental Periodicals Bibliography. Santa Barbara: Environmental Studies Inst., 1971–. Bibliographic information for sources, organized alphabetically by subject.

Database

Envirofacts **(U.S. Environmental Protection Agency)** Allows users access to databases maintained by the Environmental Protection Agency.

Web Sites

Natural Resources Research Information Pages: **www4.ncsu.edu/ffleung/nrrips.html** Organized into subject headings such as government agencies, institutions and organizations, and outdoor recreation research.

USDA Natural Resources and Environment Page: **www.usda.gov** Click on the Natural Resources and Environment link to access this comprehensive government site.

NURSING

Print Resources

Miller-Keane Encyclopedia and Dictionary of Medicine, Nursing, and Allied Health. **6th ed. Philadelphia: Saunders, 1997.** Entries explain terms, concepts, and practical applications in medicine, nursing, and related fields.

Mosby's Medical, Nursing, and Allied Health Dictionary. **Ed. Kenneth N. Anderson. 5th ed. St. Louis: Mosby, 1998.** A comprehensive source for procedures, drugs, disorders, etc.

Database

British Nursing Index **(Bournemouth University, available through SilverPlatter)** References to all major British nursing publications.

Web Sites

Nursing Websearch: **www.nursingwebsearch .com** A nursing search engine as well as annotated links organized by subject heading, including education, legal/ethical, and registered-nurse home pages.

Thornbury Nursing Research Engine: **www.nursing-portal.com/nre.html** Links to other quality nursing sites. Includes a category search and chatrooms.

PHYSICS

Print Resources

The Facts on File Dictionary of Physics. **Ed. John Daintith and John Clark. 3rd ed. New York: Checkmark, 1999.** Includes over 2,400 definitions of terminology in the field. Provides appendices about elements, physical quantities, and conversion factors.

McGraw-Hill Dictionary of Physics. **Ed. Sybil P. Parker. New York: McGraw, 1994.** General reference source for vocabulary in physics and related fields.

Physics Abstracts. **Avenel: Institution of Electrical Engineers, 1898–.** Abstracts of articles in physics and related fields organized by topic.

Databases

Inspec **(Institution of Electrical Engineers, available through OCLC FirstSearch and SilverPlatter)** Includes physics as well as electrical engineering, computers, and information technology sources. Covers mostly articles from journals but also important books, dissertations, and conference proceedings.

SPIN **(American Institute of Physics)** Indexes and abstracts current research and publications from major American and Russian journals. Focuses on physics and astronomy.

Web Sites

DC Physics: **www.dctech.com/physics/** Offers a physics-based Internet search engine and an extensive directory of other useful sites.

PhysicsWeb: **physicsweb.org** Comprehensive site on physics news, jobs, and resources.

Yahoo!'s Physics Directory: **dir.yahoo.com/ Science/Physics/** Comprehensive directory of physics topics, resources, and organizations.

PHYSIOLOGY

Print Resources

Encyclopedia of Human Biology. **Ed. Renato Dulbecco. 2nd ed. 9 vols. San Diego: Academic, 1997.** Each entry provides a comprehensive overview of the subject. Intended for a wide range of readers.

Netter, Frank H. *Atlas of Human Anatomy.* **2nd ed. East Hanover: Novartis, 1997.** Over 4,000 illustrations of the human body, each thoroughly labeled.

Shaw, Diane L. *Glossary of Anatomy and Physiology.* **Springhouse, PA: Springhouse, 1992.** Brief definitions of thousands of terms.

Web Sites

Yahoo!'s Physiology Directory: **dir.yahoo.com/ Health/Medicine/Physiology/** Provides a list of annotated direct links and a directory of links organized by subject heading.

ZOOLOGY

Print Resources

Animal Behavior Abstracts. **Bethesda: Cambridge Scientific Abstracts, 1973–.** Articles and sources from over 5,000 journals in the field. Entries include bibliographic information and abstracts.

Beacham's Guide to International Endangered Species. **Ed. Walton Beacham and Kirk H. Beetz. 3 vols. Osprey: Beacham, 1998.** Basic information on endangered species. Organized alphabetically by species.

International Wildlife Encyclopedia. **Ed. Maurice Burton and Robert Burton. 25 vols. New York: Marshall Cavendish, 1991.** General information on animals. Final volume provides both general and systematic indexes based on phylum, class, order, and family.

Databases

Animal Behavior Abstracts **(Cambridge Scientific Abstracts)** Covers all major zoological journals. Includes both field and laboratory research.

Zoological Record Plus **(BIOSIS, available through Cambridge Scientific Abstracts)** Provides an easy search of over 4,500 publications as well as books, reviews, and meetings. Covers a range of zoological topics from biochemistry to veterinary medicine.

Web Sites

Museum of Vertebrate Zoology: **www.mip.berkeley.edu/mvz/** A virtual museum with articles, news, and links to affiliated organizations.

Open Directory's Zoology Directory: **dmoz.org/ Science/Biology/Zoology/** Provides links to sites addressing topics, associations, and publications in zoology.

ENGINEERING AND COMPUTER SCIENCE

Print Resources

Applied Science and Technology Index. **New York: Wilson, 1958–.** Published annually, this work indexes over 350 English-language periodicals. Covers all engineering disciplines.

Chemical Engineering and Biotechnology Abstracts. **Cambridge: Royal Society of Chemistry, 1971–.** Covers a full range of theoretical and practical topics in chemical engineering.

The Computer Science and Engineering Handbook. **Ed. Allen B. Tucker Jr. Boca Raton: CRC, 1997.** Information on 10 subfields of computer science and engineering. Intended for an audience of engineers and other professionals.

Coulson, J. M., et al. *Chemical Engineering.* **4th ed. 2 vols. Oxford: Butterworth-Heinemann, 1996.** Articles on physical operations used in chemical and allied industries, with each chapter covering a type of operation.

Dictionary of Computer Science, Engineering and Technology. **Ed. Phillip A. Laplante. Boca Raton: CRC, 2001.** Alphabetical compilation of over 7,500 terms covering major topics in computer science.

Dubbel Handbook of Mechanical Engineering. **Ed. B. J. Davies. London: Springer-Verlag, 1994.** Chapters organized by topic. Numerous illustrations and figures to make definitions more accessible and thorough.

Electrical and Electronic Abstracts. **Piscataway: INSPEC, 1989–.** Abstracts of articles on electrical engineering and electronics found in journals, books, reports, dissertations, and more.

Encyclopedia of Computer Science. **Ed. Anthony Ralston, Edwin D. Reilly, and David**

Hemmendinger. 4th ed. New York: Grove's Dictionaries, 2000. Over 600 articles on the history of computer science, recent developments in the field, notable figures, and more.

Information Sources in Engineering. Ed. K. W. Mildren and P. J. Hicks. 3rd ed. London: Bowker-Saur, 1996. Descriptions of sources by specialized fields in engineering.

Mechanical Engineers' Handbook. Ed. Myer Kutz. 2nd ed. New York: Wiley, 1998. Comprehensive volume on all aspects of mechanical engineering, with over 70 chapters organized by topic. Includes an index.

Perry's Chemical Engineers' Handbook. Ed. Robert H. Perry, Don W. Green, and James O. Maloney. 7th ed. New York: McGraw, 1997. Information on chemical engineering including new developments, equipment, procedures, principles, calculation methods, and more.

Scott, John S. *The Dictionary of Civil Engineering.* 4th ed. New York: Van Nostrand Reinhold, 1993. Terms and concepts in civil engineering and related fields.

Standard Handbook for Electrical Engineers. Ed. Donald Fink and H. Wayne Beaty. 14th ed. New York: McGraw, 2000. Articles oriented toward practical applications of electrical engineering.

Webster, L. F. *The Wiley Dictionary of Civil Engineering and Construction.* New York: Wiley, 1997. Over 30,000 descriptions and definitions of concepts, terms, names, tools, and techniques in civil engineering and related technical fields.

Databases

Applied Science and Technology Abstracts (Wilson, available through OCLC FirstSearch) Sources include interviews, conferences, exhibitions, new product reviews, technically valuable editorials, letters, tables, and charts.

ASCE Civil Engineering Database (www.pubs. asce.org/cedbsrch.html) Bibliographic access to journals, conferences, books, standards, manuals, and more.

Bioengineering Abstracts (Cambridge Scientific Abstracts) Focuses on the medical and biological applications of engineering. Sources come from journals, conference proceedings,

and *Engineering Information*'s comprehensive database.

Chemical Engineering and Biotechnology Abstracts (Deutsche Gesellschaft für Chemisches Apparatewesen, available through Dialog@Carl) Covers over 500 journals in addition to books, technical reports, and conference information.

Computer and Information Systems Abstracts (Cambridge Scientific Abstracts) A current index of sources pertaining to computer research and applications.

Computer Information and Technology Collection (Cambridge Scientific Abstracts) Updated monthly, this database includes the latest theoretical research on and practical applications of computers.

IEEE Xplore (Institute of Electrical and Electronics Engineers) Includes IEEE transactions, journals, magazines, and conference proceedings as well as IEEE standards.

Inspec (Institution of Electrical Engineers, available through OCLC FirstSearch and SilverPlatter) Includes electrical engineering, computers, and information technology sources. Covers mostly articles from journals but also books, dissertations, and conference proceedings.

Internet and Personal Computing Abstracts (Information Today, available through Cambridge Scientific Abstracts) Over 180,000 records of sources pertaining to personal computing as well as computers in business, industry, and education.

Mechanical Engineering Abstracts (Cambridge Scientific Abstracts) Citations of journals, articles, and conference papers. Aimed specifically at specialists and engineers.

Web Sites

Academic Info's Mechanical Engineering Directory: www.academicinfo.net/engringme.html Includes a reference desk where basic information and national standards may be found.

Civil Engineering Professions: iCivilEngineer: www.icivilengineer.com Offers special features such as the academic department index, conference calendar, engineering news, and best job search sites.

Open Directory's Electrical Engineering Directory: **dmoz.org/Science/Technology/ Electrical_Engineering/** Provides links to electrical engineering sites and offers additional subject headings under which more information may be located.

Research Index Computer Science Directory: **citeseer.ist.psu.edu/directory.html** Topics include numerous annotated links to papers and presentations.

BUSINESS

Print Resources

The Advertising Business. **Ed. John Philip Jones. Thousand Oaks: Sage, 1999.** Essays are organized into chapters covering operations, creativity, media planning, and integrated communications.

Business Periodicals Index. **New York: Wilson, 1958–.** Indexes articles in English-language business journals and periodicals. Includes a section for book reviews.

Encyclopedia of Business. **Ed. Jane A. Malonis. 2nd ed. 2 vols. Detroit: Gale, 2000.** Over 700 essays on all aspects of business.

Encyclopedia of Business Information Sources. **Ed. James Woy. 15th ed. Detroit: Gale, 2001.** An annual guide to bibliographic information on over 1,000 business subjects and issues.

Finance Literature Index. **Ed. Jean Louis Heck. 4th ed. New York: McGraw, 1994.** Bibliographic citations for articles about finance in over 50 leading journals.

Harry, Mike. *Information Systems in Business.* **London: Pitman, 1994.** Background concepts, business organization, and development methodology for information systems.

International Financial Statistics Yearbook. **Washington, DC: International Monetary Fund, 2000.** A comprehensive collection of data on economic issues worldwide. Individual sections on each country provide thorough economic information.

Mahony, Stephen. *The Financial Times A–Z of International Finance.* **London: Pitman, 1997.**
Brief summaries of terms and concepts in international finance.

Mercer, David. *Marketing: The Encyclopedic Dictionary.* **Oxford, Eng.: Blackwell, 1999.** Brief definitions for basic marketing terms and longer entries for important marketing topics.

O'Brien, James A. *Management Information Systems.* **Boston: Irwin, 1993.** Chapters cover foundation concepts, development, technology, applications, and management of information systems.

Databases

Banking Information Source **(Bell & Howell)** Sources related to the financial services industry. Bibliographic information and abstracts from publications, theses, and newsletters.

Business and Industry **(Responsive Database Services, available through OCLC FirstSearch)** Facts, figures, and key events for public and private businesses and industries. Covers trade magazines, the business press, and newsletters.

Consumers Index **(Pierian, available through OCLC FirstSearch)** Information on products, services, and facilities, with a specific emphasis on consumerism and consumer protection.

FINDEX **(Cambridge Scientific Abstracts)** A guide to publicly available market and business research. Approximately 33,000 records updated quarterly.

Gale Business Resources **(Gale Group)** Detailed reports on over 1,000 U.S. and global industries include full-text essays and articles, rankings, and statistical analyses.

Wilson Business Abstracts **(Wilson, available through OCLC FirstSearch)** Indexes and abstracts for leading business magazines. Articles have citations and abstracts, while book reviews have only citations.

Web Sites

Association for Information Systems: **www.aisnet.org** Includes current news, information on conferences, and research reports.

BusinessWeb: **www.businesswebsource.com** Offers links and resources organized by type of industry. Search entire site or specific industry.

Acknowledgments (continued from p. iv)

Figure 4.3a–c: Reprinted with the permission of EBSCO Information Services.

Figure 4.4: From *The Essential Vermeer.* Copyright © 2001–2005 by Jonathan Janson. Reprinted with permission.

Figure 5.2: Reprinted with the permission of Colorado State University Libraries.

Figure 5.3: Reprinted with the permission of Colorado State University Libraries.

Figure 5.4: Reprinted with the permission of EBSCO Information Services.

Figure 5.5: Reprinted with the permission of EBSCO Information Services.

Figure 5.6a–b: Copyright © 1998–2005 by Netscape Communications Corporation.

Figure 5.7: ProFusion Search Web Search Engines screen, www.profusion.com. Copyright Intelliseek, Inc. All rights reserved.

Figure 5.9: Reprinted with the permission of Google, Inc.

Figure 5.11: Reprinted with permission.

Figure 6.2: Reprinted with the permission of Boston College Libraries.

Figure 8.2: Dean Lillard and Jennifer Gerner, excerpt from "Getting to the Ivy League: How Family Composition Affects College Choice" from *Journal of Higher Education* (November–December 1999). Copyright © 1999 by The Ohio State University Press. All rights reserved.

Page 130: Library of Congress Online Catalog screenshot. Reprinted with permission.

Page 134: Eric Dexheimer, excerpts from "Nothing to Lose: The Colorado Impact Teaches Girls about Life—Then Hoops" from *Westword* (May 13, 2004), www.westword.com/issues/2004-05-13/news/sports_print.html. Reprinted with the permission of *Westword.*

Figure 16.1: Pieter de Hooch, *Woman and Child in an Interior,* oil on canvas, circa 1658. Rijksmuseum, Amsterdam. Reprinted with permission.

Figure 16.1: Johannes Vermeer, *Woman with a Water Pitcher* (New York, Metropolitan Museum of Art). Oil on canvas; 18 x 16 in. (45.7 x 40.6 cm) Marquand Collection, Gift of Henry G. Marquand, 1889 (89.15.21).

Figures 16.3 and 16.4: Reprinted with the permission of *The Shorthorn,* University of Texas at Arlington.

Page 249: Cover of *The Feminist Difference.* Reprinted with permission.

Page 254: Cover of *Image.* Reprinted with the permission of Thomson Gale.

Page 263: Screenshot of Nobelprize.org. Reprinted with the permission of Nobelprize.org and Anders Hellengren.

Figure 3: Johannes Verspronck, *Portrait of a Man,* 1641, oil on canvas. Rijksmuseum Twenthe, Enschede, The Netherlands.

Figure 4: Johannes Verspronck, *Portrait of a Woman,* 1640, oil on canvas. Rijksmuseum Twenthe, Enschede, The Netherlands.

Figure 5: Gerard Dou, *The Prayer of the Spinner.* Oil on wood, 27.7 x 28.3 cm, Alte Pinakothek, Munich, Inv. Nr. 588. Courtesy Bayerisch Staatsgemäldesammlungen, Alte Pinakothek, Munich.

Page 281: Cover of Keith Bradsher, *High and Mighty: The Dangerous Rise of the SUV.* Copyright © 2003 by Keith Bradsher. Reprinted with the permission of Public Affairs Books, a member of Perseus Books Group, L.L.C.

Page 285: Cover copyright © The Johns Hopkins University Press. Reprinted with the permission of The Johns Hopkins University Press.

Page 290: Screenshot of EBSCO Host Research Databases abstract for Barbara J. Phillips, "Working Out: Consumers and the Culture of Exercise" from *Journal of Popular Culture* 38: Reprinted with the permission of EBSCO Information Services.

Page 307: Cover of Walter A. McDougall, *Freedom Just Around the Corner: A New American History 1585–1828.* Copyright © 2004 by Walter A. McDougall. Reprinted with the permission of HarperCollins Publishers, Inc.

Page 314: Cover of *Wired* magazine. Reprinted with the permission of *Wired* magazine.

Page 319: David Abel, from "Harvard University to Increase Wages of Its Lowest-Paid Workers," from *The Boston Globe* (February 1, 2002). Copyright © 2002 Tribune Media Services. Reprinted with permission.

Page 334: Cover of David Goodstein, *Out of Gas: The End of the Age of Oil.* Copyright © 2004 by David Goodstein. Reprinted with the permission of W. W. Norton & Company, Inc.

Page 338: Cover of *Scientific American.* Reprinted with the permission of *Scientific American.*

Index

Directory of Tutorials, Checklists, and Activities

Tutorials

Quick Reference Boxes

Checklists and Guidelines Boxes

My Research Project Activities